Analyzing Schubert

When Schubert's contemporary reviewers first heard his modulations, they famously claimed that they were excessive, odd, and unplanned. This book argues that these claims have haunted the analysis of Schubert's harmony ever since, outlining why Schubert's music occupies a curiously marginal position in the history of music theory. *Analyzing Schubert* traces how critics, analysts, and historians from the early nineteenth century to the present day have preserved cherished narratives of wandering, alienation, memory, and trance by emphasizing the mystical rather than the logical quality of the composer's harmony. This study proposes a new method for analyzing the harmony of Schubert's works. Rather than pursuing an approach that casts Schubert's famous harmonic moves as digressions from the norms of canonical theoretical paradigms, Suzannah Clark explores how the harmonic fingerprints in Schubert's songs and instrumental sonata forms challenge pedigreed habits of thought about what constitutes a theory of tonal and formal order.

SUZANNAH CLARK is Gardner Cowles Associate Professor of Music at Harvard University. In addition to her work on Schubert, her research interests range from medieval French motets to the history of music theory from Rameau to Schenker. She is the co-editor of *Citation and Authority in Medieval and Renaissance Musical Culture: Learning from the Learned*, with Elizabeth Eva Leach, and *Music Theory and Natural Order from the Renaissance to the Early Twentieth Century*, with Alexander Rehding.

Analyzing Schubert

SUZANNAH CLARK

CAMBRIDGE
UNIVERSITY PRESS

CAMBRIDGE UNIVERSITY PRESS
Cambridge, New York, Melbourne, Madrid, Cape Town,
Singapore, São Paulo, Delhi, Tokyo, Mexico City

Cambridge University Press
The Edinburgh Building, Cambridge CB2 8RU, UK

Published in the United States of America by Cambridge University Press, New York

www.cambridge.org
Information on this title: www.cambridge.org/9780521848671

First published 2011

Printed in the United Kingdom at the University Press, Cambridge

A catalogue record for this publication is available from the British Library

Library of Congress Cataloging in Publication data
Clark, Suzannah, 1969–
Analyzing Schubert / Suzannah Clark.
    p.   cm.
Includes bibliographical references and index.
ISBN 978-0-521-84867-1
1. Schubert, Franz, 1797–1828 – Criticism and interpretation.   I. Title.
ML410.S3C43   2011
780.92–dc22

                                                                    2011007625

ISBN 978-0-521-84867-1 Hardback

To my sisters: Sandra and Sally

Contents

Acknowledgements

As Sir George Grove was nearing the completion of his article on Schubert for the dictionary that would bear his name, he wrote to a friend that he feared he would deeply miss Schubert, who had been his "companion" for so long. In completing this book, I have some sympathy for Grove's sentiment. Yet writing these acknowledgements brings to the fore all the colleagues and friends that I have been lucky enough to have as real companions during the writing of this book.

The ideas for this volume first took shape while I was at Oxford. My thanks go, as always, to Emanuele Senici and I am so glad that our times at Oxford coincided. In particular, I owe an enormous debt of gratitude to my colleague at Merton College, Edward Olleson, whose formidable musical knowledge sharpened my ears to numerous nifty harmonic passages from Haydn to Brahms. I am grateful to Susan Wollenberg, who invited me to teach a joint course on Schubert's instrumental music, where I played out some of the ideas in this book and received valuable responses from Susan and the students. I also gained much joy over the years from the triumphs of each of my tutorial students in Merton and Univ. I am grateful to Eric Clarke for some important conversations about life and music analysis, as well as for animated debates over analytical quagmires with Jonathan Cross and Lawrence Dreyfus.

I consider myself extremely fortunate to have had Simon Jones as my colleague in matters pertaining to the Merton College Choir. I am grateful to the chef at Merton, Mike Wente, and to the kitchen staff and butlers for serving such superb meals with such incredible imagination. I cannot begin to count (though Oxford keeps impeccable records on such matters) the number of meals I ate with colleagues over the years at Merton, but I am especially grateful to the Warden and Fellows for bringing a sense of humor, wit, friendship, and deep intellectual exchange to them all. For morning coffees and conversations, I recall with fondness Richard McCabe, Vijay Joshi (who also kindly gave me a huge collection of scores), the college librarian Julia Walworth, and the emeritus Fellows Michael Dunnill and Roger Highfield. In fact, coffee with them was such a staple that, on returning to Merton for a visit after a two-year absence and, by habit, taking up my usual chair, I can only apologize to Michael for alarming him and leading him to think, in his advancing age, that he had seen a ghost – though, for the record, I consider him young and sprightly! I also wish to thank the wonderful porters and staff for their numerous acts of kindness.

At Oxford, I also enjoyed many "time outs" with friends I made through my ice hockey team (who never quite got the joke when I insisted I was doing my best to be more goal oriented than Schubert!): Nancy, Becca, Sally, Mima, Ali, Emma, Debs, Karen F., Karen D., Dee. Similarly, I am grateful to close friends from all across the globe, who keep me inspired: Suzanne Aspden, David Bretherton, Sharon Choa, Sean Curran, Emma Dillon, Paul Harper-Scott, Karen Henson, Gundula Kreuzer, Jenny Lewis, Melanie Lowe, Roger Moseley, Michael Puri, Enrique Sacau, Lara Shore-Sheppard, Jane Steele, Tiffany Stern, Matías Tarnopolsky, Laura Tunbridge, Sindhu Revuluri, Joshua Walden, Kathryn Whitney.

I owe a large debt to Scott Burnham, whose comments at various stages of this book helped shade its argument. Roger Parker read drafts of the first two chapters in a way that educated me on how to write the rest. These pages also owe much to the things that Carolyn Abbate queried when I first showed her what I planned to say about Schenker and hermeneutics. My way of thinking about musical form was deeply influenced by Kenneth Levy's incredible manner of teaching non-majors how to listen out for musical structure. Over the years, I have benefited enormously from the wisdom of Kofi Agawu, Margaret Bent, Bonnie Blackburn, Leofranc Holford-Strevens, Nicholas Marston, and Arnold Whittall. I am indebted to my dear friend W. Anthony Sheppard ever since grad. school and to Elizabeth Eva Leach for opera nights. Various aspects of this book have been shaped by thought-provoking conversations with fellow Schubertians: Richard Cohn, René Rusch Daley, Charles Fisk, Xavier Hascher, Marjorie Hirsch, Lawrence Kramer, Elizabeth Norman McKay, Susan Youens.

My colleagues in the Music Department at Harvard University have been unfailing in their support. My fellow connoisseurs of music theory, Christopher Hasty and Alexander Rehding, have been invaluable inter-locutors during the final stages of this book. With Alex, I additionally share the tribulations of reaching our offices way up in the North Tower of Harvard's music building and the joys of working in the midst of much merriment once we get there. The department staff, the Loeb Music Library staff, and graduate students make the atmosphere at Harvard a daily joy. I am particularly grateful to my assistant, Rowland Moseley, for his artistry and attentiveness in setting the musical examples.

I acknowledge with gratitude support from the University of Oxford for a term's leave and a matching sabbatical grant from the Arts and Humanities Research Council (UK), as well as a semester's leave granted from Harvard University. The final stages in the production of this book were carried out in the marvelous surroundings of the National Humanities Center, where I was the William J. Bouwsma Fellow during 2010–2011.

I appreciate Vicki Cooper and Rebecca Taylor of Cambridge University Press for their wonderful enthusiasm and support during the writing and production of this book.

I owe eternal thanks to my thoughtful and generous parents, Raymond and Vivien, who raised me in a home full of fun, books, and intellectual adventure, and who made numerous sacrifices for the education of their children. I dedicate this book with love to my amazing sisters, Sandra and Sally. My brother-in-law, Sumi Aota, has been incredibly kind since the moment we were first introduced. Finally, I want to express my heartfelt thanks to my partner, Cassandra Extavour, for her boundless support.

Introduction

Not long ago, a previously unknown watercolor featuring Schubert was discovered (Plate 1). Dating from July 16, 1818, it depicts Schubert peering through a kaleidoscope and his friend Leopold Kupelwieser (also the painter of the caricature) riding a draisine.[1] Both the kaleidoscope and draisine were newly invented objects at the time of the painting. The kaleidoscope originated in Scotland, invented as a scientific tool by Sir David Brewster, and around the time it fell into Schubert's hands it was all the rage in Vienna as a toy. The draisine or "Laufmachine" was invented in Germany – a kind of Fred Flintstone precursor of the bicycle, without pedals, whose function was to transport crew and materials for railway maintenance. Around 1818, it had made its way off the railtracks and into the city for leisure riding. Schubert and Kupelwieser are both portrayed as absorbed by these new technologies: Kupelwieser is so fixated on the draisine that he crashes into Schubert, and Schubert is so enthralled by the kaleidoscope that he does not see him coming.

In its original context, the watercolor was accompanied by the following commentary:

The latest example of contemporary history proves just how dangerous the landslide of new developments is from Paris. But even the seemingly harmless inventions of the kaleidoscope and the draisine have their danger, as the accompanying picture illustrates. The stout gentleman is absorbed in the contemplation of the kaleidoscope's wonderful play of colors – the dark glass makes him even more near-sighted than usual. He is about to be knocked to the ground by a passionate draisine rider, who likewise has his eye fixed only on his machine. Let this be a warning for others. There is already supposed to be a police order in the works on the strength of which every blockhead is strictly forbidden, on account of the danger, from using both new inventions.[2]

---

[1] The watercolor was discovered by Rita Steblin and first brought to public attention in her article "Schubert durch das Kaleidoskop: Die Unsinnsgesellschaft und ihre illustren Mitglieder," *Österreichische Musikzeitschrift* 52 (1997): 52–61. It appeared in a newsletter of the so-called Unsinnsgesellschaft (Nonsense Society), to which Steblin has argued Schubert belonged.

[2] It is of tangential interest that the author of the commentary believed the new inventions to come from Paris. The translation of the passage comes from an article by Rita Steblin, "Schubert through the Kaleidoscope: The 'Unsinnsgesellschaft' and Its Illustrious Members," 54–55, in a

Plate 1 Franz Schubert peering through a kaleidoscope and Leopold Kupelwieser riding a draisine. Watercolor by Kupelwieser July 16, 1818. Vienna City Library; reproduced by kind permission.

Two of the shapes in the picture – the cylinder of the kaleidoscope and the wheel of the draisine – will be familiar to analysts of Schubert's music (Example 1). In 1999, Richard Cohn recast his newly invented theory of hexatonic cycles into the geometry of tonal space shown on the left in Example 1. Tailored especially for the analysis of Schubert's music, the four cycles are interconnected through fifth relations into a cylindrical shape.

special, unnumbered English-language issue of *Österreichische Musikzeitschrift* 52, an anniversary volume on Schubert. The article was originally published as Steblin, "Schubert durch das Kaleidoskop: Die Unsinnsgesellschaft und ihre illustren Mitglieder," *Österreichische Musikzeitschrift* 52 (1997).

Example 1   Hexatonic cycles stacked in fifths (left) and circle of fifths (right)

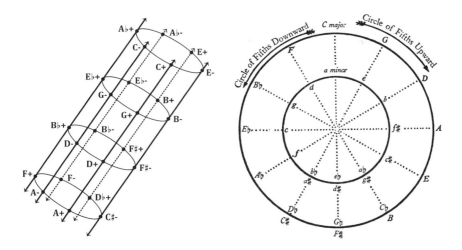

Cohn's geometry added a new dimension to the tonal space afforded by the traditional circle of fifths, which is shown on the right in Example 1.[3] The invention of the circle of fifths, a diagram of iconic status in music theory, is generally credited to Heinichen in 1711, though a circular diagram without reference to major and minor is known as early as 1677 in the Russian tradition. It was originally coined the "musical circle," for its circle of keys was in a different configuration, and, just like a scientific instrument, subsequent theorists claimed "improvements" to its design until it finally reached its currently familiar pattern.[4]

Using a little creative license, we might imagine these two music-theoretical instruments superimposed onto their concomitant shapes in the watercolor. By extension, we could also re-read the paragraph quoted above that served as the original caption for the painting and substitute "hexatonic systems" and "circle of fifths" for kaleidoscope and draisine

[3] The theoretical principles of the hexatonic model are explained in Cohn, "Maximally Smooth Cycles, Hexatonic Systems, and the Analysis of Late-Romantic Triadic Progressions," *Music Analysis* 15 (1996): 9–40. The cylinder shape was developed by Cohn in "As Wonderful as Star Clusters: Instruments for Gazing at Tonality in Schubert," *19th-Century Music* 22 (1999): 217. This particular representation of the circle of fifths is from Arnold Schoenberg, *Theory of Harmony*, trans. Roy E. Carter (Berkeley and Los Angeles: University of California Press, 1983), 155.

[4] Johann David Heinichen, *Neu erfundene und gründliche Anweisung* (Hamburg: Benjamin Schiller, 1711), 261 and for the "new improved circle," see Johann Mattheson, *Kleine General-Bass-Schule* (Hamburg: Johann Christoph Kißner, 1735), 131. On the earliest surviving circle, see Claudia R. Jensen, "A Theoretical Work of Late Seventeenth-Century Muscovy: Nikolai Diletskii's *Grammatika* and the Earliest Circle of Fifths," *Journal of the American Musicological Society* 45 (1992): 305–331.

respectively. But, one might legitimately ask, what is there to warn others about? How could such diagrams of music theory possibly be *dangerous*? How could an obsession with these technologies of tonal space possibly cause an accident of the kind depicted by Kupelwieser in Plate 1? This book is a history of obsessions with music theory in Schubert's reception – obsessive attempts to protect Schubert from being judged by music theory or to wield it precisely in order to judge him; obsessions about its role in hermeneutics and in Schubert's biography.

When Cohn promoted his theory, he rightly observed that it was a "new instrument" for "gazing at Schubert's tonality." Inspired by Donald Francis Tovey's claim that "Schubert's tonality is as wonderful as star clusters," Cohn outlines at the outset of his article the trajectory his argument will take, and remarks, poetically, that "Although we will gaze on [Schubert's] music in due time, our telescope first takes measure of Tovey's metaphor."[5] This fanciful use of celestial metaphors belies a much more serious one: here, as in his first article on maximally smooth cycles, Cohn asks: "Under what circumstances will we wish to gaze at a composition through a hexatonic lens?"[6] This is an important question, and it is this idea of music theory as a lens through which we perceive music that is of particular relevance to my book.

The impact that the choice of a "lens" of music theory has on the perception of a musical work may be put in the following fantastical terms. Imagine owning a pair of spectacles that allows only a specific shape, say circles, to be perceived by the observer. He or she would enjoy the full moon, see clocks, round tables, and wheels. Then imagine replacing these spectacles with a pair that allows only right angles to be seen. Suddenly rectangular tables would come into view, as would the corners in a room, picture frames, books, and so on. Now imagine walking into a room where everything is circular but our observer is wearing the wrong glasses. The circles are there, but the glasses do not reveal them. The result is chaos or blindness – all because of the choice of lenses.

Music theories are just like this. As they construe tonal spaces in different ways, they emphasize different patterns of logic. Applying the wrong theory can have the same sorry effect as wearing the wrong glasses. Or to put this important point again using Cohn's analogy of the telescope, it is vital to remember that music-theoretical systems are indeed "*instruments for*

---

[5] Cohn, "As Wonderful as Star Clusters," 213. Donald Francis Tovey's original comment appears in "Tonality in Schubert," in Hubert J. Foss (ed.), *The Mainstream of Music and Other Essays* (Oxford University Press, 1949), 159.

[6] Cohn, "Maximally Smooth Cycles," 31.

gazing" at music in much the same way as a telescope is an instrument for gazing at the sky. Both have the capacity to bring out things that would otherwise go unnoticed but, more perilously, just as different telescopes will enable an observer to detect different objects in the sky, so different analytical systems will force the analyst to detect different patterns in music. That is to say, where a powerful telescope will pick up an object and another would reveal only darkness, so one musical theory might reveal logic where another suggests incoherence. In both cases the "object" (whether celestial or musical) is "there"; the instrument used will, however, have a direct impact on our perception of it. It is in this way that those categories of instruments – theories and telescopes – both limit and open up our perceptions. My book traces the impact that different theoretical apparatuses have had on the perception of Schubert's music and on his place in history from his own day until now.

1 | Singing Schubert's praises: the voice of Vogl in Schubert's early history

For nearly a quarter of a century, Johann Michael Vogl (1768–1840) was the voice of Schubert's songs. He was the first to bring them to the stage; he made the *Erlkönig* his showpiece and the songs his life.[1] According to some, he was also the last to preserve the style of singing cherished in Schubert's day.[2] However, Vogl not only sang Schubert's songs in a distinctive way, he also, as it were, sang his praises using a distinctive message about the nature of Schubert's genius. As this chapter will show, this other voice of Vogl would prove to be far less ephemeral than his musical performances. It echoes throughout the memoirs of Schubert's friends and acquaintances and can be heard in early historical accounts of his music. It is traceable in the anecdotes of those who, after Schubert's death, claimed to have met him but clearly had not. It can be perceived in the image of Schubert as a composer that has persisted to this day, and it continues to influence the way in which we analyze his music.

Vogl's message is best summarized by one of his own diary entries, in which he writes that Schubert's songs are "truly divine inspirations ... products of musical clairvoyance."[3] Throughout his own life and especially

---

[1] I choose the word "stage" advisedly here. Though the concert stage was not the usual venue for song in the nineteenth century, and for the most part Vogl sang songs in the musical houses of Vienna, he did bring Schubert's songs to the stage, notably on March 7, 1821, when he sang *Erlkönig* at a concert in the Kärntnertor Theatre.

[2] Although many were critical of Vogl, a defense of his interpretation and manner of singing Schubert's songs may be found in Walther Dürr, "Schubert and Johann Michael Vogl: A Reappraisal," *19th-Century Music* 3 (1979): 126–140. Schubert's friends held mixed views on Vogl's singing, which are discussed in detail in David Montgomery, "Franz Schubert's Music in Performance: A Brief History of People, Events, and Issues," in Christopher H. Gibbs (ed.), *The Cambridge Companion to Schubert* (Cambridge University Press, 1997), 272–275 and Eric Van Tassel, "'Something Utterly New': Listening to Schubert Lieder," *Early Music* 25 (1997): 702–714. For Schubert's own praise of Vogl, see especially "Schubert to his brother Ferdinand; 12 September 1825," in Otto Erich Deutsch (ed.), *Schubert: A Documentary Biography* [hereafter *SDB*], trans. Eric Blom (London: J. M. Dent, 1946), 458. (References to documents in *SDB* will include the title given by Deutsch and, where known, the date it was written or published.)

[3] "Bauernfeld: Memoir of J. M. Vogl (1841)," in Otto Erich Deutsch (ed.), *Schubert: Memoirs by His Friends* [hereafter *SMF*], trans. Rosamond Ley and John Nowell (London: Adam & Charles Black, 1958), 226. (As with *SDB*, references to documents will include the title given by Deutsch and, where known, the date it was written or published.)

after Schubert's death (as much documentary evidence indicates), Vogl was heard to have characterized Schubert's music in this way at every opportunity. Indeed Vogl was so intimately associated with the view of Schubert as a clairvoyant genius that whenever anyone sought to address Schubert's method of composition, they cited Vogl as their authority. For instance, as Anton Steinbüchel von Rheinwall once recalled, whenever Schubert was "absorbed and lost, one would hear Vogl's usual remark spoken in an undertone, 'You see the man has no idea what goes on inside him! It is an inexhaustible flood!'"[4] Around 1850, some ten years after Vogl's death, his wife Kunigunde reminisced that he was "always of the opinion that Schubert was in a kind of trance-like state whenever he composed." She went on to specify that the knowledge (or wisdom) that may resound in Schubert's music is not that which the composer himself fully possessed: she thought this explained "how, in this state of clairvoyance, the scarcely educated boy, and later the only moderately educated youth, had glimpses into the secrets of life, feeling and knowledge."[5] As these reminiscences show, the key aspects of Vogl's growing story about Schubert were that the composer was a passive vessel through which divine inspiration passed and that he had little understanding of his own music.

The surprise is not that Vogl adopted an early Romantic notion of genius – a notion that seems harmless enough and perhaps even outdated to us – but that, through this message, he would exert such an influence on the reception of Schubert's music. Vogl's connection to this particular image of Schubert has been noted before in modern scholarship. However, its repercussions have not been fully scrutinized.[6] The most extensive exploration of the image has been carried out by Christopher H. Gibbs, who additionally has offered a broad account of how various other images of Schubert have, through repetition, entered a "canon of biographical representations," and traced how different eras fashion new anecdotes to fit their own ideas of Schubert.[7]

---

[4] "Anton Steinbüchel von Rheinwall; April 1858," *SMF*, 162. Steinbüchel did not know Schubert directly; he was a friend of Vogl.

[5] "Kunigunde Vogl to her daughter Henriette; c. 1850," *SMF*, 216.

[6] The sources I refer to here are too numerous to cite. The notion of Schubert as a passive vessel of divine inspiration is mentioned in nearly every existing article- and book-length biography of Schubert, sometimes approvingly, sometimes skeptically. See also the entry "clairvoyance" in Ernst Hilmar and Margret Jestremski, *Schubert-Lexikon* (Graz, Austria: Akademische Druck- u. Verlagsanstalt, 1997), 61–62, in which a number of sketches and sketch studies are mentioned as evidence against it.

[7] Christopher H. Gibbs, "'Poor Schubert': Images and Legends of the Composer," in Christopher H. Gibbs (ed.), *The Cambridge Companion to Schubert* (Cambridge University Press, 1997),

Gibbs offers correctives to them all. The so-called "poor Schubert" was neither as financially poor nor as pathetic as he has been represented in novels, operettas, and films. Nor was he as "neglected" as generally assumed. Rather, before his death, he was beginning to be recognized beyond his circle of friends and native Vienna – Gibbs therefore proposes that less extreme terms such as "struggling" and "undiscovered" might be more appropriate.[8] And pertinent to the present discussion, Gibbs argues that Schubert was neither as "natural" nor as "naïve" a composer as his friends assumed and as was subsequently maintained in criticism, lexicons, histories, and biographies.

Gibbs explores how these legends arose. In the case of Schubert's reputation as a "natural" composer, he suggests that witnesses who saw Schubert "dash off a song on the back of a menu" mistakenly took this to be his general mode of composition. Gibbs concedes that such a feat is possible for a short song, but not for a symphony. However, as I shall demonstrate below, careful scrutiny of the anecdotes reveals that Schubert was never actually composing in such cases, and moreover he was largely reclusive when it came to composing. Gibbs also counters the usual assumption that Schubert was a natural, unreflective composer by pointing to his (occasional) self-critical statements, his increased discrimination in what he chose to compose as time went on, the existence of sketches and drafts, as well as his use of palindromes and mirror passages, as proof that Schubert cultivated technique and planned carefully when he needed to.[9]

My purpose is not to gather further evidence in support of Gibbs's conclusion that Schubert was no clairvoyant (which, in any case, I agree with). Instead I wish to start with the observation that Vogl had much to do with spreading this image of Schubert, and then to trace more fully how it

---

39 and 48–52, and *The Life of Schubert* (Cambridge University Press, 2000), 25–26, 62–64, and 173. For other detailed critical accounts of this phenomenon, see Peggy Woodford, *Schubert* (London: Omnibus Press, 1984), 54–57 and Lorraine Byrne, *Schubert's Goethe Settings* (Aldershot: Ashgate Publishing, Ltd., 2003), 25–29.

[8] Gibbs, "Poor Schubert," 47–48.

[9] Gibbs, "Poor Schubert," 50 (for the comment on dashing off a song but not a symphony); see 45 and 41 respectively on Schubert's self-criticism and discrimination. On the existence of sketches and drafts, and on the palindromes and mirror images, see Gibbs, *The Life of Schubert*, 63. Their existence is a common argument used, as if "evidence" is needed, to discredit Schubert's clairvoyance (see n. 6). The work classically cited for this purpose is the *Great* Symphony in C Major (D. 944). While Schubert's extant sketch material tends towards torsos of movements, which do little to suggest detailed workings, different versions or contrasting settings of the same poetry have been interpreted as an indication that Schubert was indeed critical of his own work; see for instance Marius Flothuis, "Schubert Revises Schubert," in Eva Badura-Skoda and Peter Branscombe (eds.), *Schubert Studies: Problems of Style and Chronology* (Cambridge University Press, 1982), 62.

grew in nineteenth- and early twentieth-century biographies and histories of music.[10] Perhaps, however, one corrective is necessary to Gibbs's argument. He assumes that Beethoven always possessed the image of a laboring genius beside which the emergence of Schubert's "natural" image is yet another example of how Schubert was being cast in opposition to Beethoven.[11] However, many of Schubert's contemporaries – especially those in his inner circle – initially equated Schubert with Beethoven. In their view, both were natural composers. Indeed, they would hardly have insisted on a mode of composition that would have meant Schubert was second-rate. It is important to recognize that, at the time Vogl began to spin the tale, being a natural composer was high praise for any composer.

Ideas about the most convincing incarnation of genius have been subject to pendulum swings.[12] Although effortless versus labored creativity – two notions of genius – have long existed side by side, different eras have privileged one over the other. The nineteenth century witnessed one such pendulum swing. As the century wore on, the prized form of inspiration shifted from the effortless kind to the ideal of the struggling artist. Hence, Beethoven, who became the epitome of the laboring genius, was considered a "natural" composer when it was fashionable to be one at the beginning of the nineteenth century. As late as mid-century, even Wagner declared Beethoven a genius on the grounds that he had the gift of a "clairvoyant somnambulist." Inspired by Schopenhauer's views, he wrote at length about the physiological condition of the clairvoyant, who experiences apparitions in an awakened dream-like state, which do not pertain to the "real phenomenal world." These apparitions "bring forth Beethoven's melodies."[13] Beethoven eventually lost that reputation, not least in the face of the discovery of his copious sketches. So too (in large part) did Mozart, who had been regarded as the quintessential musical machine but whose image also

---

[10] Gibbs provides instances of its repetition in early lexicons ("Poor Schubert," 49). However, as mentioned above, I shall include the early twentieth century.

[11] Gibbs, "Poor Schubert," 50.

[12] Lorraine Byrne provides an excellent account of the intellectual *Zeitgeist* under which attitudes towards Schubert arose during his lifetime in *Schubert's Goethe Settings*, 25–29. For discussion of the pendulum swing to labored creativity in the course of the nineteenth century, see Peter Kivy, *The Possessor and the Possessed: Handel, Mozart, Beethoven, and the Idea of Musical Genius* (New Haven and London: Yale University Press, 2001). For a representative late nineteenth-century account of composers' sources of inspiration, see the chapter entitled "How Composers Work" in Henry Theophilus Finck, *Chopin and Other Musical Essays* (New York: C. Scribner's Sons, 1889), 59–110. Schubert is portrayed as a clairvoyant (p. 85); Beethoven is not.

[13] See Richard Wagner, *Beethoven*, trans. Edward Dannreuther (London: William Reeves, 1880), 12–14, 21–22, and 83–87; the citations above come from p. 85.

underwent revision when it became convenient for his reputation.[14] Meanwhile, Vogl's idea of Schubert's clairvoyance stuck fast.

I propose, then, to hold Vogl responsible for the stance late nineteenth-century critics took towards Schubert's music, as well as for the meager analytical and theoretical attention it initially elicited. In more subtle ways, its modern reception is also shaped by this image. If I am to pin this historiography onto the repeated utterances of Schubert's favorite singer, then it is necessary first to trace how large and persuasive the story of Schubert's working habits grew. In this chapter, we shall see it grow in the memoirs of Schubert's friends, we shall see how it was handled by Schubert's first German and English biographers, and we shall see it make its way into early histories of music, and even into an analytical essay by Schenker. Indeed, I shall trace how the story lost its innocence, particularly in the hands of Victorian critics – precisely on account of that so-called pendulum swing in the prevailing notion of genius. While Vogl and Schubert's devotees invoked divine inspiration to explain both the vast quantity of his output and the fact that Schubert did not look or behave like a genius, others would use these claims to account for perceived weaknesses in Schubert's music. Paradoxically this new critical stance towards Schubert's music depended on Vogl's anecdotes being taken seriously.

I turn first, then, to the memoirs of Schubert's friends, many of which date from 1857 to 1858. They were written in response to a request from Schubert's would-be biographer Ferdinand Luib, whose projected biography never appeared but whose material was used by Heinrich Kreissle von Hellborn for his monumental biography, which was expanded in 1864 from an initial shorter biographical sketch published in 1861.[15] We shall see in due course what Kreissle made of the recollections. In the meantime, I shall scrutinize them first-hand for their stories of Schubert's clairvoyance, and for evidence of Vogl's role in propagating the idea that Schubert had such an ability.

[14] See, for example, the various essays on Mozart's sketches in Christoph Wolff (ed.), *The String Quartets of Haydn, Mozart and Beethoven: Studies of the Autograph Manuscripts* (Cambridge, MA: Harvard University Department of Music, 1980).

[15] Heinrich Kreissle von Hellborn, *Franz Schubert: Eine biographische Skizze* (Vienna: L. C. Zamarski and C. Dittmarsch, 1861). The longer version was serialized in 1864 in *Niederrheinische Musik-Zeitung für Kunstfreunde und Künstler* and *Signale für die musikalische Welt*, and appeared in book form one year later: see Heinrich Kreissle von Hellborn, *Franz Schubert* (Vienna: Carl Gerold's Sohn, 1865). There are various translations into English: the first appeared in abridged form with a translation by Edward Wilberforce, *Schubert: A Musical Biography* (London: Wm. H. Allen & Co., 1866); the most complete translation is *The Life of Franz Schubert*, trans. Arthur Duke Coleridge (London: Longmans, Green and Co., 1869).

Vogl's Schubert

Appropriately enough, the accounts of Vogl's first encounter with Schubert in 1817 convey an early formulation of the singer's view. The most detailed account comes from one of Schubert's closest friends, Joseph von Spaun, who, in his response to Luib's request for biographical information about Schubert, recalled – and undoubtedly embellished – how they met.[16] According to Spaun, Vogl was at first reluctant to meet the unknown composer. He was repeatedly approached by Schubert's friends, especially Franz von Schober, and though still reluctant, finally agreed to attend an evening at the latter's house. There are different versions about what happened next.

In Spaun's earlier account, Schubert cautiously presented the singer with his newly composed setting of Mayrhofer's "Augenlied," and Vogl immediately appreciated his talent. Given that, in this case, Spaun was casting the story in its first public record, for Schubert's obituary notice of 1829, some exaggeration of Vogl's enthusiasm is unsurprising.[17] By contrast his later account, from 1858, portrayed Vogl's guarded response. According to this version, it was Vogl who took the initiative and picked up the nearest sheet of manuscript paper, which happened to have "Augenlied" written on it. Summoning only a hum to Schubert's accompaniment of it, he apparently "coldly" judged it "not bad." Spaun boasts, however, that it is evident from this that even one of Schubert's most unimportant songs had the capacity to elicit some interest in this most discerning singer. Next, Vogl apparently attempted "Memnon" and "Ganymed," among other songs that Spaun does not specify. Still only dignifying these with a mezza voce rendition, Vogl was said to have parted company without promising ever to return. However, before leaving, he supposedly spoke to Schubert, conceding, "There is something in you but you are too little a comedian, too little of a charlatan; you squander your fine thoughts without making the best of them."[18]

Spaun's 1858 version of the encounter invokes the topos of the older master, who, despite his best efforts to the contrary, finds himself having to acknowledge the talents of a younger, usually innocent genius who

---

[16] "Josef von Spaun: Notes on my Association with Franz Schubert (1858)," *SMF*, 131–132. According to Deutsch (*SMF*, 43), these memoirs appear not to have reached Luib.

[17] "Josef von Spaun: On Schubert (1829) [Obituary notice]," *SMF*, 22. Vogl was also portrayed as immediately and enthusiastically recognizing Schubert's talent in his own obituary; see "C. S.: Obituary notice of J. M. Vogl (1841)," *SMF*, 305.

[18] "Josef von Spaun: Notes on my Association with Franz Schubert (1858)," *SMF*, 132.

inevitably does not look the part. Spaun hardly need have added that Vogl was secretly much more impressed than he was willing to let on to either Schubert or his friends on that occasion, nor did he really need to explain that when Vogl came across a setting of "Lied eines Schiffers an die Dioskuren" shortly after meeting Schubert, he was struck by its depth and maturity, yet baffled by how it could emanate from such an unlikely source – from, that is, such a "little young man."[19] Vogl's later insistence on Schubert's clairvoyance may well have started and persisted as a means of accounting for the discrepancy he sensed between the composer's physique and somewhat mundane existence, on the one hand, and the impression of his music, on the other.

In any case, some 63 years after Schubert's death, a hearsay account by the wife of the man who brought the two together would supply an unsurprising twist to the tale.[20] According to Thekla von Schober, Vogl's first encounter with Schubert now centered around Schubert's most famous poetic setting: the "Erlkönig." In her account, much like in Spaun's earlier account, there is no trace of a reticent Vogl. Instead Schubert was enthusiastically dispatched to a piano to sing his prize song. Immediately taken by it and its composer, Vogl apparently exclaimed, "Good heavens, man, you compose like a god!"[21]

The truth of the event matters little, though one can certainly imagine that a singer of Vogl's stature probably was approached frequently by budding composers and probably was routinely unenthusiastic. We perhaps need not decide which words he actually spoke on that occasion – even though Spaun's 1858 account rings truest – because these accounts all convey opinions that Vogl uttered often during his lifetime, namely: Schubert did not properly hone his talents; he was divinely inspired. Notably absent from all of the versions of Vogl's first impression is the idea that this divine inspiration was a force that Schubert did not understand. Vogl presumably became convinced of that detail once he got to know the composer.

After Schubert's death, many reminisced about what it was like to have witnessed Schubert compose. With tinges of nostalgia, they clearly saw him through Vogl's eyes. As one of Schubert's schoolfriends, Albert Stadler,

---

[19] "Josef von Spaun: Notes on my Association with Franz Schubert (1858)," *SMF*, 132.

[20] Thekla was the wife of Franz von Schober, who first introduced Vogl to Schubert. We do not have a direct account of the meeting from Schober, and this account by Thekla was recorded 26 years after her husband's death. Apparently Schober attempted to write memoirs of Schubert but found himself not up to the task; see "Schober to Bauernfeld, 19 January 1869," *SMF*, 205.

[21] "Thekla von Schober (1891): Franz Schubert and Franz von Schober," *SMF*, 210.

wrote in 1858, also with the aim of contributing to Luib's planned biography, the composer would often retreat to a writing table and, despite the noise from the chatter of his friends, would compose with great ease and speed: he would "bite his pen, drum with his fingers at the same time, trying things out, and continue to write easily and fluently, without many corrections, as if it had to be like that and not otherwise."[22]

If Stadler had ended his observation there, it would have suggested that Schubert had a measure of control over his musical creations. Instead he goes on. Significantly, he turns to recollections of a letter in which Vogl had written, "there are two kinds of composition, one which, as in Schubert's case, comes into existence during a state of clairvoyance or somnambulism, without any conscious action on the part of the composer, but inevitably, by act of providence and inspiration – one may well be astonished and charmed at such a work, but not criticize it. The second way of composition is through willpower, reflection, effort, knowledge, etc."[23] Stadler provides no assessment of which kind of compositional method is more highly regarded, nor does he question Vogl's claim about Schubert. Instead he moves on to another (and unrelated) thought. The implication, of course, is that Vogl was the authority on the subject.

There are many other stories of Schubert composing anywhere and instantaneously. Two anecdotes, however, contain a small yet significant detail, which puts his apparently public flashes of inspiration into an important context. On one occasion in July 1827, Schubert was at the Fröhlich sisters' house. The eldest of the Fröhlich sisters, Anna, had requested a poem from the great Viennese playwright Franz Grillparzer for the birthday of her pupil Louise Gosmar, and on Schubert's visit she asked him to set the poem to music. There are two extant versions of the anecdote, one from Leopold von Sonnleithner (who was unlikely to have been present) in 1857; the other from Gerhard von Breuning, who claims to have transcribed from memory Anna Fröhlich's own account (albeit four years after her death).[24]

---

[22] "Albert Stadler: Salzburg, 17 January 1858," *SMF*, 146.

[23] "Albert Stadler: Salzburg, 17 January 1858," *SMF*, 146. For reasons that will become clear later, the above quotation includes a portion of the letter cited by Kreissle, which Stadler omitted in his memoir. See Kreissle, *The Life of Franz Schubert*, vol. I, 122–123 n. 1. According to Kreissle, the letter was dated 15 November 1831.

[24] "Leopold von Sonnleithner: Vienna, 1 November 1857," *SMF*, 111, and "Gerhard von Breuning: Aus Grillparzers Wohnung (1884)," *SMF*, 252. Sonnleithner most likely "remembered" this event because Louise Gosmar became his wife, and he learned the story from her. However, given that the song "Ständchen" (D. 920) was intended as a surprise for her, she clearly did not witness the event either. It also possible that Sonnleithner heard this story from Grillparzer, who was his cousin.

Sonnleithner describes how Schubert was presented with the poem by Anna, whereupon he rushed to an alcove to read through it, and immediately declared with a smile, "I've got it already, it's done, and it's going to be quite good." Sonnleithner adds the important detail that Schubert returned with the completed composition a "day or two" later.[25] Anna's account, memorialized by Breuning, is identical, except that Schubert was not observed to have rushed to an alcove; he merely leant against the piano to read the poem. He is said to have exclaimed the poem to be beautiful, looked at the sheet for a while and then said "There, it is finished now, I've got it already."[26] "Only three days later" (she was clearly impressed by the speed), he presented her with the music. Again, this final detail is revealing: although many witnessed Schubert's flashes of inspiration when he read through a poem and he declared his composition "done," it seems few actually witnessed him compose. He preferred to do so in private.

Anna's account goes on yet further, for, as it turns out, she had to complain to Schubert about his setting: he had written the piece for mezzo-soprano (that is, for Anna's sister Pepi to sing) and four male voices; Anna needed it recast for women's voices only. She claimed to have said to him: "No, Schubert, I can't use it like this, it's meant to be a tribute from Gosmar's women friends only." Schubert obliged with a revised setting, which he does seem to have done immediately, "sitting over there in the right-hand window recess of the ante-room."[27] Sonnleithner was partially right, then: Schubert did disappear off to an alcove, but he was arranging not composing. When later biographers picked up on such anecdotes, they would surmise that Schubert had only to "read the poem, and the appropriate tune, married to immortal verse (a marriage, in his case, truly made in heaven), rushed into his mind, and to the end of his pen."[28] All but the last detail captures Schubert's compositional process: as quick as Schubert was at composition, the degree of spontaneity does seem to have been exaggerated.

The reliance on Vogl's opinion that Schubert was somehow clairvoyant seems therefore to stem from Schubert's claims to have "finished" or "got it" after a quick read through a poem. Schönstein's memoirs of another such occasion provide ample evidence of this habit. During a sojourn in Zseliz in 1824 (at which Schönstein was present), Karoline, the Countess Esterházy, asked Schubert to set the poem "Gebet" (D. 815) as a four-part

---

[25] "Leopold von Sonnleithner: Vienna, 1 November 1857," *SMF*, 111.

[26] "Gerhard von Breuning: Aus Grillparzers Wohnung (1884)," *SMF*, 252.

[27] "Gerhard von Breuning: Aus Grillparzers Wohnung (1884)," *SMF*, 252.

[28] Sir George Grove, "Schubert," *Grove's Dictionary of Music and Musicians*, ed. J. A. Fuller Maitland (London: Macmillan, 1908), 330.

song. She made her request at breakfast. First Schubert read the poem, "smiled inwardly, as he usually did when something appealed to him" (the same smile, it seems, that Sonnleithner reported in his anecdote above), and he "retired forthwith, in order to compose." Note again: he *retired* and composed in private.

The song was ready by evening. Schönstein writes of his astonishment that such a substantial piece could be written in one day. Indeed, he is certain that anyone who knows the piece will not believe that Schubert could have composed it in "barely ten hours." "It certainly seems incredible, but it is nevertheless true," Schönstein avows, forestalling any potential skepticism. He did not witness Schubert compose yet he came up with the only explanation he could think of for the achievement: "Schubert was the man for that kind of thing, this heaven-inspired clairvoyant who, as it were, simply shook his most glorious things out of this sleeve (to use a colloquial expression)."[29]

Schönstein was reluctant to give Vogl all the credit for noticing special powers. He claims to have already had an inkling of Schubert's clairvoyance, before "Vogl told me himself" of another incident which "*confirmed anew my previously formed opinion* that Schubert was a kind of musical clairvoyant" (italics mine).[30] This particular story goes like this: Vogl was singing with Schubert in his usual way and handed him a song that Schubert had composed about two weeks earlier. A copyist had in the meantime transposed it to a lower key for Vogl's benefit; therefore it was no longer in Schubert's own hand. After running through it, Schubert is said to have exclaimed, "You know that song isn't bad! Who's it by?" Schönstein, presumably following Vogl's lead, concluded that Schubert no longer recognized his own composition.[31]

Others repeated the same tale – all to illustrate Schubert's purported unconscious creativity. A schoolfriend of Schubert, Max Löwenthal, latched on to it in a diary entry from 1838, and surmised that Schubert "created his admirable song compositions so unconsciously that, at times, he even completely forgot what he had written."[32] Karoline Pichler, a pupil of Mozart and host to a lively salon frequented by Beethoven, Schlegel, Grillparzer, and Schubert, drew the same conclusion. In her rendition, note the stress placed on the source of the anecdote: Schubert "brought into existence what was beautiful and moving in his compositions almost

---

[29] "Karl Freiherr v. Schönstein: January 1857," *SMF*, 102.
[30] "Karl Freiherr v. Schönstein: January 1857," *SMF*, 101.
[31] "Karl Freiherr v. Schönstein: January 1857," *SMF*, 101.
[32] "Max Löwenthal: Diary (1838)," *SMF*, 296.

unconsciously, indeed perhaps I may refer here to an anecdote which I had from the mouth of our famous singer, Vogl, himself." After redescribing how Schubert did not recognize his own composition, she emphasized again that his music was "so unconscious, so involuntary."[33] Christopher H. Gibbs, in his revisionist biography, follows Maurice J. E. Brown in suggesting, utterly plausibly, that Schubert's sense of humor might have been lost on Vogl – and indeed Schönstein, Löwenthal, and Pichler. Gibbs argues that Schubert might well have been commenting ironically on Vogl's interventionist attitude towards his songs, embellishing and transposing them as he was clearly wont to do.[34]

Neither Löwenthal nor Pichler bothers to mention which song Schubert had supposedly forgotten, and Schönstein confesses that he no longer remembered the name of it. However, in yet another account of this incident, this time by Vogl's wife Kunigunde – ever the one to find an apt song to underscore an anecdote – the song is identified as "Der Unglückliche."[35] As it turns out, Karoline Pichler wrote the text of "Der Unglückliche." As it also turns out (although it seems maladroit to critique the colorful embellishments of such tales), there are numerous extant sketches for "Der Unglückliche." Indeed some scholars have questioned the validity of Kunigunde's memory because all evidence suggests that Schubert labored over this one![36] At any rate, the repetition of the story is of more significance than the overlapping or not of details, and it seems that Vogl repeated himself often, holding dear to the idea that Schubert was the quintessential clairvoyant composer, more vessel than creator.

Soon enough, stories of Schubert's compositional methods grew to apocryphal proportions. In 1856, a certain John Ella reported that he went to a coffeehouse with Kapellmeister Reuling, who informed him that they were sitting in the same spot in which Schubert "sketched many of his songs whilst smoking his cigar in the company of Beethoven."[37] Reuling

---

[33] "Karoline Pichler: Memoirs (1844)," *SMF*, 302. In the same memoir, Pichler explains that Haydn and Mozart must also have possessed the same mysterious powers. She bases her conclusion on her personal experience of having met them both: as in Schubert's case, their personalities did not seem to suggest greatness.

[34] See Maurice J. E. Brown, *The New Grove Schubert* (New York: Macmillan Publishers Ltd, 1982), 17. Gibbs, *The Life of Schubert*, 62.

[35] "Kunigunde Vogl to her daughter Henriette (Vienna, *c.* 1850)," *SMF*, 217.

[36] See, for example, Walther Dürr, "Entwurf – Ausarbeitung – Revision: Zur Arbeitsweise Schuberts am Beispiel des Liedes *Der Unglückliche* (D 713)," *Die Musikforschung* 44 (1991): 221–236.

[37] "John Ella: Note on Schubert," *SMF*, 263. Ella mentions that this took place in 1845, on his first visit to Vienna. Ella (1802–1888) was an English writer on music and founded the Musical Union in London. Reuling (1802–1877) met success as a composer of numerous dramatic works and was first appointed Kapellmeister of the Josephstadt Theatre and then to the Kärntnertor

claimed that Beethoven used to blow the cigar ashes onto the manuscript and could be heard in a "mock-heroic strain" (no less) to say "Behold Phoenix rising out of the ashes!" One could, of course, easily separate fact from fiction in this story, as Otto Deutsch has done: Schubert smoked, but not cigars; he went to coffeehouses, but not to compose; he did not socialize with Beethoven.[38]

More interesting, however, is how this story mythologizes the essence of Vogl's representation of Schubert. The Phoenix is a mythical bird, which dies, consumed by flames, and then springs forth anew from its own ashes. An heir to itself, only one Phoenix is said to live at any one time; it is unique. As some versions of Classical legend have it, the sun god would stop his chariot to listen to the bird sing its beautiful song. On the one hand, Schubert's association with the Phoenix is complimentary: perhaps, like the Phoenix, Schubert too was unique, and surely the reference to song – and to a listener entranced by it – is apposite. On the other hand, it robs Schubert of the credit of an active part in the creation of his musical products: like the Phoenix, Schubert's music was said to emanate from an unlikely source and to emerge fully formed, without, that is, going through any biological or organic process – without indeed going through the struggle of creation.

How might Schubert himself have viewed Vogl's portrayal of his mode of inspiration? In 1816, he wrote a musical commentary on the matter. At first blush, the composer's choice of piano prelude for his setting of Mayrhofer's "Geheimnis: An Franz Schubert" (as "Geheimnis," D. 491) indicates that Schubert may have been complicit in fostering the view that his inspirations were "divine." Mayrhofer's poem begins with the line, "Sag an, wer lehrt dich Lieder, so schmeichelnd und so zart?" ("Tell me, who teaches you such flattering, tender songs?"). Schubert's musical answer is given in Example 1.1. A lone, *pianissimo* arpeggiation in the right hand flutters down to a cadence before the voice enters. This piano prelude suggests that his songs come from on high. It might seem that Schubert himself was complicit in promoting the prominent nineteenth-century view of his divine inspiration.

Theatre in Vienna. This anecdote appeared in a program note for one of the Union's chamber concerts on June 24, 1856. See Deutsch's comment, *SMF*, 263.

[38] Deutsch provides these correctives in the notes to Ella's anecdote, *SMF*, 263. This anecdote brings to mind E. M. Forster's vivid imagery of the goblins in the Scherzo of Beethoven's Fifth Symphony – goblins that Beethoven marshalled into position on the music stave and then blew away with a puff of air: "Beethoven took hold of the goblins and made them do what he wanted. He appeared in person. He gave them a little push, and they began to walk in a major key instead of in a minor, and then – he blew with his mouth and they were scattered!" *Howards End* (New York: Alfred A. Knopf, 1921), 40.

Example 1.1 Schubert, "Geheimnis" (D. 491), mm. 1–7

Yet there may be a way of reading his setting of "Geheimnis" as ironic. Many have considered the song an uninspired work – which is an irony in itself. They assume that Schubert was merely returning a favor to Mayrhofer.[39] But what if Schubert is portraying his music as least inspired when tapped straight from a muse? Indeed, the rest of this song contains a number of characteristic modulations. Two are hexatonic; one of which is masterful in execution, the other awkward. The masterful one comes amidst a more poetic aspect of the text about an old man crowned with reeds who pours out his urn and water flowing in a meadow. Significantly, I think, the awkward modulation prepares the return of a singer-persona within the poem. This comes at the very point where Mayrhofer suggests that Schubert, like the singer, must wonder at God's creation: "Er singt, er staunt in sich; was still ein Gott bereitet, befremdet ihn wie dich" ("He sings, he marvels inwardly; he wonders at God's silent creation, as do you").

Another biographical anecdote compiled by Deutsch further suggests that we ought to read the prelude of "Geheimnis" with heavy doses of

---

[39] See, for example, John Reed, *The Schubert Song Companion* (Manchester: Mandolin, 1997), 238–239.

irony. Franz Lachner's anecdote dates posthumously from *c.*1905 but recalls in detail a conversation he had with Schubert when he paid him a visit in early 1826.[40] The composer apparently greeted him with "Let's have some coffee!" whereupon he got out his coffee mill and began grinding beans. In words reminiscent of other moments of inspiration, he exclaimed, "I've got it, I've got it, you crusty little contraption!" He then hurled the machine and beans all over the room and cried out, "Oh a coffee-mill like this is a wonderful thing. Melodies and themes just come flying in. You see, it's this Ra-ra-ra, that's what it is! It gives us inspirations, it transforms us into the wonderful realm of the imagination!" Lachner laughed, seemingly joining in the mockery with "Ah, so it's your coffee mill that composes, not your head?" To which Schubert replied, "That's it, Franzl, one's head sometimes searches for days for an idea which the little machine there finds in a second. Listen!" Lachner quickly noted down the melodies. Schubert then gathered up the beans, resumed grinding, and together they drank Schubert's source of inspiration. If we are taken in by this story, it seems we should be grateful for Lachner's transcription skills: the melodies belong to the String Quartet in D Minor (*Der Tod und das Mädchen*, D. 810).

However, as Deutsch points out in his commentary, "the origin of the anecdote about the coffee mill cannot be established with certainty."[41] Never mind. The important point from the perspective of the reception of Schubert is that he was portrayed as mocking the idea that he – literally – grinds out his music by interpreting signals from another source. Equally important is that Lachner is portrayed as taking the moment of inspiration seriously. He transcribes the music. Just in case. He needn't really have bothered: Schubert had composed the quartet some two years before this event supposedly took place.

A central part of the image that Vogl generated, then, is the absence of those qualities attributed to the second type of composition, noted earlier, namely: willpower, reflection, effort and, above all, knowledge. Schubert was assumed to lack all of these qualities. This assessment has had an enormous impact on the shape of Schubert's early reception and modern scholarship, as well as on the way in which listeners are invited to hear Schubert's music and to assess its intellectual content. It is apt, then, that

---

[40] "Another Lachner Anecdote (1905)," *SMF*, 292–293.

[41] "Another Lachner Anecdote (1905)," *SMF*, 295. Deutsch provides a brief publication history of this anecdote in his commentary, 295. Lachner was influential in his day as an operatic and festival conductor in Vienna and Munich and was a prolific, though now largely forgotten, composer in his own right.

on Vogl's death, Vogl was described as Schubert's "first patron and bene-factor, the truest interpreter of his overflowing, trance-like genius."[42] This description brings together, if perhaps unwittingly, both Vogl's role in the dissemination of Schubert's songs and his characterization of his composi-tional method.

Yet for every story that depicts Schubert suddenly caught in a frenzy of composition, writing in a coffeehouse, composing in a transfixed state or rushing to an alcove, there are competing, more mundane versions of compositional events. We are also told repeatedly by Schubert's closest friends – especially those with whom he lived – that Schubert's normal time and place of composition was in his room, at a writing desk, between nine o'clock in the morning and two in the afternoon, a schedule he apparently kept daily.[43] If ever a fact could deflate the image of the Romantic com-poser, it would be the existence of routine – for it is hardly befitting of divine inspiration to hold office hours.

Although all of these same friends participated in Vogl's nostalgia for a clairvoyant Schubert, there were some dissenting voices – though, as we shall see, even they joined the chorus and called Schubert a somnambulist at some point. Even upon Schubert's death, his friends disagreed over whether or not he possessed the intellectual power and enough education to understand his own art. Johann Mayrhofer thought not. In the obituary he penned in 1829, he wrote: "Devoid of a more profound knowledge of composition and thorough-bass, he [Schubert] actually remained a natural artist."[44] Joseph von Spaun claimed the opposite in his obituary: Schubert, he insisted, was perfectly capable of accounting for the "peculiarities of his work in a manner which most decisively contradicted the opinion, held

---

[42] See "Albert Stadler to an unknown lady," *SMF*, 215.

[43] Actually there are varying accounts of his specific working hours. According to Hüttenbrenner, Schubert spent 6 a.m. to 1 p.m. composing when Schubert lived with Mayrhofer ("Anselm Hüttenbrenner for Liszt: Fragments from the Life of the Song Composer Franz Schubert . . . Vienna 1854," *SMF*, 182) and it was Spaun who suggested he worked from 9 a.m. to 2 p.m. ("On Schubert (1829)," *SMF*, 25). All agree, however, that he held to a routine, though Sonnleithner blamed Schubert's failure to obtain the post at the Kärntnertor Theatre on a period of excessive behavior that meant he would lie in bed until 10 or 11 a.m. and be punctual for nothing ("Leopold von Sonnleithner: Vienna, 1 November 1857," *SMF*, 109–110). Sonnleithner seems to have been annoyed that Schubert was neither composing assiduously nor earning his own living.

[44] "Johann Mayrhofer: Recollections of Franz Schubert (*Neues Archiv für Geschichte, Staatenkunde, Literatur und Kunst*, Vienna, 23 February 1829) [obituary notice]," *SMF*, 13. Schubert lived with Mayrhofer from 1818 to 1820, and the latter's intellectual and melancholic outlook on life had a considerable impact on Schubert's output. The two seemed to have parted ways in Schubert's later years, as Mayrhofer regretfully admits in the obituary.

here and there, that he produced his finest music as it were by inspiration pure and simple, without any conscious activity of his own."[45]

Yet, when it was convenient to do so (some thirty years later), Spaun was also not adverse to appealing to Schubert's clairvoyance. As a form of defense against those who attacked Schubert's public image (it was either too boring or too lewd), Spaun understandably sought to emphasize the composer's "divine" inspiration, a condition that rendered him more obviously special. In writing for Luib in 1858, he alluded to those who saw a "dull fellow with no feeling" in Schubert's public guise. "In the afternoon" – when the public saw him – "he was admittedly another person," Spaun conceded.[46] He therefore spoke of having been privy to witnessing his demeanor in the act of composition: "Anyone who has seen him of a morning occupied with composition, aglow, with his eyes shining and even his speech changed, like a somnambulist, will never forget the impression."[47] It could not be clearer that reports of Schubert's clairvoyance were seen as an answer to his disconcertingly ordinary – or even, as many claimed, unattractive – appearance.

At a very early stage, then, there were competing claims about Schubert: some argued he was aware, others that he was unaware of the reasons behind the shape of his musical content. The image of a studious, knowledgeable musician – especially one who could defend his "peculiarities" – never caught on.

Joseph Hüttenbrenner regretted this impulse, and railed against Mayrhofer for his damaging obituary, although he admits he too was once under the false impression that Schubert was a clairvoyant:

Schubert the natural composer. Who is a natural composer? We called Schubert a natural composer at first. I did. Mayrhofer did in his article, "Franz Schubert," in the "Oesterreichisches Archiv" of the year … no … Mayrhofer understood nothing about music; I fell out with him over this; his opinion of Schubert – can

---

[45] Spaun, "Österreichisches Bürgerblatt für Verstand, Herz und gute Laune," *SDB*, 878. The real pity, of course, is that Spaun did not reveal what it is that Schubert said about music or his own "peculiarities." This is almost the same document as referred to earlier as "On Schubert (1829)," *SMF*, 18–29. However, the thought cited above is not in the latter version. An anonymous entry in the Dresden *Abendzeitung* (19 August 1825) is also tantalizing in this regard: the author praised Schubert's songs, saying they testify to a "profound feeling, combined with considerable musical theory," but unfortunately does not spell out what he means (see *SDB*, 418).

[46] "Josef von Spaun: Notes on my Association with Franz Schubert (1858)," *SMF*, 138. Bauernfeld was another to acknowledge to Luib that Schubert was "inwardly a poet and outwardly a hedonist"; "Eduard von Bauernfeld: 24 November 1857," *SMF*, 45. However, he did not resort to presenting Schubert as a somnambulant genius, although much later he attributed the more trite music to Schubert writing "just as it came into his head, in the first surging, exuberant and immature flush of youth"; "Bauernfeld: Some Notes on Franz Schubert (1869)," *SMF*, 234.

[47] "Josef von Spaun: Notes on my Association with Franz Schubert (1858)," *SMF*, 138.

one degrade and insult Schubert more? Meanwhile Sechter, Assmayr, Preyer were of the same opinion – they declare Beethoven and Schubert to be merely natural composers?!! Pereant![48]

In his commentary, Otto Erich Deutsch deems this particular reminiscence by Hüttenbrenner to be "somewhat confused owing to senility."[49] Indeed, after the onset of his dementia, Hüttenbrenner was equally capable of saying the exact opposite (though Spaun contradicted himself too, and he supposedly had his wits about him). Also around 1858, Hüttenbrenner found it irresistible to muse that, "when composing, Schubert looked to me like a somnambulist. His eyes shone, standing out as if they were made of glass."[50] That said, the content of Hüttenbrenner's outburst should not be summarily dismissed. It reveals that Schubert's circle of friends were also of the view that Beethoven was a natural composer, and confirms that by mid-century attitudes were changing. Hüttenbrenner's falling-out with Mayrhofer is both testimony to the shifting trends in ideas about genius and a tacit acknowledgement that something was at stake.

On yet another occasion *c.*1858, Hüttenbrenner again asserted that no one should suffer the "reproach" of being called a "natural composer." To label someone thus was an indictment against their harmonic and contra-puntal skill.[51] Two years later, he was still seething over Schubert's – and Beethoven's – tarnished reputation: he complained to Beethoven's famous biographer Alexander Wheelock Thayer about "The orthodox people in the Vienna Court Chapel who stupidly presume to call Beethoven and Schubert natural composers ?! because they cannot write a fugue."[52] A further six years later, he wrote almost exactly the same words in a letter to an unknown recipient: "The gentlemen of the Imperial Court Chapel ... say *Beethoven* and *Schubert* are natural composers, they cannot write a fugue. Herr Bibl, first organist at the Metropolitan Church, says the same."[53] This time Hüttenbrenner goes on to point out numerous fugues or fugal passages by both. Again, Deutsch argues that Hüttenbrenner's writings "all show the writer's mental deterioration."[54] While it is true that they are not lucid, they

---

[48] "Josef Hüttenbrenner's Notes," *SMF*, 76. The ellipses are in the original.

[49] "Josef Hüttenbrenner's Notes," *SMF*, 76.   [50] See "Schubertiana," *SMF*, 76.

[51] "Josef Hüttenbrenner [c. 1858]," *SMF*, 76. The date of 1858 was inserted by Deutsch.

[52] "Josef Hüttenbrenner to Thayer, Vienna, 8 October 1860," *SMF*, 190. Luib was also engaged in a biography of Beethoven, and he seems to have given some of his material to Thayer. See Deutsch, "Introductory Note," 42–43. Although Schubert and Beethoven never crossed paths, they knew many people in common.

[53] "Josef Hüttenbrenner to an unknown recipient, Vienna, 7 and 12 March, 1968," *SMF*, 192. Italics in original.

[54] See Deutsch's comments on Hüttenbrenner, *SMF*, 193.

do reveal that he seems to have become obsessed with the damage that Vogl's story had done to Schubert's reputation, and he feared the same for Beethoven. Clearly Beethoven did eventually shed the image of the natural composer. Schubert never really has.

Kreissle's Schubert

One detailed reaction to the biography of Schubert by Heinrich Kreissle von Hellborn survives from the pen of Joseph von Spaun, who made notes possibly intended for a published review.[55] Spaun's quibbles may seem unjustified, given that he himself wrote similar impressions of Schubert for Luib in 1858,[56] but he complained that Kreissle's readers would be left with the wrong impression of Schubert's musicianship:

anyone inclined to believe that Schubert was only an excellent natural composer, a belief into which several intimations in the biography could mislead one, would make a great mistake. He possessed the most thorough musical knowledge and had studied the works of the great masters, both old and new, in the greatest detail. Bach and Handel he worked through thoroughly and held in very high esteem; all Gluck's operas he could play almost from memory and there was probably not a note by Mozart, Beethoven and Haydn that he did not know. With such knowledge one is no mere natural composer.[57]

Spaun conceded that Schubert could be faulted for not revising his work and for not excising some tedious passages,[58] but according to him, Schubert could have revised his work if he had the inclination or time. Had Spaun read Kreissle's biography more carefully, he would have known that Kreissle made exactly the same point. Indeed Kreissle came to Schubert's defense often enough.

---

[55] Spaun was presumably responding to the serialized biography (see n. 15 above). "Josef von Spaun: (2) Some Observations on the Life of Schubert by Herr Ritter von Kreissle-Hellborn (1864)," *SMF*, 359–368. Deutsch points out (p. 370) that these notes were never published by Spaun.

[56] As mentioned in n. 16, Deutsch indicates (*SMF*, 43) that Spaun's memoir, "Josef von Spaun: Notes on my Association with Franz Schubert (1858)," may not have reached Luib, in which case it seems unlikely they were part of the papers Kreissle received. However, Kreissle does mention Spaun as one of his sources (see n. 116 below). Whether or not Kreissle had access to this particular document, it is significant that Spaun contemplated characterizing Schubert as a somnambulist in a memoir he intended for public consumption.

[57] "Josef von Spaun: (2) Some Observations on the Life of Schubert by Herr Ritter von Kreissle-Hellborn (1864)," *SMF*, 362–363.

[58] "Josef von Spaun: (2) Some Observations on the Life of Schubert by Herr Ritter von Kreissle-Hellborn (1864)," *SMF*, 363.

While the early chapters of the biography comprise many anecdotes cited verbatim from the memoirs collected by Luib, by the later chapters Kreissle began to add his own commentary, openly questioning the opinion of Schubert's friends. It fell to the final chapter of Kreissle's biography to tackle Vogl's conviction about Schubert's clairvoyance – and here, Kreissle placed the weakness of understanding not in Schubert but in his commentators:

> although men [Vogl, Schönstein, and Schober] are utterly mistaken in ascribing his inventive genius and power to a state of clairvoyance, irrespective of ordinary cultivation, the characteristic fact still remains, that even men who were deeply interested in him, and occasionally seized an opportunity of watching him in his working hours, tried to explain, by references to supernatural means, a process incomprehensible to them, but one which was developed completely in the works of this great composer.[59]

Nonetheless in the last few of pages of the biography, Kreissle seems almost to give credence to the opinion of Schubert's friends. He remarks, "If ever there lived a 'naïf' music-composer in the highest sense of the epithet, that man assuredly was Franz Schubert." Note how Kreissle stresses that he means naïveté "in the highest sense" of the term. Indeed, he links it to Schubert's apparently effortless writing: "That the *limae labor* ['painstaking polishing'] was a very rare thing with Schubert, is a well-authenticated fact, and evidenced most unmistakably by his own manuscripts."[60] He goes on to explain that this is why there is less of a concentrated power and polish in Schubert's music, and why he was prone to repetition. But for Kreissle, Schubert's foibles had everything to do with the haste in which he wrote, rather than any lack of knowledge or ability.

Kreissle's final appraisal of Schubert is as positive as any of his friends could have hoped for: in sum, he found that Schubert achieved "entire originality," "exuberant inventiveness," "vigour and glow," "deep true senti-ment," "warmth and dramatic life" in his music, and he possessed a "versa-tility and original power" and an intellect that inspired the next generation of composers.[61]

Kreissle equally questioned misgivings about Schubert's level of educa-tion. In a chapter on Schubert's "characteristics," he concluded: "it would be incorrect to assert that his education was generally defective, and that

---

[59] Kreissle, *The Life of Franz Schubert*, vol. II, 264. Kreissle specifies in a footnote that the "men" he was talking about are Vogl, Schönstein, and Schober.

[60] Kreissle, *The Life of Franz Schubert*, vol. II, 263.

[61] Kreissle, *The Life of Franz Schubert*, vol. II, 262 and 265.

the many beautiful things he gave to the world were the unreasoning efforts of a dreamlike imagination. The few letters we possess . . . prove that their author's heart and understanding were in the right place."[62] Although Kreissle clearly argued that it would be overstating the case to say that Schubert lacked education, numerous comments by Schubert's friends, which appeared after his biography was published, suggest the message did not get through. While Spaun's comments languished unpublished, others echoed his protest in similar terms – and appeared in print. Nearly thirty years after Vogl's death, and a decade after the appearance of Kreissle's biography, the debate about Schubert's level of education would continue to rage.

In an extensive and very measured memoir, which appeared in Vienna's *Die Presse* on April 17 and 21, 1869, Eduard von Bauernfeld reflected on Schubert's reputation for lacking literary education and for being a "kind of talented 'drunken savage.'"[63] A highly educated man himself, Bauernfeld's public correction of "certain mistakes" about Schubert offers important insights into what he and his friends valued about Schubert's creativity, as they reflected on the reputation they were complicit in constructing. According to him (and similarly to Spaun), Schubert knew the masters, knew the theory of his art, and was well versed in literature; he was familiar with history and "even" (Bauernfeld's emphasis) philosophy:

Schubert, admittedly, had no real academic education; his studies scarcely went beyond the Gymnasium and, throughout the whole of his short life, he remained self-taught. In his own subject he knew the masters and the master-works fairly thoroughly and, under Salieri's guidance, had also given adequate attention to the theory of his art. Moreover in literature, too, he was anything but unversed and the way he understood how to interpret, with inventiveness and vitality, the different poetic individualities, like Goethe, Schiller, Wilhelm Müller, J. G. Seidl, Mayrhofer, Walter Scott and Heine, how to transform them into new flesh and blood and how to render faithfully the nature of each one by beautiful and noble musical characterization – these recreations in song should alone be sufficient to demonstrate, merely by their own existence and without any further proof, from how deep a nature, from how sensitive a soul these creations sprang. A man who so understands the poets is himself a poet! And a man who is a poet and who indulges convivially with friends and congenial companions from time to time is still far from being a drunken savage! Nor was it a rare thing for this savage to venture on serious reading; there exist extracts, in his handwriting, from historical, even from philosophical, writings; his diaries contain his own, sometimes extremely original,

---

[62] Kreissle, *The Life of Franz Schubert*, vol. II, 154.
[63] "Bauernfeld (3): Some Notes on Franz Schubert (1869)," *SMF*, 229.

thoughts, as well as poems, and his favourite companions were artists and people with artistic affinities.[64]

Still in 1877, another acquaintance of Schubert's, Maria Mitterbacher, expresses exasperation over the persistent belief in Schubert's lack of knowledge: she outright protested against those who said that his music "was superimposed on him like a garment and that, in reality, he was a beer barrel, who did not know himself what he wrote. But that is simply ridiculous!"[65] She was reacting against the project that Adorno identified as the "transformation of Schubert the man into that repulsive specimen of petit bourgeois sentimentality," which culminated in Rudolph Hans Bartsch's *Schwammerl: Ein Schubert Roman* (1912) and Heinrich Berté's popular operetta *Das Dreimäderlhaus* (1916).[66] Such sentimental views of Schubert were by no means restricted to the Austrians, as the English fostered this view with verve.

Grove's Schubert

If Schubert's first biographer made a modest effort to deflate Vogl's image of Schubert, then Schubert's second major biographer made every effort to revive it. Indeed, the notion of Schubert's clairvoyance and accompanying lack of knowledge would have a far more powerful – and eventually detrimental – effect on Schubert reception thanks to Sir George Grove's biography written almost twenty years after Kreissle's. Grove, who is usually credited with writing a highly sympathetic portrayal of the composer, breathed new life into Vogl's belief. He made far more than Kreissle ever did of anecdotal testimony to Schubert's poor education, to his lack of formal and contrapuntal know-how, and to his clairvoyant musicianship.

Grove's dictionary article follows the basic structure of Kreissle's biography, giving a year-by-year account of Schubert's short life from his time in the Imperial Court Chapel choir in 1808, when he also began his studies at the *Konvict* school for choristers, aged 11. After detailing the main events

---

[64] "Bauernfeld: Some Notes on Franz Schubert (1869)," *SMF*, 229–230.

[65] "Frau Maria Mitterbacher, née Wagner: Memoirs (1877)," *SMF*, 298. Mitterbacher knew Schubert in her youth and, by her own account, witnessed Schubert perform many of his own songs.

[66] Theodor W. Adorno, "Schubert (1928)," trans. Jonathan Dunsby and Beate Perrey, *19th-Century Music* 29 (2005): 8. When *Das Dreimäderlhaus* made its way to London in 1922, it went by the name *Lilac Time*.

of each year, Grove lists, with occasional commentary, the pieces Schubert composed. In this respect, he offers a more substantial sense of Schubert's output than Kreissle did, largely on account of his travels to Vienna, during which he unearthed many otherwise unknown works. The entry ends with an overview of Schubert's posthumous reputation. Grove highlights in particular the esteem in which Schumann and Liszt held him, and he welcomes Schubert's growing reputation in England – owed in large part to himself! He goes on to explore the (meager number of) portraits of Schubert, his attitude to religion, and his lifestyle; finally, he provides a detailed commentary on the harmonic and formal aspects of Schubert's instrumental and song output.[67]

Beginning as Grove did with Schubert's school years, he blames Schubert's friends and early teachers, among them Antonio Salieri, for not doing more to educate Schubert on how to hone his natural talent. They have "a lot to answer for," quips Grove, for they left Schubert in a state of permanent embarrassment, which, Grove claims, Schubert attempted to rectify by studying with Sechter during what would turn out to be the last few weeks of his life.[68]

The idea of Schubert's intellectual weakness dies hard. Every modern biography touches on the matter and offers a corrective, as if for the first time. Given the litany of attempts to dispel the myth of Schubert's poor schooling, one might wonder why Grove's characterization of Schubert even persists. Indeed, in 1940 Howard D. McKinney and W. R. Anderson went so far as to scrutinize Schubert's school report cards and compare them to those of his peers.[69] They argue that, contrary to popular assumption, he was one of the brightest in his class, which is what enabled him to teach in his father's school from such a young age. Although his contemporaries indicate he neglected his other subjects in favor of his compositional activities, McKinney and Anderson reveal that this did not have an adverse affect on his school results. With regard to musical training, they argue that Schubert received a superior general education to either Mozart or Beethoven. They also conclude that the fact that he turned to Sechter later in life has overshadowed the musical training he received early in his

---

[67] Grove, "Schubert." Grove's insights into Schubert's harmony and form offer one of the best glimpses into mid-nineteenth-century perceptions of Schubert's harmonic and formal practice. These aspects of Schubert reception will be treated in Chapter 2.

[68] Grove, "Schubert," 282, 288–289, and 324.

[69] Howard D. McKinney and W. R. Anderson, *Music in History: The Evolution of an Art* (New York: American Book Company, 1940), 549–550.

schooling.[70] This hardly put the matter to rest. Similar territory is covered, as if anew, by recent biographers. Most recently, for example, Christopher H. Gibbs downplays the significance of Schubert's attempt to study with Sechter and puts Schubert's education into relief once more.[71]

Grove made the most out of his belief in Schubert's poor education and blames a number of Schubert's apparent shortcomings on the neglect of his teachers. Firstly, his themes (in the instrumental music) display an "untutored *naïveté*" (the italics are Grove's). Secondly, instead of engaging in contrapuntal treatment, as Grove believed was called for in good instrumental music, "his want of education" drove him to repeat passages, usually immediately and almost note for note in various keys, which he did for no good reason other than that he liked them. Hence the "diffuseness" in his forms. While in the songs such repetition "does not offend," Grove took it as a fault in the instrumental music. In particular, it led to an "incalculable amount of modulation." Yet, Grove wondered: "if we knew what he was thinking of, as we do in the songs, we might possibly find the repetition just."[72]

It is a pity Grove did not ponder over what might constitute a plausible justification for these traits in Schubert's instrumental music, as he did in the songs. Toward the end of the dictionary entry, Grove explains in detail that Schubert's modulations were an expressive force in the songs, invariably matching the demands of the words. It never occurred to him to credit Schubert with creating a different aesthetic for instrumental music, where repetition and modulation – or even diffuseness – might count as aesthetic devices. Instead, he put his faith in the apparently immutable Classical or Beethovenian aesthetic ideals and formal definitions of "how music ought to go."[73]

---

[70] McKinney and Anderson, *Music in History*, 550–551. Hidden within this largely forgotten textbook is a remarkable reevaluation of the history of Schubert's image – remarkable because it would take another two decades before musicologists generally embraced the stance of McKinney and Anderson. They argue, for instance, that Schubert's image as a sentimental, morose composer, perplexed by the world he inhabited was the product of the "misguided adulations of his sincere admirers" (p. 549). They regard Sir George Grove as the first to crystallize this viewpoint – they call him Schubert's first biographer – and see others as following suit (p. 550). Although Grove's portrait was not without precedent, their reference to Grove illustrates his influence in shaping Schubert's early history. It also shows how Grove's biography eclipsed Kreissle's, despite the latter's availability in English translation.

[71] See, for instance, Gibbs, *The Life of Schubert*, 166–167.   [72] Grove, "Schubert," 325 and 327.

[73] The particular turn of phrase was coined by Scott Burnham, *Beethoven Hero* (Princeton University Press, 1995), xvi. For a similar discussion on paradigms of tonality and sonata as "the way music goes," see Susan McClary, *Feminine Endings: Music, Gender, and Sexuality* (University of Minnesota Press, 1991), 16.

As we saw earlier, however, Kreissle had been willing to suggest that Schubert launched a new aesthetic. Nevertheless, it was not really until the early twentieth century, with the reassessments by Theodor W. Adorno and Sir Donald Francis Tovey of Schubert's use of repetition, modulation, and sense of temporality, that anyone thought to construe the most conspicuous features of Schubert's aesthetic in their own terms. One of the first detailed analyses of the "heavenly length" of Schubert's monumental *Great* Symphony in C Major (D. 944) depended on – of all things – the preanalytical act of adding measure numbers to the measureless scores of the nineteenth century. Yet its author Edmondstoune Duncan was merely ridiculed for wasting his own precious time in counting the measures of such long-winded works: "There is no denying the prolixity of (for example) the C major Symphony – it is notorious and inescapable. There are more than 200 pages in the miniature full score. Mr. Edmondstoune Duncan counted up, in the leisurely days before the War, the number of measures in the Finale alone, and arrived at a total of 1,159 .... Of many of his works it may be declared with truth that there is disparity between the worth of the thing said and the time that is taken to say it."[74] Thus, although Grove intended to promote Schubert and his music to the British public, it seems fair to say that, having insisted so strongly that the music was flawed, he was equally responsible for halting serious study of Schubert's music among critics and theorists until well into the twentieth century. Moreover, Grove rehearsed the absence in Schubert of many features that were traditionally associated with genius: his stature and demeanor did not suggest it (p. 322), no feats of memory or quotable aspects of his life are recorded (p. 324), he had difficulty expressing himself through means other than music (p. 324), he led a regular, if not monotonous, lifestyle (p. 323), and he was "strangely uncritical" about which poems he set to music (p. 324).

In light of this inventory, it perhaps comes as little surprise that Grove would explicitly endorse Vogl's characterization of Schubert, as a means of elevating Schubert back into the realm of genius. After citing the passage in Vogl's diary in which Schubert's clairvoyance was mentioned, Grove adds:

The word *clairvoyance* [Grove's emphasis], too, shows that he [Vogl] thoroughly entered into Schubert's great characteristic. In hearing Schubert's compositions it is often as if one were brought more immediately and closely into contact with

---

[74] Lawrence Gilman, "Music of the Month: Songs of a Rustic Angel," *North American Review* 213 (1921): 847–848. Edmondstoune Duncan's analysis appears in *Schubert* (London: J. M. Dent, 1905/rev. 1921), 206–214.

music itself than is the case in the works of others; as if in his pieces the stream from the great heavenly reservoir were dashing over us, or flowing through us, more directly, with less admixture of any medium or channel, than it does in those of any other writer – even of Beethoven himself. And this immediate communication with the origin of music really seems to have happened to him. No sketches, no delay, no anxious period of preparation, no revision, appear to have been necessary. He had but to read the poem, to surrender himself to the torrent, and to put down what was given him to say, as it rushed through his mind. This was the true "inspiration of dictation," as much so as in the utterance of any Hebrew prophet or seer. We have seen one instance in the case of the "Erl King."[75]

After Schubert's death, there could, of course, be no new, genuine witnesses to his working habits. Instead, Grove felt the compositions themselves bore witness to Schubert's somnambulism. Their fluidity, their dreamlike or otherworldly sound quality, as well as their sheer quantity, made the idea of somnambulism irresistible. And Grove, who was privy to so many of Schubert's manuscripts during his travels to Vienna, could testify first-hand that he saw little evidence of either sketching or editing.

Having claimed that Schubert lacked education and having propagated explicitly Vogl's view of Schubert's creative process, it presumably seemed to Grove only fitting to conclude that "In listening to [Schubert] one is never betrayed into exclaiming, 'How clever!' but very often 'How poetical, how beautiful, how intensely Schubert!'"[76] Despite praising Schubert's music for its "individuality," distinct modulations and unparalleled beauty, Grove presents a deterrent for any would-be theorist who might be tempted to theorize Schubert's output when he declares that Schubert's inspiration is not to be confused with innovation (and note how "innovation" is defined in strictly Beethovenian terms):

[Schubert] never seems to have aimed at making innovations or doing things for effect. For instance, in the number and arrangement of the movements, his symphonies and sonatas never depart from the regular Haydn pattern. They rarely show aesthetic artifices, such as quoting the theme of one movement in another movement, or running them into each other; changing their order, or introducing extra ones; mixing various times simultaneously – or similar mechanical means of producing unity or making novel effects, which often surprise and please us in Beethoven, Schumann, Mendelssohn, and Spohr. Nor did he ever indicate a programme, or prefix a motto to any of his works. His matter is so abundant and

---

[75] Grove, "Schubert," 289. The passage from Vogl's diary which Grove refers to was quoted at the outset of this chapter.

[76] Grove, "Schubert," 326.

so full of variety and interest that he never seems to think of enhancing it by any devices. He did nothing to extend the formal limits of Symphony or Sonata, but he endowed them with a magic, a romance, a sweet naturalness, which no one has yet approached. And as in the general structure so in the single movements.[77]

Again we see that Grove was unwilling to set aside accepted (read: Beethovenian) models of form and organicism in order to ascribe to Schubert any formal or technical novelty. And again, by contrast, it is worth noting that Kreissle found many an occasion to do so.

For example, Kreissle lamented that the general public was slow to recognize the value of Schubert's *Great* Symphony, which, concurring with Mendelssohn and Schumann, he ranked as the most important orchestral work next to Beethoven's symphonies because it possessed an "individuality of form." Similarly, the scherzo of the symphony was under-appreciated by the public but was "of the profoundest originality."[78] In another genre also, Kreissle was prepared to believe that Schubert could have been an innovator had he lived long enough: he "might have appeared as an operatic reformer and the founder of a true German musical drama... It can hardly be disputed, by unprejudiced persons, that Schubert had the stuff in him requisite for such an undertaking."[79] Grove had far less confidence in the possibility.

Had Grove muted rather than ventriloquized the voice of Vogl, English critics, who naturally were Grove's most immediate audience, would have been far more likely to embrace Schubert – even if they remained suspicious about the sentimentalism in his music. If critics and theorists listened to Grove more than to Kreissle, who amongst them could possibly serve as the equivalent to a Czerny or an A. B. Marx for Schubert's music? Indeed, apart from Kreissle's praise of Schubert's individuality of form, his "profoundest originality," and his potential to reform opera, there was little suggestion in the nineteenth century that Schubert's music might constitute fodder for music theory. Such an idea would have to wait until the anniversary of Schubert's death, when Tovey published the essay mentioned earlier – a remarkable, pithy treatise – on Schubert's tonality.[80] Meanwhile, as David Gramit and Scott Messing have eloquently shown, Victorian England was gripped by the "cardinal virtues" of "industry and efficiency." Moreover, a

---

[77] Grove, "Schubert," 326.   [78] Kreissle, *The Life of Franz Schubert*, vol. II, 230.

[79] Kreissle, *The Life of Franz Schubert*, vol. II, 238.

[80] Donald Francis Tovey, "Tonality," *Music and Letters* 9 (1928): 341–363.

consensus had grown amongst the Victorians that there was an inextricable link between an artist's aesthetic work and moral conduct.[81]

One book in particular made its mark on the Victorian imagination: in 1871, Hugh Reginald Haweis wrote a book called *Music and Morals*. Its immense influence may be quantified by its numerous reprintings – it was in its nineteenth impression by 1900 and continued to be reprinted well into the twentieth century. Haweis was responsible for articulating the view that an artist's moral conduct was more important than the works themselves in making aesthetic judgements. In the wake of this particularly influential book, Grove's digest of Schubert's shortcomings ultimately left Schubert's detractors with little work to do in attacking the composer.[82]

Schubert's detractor: Henry Heathcote Statham

No sooner had the ink dried on Grove's 1882 essay than Henry Heathcote Statham, an amateur musician like Grove himself, began to warn readers not to be persuaded by the "exaggerated value" Grove assigned to Schubert in his dictionary – both through the manner in which Grove promoted a music that, to Statham, was so obviously flawed and by the disproportionate amount of space he devoted to Schubert in his dictionary. Statham was primed with these criticisms from a review he had written of earlier volumes in the dictionary. He complained about the "curious disproportion" allotted to Bach (5 pages), Handel (10), Beethoven (50), and Mendelssohn (60).[83] He was already in disbelief that Mendelssohn should have garnered so much attention; thus when Schubert's entry was later published and exceeded even Mendelssohn's in length, he felt compelled to write another review.[84]

---

[81] David Gramit, "Constructing a Victorian Schubert: Music, Biography, and Cultural Values," *19th-Century Music* 17 (1993): 65–78 (citation on 68) and Scott Messing, *Schubert in the European Imagination: The Romantic and Victorian Eras*, vol. I (New York: University of Rochester Press, 2006), 182–188.

[82] For an excellent study of Haweis and his influence on the British reception of Schubert, see Scott Messing, *Schubert in the European Imagination*, 182–186.

[83] Henry Heathcote Statham, "Grove's Dictionary of Music," *Edinburgh Review* 153 (1881): 214–215.

[84] Henry Heathcote Statham, "Schubert – Chopin – Liszt," *Edinburgh Review* 158 (1883): 475–478. Grove wrote the entries on Beethoven, Mendelssohn, and Schubert. Eric Blum also pointed to the length of the entry on Schubert when he edited the special 1951 reprint of Grove's entries (published as they were retired from the dictionary); Grove, *Beethoven, Schubert, Mendelssohn*, ed. Eric Blum (London: Macmillan, 1951).

Wherever Grove saw merit in Schubert's music, Statham emphasized its poor construction and ill-conceived design; where Grove eagerly sought to dig out all of Schubert's music from oblivion, Statham urged listeners to let much of it remain in obscurity. He also categorically denied Schubert a place on the "pedestal" that he believed should only be "occupied by the few great musicians of the world."[85] Indeed, he kicked Schubert off the pedestal using the very terms employed by Grove to perch him there.

Statham's essay on Schubert first appeared as a review of Grove's in 1883 in the *Edinburgh Review*, and almost a decade later was published as part of a chapter in a book entitled *My Thoughts on Music and Musicians*.[86] The book begins with a chapter on form, is followed by numerous chapters on individual composers, and ends with a chapter on the venerable tradition of English organ music.[87] Statham's personal interests shaped this format. The first chapter probably owes its existence to his profession (he was an architect) and the last undoubtedly to his hobby (he was an organist). The first chapter also explains why Statham assigned the status he did to Schubert. It originated as a lecture entitled "The Intellectual Basis of Music," which Statham delivered to the Royal Institution (of Great Britain) in 1882.[88] This "intellectual basis" is intimately connected with proper constructions of form and his belief in the supremacy of absolute music, notions that certainly mark him out as a man of his age and of distinctly Victorian sensibilities, and that are perhaps even less surprising given that he was an architect by profession. His rebuttal of Grove's reading of Schubert is heavily indebted to this project of intellectualism.

Statham distinguished himself from much nineteenth-century music theory by insisting that the construction of the tonal system was independent of the physics of sound. This departure from consensus, though not unique to Statham, was in his view important enough that he started his book by explaining it in detail. Rejecting the notion that music has its origin in the imitation of nature, he proposes that the genius of the composer is entirely the domain of the mind. The scale was "contrived by man," and although the major triad bears a close resemblance to the overtone series, he argues that

[85] Henry Heathcote Statham, *My Thoughts on Music and Musicians* (London: Chapman and Hall, 1892), 325.

[86] See notes 84 and 85.

[87] Schubert joins company with Chopin and Mendelssohn in a chapter of Statham's book; all other chapters are devoted to a single composer. The trio of Schubert, Chopin, and Liszt in the *Edinburgh Review* (1883) was circumstantial; as Statham explains, he was merely reviewing recently published books.

[88] The lecture was advertised for two weeks running in *Nature: International Journal of Science* 26, no. 656 (1882): xxix and 26, no. 657 (1882): xxxvii.

this coincidence does little more than perhaps explain why it provides a more satisfactory finish to musical works than the minor mode.[89] The creation of masterworks is the art of controlling discords in relation to concords, which has its basis in logical method, or, as he called it, "reasoning in tones."[90] This reasoning, in Statham's view, operates as much on the formal as on the surface level because he takes the "harmonic treatment of a composition as analogous with structure."[91] He is dismissive of music that does not abide by these conditions: "No music, worth calling music, is to be had except in subordination to this process of rational and logical harmonic progression."[92] This belief is bad news for the Schubert known to him through the lenses of Grove.

If music emanates from the mind, the "clairvoyant" characterization of Schubert's compositional process threatens his claim to greatness. Statham is certainly capable of a sobering critique of music theory. After careful reflection, he discredits the claims for a mysterious origin of music by such "scientific investigators" as Tyndall and Helmholtz (these are the two he mentions specifically). Yet he does not question the possibility of musical clairvoyance, which equally ascribes to music a mysterious origin.

Intellectual prowess was for Statham imperative not only to the construction of proper harmony and formal structure, but also to great melody. Although melody is a parameter that belongs to the realm of the "pure aesthetic" (i.e. is not regulated by traditional strictures), it too is subject to the laws of balance and organic unity.[93] Interestingly the power to create distinct melodies, especially prolifically, is "more than any other faculty, the measure of the power and originality of musical genius."[94] Given Schubert's reputation for melodic imagination, one might expect this statement to pave the way for a declaration of Schubert's genius. This is not forthcoming, however. Statham's yardstick is the generation of "distinct" melodies, and under this rubric Schubert ties for second place. Not surprisingly, Beethoven places top. The "proof," as Statham saw it, lies in Beethoven's piano sonatas, which he regarded as remarkable for the sheer variety of melody, each one distinct to its sonata movement.

---

[89] On the origin of the scale see Statham, *My Thoughts on Music and Musicians*, 14, and on the origin of the triad, 25–26.
[90] Statham, *My Thoughts on Music and Musicians*, 32.
[91] Statham, *My Thoughts on Music and Musicians*, 39.
[92] Statham, *My Thoughts on Music and Musicians*, 41.
[93] Statham, *My Thoughts on Music and Musicians*, 1 and 8.
[94] Statham, *My Thoughts on Music and Musicians*, 11.

Schubert thus joins Mendelssohn as a "gifted" composer but of the "second order." Although Schubert's or Mendelssohn's melodies are indeed "distinct and individual" – Statham will split hairs here – they are collectively speaking too singular in style and suffer "a lack of sharply defined character."[95] The overall "family resemblance" of Schubert's music affects the listening experience, inducing ennui. The songs may at first hold interest but, Statham protests:

A long morning of them, even with a singer capable of fully entering into their meaning, leaves one (*experto credite*) with a consciousness of having been overdosed with sentiment; of having gone through a great deal of repetition and mannerism, beautiful at first but cloying after a time; with a longing for something more bracing and manly in style and feeling.[96]

It is comments such as these that, as both Gramit and Messing have observed, betray Statham's Victorian discomfort with the feminine aspect of Schubert's expression.[97] Statham's main complaint is therefore almost predictable. Schubert's songs do not measure up to the prized stylistic yardstick of his day: "the heroic note is not in his songs," but instead they "represent either merely rustic love, or that sad and clinging sentiment which belongs to the weaker and not to the nobler side of the passion."[98]

Statham also positioned himself squarely on the side of those who argued for the supremacy of absolute instrumental music, a position he held is true at the level of both tone and form. Firstly, he argues that only a non-musician would agree with the oft-repeated claim that the human voice produces the most pleasing tones. A discerning musician, he claims, would trade any vocal performance for an equal instrumental one, even, he supposes, if it that meant vocal music had to be cast into oblivion.[99] He was adamant about this, to the extent that he considered the vocal outburst in the finale of Beethoven's Ninth Symphony to be "wrong-headed."[100] Secondly, when turning from surface-level parameters such as tone, melody, harmonic progression, and timbre to large-scale formal matters, Statham argued that he need only confine his attention to instrumental music. He acknowledges that the same general principles of form apply to vocal music, but contends that only instrumental music exhibits "abstract ideal form," unfettered as it is

---

[95] Statham, *My Thoughts on Music and Musicians*, 11.

[96] Statham, *My Thoughts on Music and Musicians*, 324.

[97] Gramit, "Constructing a Victorian Schubert," 65–78 and Messing, *Schubert in the European Imagination*, 196.

[98] Statham, *My Thoughts on Music and Musicians*, 324–325.

[99] Statham, *My Thoughts on Music and Musicians*, 4.

[100] Statham, *My Thoughts on Music and Musicians*, 310.

by the "interruption" of words. Indeed, in his view, instrumental music as a genre should have "no pretence to declamatory meaning of any kind."[101]

In this context, the blatant lyricism in Schubert's instrumental output left him little choice but to dismiss it. His conclusions are again predictable: Schubert's instrumental music was not based on abstract ideas but was contaminated by the declamatory, albeit without any concrete association of specific words. Schubert's emerging association with the lyrical, together with his long-standing reputation as a songwriter, signaled to Statham that he was experiencing the music of a lesser composer. To think otherwise would disrupt his carefully constructed worldview of musical hierarchy.

Despite dismissing vocal music, Statham nonetheless had standards for it, standards which, alas, Schubert did not meet. Statham latched onto Grove's comment that Schubert set whatever poetry he was given or came across because he "did not care" about its quality.[102] For Grove, this was merely another endearing side to this carefree composer and another symptom of the composer's fertile musical creativity. For Statham, it was categorical evidence that he lacked an intellectual approach even to his vocal music. Statham declared more decisively than Grove that Schubert possessed "no perception whatever" of the relative literary value of the texts he set.[103] One wonders what either would have made of Anselm Hüttenbrenner's assertion that Schubert often rejected poetry he did not think was suited to music.[104] To be sure, hints of any capacity for discernment on the part of the composer would have shattered the illusions of both critics, though in different ways. Grove's Schubert would have had to have been construed as less naïve, Statham's as possessing a modicum of wisdom.

In Statham's view, another person who overrated Schubert was Franz Liszt, who extolled Schubert as "the most poetic of composers."[105] Grove had taken praise for Schubert by another composer – especially one of Liszt's stature – as corroboration of his own view of Schubert's worth. But Statham counters this claim by questioning the messenger. Liszt, he argued,

---

[101] Statham, *My Thoughts on Music and Musicians*, 42 and 3. The long-standing assumption of the transferability of theoretical practice from instrumental music to vocal music will be questioned in Chapter 2.

[102] Compare Grove, "Schubert," 324, where he also says Schubert was "strangely uncritical" when it came to the poetry he set; cited by Statham, *My Thoughts on Music and Musicians*, 320.

[103] Statham, *My Thoughts on Music and Musicians*, 320.

[104] "Anselm Hüttenbrenner for Liszt: Fragments from the Life of the Song Composer Franz Schubert . . . Vienna 1854," *SMF*, 182–183.

[105] This was cited in Grove as a sign of Schubert's growing reputation; see "Schubert," 326.

is hardly to be associated with "calm or well-balanced judgment."[106] He also suggests that Liszt was probably making no more than a throwaway comment, which Schubert's admirers have been only too eager to repeat in earnest. At any rate, Statham felt this was far too grand a compliment for a composer who produced music "without study, without thought or care for its meaning, or for the value of the words, without what can be called intellectual perception, by a mere spontaneous process of letting composition run through to the end of the composer's pen."[107]

Liszt's comment, he proposes, might more accurately be construed as "the most Romantic of composers," which he suspects is what Liszt actually meant to say. The revised epithet befits Schubert because Romantic composers are the "school of fluent and passionate expression with deficient formative and shaping power."[108] Put this way, it is evident that behind the superlative in Statham's exalted new phrase lies a less euphoric conclusion: of all the so-called Romantic composers, Schubert had the most deficient power to shape and form his ideas.

In coining this new phrase for Schubert, however, Statham also changed the subject. While Liszt was referring to the songs, Statham was thinking of the instrumental music. Thus Schubert fell from the pedestal, only to land on a ground that had shifted. Fittingly, Statham enlisted Vogl's words to deliver this final blow. He wrote that Vogl's first impression of Schubert's songs is above all the lasting impression of his instrumental music: Vogl's comment – "You squander your fine thoughts instead of making the most of them" – is, wrote Statham, "tenfold more applicable to his longer instrumental compositions."[109] As we can plainly see, Vogl's resonant voice was made to echo in new quarters: the instrumental music. A few steps back, Statham had conceded that Schubert's best songs are "very perfect and finished in form."[110] However perfect they might be, they were not fitting material for assessing the relative value of a composer. They did not belong to the most serious or important class of composition. Sustainable verdicts on composers are to be made on the basis of how

[106] Statham, *My Thoughts on Music and Musicians*, 323. An anonymous reviewer of Statham's book points out that, while Statham used Beethoven's praise of Handel to secure the latter a place among the great composers, Beethoven's praise of Schubert surely means that Statham's attitude toward Schubert "recoils like a boomerang on his own head." See the anonymous review of *My Thoughts on Music and Musicians* in *The Musical Times and Singing Class Circular* 33, no. 587 (1892): 45.

[107] Statham, *My Thoughts on Music and Musicians*, 322–323.

[108] Statham, *My Thoughts on Music and Musicians*, 323.

[109] Statham, *My Thoughts on Music and Musicians*, 327.

[110] Statham, *My Thoughts on Music and Musicians*, 323 and 325.

they handled large-scale instrumental form. Schubert, we are told, mishandled it.

Statham took an equally dim view of Grove's excuses for Schubert's poor sense of form. As we saw above, Grove lamented Schubert's lack of education and suggested that, had he been trained like either Mozart or Mendelssohn, he would have "gained that control over the prodigious spontaneity of his genius which is his only want, and have risen to the very highest level in all departments of composition, as he did in song-writing."[111] Impossible, Statham retorts. The only time Schubert was ever portrayed by his contemporaries as angry was when someone attempted to suggest improvements to his work. Faults remain in his music because he categorically refused advice – another sign of his lack of intellectual engagement.

In this fashion, then, Statham managed to dissolve the aura surrounding Schubert's purported clairvoyancy. When Vogl assigned the trait to Schubert, he no doubt assumed it was an immutable sign of genius that would gain for Schubert everlasting and incontestable entry into the pantheon of great composers. Vogl could not have predicted that, of the two modes of composition he mentioned in that letter to Stadler, he had chosen the one that not only was rapidly going out of fashion but also would leave the composer open to fierce criticism.

It is an ironic twist that Statham debunked the theory that Schubert is a great composer through tactics which were not dissimilar to Vogl's means of elevating him: he appealed to the then-fashionable form of genius. He concludes that Schubert does not satisfy "the famous definition of genius as 'an infinite capacity for taking pains.'"[112] He invokes the definition in quotation marks as if to suggest he is citing an authority, and he calls it famous as if to assert that its criterion is timeless rather than fashionable.[113]

---

[111] Grove, "Schubert," 282; cited by Statham, *My Thoughts on Music and Musicians*, 317.

[112] Statham, *My Thoughts on Music and Musicians*, 317.

[113] In *A Study in Scarlet* (1887), Sherlock Holmes says "They say that genius is an infinite capacity for taking pains ... It's a very bad definition, but it does apply to detective work"; see Sir Arthur Conan Doyle, *The Complete Sherlock Holmes*, vol. II, ed. Kyle Freeman (New York: Barnes and Noble Classics, 2003), 27. In a commentary to this passage, Freeman argues (p. 697) that the definition is a common bastardization of Thomas Carlyle's aside "'Genius' (which means transcendent capacity of taking trouble, first of all)," in *History of Friedrich II of Prussia, Called Frederick the Great (1858–1865)*. For a flavor of the debate around Statham's time on this particular wording of the definition, see Anon., "Am I a Genius?" *The Critic* 8, no. 192 (1887): 120, where the phrase was attributed to Carlyle and seen as a sign of talent rather than genius. Elsewhere it was attributed to Samuel Johnson. In *Notes and Queries: A Medium for Intercommunication for Literary Men, General Readers, etc.* s. 5 v. 12 (July 26, 1879): 68, a certain R. F. S. asked readers the source of this wording of the definition, which sparked regular communications and articles on the topic well into the mid-1880s. For a summary of popular beliefs, see William Shepard Walsh, *Handy-book of Literary Curiosities* (Philadelphia:

In fact, around the time that Statham was writing, the authorship and exact wording of this definition of genius were hotly debated, as was the question of whether creativity with effort was more a sign of talent than genius. The debate raged in popular magazines of the time and even found its way into the mouth of the fictional character Sherlock Holmes. In light of this context, as well as Haweis's influential adage that "genius of the nineteenth century is analytic,"[114] Statham's aesthetic judgement comes across as a textbook response to the material in Grove's essay. Accordingly, Statham believed it would be far more accurate to portray the composer as indolent, undiscerning, and intellectually inferior. As if to ensure that the status of greatness would be kept well out of Schubert's grasp, Statham also preempted any objections that Schubert was in fact industrious or studious. Those who assert that Schubert's copious output illustrates that he was not indolent are misguided because, according to Statham, writing in quantity without a sense of quality is simply another form of indolence. Schubert may well have been self-taught, but "he did not teach himself enough."[115] While Schubert's refusal to labor over his material constituted his ultimate intellectual failure throughout nineteenth-century reception history, changes in the definition of genius meant that Vogl's message – repeated and elaborated upon by Grove – was especially poised to turn into something nasty.

From Vogl's voice to Schubert's body

Schubert's physical appearance had always been an issue for commentators. Kreissle's detailed description of the composer's physique was hardly flattering. It was apparently based on the verbal and written statements of Spaun, Schober, Sonnleithner, Kupelwieser, Bauernfeld, Schindler, Mayrhofer, Stadler, and Anna Fröhlich.

The presence and personal appearance of the composer were anything but attractive.

His round and puffy face, low forehead, projecting lips, bushy eyebrows, stumpy nose, and short curly hair, gave him that negro look which corresponds with that conveyed by the bust which is to be found at the Währing churchyard. He was under the average height, round-backed and shouldered, with plump arms and

---

J. B. Lippincott Co., 1892), 410. The debate around this phrase and definition and its use in psychology and the arts for defining genius raged well into the twentieth century.

[114] Quoted in Messing, *Schubert in the European Imagination*, 184.

[115] Statham, *My Thoughts on Music and Musicians*, 326 and 317.

hands, and short fingers. The expression of his face was neither intellectual nor pleasing, and it was only when music or conversation interested him, and especially if Beethoven was the topic, that his eye [*sic*] began to brighten and his features light up with animation. However uncomely, nay, almost repulsive, his exterior, the spiritual and hidden part of the man was notable and abundantly endowed.[116]

In the unpublished notes mentioned previously, Spaun objected to this portrayal of Schubert, clearly not knowing that he himself was partially to blame for it:

Schubert is not described correctly either from a physical or from an intellectual standpoint. His face is portrayed as almost ugly and negroid; but anyone who knew him will be forced to contradict that . . . [While one cannot say] Schubert was handsome, he was well formed . . . So far as his body was concerned, one might imagine him as a fat lump, from the descriptions in the biography. But that is entirely incorrect. Schubert had a solidly built, thick-set body but there was no question of his being fat or of having a paunch. His very youthful friend, Moritz Schwind, exceeded him in girth even in those days.[117]

Grove softened Kreissle's description by attributing Schubert's bad posture to long hours spent composing, by interpreting the "projecting lips" as a sign of assertiveness, and by looking to Schubert's jaw for a piece of the accepted physiognomy of greatness. Moreover, instead of portraying his typical facial expression as unintellectual, as Kreissle had done, for Grove it was merely uninteresting:

[Schubert's] exterior by no means answered to his genius. His general appearance was insignificant. As we have already said, he was probably not more than 5 feet and 1 inch high, his figure was stout and clumsy, with a round back and shoulders (perhaps due to incessant writing), fleshy arms, and thick short fingers. His complexion was pasty, nay even tallowy; his cheeks were full, his eyebrows bushy, and his nose insignificant. But there were two things that to a great extent redeemed these insignificant traits – his hair, which was black, and remarkably thick and vigorous, as if rooted in the brain within; and his eyes, which were truly "the windows of his soul," and even though the spectacles he constantly wore were so bright as at once to attract attention. If Reider's portrait may be trusted – and it is said to be very faithful, though perhaps a little too *fine* – they had a peculiarly steadfast penetrating look, which irresistibly reminds one of the firm rhythm of his

---

[116] Kreissle, *The Life of Schubert*, vol. II, 152–153. Although he claimed all the sources mentioned above (p. 153, n. 2), Kreissle's description is close to the most detailed extant written description, which is in "Leopold von Sonnleithner: Vienna, 1 November 1857," *SMF*, 121.

[117] "Josef von Spaun: (2) Some Observations on the Life of Schubert by Herr Ritter von Kreissle-Hellborn (1864)," *SMF*, 361.

music. His glasses are inseparable from his face ... He had the broad strong jaw of all great men, and a marked assertive prominence of the lips. He had a beautiful set of teeth (Benedict). When at rest the expression of his face was uninteresting, but it brightened up at the mention of music, especially that of Beethoven.[118]

The manner in which Grove begins his description of Schubert's physique reasserts the suspicion mentioned earlier that at the heart of claims for Schubert's clairvoyance was the need to reconcile Schubert's ordinary (even unappealing) appearance with his remarkable music. Franz Xaver Freiherr von Andlau put his first impression of Schubert succinctly: "one would never have suspected in this wooden appearance, in the unprepossessing exterior, the greatly gifted creator of so many wonderful songs."[119] Others concocted elaborate narratives to cope with their outright shock when they laid eyes on Schubert for the first time. Louis Schlösser, for instance, revealed his surprise at how different the composer looked from how he had pictured him from his music:

Having already been charmed by his songs at home, I was all the more delighted to be able to see and hear the composer himself and his admirable interpreter, the singer Vogl. I had read the names of the two inseparables on the bills and had immediately taken my seat quite close to the orchestra, so as to be able to observe everything in the greatest detail. O! strange play of the imagination that so likes to adorn the creator of consummate tone pictures with the advantage of physical beauty as well! Great was my disappointment when Schubert, whose personality interested me so extraordinarily, appeared on the platform and I saw, in this rather awkward, almost clumsy, figure, in the strongly domed head, in the gentle, though anything but spirited, features, the tone poet whom my dreams had identified with the grace of form of the youthful Antinous. Had it been a question of external advantages, nothing would have more convincingly disproved the saying "that a beautiful soul also inhabits a beautiful body" than the case in point; but the sense of being in the presence of unusual genius caused all thought of the physical to vanish and it disappeared completely when Schubert went to the piano and started by playing the first of his two trios in E flat and B flat and then accompanied "Der Wanderer" and "Erlkönig" which were sung by Vogl. Melodic waves of sound must have vibrated in his soul when, after storms of applause and recalls, he added a free fantasy which finally led into one of his delicious impromptus. A profusion of the loveliest tonal blossoms showered over the audience, who were carried away with admiration. Music was the atmosphere in which he lived and breathed, in which his

---

[118] Grove, "Schubert," 322.

[119] "Franz Xaver Freiherr von Andlau (1857)," *SMF*, 222. Andlau lists some of the songs he found particularly moving and pleasurable, though as Deutsch points out in his commentary (p. 222), not all of them are by Schubert.

subjectivity unconsciously attained its highest development, and in which his whole being attained a state of ecstasy.[120]

Otto Erich Deutsch concluded that Schlösser's description of the concert was fictional, for two reasons. Firstly, Schlösser was in Vienna between the spring of 1822 and May 1823, and so he could not possibly have heard the piano trios or either set of the impromptus – they had not yet been composed. Secondly, Schubert never improvised in public.

It is, of course, possible that Schlösser did attend such a concert but forgot which pieces he had heard and was wrongly under the impression that Schubert was improvising. But even if the whole concert was an invention of his imagination, the illuminating fact remains that he felt compelled to tell a story about the discrepancy between the sound of Schubert's music and his looks. On hearing Schubert's songs, he mythologized their creator, imagining the ideal type of youthful beauty – a perfect, sensuous, handsome lover: Antinous, no less (the lover of the Emperor Hadrian and not, surely, the Antinous who was the greedy, cruel villain of the *Odyssey*). On seeing Schubert, Schlösser was only able to put aside the disappointment of Schubert's physique once the sound of the music started. And note how the memory of the concert ends with reference to Schubert's unconscious creative method, underscoring the need to separate Schubert's body from his music.

In the rest of this memoir, Schlösser also shared his first impressions of visiting Schubert's home – the site of composition. Again he points to an incongruity, this time between the beauty of Schubert's songs and the starkness of the room. And again he did not miss the opportunity to declare that when he heard Schubert at the piano the composer was transformed: "How his eyes shone." Moreover, he repeats what had become the standard narrative regarding Schubert's creativity: his "melodies and forms thronged his creative faculty in richest profusion so that he needed but to capture them and dam them up, to prevent the broad stream from overflowing its banks. Apart from the astonishing quality of songs, the great number of voluminous works bears convincing testimony to this."[121]

To be sure, the idea that a great composer should be physically attractive seems strange when frankly stated. But in the biographies, references to Schubert's portly stature had their innocent origins. Biographers often noted that, as a term of endearment, Schubert's close friends nicknamed him "Schwammerl" (meaning "little mushroom," but also translated as

---

[120] "Louis Schlösser: (1) Memoirs of Schubert (1883)," *SMF*, 328–329.
[121] "Louis Schlösser: (1) Memoirs of Schubert (1883)," *SMF*, 330.

"tubby" or "sponge"). Some would explain that it remained unclear whether the nickname arose because Schubert was short and stout or because of his drinking habits.[122] Primed by a few decades of intense debate over the intimate association between an artist's moral conduct and the aesthetic value of his work, the link among an artist's morality, music, *and* body was a small leap, especially for Victorian sensibilities. Schubert was deemed a vessel through which both music and beer flowed. Soon enough, Schubert's music bore the same imperfections as his body.

Statham stuck closely to the aesthetic link between music and morals in judging Schubert's music as inadequate, but note the choice of vocabulary: "flabby" (in the second paragraph below), a word that easily translated into criticism based on Schubert's physique:

The relation between Schubert's character and his music is illustrated more strongly in regard to his instrumental composition than in the other branch of his art.[123]

The materials for exquisite musical structures are there, but the will or the power to combine them into an effective whole is wanting; and even those of his longer compositions which are quite balanced and symmetrical in form almost always affect one as too long, owing to their loosely-knit structure and want of *verve* and finish of detail; as Garrick said of Adam Smith's conversation, they are "flabby," and therein reflect their author's whole life and character. Schubert's life and works, indeed, suggest a lesson almost as much moral as artistic – that the most strong and healthy form of art, as of character, is not to be developed by giving one's self up to emotional impulses, however beautiful and attractive; that the strong artist, as well as the strong man, is he who is the master, not the servant, of his fancy and inspiration.[124]

As we shall see, the notion of a link between Schubert's body and music as both "flabby" would gain momentum after Statham. Discussions that shifted the focus of Schubert biography from character to physique were increasingly widespread towards the end of the nineteenth century. One particularly anxious commentator explained in an anonymous essay, "Manliness in Music," that effeminate music was to blame for the "weakening of moral

---

[122] Anselm Hüttenbrenner revealed his nickname in "Anselm Hüttenbrenner for Liszt: Fragments from the Life of the Song Composer Franz Schubert . . . Vienna 1854," *SMF*, 185, and Deutsch concluded it referred to his figure, *SMF*, 189. See also a letter "Doblhoff to Schober, Vienna 12 November 1823," in which Schubert is referred to as "Schwämmelein," *SDB*, 296, and again Deutsch's clarification of its meaning "tubby" rather than "tipsy" on account of the latter's proximity to the Viennese dialect word "Schwammer," *SDB*, 297.

[123] Statham, *My Thoughts on Music and Musicians*, 326.

[124] Statham, *My Thoughts on Music and Musicians*, 328–329. Italics in original.

and physical fibre" amongst British men. In a spirited defense against the attack that "all male musicians [are] unmanly and invertebrate," the author retorts: "No musician need be unmanly; and the best have almost invariably been remarkable for a robustness of mind and character, if not of physique."[125] The shift in emphasis from morals to both morals *and* the body is plainly evident.

There are two recent detailed scholarly examinations of this aspect of Statham's response to Grove. Both David Gramit and Scott Messing convincingly illustrate that Statham's extreme reaction to Grove's entry on Schubert was a response more to the latter's characterization of Schubert as a man and composer than to Schubert's actual compositions. Grove constructed Schubert as even more feminine and naïve than previous German and English biographers had.[126] Indeed, it seems as if Grove himself was naïve to think he could convince his compatriots of Schubert's worth by bringing to the fore those qualities they most mistrusted in a man. Statham's reaction therefore serves as a record of the problematic connotations effeminacy had for Victorians, particularly for Victorian men who wished to engage with music while maintaining their manly dignity.[127] In this context, Statham's aesthetic judgement comes across as a textbook, if vehement, response to Grove's characterization of Schubert the man. Nonetheless, both Gramit and Messing present Statham as something of an isolated figure.[128]

Messing based his conclusions on a comparison of Statham's comments with more favorable reviews of Grove, while Gramit based his on two important monographs from the early twentieth century, one a biography by Edmondstoune Duncan, the other a volume by Richard Capell devoted exclusively to Schubert's songs.[129] Despite the fame of Gramit's sources, their testimony is narrow, for it is perhaps to be expected that a monograph, whose author is clearly devoted to his or her subject, is more inclined to elevate the status of the composer in question. Certainly such authors

---

[125] Anon., "Manliness in Music," *The Musical Times and Singing Class Circular* 30, no. 558 (1889): 460–461. For another discussion of this essay, see Messing, *Schubert in the European Imagination*, 187.

[126] For a close analysis of the effeminizing depiction of Schubert to English audiences through Wilberforce's choice translation and abbreviation of Kreissle's biography and for Grove's subsequent exaggeration of these qualities, see Gramit, "Constructing a Victorian Schubert," 69–72.

[127] This point is accounted for in detail in Gramit, "Constructing a Victorian Schubert," 75–76.

[128] Gramit claimed Statham had less of an impact on subsequent criticism on Schubert than the enthusiastic Grove did; see Gramit, "Constructing a Victorian Schubert," 77. Messing argued that Statham was "the lone voice of dissent" among reviewers of Grove's dictionary entry; see *Schubert in the European Imagination*, 198.

[129] Duncan, *Schubert* and Richard Capell, *Schubert's Songs* (London: E. Beun, 1928).

would be unlikely to share Statham's view that the object of their study had received too much attention. Statham's attitude is more perceptible in general history books, in which authors feel it is pertinent to calibrate a composer's contribution to history. As we shall see, it was mainly in general histories that Schubert's physique was pressed into service to explain the diffuseness in his instrumental music.

That said, there is one monograph on Schubert in which the author is wholly unforgiving of Schubert's shortcomings. Within its first paragraph, Arthur Hutchings writes:

Indeed a certain flabbiness, manifesting itself in lack of ambition or of definite purpose, as in other ways, is one of Schubert's chief weaknesses.

It is a curious inclusion in the opening of a composer monograph, and Hutchings later tempered this thought and revised this very sentence for a new edition in 1973:

Some of his greatest music is easy-going; some of his weakest is flabby.[130]

Hutchings's original use and retention of the word "flabby" illustrates his awareness of the critical discourse on Schubert. Indeed later in the book (and in all editions), he openly remarks that:

The very nature of Schubert's writing, its place in history, made it easy for his weak places to be called flabby.[131]

Two general histories by Daniel Gregory Mason and Cecil Gray stand out in linking Schubert's music and his body. Both authors were engaged in monumental projects and sought to fit Schubert into the broadest of historical schemes. Mason's view of Schubert appeared in multiple formats and was finally published in *The Romantic Composers* (1906), which was part of a trilogy alongside *Beethoven and His Forerunners* and *From Grieg to Brahms*.[132] Cecil Gray's *The History of Music* (1928) was the musical representative in a massive multi-authored series of over a hundred volumes entitled "History of Civilization," whose stated aim was "a complete history of mankind from prehistoric times to the present day in numerous volumes designed to form a complete library of social evolution."[133] The

---

[130] Arthur Hutchings, *Schubert* (London: J. M. Dent, 1945), 1 and *Schubert*, rev. edn. (London: J. M. Dent, 1973), 1.

[131] Hutchings, *Schubert*, 88.

[132] Daniel Gregory Mason, *The Romantic Composers* (New York and London: Macmillan, 1906).

[133] For this aim, see the advert on the unnumbered page following 284 in Cecil Gray, *The History of Music* (London and New York: Kegan Paul, Trench, Trubner, 1928).

series, when it was still in its projected stage, was given numerous favorable previews and, as one might expect of this time period, was seen as a largely scientific endeavor. It therefore gained a substantial preview in the scientific journal *Nature*, which praised it as "the most important contribution so far undertaken towards the task of organization and systematization of the social sciences."[134]

It may seem odd that I point to these two studies in a discussion about Schubert biography, since both authors viewed biography as largely irrelevant to the understanding of music history. As if to counter their Victorian intellectual heritage, both complained in the prefaces to their books that biographical information had come to occupy a disproportionate amount of space in histories of music. Mason therefore promised to deal "as briefly as possible with colorless biographical facts" and only to make use of "characteristic anecdotes, of contemporary descriptions of appearance, manners, etc., and of letters and table-talk" when it became a relevant means of shedding light on a composer's work.[135] Mason's statement, also in the preface, that "no man can express anything in [music] except through a technical mastery which has little to do with character" is intriguing in light of the exception he goes on to make for Schubert.[136] In his book, Schubert's *lack* of technical mastery is shown – thanks to a citation of Statham, no less – to have everything to do with the composer's character and appearance.[137] Similarly, Gray too asserted that he would only use "relevant facts which help to shed light upon some particular aspect of a composer's work."[138] Clearly, both suggest a consciously new approach to biography.

It must be pointed out that Gray had made creative use of biographical detail previously in his career. A few years before writing his *History of Music*, he wrote a book-length study of Carlo Gesualdo, known for the brutal murder of his wife. Hardly therefore possessing an exemplary biography, Gray came up with a colorful solution to the problem of Gesualdo's horrific act (or "lack of moral fibre"): he wrote a chapter on murder as an art form.[139]

The conspicuous absence of any discussion of Gesualdo's biography in Gray's *History of Music* puts into relief the strong presence of biography in

---

[134] See Gray, *The History of Music*, two unnumbered pages following 284.
[135] Mason, *The Romantic Composers*, vi.   [136] Mason, *The Romantic Composers*, vi.
[137] Messing also highlights this citation, but he makes a different point from mine; see *Schubert in the European Imagination*, 201.
[138] Gray, *The History of Music*, vii.
[139] Cecil Gray, *Carlo Gesualdo: Prince of Venosa, Musician and Murderer* (London: Kegan Paul, Trench, Trubner, 1926).

the case of Schubert. Gesualdo is sprinkled throughout Gray's history, cited mostly for his remarkable, original chromaticism. A comparison with Schubert's equally original harmonic palette would have been striking here, but instead his biography serves to diminish his accomplishments. And this points to a common strategy in Gray's and Mason's histories: biography is invoked in Schubert's case to explain away the foibles in his music.

Given that Mason promised to eschew "colorless biographical fact," it may seem surprising to find that he details Schubert's physique at length:

Physically Schubert was a short, stout man, with round shoulders, thick, blunt fingers, low forehead, projecting lips, stumpy nose, and short curly hair. Very near-sighted, he wore spectacles from boyhood. His friends' somewhat boorish wit compared him to a negro, a cabman, and even a tallow-candle, and afflicted him with the nickname of "Schwammerl," or "The Sponge" – whether in reference to his fondness for beer or to his superfluous flesh does not transpire.[140]

No other composer in Mason's trilogy is described in such detail. Conscious of this difference, Mason contemplated the purpose of introducing Schubert's appearance into his study and concluded that these "bits of otherwise insignificant personal detail" explain the nature of his music.[141] The shape of Schubert's body will matter to the aesthetic judgement of his music. Here Mason chooses to invoke Statham, explaining that the "weaker aspect of Schubert [is] connected with his lack of intellectual vigor and possibly with a certain flabbiness of moral fibre."[142]

Although Mason concedes Statham might have been extreme in his view, such concession is camouflage for his general sympathy for Statham's thinking. This is unsurprising given that, like Statham, he was noted for a self-disciplined, intellectual approach to music and for eschewing excessive emotion.[143] Indeed, Mason's readers were introduced to the idea that Schubert's appearance explains his music some eighteen pages earlier, where he goes a step further than Statham ever did, tying the faults of

---

[140] Mason, *The Romantic Composers*, 70–71.   [141] Mason, *The Romantic Composers*, 71.

[142] Mason, *The Romantic Composers*, 98. Messing makes the interesting point that Statham had already linked Schubert's weaknesses to his body insofar as he criticized the composer for lacking a "backbone"; see *Schubert in the European Imagination*, 197. While it is true that the word suggests "bodily debility," as Messing puts it, I interpret Statham's use of the term as referring to his character – and still therefore influenced by the morals and music ideology of Haweis. My view is not intended in any way to exonerate Statham, but merely to emphasize that Mason and Gray represent a new phase in Schubert reception.

[143] Boris Schwarz and Nicholas E. Taw, "Mason, Daniel Gregory (ii)," *New Grove Dictionary of Music and Musicians*, vol. XVI, ed. Stanley Sadie (New York: Macmillan, 2001), 34.

Schubert's music to his body. Writing in his own voice, without attribution to anyone else, Mason concludes: Schubert's "works are thus, if one may say so, like his person, embedded in superfluous flesh."[144] Nor is this the only time that Mason emphasized Schubert's portliness. In a monthly magazine he edited, he further endorsed this characterization of Schubert by choosing the following caption to accompany the composer's portrait: "Schubert's personal appearance was singularly unattractive. He was short and rather fat, with somewhat shapeless features and flabby complexion. His eyes, however, in spite of an excessive near-sightedness, are said to have been bright and expressive."[145]

In *The Romantic Composers*, Mason went so far as to detail precisely how Schubert's personal traits manifest themselves in the music, something neither Statham nor Gray cared to do. Shortly after the description of Schubert cited above, and immediately after claiming that his lifestyle entailed "devotion to day-dream and revery [*sic*], even [an] indolence and resulting sponginess of physique," Mason observes the effects of these traits on the music:

matters of ordinary observation [i.e. Schubert's physique and lifestyle] are re-enforced by the internal evidence of his music, as for example the preference for short pieces, each vividly expressive of a single mood; the pervasive tone of tender sadness, frequently irradiated by charming fancy, but seldom swept aside by tumultuous passion and energy; the fondness for minor keys, delicious modulations, and persistent hypnotizing rhythms; the incapacity for complex structure and sustained imagination. Here, obviously, is no hero of abstract thought, like Bach, or of intellectual and emotional passion, like Beethoven, but a gracious sentimentalist, a man of feeling, a sort of Burns or Heine of music.[146]

It should perhaps come as no surprise that Mason also tackled the issue of Schubert's legendary mode of composition. Although he managed to cast Schubert as innovative, both as a song and as an instrumental composer – something that had eluded even Grove – Mason soon forgot that he had justified the unevenness of Schubert's output on the grounds that any composer who lives at the cusp of two historical periods is bound to produce an uneven output. Instead he attributes the "gold" to musical skill and the "sand" to biographical shortcomings. Writing in particular about the early compositions, he noted: "What they chiefly reveal is the ingenuousness, one

---

[144] Mason, *The Romantic Composers*, 80.
[145] Mason (ed.), *Masters in Music: Volume IV* (Boston: Bates and Guild Co., 1904), unnumbered page between 96 and 97.
[146] Mason, *The Romantic Composers*, 71–72.

might almost say the unconsciousness, with which he habitually composed."[147] As Mason went on to suggest, Schubert's clairvoyance was the root of the formal problems manifested in the instrumental forms:

The chief faults of Schubert's instrumental works – and they are grave ones – result in part from his way of composing, and in part from the untraversable opposition between the lyrical expression native to him and the modes of construction suitable to extended movements. Schubert was an easy-going, careless, and indolent writer. He wrote music as most people write letters . . . What all this means, practically, is that he did not "compose" at all in the strict sense of placing together tones with care and forethought, but merely improvised on paper. As a result, while he certainly attained a delightful spontaneity of effect, he also fell into the pitfalls of monotony and diffuseness.[148]

After providing the second theme of the G Major String Quartet (D. 887) as an example of the repetition and diffuseness that arise from this indolent, unintellectual, lyrical compositional impulse, Mason launched into the comment, cited previously, that Schubert's music and body both exhibit superfluous bulk.

Gray found an even more unpalatable way to phrase this thought. He wrote that "There was a lack of intellectual fibre and grit about his personality – a flabbiness and superfluity of adipose tissue in his mind as in his body."[149] Although he made few remarks about Schubert's actual music, he alleged that even the best of Schubert's instrumental compositions are "all in varying degrees diffuse in form, slipshod in craftsmanship, and unequal in content; side by side with the most exquisite moments we find whole stretches of listless and flaccid music-making and sterile repetition."[150] It was equally the case for Gray that Schubert's purported lack of intellect determines his place in history: Schubert was "the most completely lacking of all great composers in the purely cerebral power which is the necessary concomitant of the highest artistic achievements."[151] Gray gained quite a reputation for these comments, and one scholar went so far as to assert that his comments on Schubert's flabbiness were one reason for the "contemptuous silence" on his death.[152]

Whether or not Gray was directly influenced by Statham or Mason is impossible to say. It does, however, seem a striking coincidence that, like

---

[147] Mason, *The Romantic Composers*, 80–81.   [148] Mason, *The Romantic Composers*, 97–98.
[149] Gray, *The History of Music*, 193.   [150] Gray, *The History of Music*, 193.
[151] Gray, *The History of Music*, 191.
[152] Richard Gorer, "Cecil Gray," *Music Review* 12 (1951): 307.

Statham, he contemplated the benefits of tampering with Liszt's epithet about Schubert being "the most poetic of musicians." Gray substituted "musicianly" for "poetic," arguing that Schubert should be considered "the most *musicianly* of all musicians who ever lived." He admitted intending this in a "depreciatory sense" and claimed it more accurately represented Schubert's full and uneven output. In the same chapter, however, he carefully set different standards for Mozart and Beethoven; these, he argued, should be judged on the basis of selected works.[153]

Faced with the issue of Schubert's clairvoyance, Gray needed first to save Mozart's reputation from the same apparent flaw. He corrects the widespread assumption that Mozart was a "musical machine, pouring forth marvellous works in heedless and effortless profusion, almost unconsciously."[154] His evidence is Mozart's own claim that he studied the works of great composers and worked hard to compose the "Haydn" Quartets, which were "the fruit of long and painstaking labour." Moreover, Mozart's intensive study of counterpoint in 1782 – requiring "severe discipline" – seemed the logical explanation behind the "superlative greatness" of Mozart's late style.[155] Evidence that Schubert too studied great masters and that he was about to study counterpoint with Sechter were summarily dismissed – not because Schubert's untimely death meant we never heard the benefits of those lessons, but because, much like Statham, Gray was skeptical that Schubert would have reaped much reward from them: the "probabilities are against any such development." Despite Schubert's extraordinary "natural gifts," he lacked the intellectual inclination to handle them.[156]

In the midst of his discussion of Schubert, Gray reminds readers of the revisionist history he carried out earlier in his book regarding Mozart – only to insist that Schubert deserves the reputation that had so tarnished Mozart. He writes: "[Schubert], indeed, and not Mozart, is the very type of the conventional music-machine, contentedly turning out work after work, day after day, without any expenditure of mental effort, and unrestrained by any faculty of self-criticism."[157] If he was confident that separating Mozart from the image of a musical machine would ensure his entry into the pantheon of great composers, he must have known that linking Schubert to such an image would keep him out.

References to Schubert's body – of the sort made by Mason and Gray – eventually died down. But questions over his intellect and clairvoyance

---

[153] Gray, *The History of Music*, 191–192, 181 (on Mozart) and 187–189 (on Beethoven).
[154] Gray, *The History of Music*, 179.   [155] Gray, *The History of Music*, 181.
[156] Gray, *The History of Music*, 193.   [157] Gray, *The History of Music*, 191.

raged on. Indeed, well into the twentieth century, students of Schubert would continue to encounter the idea that Schubert was a clairvoyant in important English and German tomes intended to educate the young or interested amateur, such as *The Oxford History of Music, Encyclopaedia Britannica*, Schenker's *Tonwille*, and Ferguson's *A History of Musical Thought*. In *The Oxford History*, Hadow endorses the view that "His genius was, as Vogl states, *clairvoyant*." In the entry on "song" in the *Encyclopaedia Britannica*, the author also cites Vogl: "He composed in a state of *clairvoyance*."[158] Are the italics in these two sources a visual signal that their source was Grove, who also italicized the word? At any rate, both convey the idea emphatically and gloss it with comments that Schubert could compose under any conditions and in any circumstances. In his *Tonwille* series, Heinrich Schenker addresses himself to the Austro-German youth. Far from citing Vogl as an authority, Schenker expresses considerable annoyance with Vogl – but not for crediting Schubert with clairvoyance, which he in fact endorses. Instead, he berates Vogl for modifying some of Schubert's songs in arrogant disregard for the composer's superior thoughts. The clairvoyant idea is transmitted via an unattributed quotation from Stadler's letter to Luib; its particular form suggests that Schenker had read Kreissle.[159] Finally Donald N. Ferguson's textbook contains remarkably subtle interpretations of Schubert's music, especially the songs. He argues in particular that Schubert responded to each poem in setting his songs, in such a way that no method can be detected. This comment will inspire my own analyses in Chapter 2, but the striking thing in this context is that, for Ferguson, part of this lack of visible method again boils down to Schubert's purported compositional process. And so Vogl's fairytale about Schubert's composing is repeated once more. "There was," Ferguson recounts

never a writer to whom method meant so little. Beethoven's process of development, imposing and fluent as it appears in the music itself, was, as we know from

---

[158] W. H. Hadow, *The Oxford History of Music*, vol. V *The Viennese Period* (Oxford: Clarendon Press, 1904), 338. Walter A. J. Ford, "Song," in *Encyclopedia Britannica: A Dictionary of Arts, Sciences, Literature and General Information*, vol. XXV, 11th edn. (New York: Encyclopaedia Britannica Company, 1911), 409.

[159] See n. 23 above, and also see the discussion below on this quotation. Heinrich Schenker, *Der Tonwille: Pamphlets in Witness of the Immutable Laws of Music, Offered to a New Generation of Youth*, vol. II, ed. William Drabkin (Oxford University Press, 2005), 37. Schenker goes on to imply that all German geniuses (he lists Bach, Handel, Haydn, Mozart, and Beethoven) are clairvoyants, ignored by the German people (p. 37).

countless sketches, the result of laborious and hesitant efforts. Of Beethoven's method Schubert adopted but little; for he could not labor over composition. To ponder a process was for him to wither inspiration. There is no writer consequently whose method is so inimitable.[160]

Vogl's voice, muting analysis

With these negative connotations surrounding Schubert's creative method and intellectual capabilities being so ubiquitous, it is small wonder that Schubert's music elicited little sustained theoretical attention in the nineteenth century. In the eyes of the commentators discussed above, the songs did not constitute the appropriate genre for such an erudite enterprise as writing music theory, and Schubert's equally "unconscious" instrumental creations were considered to be so riddled with imperfections that it seemed especially risky to construct any theoretical statements around them.

Such comments as the following were not uncommon in late nineteenth- and early twentieth-century criticism: "The music of Schubert is … so melodious in character as to be appreciable by every hearer without effort, and without the consciousness of nerving himself up to a laborious grappling with the classical."[161] "In these [chamber] works, we do not look for architectonic power – we must admit, in fact, at the risk of seeming ungracious, that Schubert is diffuse at times – but our senses are so enthralled by the imaginative freedom and by the splendor of color, that all purely intellectual judgment is suspended."[162]

Even Vogl advocated this view. Earlier in this chapter, I quoted a letter from Vogl to Stadler. In Stadler's own memoir (see n. 23 above), he did not quote Vogl's full statement. I cite the passage in full below (I have placed the additional words in italics):

There are two kinds of composition; one which, as with Schubert, comes forth to the world in a state of clairvoyance or "somnambulism," without any freewill on the part of the composer, the forced product of a higher power and inspiration – *one may well be astonished and charmed at such a work, but emphatically not criticise*

---

[160] Donald N. Ferguson, *A History of Musical Thought* (New York: F. S. Crofts & Co., 1935), 322.
[161] William S. B. Mathews, *How to Understand Music*, vol. II (Philadelphia: Theodore Presser, 1888), 9.
[162] Walter Raymond Spalding, *Music: An Art and a Language* (Boston and New York: Arthur P. Schmidt Co., 1920), 166. I return to this passage in Chapter 3.

it. The second way of composition is through willpower, reflection, effort, knowledge, etc."[163] (italics mine)

The products of divine inspiration are to be wondered at, not judged. The logical outcome of this view is that such music is not to be theorized either – especially if, as in Schubert's case, it is so often deemed imperfect, suggesting an inadequate line to the muses. His source and mode of composition therefore became seen as all too anti-rational and anti-intellectual to constitute fodder for the technical scrutiny to which other music, notably Beethoven's, was being subjected. Moreover, why even begin to expend energy theorizing about the music of a composer who himself expended so little energy writing it?

If Schubert's reputation for clairvoyance stifled the analysis of his music, music theory was occasionally appealed to in order to stifle Schubert's reputation. Perhaps not unexpectedly, Statham turned to music theory in order to judge the value of Schubert's music. In his words:

The belief in Schubert's greatness as an instrumental composer is, however, a forced one; and *the more the public learn about musical composition and musical form, the more certainly they will eventually find this out*.[164] (italics mine)

Here Statham brings two threads together. As the public learns about how music composition is done – what, in other words, is the winning compositional process – and once the public is well-informed about musical form, presumably through the proper understanding of music theory, everyone will grasp Schubert's proper place in history.

In the nineteenth century, Schubert's compositional efforts were never interpreted as battling directly with the tenets of Classical form or diatonic syntax. Rather, they were taken to deviate from them – like the somnambulist whose path is unclear. In a way, they had to be dismissed in this way: dangerous waters lurked ahead for critics who risked presuming that Schubert's music ought to be accounted for theoretically. From a theoretical standpoint, to take Schubert's form and syntax seriously would be to gnaw away at music theory's tenets. And so Vogl's message about that legendary muse whose flow of melodic inspiration Schubert was incapable of redirecting continued to be repeated. If the gradual discovery of Schubert's output – perhaps especially the instrumental music – brought with it any inkling that

---

[163] The full passage is cited by Kreissle, *The Life of Franz Schubert*, vol. I, 122–123, n. 1. Translation modified.

[164] Statham, *My Thoughts on Music and Musicians*, 326.

the basic tenets of harmonic and formal theory needed revisiting, then the accident of history that led many of Schubert's manuscripts to lie undiscovered until the end of the nineteenth century risked exposing music theory as an accident of history too. It was imperative that Schubert was pushed to the margins of history. As Adorno famously observed, the best way to do that was to make him into an ineffectual bourgeois personality of precisely the kind ultimately portrayed in *Lilac Time*.[165]

The twentieth century brought about a radical shift in stance, through such essays as Adorno's, but also through Tovey's appraisal of Schubert's harmony, as well as other voices who finally called for Schubert to be judged on his own terms.[166] As we shall see in Chapter 2, twentieth-century scholars were keen to embrace new theoretical paradigms for explaining Schubert's songs. They sought "purely musical" formal designs for their large-scale harmonic stations, often at the expense of the text. By contrast, as we shall see in Chapter 3, twentieth-century scholars were remarkably slow at inventing new paradigms to accommodate his unique sonata forms even though they consistently argued that existing models were unsuited to his lyric formulae. Instead of exploring new purely musical formal designs, scholars have turned to narratives to explain Schubert's harmony. As we shall see in Chapter 3, their narratives invariably leave unchallenged the notion that Schubert's instrumental forms are "diffuse." Only since the late 1990s have theorists seriously contemplated new harmonic paradigms for his sonata forms.

My purpose in the rest of this book will be to home in on those passages in Schubert's music that may serve as a means of questioning some of the most cherished tenets of music theory. In other words, instead of using music theory to analyze Schubert, I shall use Schubert to analyze music theory. I begin this journey by scrutinizing analytical approaches to Schubert's songs, and I introduce a new way of modeling Schubert's harmonic procedure. My theoretical model concurs with an old mode of thought, one prevalent in the early twentieth century, namely that, as Ferguson sensibly put it in his textbook, "the form of the music is constantly created by the text." As Finney similarly observed in 1935 in his textbook, "No arbitrary attempt is made to carry out a preconceived musical plan"; "it is futile to speak of a 'musical form' for the art song as a structural shape that can be subtracted from its materials and viewed as an abstraction." In other words, each song "makes its own formal

---

[165] Adorno, "Schubert (1928)," 8.   [166] Tovey, "Tonality."

laws."[167] In line with this thinking, my theoretical model emphasizes how the text dictates the musical treatment and yields the structure. As it happens, one of the most conspicuous songs that will provide me with such an opportunity is one that Vogl sang when he gained his first impressions of Schubert: "Ganymed."

---

[167] See Ferguson, *A History of Musical Thought*, 316 and Theodore M. Finney, *A History of Music* (New York: Harcourt, Brace and Company, 1935), 430. Numerous other studies from around this time period could be mentioned (and are mentioned in Chapter 2). However I make reference to these two studies here because both are general histories and contrast with Mason and Gray in outlook – although see above for Ferguson's rhapsody on Schubert's compositional process in contrast to Beethoven's.

2 | "A word will often do it": harmonic adventure in Schubert's songs

In writing Schubert's obituary in 1829, Johann Mayrhofer (1787–1836) noted that 19 January 1822 marked an important day for the understanding of Schubert's songs. On that day an anonymous review of some of them appeared in the Viennese *Allgemeine musikalische Zeitung*. The songs under scrutiny, it might be worth revealing, included settings of poetry by none other than Mayrhofer himself.[1] Nonetheless, in all modesty, the event was important for Schubert too: this was the first extensive review devoted to his songs. It extols Schubert for his "truly expressive song," his "rich lyrical gift" and his captivating accompaniments.[2] These traits, of course, continue to be regarded as important to Schubert's transformation of the German lied.[3]

The next major piece of criticism appeared as soon as a month later, in another Viennese newspaper.[4] This time the author signed his name: he was Friedrich von Hentl, and his review promised to be a probing discussion of all of Schubert's songs published up to that point, namely Opp. 1–7. He too singles out Schubert's lyricism and accompaniment for praise. According to him the vocal line is not solely responsible for carrying the expression of the words, as was primarily the case for Schubert's predecessors. In Schubert's songs, the accompaniment also holds a distinctive expressive force. Hentl additionally drew attention to the unique qualities

---

[1] For this comment in Mayrhofer's obituary, see "From the *Neues Archiv für Geschichte, Staatenkunde, Literatur und Kunst*, 23 February 1829: Recollections of Franz Schubert," in Otto Erich Deutsch (ed.), *Schubert: A Documentary Biography*, trans. Eric Blom (London: J. M. Dent, 1946), 862 (hereafter *SDB*); the review he refers to is reproduced as "From the Vienna *Allgemeine musikalische Zeitung*, 19 January 1822," *SDB*, 206–8.

[2] Although the review of January 19, 1822 is unsigned, it is generally assumed to be the work of Friedrich August Kanne (1778–1833), who was the editor of the Viennese *Allgemeine musikalische Zeitung* from 1821 until 1824, when it ceased publication; see Deutsch's commentary in *SDB*, 208.

[3] Thrasybulos G. Georgiades, *Schubert: Musik und Lyrik* (Göttingen: Vandenhoeck and Ruprecht, 1967), Kristina Muxfeldt, "Schubert's Songs: The Transformation of a Genre," in Christopher H. Gibbs (ed.), *The Cambridge Companion to Schubert* (Cambridge University Press, 1997), 121–137, Susan Youens, "Franz Schubert: The Prince of Song," in Rufus Hallmark (ed.), *German Lieder in the Nineteenth Century* (New York: G. Schirmer, 1996), 31–74.

[4] March 23, 1822, in *Weiner Zeitschrift für Kunst*.

of Schubert's harmony, but he avoided discussing the mechanics of it in any detail: "Others will judge the theoretical aspect of these works and say how far justice is done to the technics of an art where no lapse may be tolerated, since definite rules exclude wilfulness."[5] So much for the analysis of Schubert's harmony.

There is, however, one sign that Hentl might relent and delve into technical matters after all. Although Schubert's melodies tend to shift rapidly from one emotional state to another in order to paint the details of the text, suggesting disorder on the surface, their underlying cohesion may, he claims, be explained by appealing to that most prized and scruti-nized concept of the nineteenth century: organicism. Hentl concludes, "Each note must remain where it is if the melody is not to be ruined – a sure touchstone of its organic constitution!" Yet any hope that he might reveal the inner workings of this organicism is immediately dashed: "The characterization [of the melody]," he goes on to say, "is so incisive as to require no explanation in order to be generally felt."[6]

As we can see, then, Schubert's earliest, sympathetic critics readily point to the novelty of Schubert's melodies, harmony, and accompaniments. However, they provide frustratingly few clues about how their effect is achieved. Hentl serves as a good example: when it comes to comprehending Schubert's melody, he argues no explanation is needed, and when it comes to analyzing Schubert's harmony, he suggests someone else should do it.

Hentl might have been none too pleased that the first detailed analysis of Schubert's musical language would fall, as it were, to a member of the opposition. A series of reviews appeared during Schubert's lifetime in the Leipzig *Allgemeine musikalische Zeitung* spanning the years 1824–8. According to Otto Deutsch, these were penned by Gottfried Wilhelm Fink, a frequent contributor to the journal before becoming its editor in 1827. He was a staunch conservative, famous for his book-length attack on A. B. Marx.[7] He found much to object to in Schubert's song settings: the melodies were often unsingable, the accompaniments were overdone, the form departed from his favored strophic model. However, he devoted greatest attention to what bothered him most: Schubert's harmony.

---

[5] Hentl, "From the *Weiner Zeitschrift für Kunst*, 23 March 1822," *SDB*, 214.

[6] Hentl, "23 March 1822," *SDB*, 217. I have substituted the word "explanation" (*Auseinandersetzung*) for "analysis" in the published translation. Although "analysis" is undoubtedly meant (in the sense that an ensuing explanation would have dealt with unity created through pitch etc.), a more literal translation avoids the danger of suggesting that my argument turns on the choice of word in the translation.

[7] Gottfried Wilhelm Fink, *Der neumusikalische Lehrjammer, oder Beleuchtung der Schrift: Die alte Musiklehre im Streit mit unserer Zeit* (Leipzig: Mayer and Wigand, 1842).

Fink was horrified generally by the new harmonic trends of his day, which he said consisted of an "unwarrantably strong inclination to modulate again and again, with neither rest nor respite . . . a veritable disease of our time and threatens to grow into modulation-mania."[8] It seems that, in Fink's mind, Schubert suffered the worst bouts of this disease. As he put it, Schubert's modulations are "free, very free, and sometimes rather more than that."[9] Fink repeated himself often on this topic.[10] Some three years later, for instance, he said that Schubert modulates "so oddly and often so very suddenly towards the remotest regions as no composer on earth has done."[11]

The suspicion that Schubert's modulations are free and odd has haunted the reception of his music ever since. As we saw in the previous chapter, the nineteenth-century attitude was that this freedom and oddity were signs of Schubert's mismanagement of musical form and lack of technical knowledge, a view that much recent Schubert scholarship attempts to overturn by promoting instead a more pluralist view that his formal structures are constructions of a different subjectivity.[12] This radical change in stance, however welcome it might be, should not divert our attention away from the fact that Schubert's harmonic infractions nonetheless remain carefully guarded, for during the twentieth century they became prized hermeneutic possessions. Modern scholars resist overturning entirely the impression that Schubert was prone to some sort of modulation mania – his modulations continue to be characterized as excessive, digressive or meandering. Yet, as this chapter will expose in relation to the songs (detailed study of Schubert's sonata-form structures will occupy chapters 3 and 4), modern views of Schubert's harmonic infractions are based on a very different definition of tonal order from Fink's. Our twentieth- and twenty-first-century notion is a product of the institutionalization of music theory, in which, amongst other influential factors, modulation became reckoned on ever-broader structural levels. To put it another way, if Schubert was a strain on Fink's ears, his modern legacy is that he is a strain on music theory.

Although Fink is critical of Schubert, it could be said to be fortunate that he built his case against the composer by enumerating Schubert's harmonic

---

[8] Gottfried Wilhelm Fink, "From the Leipzig *Allgemeine musikalische Zeitung*, 24 June 1824," *SDB*, 355.

[9] Fink, "24 June 1824," *SDB*, 354.

[10] During Schubert's lifetime, Fink wrote no fewer than five reviews on the songs between June 1824 and January 1828.

[11] Fink, "From the Leipzig *Allgemeine musikalische Zeitung*, 25 April 1827," *SDB*, 636.

[12] The most influential piece of writing on this topic is, of course, Susan McClary, "Constructions of Subjectivity in Schubert's Music," in Philip Brett, Elizabeth Wood, and Gary Thomas (eds.), *Queering the Pitch: The New Gay and Lesbian Musicology* (New York: Routledge, 1994), 205–233.

offences. Fink is a uniquely valuable early nineteenth-century critic of Schubert's music. In many ways he is all we have got. While others also point to the existence of Schubert's predilection for excessive modulation, Fink is the only contemporary of Schubert who ventured into detailed analysis of the harmony.[13] Even those who praised Schubert were remarkably laconic, finding as they did excuses not dissimilar to Hentl's. At the end of Schubert's career, for example, an anonymous reviewer of the publication of the first part of *Winterreise* (D. 911) mentions Schubert's "technical beauties" in the cycle but says that analysis of them cannot be attempted because the *Theaterzeitung* is the wrong journal for theoretical matters.[14]

A close reading of Fink's analyses will therefore reward us with a rare glimpse into an early nineteenth-century reaction to Schubert's harmonic practice. My first task, therefore, will be to glean more information from Fink by examining in detail two songs he discusses in his first review, in which he differentiates between acceptable and unacceptable modulations. My findings will be tested, more briefly, against a number of other songs to which Fink refers in the course of his subsequent reviews. I argue, based on close readings of his comments, that it was the *manner* of Schubert's modulations – rather than the fact that they occurred – that most significantly disturbed his ears.

Before proceeding with my examination of Fink, I shall outline the aims of the subsequent sections of this chapter. The section "Modeling analysis" is a kind of historiography of music-theoretical scholarship on Schubert's songs, starting with responses to "new musicology" debates of the 1980s and 1990s. I shall first explore in detail two studies that were intended to serve as models for how to do an analysis of song. These studies, by David Lewin and Kofi Agawu, may be read as responses to the attacks on music analysis which, in the opinion of new musicologists, was all too often exercised in a cultural and historical vacuum. I explore the place that Lewin and Agawu assign to both music theory and analysis in the practice of song hermeneutics.

---

[13] Another review (of a performance of Schubert's song, rather than a publication, as in Fink's case) that has garnered much attention is Anon., "From the Vienna *Allgemeine musikalische Zeitung*," *SDB*, 166. In it, the author refers to a performance of *Gesang der Geister über den Wassern* (D. 714) as "an accumulation of every sort of senseless, disordered and purposeless musical modulation and sidetracking," without however going into any of the kind of helpful detail that Fink does. Scholars have consequently used the statement to speculate what Schubert's listeners were reacting to. See especially Walther Dürr, " 'Ausweichungen ohne Sinn, Ordnung und Zweck' – Zu Tonart und Tonalität bei Schubert," in Erich Wolfgang Partsch (ed.), *Franz Schubert – Der Forschrittliche? Analysen – Perspektiven – Fakten* (Tutzing: Hans Schneider, 1989), 73–104 and Hartmut Krones, "'Ein Accumulat aller musikalischen Modulationen und Ausweichungen ohne Sinn, Ordnung und Zweck': Zu Schuberts 'schauerlichen' Werken der Jahre 1817–28," *Österreichische Musikzeitschrift* 52 (1997): 32–40.

[14] Anon., "From the *Theaterzeitung*, 29 March 1828," *SDB*, 758.

Lewin, who analyzes "Auf dem Flusse" from *Winterreise*, provides a golden opportunity to witness the power of music theory in this apparently more responsible interpretative practice. He argues that the music's yes-or-no answer to a question posed in the poem hinges on the ability to relate one key to another. As we shall see, Lewin's theoretical dexterity – he uses both Schenker and Riemann in imaginative ways – enabled him to claim that Schubert set the poem in a manner that implies both "yes" and "no" to the question, an ambivalence he claims is latent in Müller's poem. At the same time, I shall trace why Lewin's all-important harmony is absent from Schenker's own graph of "Auf dem Flusse." As we shall see, while Lewin goes to great lengths to seek a meaning for this harmony, Schenker went to equivalent lengths to downplay it in order to preserve his principle of monotonality. If such a harmony – conspicuous, incidentally, in the song – can come so starkly in and out of focus through different applications of music theory, then the moral of the story I wish to draw is that music theory plays a far more potent role in shaping musical meaning than is generally admitted. That is to say, by and large we have come to take for granted that – barring misreadings – music theory supplies us with "honest answers" to such apparently straightforward questions as how harmonies relate to one another.

Schubert becomes a good test case in this respect, as he pushed the boundaries of Classical syntax and harmonic-formal logic. A review of the literature on Schubert's songs reveals that what remains unsettled even to today is which model of harmonic analysis is best suited to Schubert's music. Lately, much faith has been placed in neo-Riemannian theory for its potential to elucidate aspects of Schubert's harmony that remain inscrutable – or, perhaps, awkwardly explained – through Schenkerian and other diatonic models. In the "Analytical models" section of this chapter, I shall point to some important neo-Riemannian developments, but I shall focus primarily on two new harmonic models formulated by Thomas Denny and Harald Krebs specifically to address Schubert's most adventurous songs, namely those that begin and end in different keys.[15] Neither paradigm has caught

---

[15] Thomas Denny, "Directional Tonality in Schubert's Lieder," in Erich Wolfgang Partsch (ed.), *Franz Schubert – Der Forschrittliche? Analysen – Perspektiven – Fakten* (Tutzing: Hans Schneider, 1989), 37–53, Harald Krebs, "The Background Level in Some Tonally Deviating Works of Franz Schubert," *In Theory Only* 8/8 (1985): 5–18; "Alternatives to Monotonality in Early Nineteenth-Century Music," *Journal of Music Theory* 25 (1981): 1–16; "Tonart und Text in Schuberts Liedern mit abweichenden Schlüssen," *Archiv für Musikwissenschaft* 47 (1990): 264–271; and "Some Early Examples of Tonal Pairing: Schubert's 'Meeres Stille' and 'Der Wanderer,'" in William Kinderman and Harald Krebs (eds.), *The Second Practice of Nineteenth-Century Tonality* (Lincoln and London: University of Nebraska Press, 1996), 17–33. See also Krebs, "Third Relation and Dominant in Late 18th- and Early 19th-Century Music," 2 vols. (PhD thesis: Yale University, 1980).

on, suggesting that students of Schubert's songs prefer to fashion anew theoretical constructs in order to carry out their readings of Schubert's songs – indeed this highlights just how difficult it is to settle on a methodology for analyzing them. Two aspects of Denny's and Krebs's work will occupy my attention: firstly their methodologies of arriving at "purely musical" (to use a term of Agawu's) explanations for Schubert's keys and, secondly, their habits of hermeneutics. While neither Denny nor Krebs sought to produce "complete" analyses of the kind demanded by new musicologists or advocated by Lewin and Agawu, both do in fact make brief nods to the broader picture of musical meaning. I shall therefore take the opportunity to trace how they construct musical meaning.

The link between Denny and Krebs and the next section of this chapter is their analyses of "Ganymed," which I shall additionally compare to Lawrence Kramer's reading of the song. "Ganymed" fits neatly into one of Krebs's models, but bursts the seams of all of Denny's. Denny therefore turns to Schenkerian analysis, an odd gesture given that it was the very system he rejected at the outset of his study. Kramer has analyzed the song twice during the course of his career, first by using a method of organizing Schubert's harmonic stations into patterns of root motions, which bears striking similarities to Denny's proposed paradigm, then by turning to Schenker. As it turns out, they all interpret Schubert's setting (which begins and ends in different keys) against the norms of the Schenkerian *Ursatz* (which is monotonal) and they all agree that Schubert's "deviance" was inspired by the text.

In the penultimate section of this chapter, I suggest, however, that Schubert got the idea for the structure of his setting from Johann Friedrich Reichardt, whose setting also begins and ends in different keys. Rather than the background structure being some theoretical model or principle of monotonality, I argue that the proper "background structure" of Schubert's harmonic structure is Reichardt's. Schubert's transformation of this lied brings us back to where my chapter started, with the kinds of observations made by Fink. Schubert, as it were, "composes out" Reichardt's background structure, transforming the manner of modulation at the foreground level. It is by comparing Schubert's song to his predecessor's, rather than to established theoretical models, that we catch a glimpse of what must have sounded fresh and novel about Schubert's harmony to his first listeners – and disconcerting to his first critics. Similarly, the comparison offers us a fresh hearing and the opportunity to rethink the ways we have thus far modeled Schubert's harmony in the context of song, a topic which occupies this chapter's final section.

A nineteenth-century way of hearing

After citing Schubert's song "Auf der Donau" (D. 533) as an extreme example of Schubert's propensity for modulation, Fink outlines the keys it visits. The song

> begins in E♭ major, which has disappeared at the seventh bar; then comes C minor, A♭ major and minor, C♭ major &c., and F♯ minor, where it stays for some time and closes.[16]

To modern readers, it will seem curious that a critic, who was enraged by modulations that go too far, makes no specific comment about the fact that the song begins and ends in a different key. Fink's annoyance with this song seems to have more to do with the disappearance of the tonic by the seventh measure. Let's examine the passage.

As can be seen in Example 2.1a, the first six measures oscillate between tonic and dominant, clearly establishing E♭ major. The offending seventh measure has an Ê♭ in the vocal line. What is the problem? This Ê♭ even looks like a resolution of the common cadential gesture $\hat{5}-\hat{7}-\hat{8}$ (B̂♭–D̂–Ê♭), the eighth-note rest notwithstanding.[17] The problem for Fink is that the accompaniment delivers a submediant (C minor) harmony below this Ê♭ instead of the tonic. It seems, then, that Fink is disconcerted by a mere vi chord. He surely must have encountered this progression numerous times elsewhere, even in the repertoire he held so dear. Is he, then, an incompetent critic? The short answer is no.

The longer answer entails moving on to the next Ê♭, which appears in the voice two measures later. Another $\hat{5}-\hat{7}$ gesture over a dominant suggests a resolution to C minor in m. 9 for the start of the next poetic line. Schubert avoids harmonizing the Ê♭ as $\hat{3}$ of C minor. Instead, he delivers yet another VI chord. Ê♭ is now supported by an A♭ major harmony and is therefore a $\hat{5}$ in its new context. Despite, then, the strong presence of the note Ê♭ in the voice in mm. 7 and 9, emphasized as it is at the beginnings of the short phrases, the key of E♭ has indeed disappeared from underneath it, as Fink observes. In this way, m. 7 is worth commenting on because it marks the point at which Schubert begins to part company with his opening tonic harmony, although not its tonic pitch.

---

[16] Fink, "From the Leipzig *Allgemeine musikaliche Zeitung*, 24 June 1824," *SDB*, 354.

[17] In order to distinguish pitches from keys, I have adopted the caret symbol of Schenkerian theory over the name of a pitch. Ê♭ refers to the pitch, E♭ to the harmony or key.

Example 2.1a   Schubert, "Auf der Donau" (D. 553), Section A

The vocal line in mm. 15–16 presents another opportunity for a cadence. It outlines $\hat{4}-\hat{7}-\hat{8}$, landing on an $E\flat$ no less. While this time an $E\flat$ major harmony is indeed articulated in m. 16, it functions as a dominant and is prepared by a German sixth. By transforming the $E\flat$ major harmony from tonic to dominant function, it aptly sets the word "geistergleich," meaning "ghostly." It is not until the end of the following phrase that the piano and voice synchronize for the first time to produce an authentic cadence, as annotated in Example 2.1a. It marks the end of Section A. The song has

Example 2.1a (cont.)

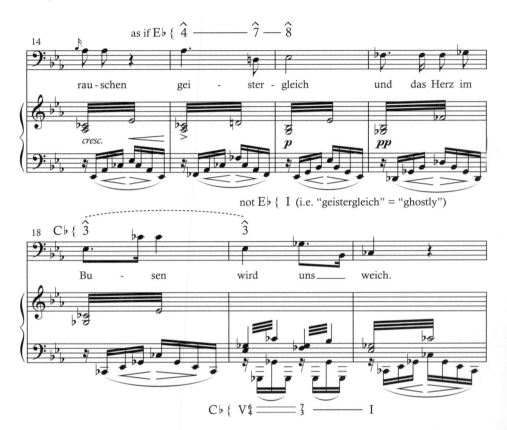

reached C♭ major, where the salient Ê♭s at the opening of mm. 18 and 19 serve now as 3̂s. The elusive departures and arrivals of all but the last key seem to be why Fink is critical of this song.

Fink does not comment on the B section of "Auf der Donau," except to say that the thirteen trills deep in the piano's bass line are "details about which it is not worth while making words."[18] His contempt is palpable. His harmonic analysis resumes with the thematic return of the A section, now in F♯ minor. Fink says nothing of the change in mode from major to minor. As noted in the citation above, he simply observes that F♯ minor is where the song "stays for some time and closes."

Example 2.1b begins with the return of the A section at m. 38. The first thing to note is that m. 42 shares the same harmonic progression and voice-leading circumstances as m. 7. Why then are Fink's ears not offended again? How is it that the song now "stays for some time" in F♯ minor? If the

---

[18] Fink, "24 June 1824," *SDB*, 355.

Example 2.1b   Schubert, "Auf der Donau," Section A′

harmonic moves are identical (both dominant to submediant), why is his impression of it different the second time? Is Fink an unobservant critic? Again, the short answer is no, and the longer answer demands that we press on to m. 44.

Close scrutiny of the parallel passages in mm. 8–9 and 43–44 reveals that, although the harmonic functions are the same, the manner in which the progression is presented is more stable the second time around. The

Example 2.1b (cont.)

resolution of the voice in m. 44 is smoother than in m. 9. It will be remembered that the B̂♮ in the voice in m. 8 did not resolve up a semitone. The corresponding passage in m. 44 does, however, resolve upwards, from Ĉ♯ to D̂. Moreover, the F̂♯ in the voice a measure later (m. 45) is supported by an F♯ major harmony. The next one in m. 47 is again supported by an F♯ major harmony, with the German sixth again lending it a dominant function, this time aptly underscoring the word "verdorrt" ("faded"). Nonetheless, m. 47 marks the real beginning of a gravitation towards F♯, as the harmony is brought around to F♯ minor, with mm. 50–51 finally articulating a V$^6_5$–i cadence in F♯ minor. After this point the song unquestionably remains in F♯ minor: for some 15 measures it almost exclusively repeats V–i cadences, with plenty of assertions of F̂♯ as 1̂ in the voice.

What is there to learn from this analysis? It is my contention that when Fink complains about Schubert's "free" and "odd" modulations, he is less concerned about *which* keys Schubert goes to than he is about the *manner* in which Schubert reaches them. Examination of Fink's contrasting reaction to another song will, I think, confirm this suspicion.

Fink claims that in "Selige Welt" (D. 743) "even the most remote modulations are mild and therefore praiseworthy."[19] To appreciate his comment, we need to find out what "mild" means. The song is in A♭ major and by the ninth measure C♭ major has arrived. In "Selige Welt," the keys are introduced differently from in "Auf der Donau." A♭ major is first established with an authentic cadence in the piano prelude and echoed at the end of the first textual couplet in m. 5 (see Example 2.2). The voice closes the couplet in A♭ major, and an emphatic *f* in the piano articulates the cadence again with massive chords reaching outwards to span five octaves in m. 6. The cadence is unmistakable. The voice and piano rebegin with the material and dynamic level from the voice's first entry of the song. This time a subtle inflection of A♭ major to minor is introduced by the Ĉ♭ under "hin und *her*" (back and *forth*). The result is cataclysmic, one might expect Fink to exclaim. The song is catapulted into C♭ major. A♭ major has disappeared by the ninth measure, one might expect Fink to protest. However, as Example 2.2 shows, the arrival of the new key is underscored by a strong V–I cadence in mm. 8–9, emphasized by an *f* dynamic for the dominant and an *ff* for the tonic. The voice partakes fully in the cadential move, leading up to the tonic by stepwise motion from 5̂ to 8̂. There is no mistaking this cadence either, but for good measure the pianist bangs it out again across the full range of the keyboard, this time landing on the downbeat in m. 10. For the next few measures C♭ major enjoys some stability, supported as the ensuing phrases are by tonics and dominants. This procedure, unlike the evasive harmonic entrances found in "Auf der Donau," is "mild" to Fink's ears, and it is therefore praiseworthy.

Although the B section of "Selige Welt" is only seven measures long, it touches on no fewer than four keys. The first key picks up where the A section left off, in C♭ major. The rocking of the boat on the water is depicted by the

---

[19] Fink, "24 June 1824," *SDB*, 354–5.

Example 2.2 Schubert, "Selige Welt" (D. 743)

Example 2.2 (cont.)

complementary I–V^7; V^7–I phrase and the word repetition. Each phrase begins with the same Ĝ♭, while, as it were, the waves shift underneath, changing the Ĝ♭ from 5̂ to 1̂. The tenor of the poem changes between the A and B sections. While in the A section the protagonist was content to drift aimlessly on "life's sea" ("Ich treibe auf des Lebens Meer"), in the B section he attempts to be active and seek a "blessed island" ("eine selige Insel"). This is folly, he recognizes, as no such place exists ("doch eine ist es nicht").

The portrayal of harmonic restlessness is different in each section, as befits the two modes of restlessness in the poem. In section A, Schubert's favorite technique of introducing a chromatic pitch (the Ĉ♭ of 'hin und *her*') veers the harmony towards the tonicization of C♭ major. The actual arrival of the new key is emphatic, as is the establishment of the tonic of the song in the first place. The protagonist's willingness to go with the flow, as it were, is portrayed by the synchronized assertions of keys in both the piano and voice. If the harmony is coordinated, the sense of drifting through life's sea is depicted through the unpredictable phrase rhythm and placement of distinct rhythmic features within each phrase.

The initial sense of calm and control over the harmony and phrase rhythm that begins the B section and coincides with the protagonist taking control over his destiny is disrupted in m. 14 as the protagonist becomes aware that the idyllic island he is seeking does not exist. Although the harmonies continue to involve tonics and dominants, they are modulatory rather than stabilizing. However, there is a thread that runs through each key. As shown in Example 2.2, the Ĉ♭ in m. 9 is taken up again in m. 14, each rhyming words "gahn/Wahn." In m. 15, the voice arrives on a B̂♮ and the piano takes up the pitch in m. 16. The journey and harmonic role of this common tone is depicted in Example 2.3, which illustrates how the Ĉ♭/B̂♮ changes from a 3̂ in A♭ minor to a 1̂ in C♭ major to a 3̂ in G major to a 5̂ in E minor. In all of these cases it is a consonance within its triad, but once the piano takes over in m. 16, B̂♮ becomes the pitch that requires resolution to C minor in m. 17 and the thread of the common tone ends, as shown in the example.

The nifty move in m. 17 (see Example 2.2), which brings about the return of the opening material, is a characteristic Schubertian maneuver: after the arrival of C minor, Schubert extracts the pitch Ê♭ from the triad, which serves as the dominant preparation for A♭ major, as is shown in the analysis in Example 2.3.[20] The LPR transformations in the example are

---

[20] Perhaps the most famous example of this maneuver is the entry of the second theme in the exposition of the first movement of the *Unfinished* Symphony. The end of the transition remains in B minor, from which 3̂ is extracted and becomes the dominant 5̂ that prepares the entry of G

Example 2.3   Harmonic reduction of Schubert, "Selige Welt"

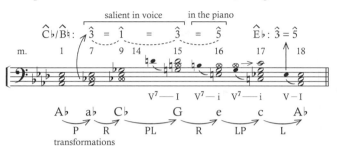

neo-Riemannian symbols. L, P, R refer respectively to "Leittonwechsel," "Parallel," and "Relative" between two major and minor triads.[21] In each case, there are two common tones and one displaced tone. The P between the tonic major/minor shows a single semitone displacement from $\hat{C}$ to $\hat{C}\flat$ between the two common tones $\hat{A}\flat$ and $\hat{E}\flat$. The R between the next two triads depicts the tone displacement from $\hat{A}\flat$ to $\hat{G}\flat$ and the common tones $\hat{C}\flat$ and $\hat{E}\flat$. An L transformation may be found at the end of Example 2.3, where C minor and A♭ major share the tones $\hat{C}$ and $\hat{E}\flat$ but differ by a single semitone displacement of $\hat{G}$ to $\hat{A}\flat$. Both R and L are diatonic relations, thus chromatic thirds are labeled as compounds, which in the example are PL and LP. The order of the compound symbols matters: to get from C♭ major to G major, one must imagine first C♭ major transforming into B minor through P (to employ enharmonic equivalence), and then imagine $\hat{F}\sharp$ displacing by a semitone to $\hat{G}$ for the L transformation in order to produce G major.

The advantage to neo-Riemannian labels, as opposed to Roman numerals, is that harmonic moves are accessed as transformations of their immediate predecessors, rather than in relation to an overall tonic, although larger-scale harmonic ports of call can also be labeled. Example 2.4 provides one such example, where the "half-step" move from C♭ major to C minor that opens and closes the B section of "Selige Welt" is labeled SLIDE, which is a label adopted by neo-Riemannian theorists from David Lewin.[22] However, the purpose of my transformation analysis in Example 2.3 is to highlight

---

major. The difference in this song is that Schubert uses it to come back to the tonic rather than to venture away from it, thus it is retransitional rather than transitional.

[21] Only the label for the "Leittonwechsel" is original to Riemann, as his "Parallel" means our relative, and our parallel was called "Variante" by him.

[22] David Lewin, *Generalized Musical Intervals and Transformations* (New Haven: Yale University Press, 1987), 178. The SLIDE operation is defined as preserving the third of a triad while changing its mode. In the case of Example 2.4, the $\hat{E}\flat$ is preserved such that C♭ major becomes C minor.

Example 2.4 Graphic representation of Charles Rosen's interpretation of Schubert, "Selige Welt," Section B

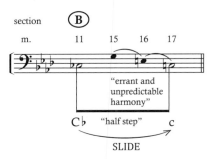

the relationships between each articulated tonic: all but the first one (P) is a third relation (R, PL, R, LP, L). Among these keys, there is no large-scale dominant in relation to A♭ major. The role of the dominants in this song is instead articulative or purely cadential, as shown through the Roman numerals in the example. According to my analysis, the neo-Riemannian transformations operate at a higher hierarchical level than the surface-level cadential dominants.

A Schenkerian analysis of this song would yield a very different interpretation. Example 2.5 illustrates a standard Schenkerian reading of "Selige Welt." It shows an interrupted structure, with a bass arpeggiation that is infused with mixture. The E♭ major harmonies in mm. 17 and 20, which are merely cadential in my neo-Riemannian analysis, serve as the two structural dominants in the Schenkerian reading. The Schenkerian perspective lies behind at least one modern commentator's characterization of Schubert's harmony. Charles Rosen makes a distinction between the harmony of sections A and B of the song. He calls the harmonic material in section A "fairly conventional" compared to the harmonic movement in section B, which he calls "more idiosyncratically Schubertian." As he explains, the B section comprises "basically a half-step move from C flat major to C minor, prepared by straying through the harmonies of G major and E minor ('the madman seeks his fortunate island')."[23] This comment may be represented by Example 2.4, in which the outer keys are structural and the inner keys stray around. Rosen prefers to home in on the "errant and unpredictable" (his words) quality of Schubert's harmonic stations, reading Schubert's choice of keys as a measure of his portrayal of the madman's futile efforts to direct his boat towards a definite goal. Unlike

---

[23] Charles Rosen, "Schubert's Inflections of Classical Form," in Christopher H. Gibbs (ed.), *The Cambridge Companion to Schubert* (Cambridge University Press, 1997), 77.

Example 2.5   Schenkerian reading of Schubert, "Selige Welt"

I — ♭III-(   )iii — V

Fink, Rosen bases his distinction between "mild" (or conventional) modulations in the opening A section and the "odd" (or errant and unpredictable) ones in the B section on the basis of large-scale design.

Whether reading "Selige Welt" through a Schenkerian or neo-Riemannian lens, there is no denying that the modulations are remote. Indeed, the only key in the collection that is diatonic to A♭ major is C minor. But to my mind, my analysis in Example 2.3 better captures the spirit of Fink's comment that *"even the most remote modulations are mild and therefore praiseworthy."* While some of the modulations in this song are more remote than others, even the most extreme ones are rendered "mild" because they are prepared by an authentic cadence. Certainly Fink cannot have been referring to the song's character, for the cadences that establish the keys are far from mild in terms of both dynamics and tessitura.

Fink's references to the other songs in his first review further support my reading. He identifies some songs as having acceptable modulations and others as having unacceptable ones, yet all contain remote modulations. An examination of the music again reveals that the distinction corresponds to modulations with authentic cadences and those without. It is therefore the surface presentation of the modulations that concerns Fink more than their remoteness. Moreover – and it is an important distinction compared to modern approaches – Fink seemed unconcerned by the need to find a logical overarching design in the sets of keys. Thus, for instance, in "Schlummerlied" he finds "a few desperate modulations towards the middle" (*SDB*, p. 354) and in "Gruppe aus dem Tartarus" "the modulations are very glaring" (*SDB*, p. 355). The "desperate" modulations must refer to the passages in mm. 9–11, 20–22, and 31–33 in which the harmonies shift each time from F major, the home tonic, to A major, B♭ major, and C major – all without any hint of dominant preparation. "Gruppe aus dem Tartarus" is highly chromatic from the start, and the melodic line often traces a chromatic scale; rarely are the harmonic stations in the song articulated with an authentic cadence. Therefore Fink is critical of both.

By contrast, Fink acknowledges that "Schatzgräbers Begehr" (Op. 24, no. 4) also contains remote modulations but argues that Schubert "deals with them easily" (*SDB*, p. 355). This comment is particularly interesting in light of the song's chromatic bass line, which is not dissimilar to the one in "Gruppe aus dem Tartarus" (though the latter admittedly contains a greater frenzy of activity in the accompaniment). Significantly, and unlike "Gruppe aus dem Tartarus," the new tonal stations are articulated each time with an authentic cadence.

In a later review dated 25 April 1827, Fink complained that, in "Du liebst mich nicht," "the quite short and very simple melody has to be dragged through almost every key and several times from one extreme to the other by a mere two progressions" (*SDB*, p. 636) – note the complaint is twofold: the key changes take the song almost everywhere (Schubert's modulations are "free, very free") and extreme keys are connected with too few progressions (Schubert modulates "so oddly and so very suddenly"). Fink's quibble in his review from 23 January 1828 about the return of C major in m. 68 in "Die Allmacht" (D. 852) is particularly illuminating. Again he complains that the new key "should be more closely related to what has gone before by metrical relationship and harmonic modulation" (*SDB*, p. 719). C major is the home tonic of the song, so it might seem strange that he did not put his remark the other way around – something like, "the material before the return to the tonic should be more closely related to it." Instead he makes his judgement calls as the music proceeds, based on surface-level details rather than large-scale plans.

As shown in the box in Example 2.6, however, the entry of C major in m. 69 is even prepared with an authentic cadence. So what is there to complain about? The offence this time seems to be that the dominant harmony is neither sufficient in length nor powerful enough to allow the ear to adjust after the extensive passage of over 30 measures in A♭ major that precedes it. According to Fink, Schubert's handling of the move from the flattened submediant to the tonic through a dominant harmony is topsy-turvy: the normally ornamental upper chromatic neighbor note is treated as an extended key area, while the normally all-important dominant is too brief. In other words, a cadential formula that ought to have gone as in Example 2.7a is instead weighted aurally as Example 2.7b.

The graph in Example 2.7b indicates a lower-level articulative dominant, with a more salient LP move – much like the harmonic framework of

Example 2.6 Dominant preparation of tonic return in m. 69 in Schubert, "Die Allmacht" (D. 852), mm. 59–74

Example 2.7   (a) Diatonic interpretation of ♭VI–V–I Schubert, "Die Allmacht,"
mm. 32–74; (b) interpretation of mm. 32–74 according to aural salience of harmonies

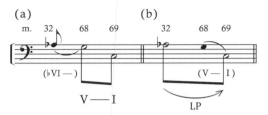

"Selige Welt," which Fink considered "mild and therefore praiseworthy." If
"Die Allmacht" also has a dominant harmony to prepare for the return to C
major, why is it not similarly praiseworthy? It seems that my statement
above about the distinction between acceptable and unacceptable modulations on the basis of the presence or absence of an authentic cadence
requires the following nuance. The preparation for the new key through its
dominant needs to be proportional both to the salience of a previous key
and to how long the ear therefore requires to adjust. A quick succession of
keys, as in "Selige Welt," can withstand brief dominants.

In the four years during Schubert's lifetime that Fink occupied himself
with Schubert criticism, he remained consistent in his criticism about
Schubert's harmony and continued to complain about the modern predilection to modulate often and without proper preparation.[24] Fink's
complaints are an important testimony to an early nineteenth-century
way of hearing. While Schubert was, for him, a composer who modulated
too much and too far, seduced as he was by the fashion of his day, Fink
seems to have understood that a well-placed authentic cadence has the
capacity to render any key acceptable. Or, to put it the other way around,
to Fink's mind, a remote key becomes justifiable from a musical point of
view if its presence is announced frankly at the local level. The dominant is
a preparatory harmony and need not be a large-scale structural necessity,
as it is for Schenker, for example. Indeed, this has implications for the

---

[24] By contrast, over the course of the four years he softened his view of the melodies and
accompaniment, applauding Schubert for finding the predominant emotion in a poem and (on
the most successful occasions) evoking it through simple melodies, while allowing the
accompaniment to further paint the poem. With regards to harmony and form, he continued to
maintain that Schubert "oversteps the species at hand," although he conceded in his review of
January 23, 1828 that Schubert had a "sound knowledge of harmony" and that sometimes his
choices were justified by the words (*SDB*, 718). Nonetheless he lived in hope that Schubert
would either grow out of the habit of modulatory excess or come to realize that it was merely a
trend of his day and therefore abandon it.

relevance of neo-Riemannian theory, particularly with regards to the third relations that define many of the harmonic stations articulated in these songs. It is against this nineteenth-century backdrop that I wish to examine modern-day approaches to analyzing Schubert's songs. My first port of call, as explained earlier, is the two studies on the methodology of song analysis.

Modeling analysis

A growing awareness that song analysis too often consisted of a scrutiny of the music without sufficient regard for the text prompted perhaps the most famous indictment against analysis of the 1980s, namely Joseph Kerman's "How We Got into Analysis, and How to Get Out."[25] Kerman criticized Schenker for entirely ignoring the text in his analysis of the second song from Schumann's *Dichterliebe*, and especially his followers for quibbling over the *Kopfton* – is it a $\hat{5}$ or $\hat{3}$ line? They all, he argued, missed the essence of the song setting because they paid attention neither to the text nor to the context in which Schumann composed his song.[26]

At least two important studies by music theorists have aimed to remedy this situation and to model a methodology for, as it were, a more complete analysis of song. The earliest is by David Lewin, whose analysis of "Auf dem Flusse," from *Winterreise*, was intended to serve as a model by example. It aimed to show how the relationship between musical structure and textual imagery might operate. To this end, he examined the structure and meaning of the poem and, on the musical side, scrutinized such matters as Schubert's choice of key, the proportion of musical time assigned to each strophe (he notes that half of the song-time is devoted to four of the five stanzas), the rhythmic features and the melodic contour. He appealed frequently to Schenkerian concepts, though he was critical of Schenker's

[25] An earlier version of this article appeared under the title of "The State of Academic Music Criticism," in Kingsley Price (ed.), *On Criticizing Music: Five Philosophical Perspectives* (Baltimore: Johns Hopkins University Press, 1981), 38–54. The essay with the more famous title was originally published in *Critical Inquiry* 7 (1980): 311–331 and is reprinted in *Write All These Down: Essays on Music* (Berkeley and Los Angeles: University of California Press, 1994).

[26] It is therefore ironic that Kerman reproduces Schenker's graph without quoting or referring to Schenker's own accompanying text in the other volume of *Free Composition*. Schenker's text is crucial to understanding why the middle of the song contains so much detail in the graph: the chromatic procedure in that spot was the focus of Schenker's theoretical point. Kerman's complaint about the minimal detail in Schenker's analysis of the outer parts of the song is therefore addressed in the accompanying prose to the graph.

own reading, and in one place invoked Riemann for both his function theory and dualism. As we shall see, the trickiest issue for Lewin was how to deal with a G♯ minor passage in the fifth strophe.

At the outset of his study, Lewin remarks, "A Schubert song takes as structural premises not only musical syntax, as it was understood at the time, but also *the structure of the individual text at hand*."[27] Indeed. But, writing as he was in the early 1980s in the wake of attacks on formalism, Lewin's purpose was primarily to remind readers that a song comprises text as well as music. For our purposes, however, it is important to note that Lewin points to the *structure* of the text, not to individual words. Indeed, the opening sentence of his study similarly reads: "I propose here to explore the relation of *musical structure* to textual imagery in Schubert's song *Auf dem Flusse*."[28]

This already marks Lewin squarely as a twentieth-century critic. Compare Schubert's greatest nineteenth-century advocate, Sir George Grove, who explained that Schubert's music "changes with the words as a landscape does when sun and clouds pass over it." Schubert's sensitivity to the text is so meticulous that, Grove adds, "A word will often do it."[29] This latter comment is the flagship quotation for the title of this chapter because it encapsulates the distinction between the nineteenth-century literary tradition (which still persists in German and some Anglo-American scholarship today) and the modern theory-laden and specifically Anglo-American tradition, which is the main focus of my critique in this chapter.[30] Whereas the former group focuses on the minutiae of the words as the motivating factor in Schubert's harmonic shifts, the latter tends to see the overall meaning of the poem as reflected in the large-scale patterns of Schubert's harmonic adventures, an approach undoubtedly influenced by the absorption of Schenkerian

---

[27] David Lewin, "*Auf dem Flusse*: Image and Background in a Schubert Song," *19th-Century Music* 6 (1982): 47–59; reprinted with additions in Walter Frisch (ed.), *Schubert: Critical and Analytical Studies* (Lincoln and London: University of Nebraska Press, 1986), 126–152. Citations are taken from the reprinted version. This citation is from 127; italics mine.

[28] Lewin, "Image and Background," 126; italics mine.

[29] George Grove, "Schubert," *Grove's Dictionary of Music and Musicians*, ed. J. A. Fuller Maitland (London: Macmillan, 1908), 329 and 331.

[30] I should explain my terms here, although I shall return to this topic in greater detail below. I am making a distinction between the hermeneutics of song based on close literary readings that use a kind of generic music-analytical method and the hermeneutics of song where literary readings have played second fiddle, as it were, to theory-based analysis, such as Schenkerian analysis. In the case of the latter, scholars have often been tempted (as I shall demonstrate in this chapter) to theorize musical structures separately from the text. I have borrowed the distinction between these two traditions of thought from Agawu, "Music Analysis versus Musical Hermeneutics," *American Journal of Semiotics* 13 (1996): 9–11.

thinking. Thus, although Lewin certainly pays great attention to surface detail, he does so in the service of comprehending details in relation to large-scale logic.

Subsequent to Lewin's study, Kofi Agawu codified what an ideal song analysis might involve. He identified six basic activities, which he mapped out into three stages, as follows:

Stage 1a	Informal data-gathering: collect as many significant musical features of the song as possible.
Stage 1b	(More) formal data-gathering: use an explicit method (such as a voice-leading graph) to generate more data and to revise or reorganise previously collected data.
Stage 1c	Preliminary interpretation (1): develop metaphors for "purely musical" devices.
Stage 2a	Develop a contextual reading of the text.
Stage 2b	Preliminary interpretation (2): compare the results of 2a with those of 1a, 1b and 1c.
Stage 3	Explicit interpretation: "narrativize" the various profiles and data assembled in stages 1a, 1b, 1c, 2a and 2b, adding information from "external" sources, including style, biography and reception.[31]

As is clear from the stages listed above, a "comprehensive" analysis should seek to address the music, the text, and the context in which a song was formulated, much as Kerman also advocated.[32] Although Agawu organizes these activities into numbered stages and sub-stages, he explains that these need not represent the order in which the analysis of song is carried out.[33] Nonetheless, there is a clear indication that musical analysis is the foundation on which the other interpretative activities rest. There is nothing controversial about this statement – indeed it summarizes the long-standing practice of hermeneutics.[34]

---

[31] Agawu, "Theory and Practice in the Analysis of the Nineteenth-Century *Lied*," *Music Analysis* 11 (1992): 11.

[32] While Kerman (and others) suggested that the analyst has an obligation to contextualize his or her analysis, in another study Agawu reminds us that in certain circumstances it is legitimate not to. See Agawu, "Music Analysis versus Musical Hermeneutics," 9–24.

[33] Agawu, "Theory and Practice," 11.

[34] For a further discussion of the interface between analysis and hermeneutics, see Agawu, "Music Analysis versus Musical Hermeneutics," 9–24. See also Ian Bent (ed.), *Musical Analysis in the Nineteenth Century*, vol 2: *Hermeneutic Approaches* (Cambridge University Press, 1994), 4–8, where he explains (*pace* Dahlhaus) that the beginnings of hermeneutics stemmed from the conviction that behind music that is initially incomprehensible, there lies meaning. Its hermeneutic understanding, though revealed through the analysis of the musical text, transcends the technical understanding of the work.

But this practice deserves more scrutiny than it has had to date, particularly with regard to the assumptions made about the role of analysis and music theory in hermeneutics. The rest of this chapter will therefore linger on Stage 1b, the stage in which one is invited to apply an explicit analytical method to the material gathered in Stage 1a for the purpose of carrying out readings in further stages. Agawu recommends Schenkerian analysis (a voice-leading graph), which is unsurprising, as it is the method to which, until very recently, most (again Anglo-American) scholars of nineteenth-century song have turned as a matter of course.[35] To be sure, the data collected in Stage 1a, which is meant to comprise significant musical features, will already be influenced by the analyst's music-theoretical leanings, but I shall focus in particular on how Schenker's canonical technique of analysis directs the analyst – nay, the hermeneut whom Agawu is trying to encourage – towards a very particular organization of the collected data.

It is worth recalling once more that Lewin reminded his readers that an important structural premise in a Schubert song was the "musical syntax, *as it was understood at the time*" (emphasis mine). There is no hint that Lewin wished to propose a historicist approach to song analysis, but it is worth observing here that Fink's understanding of harmony suggests a very different organization of data from the one elaborated by Schenker. The distinction has everything to do with the role of the dominant and the

---

[35] The bibliography on nineteenth-century song and Schenker is too vast to cite here. The studies on Schenker and Schubert examined in this chapter are among the most important contributions in the field. Important contributions regarding other composers include Deborah Stein, *Hugo Wolf's Lieder and Extensions of Tonality* (Ann Arbor: UMI, 1985) and Kofi Agawu, "Structural 'Highpoints' in Schumann's *Dichterliebe*," *Music Analysis* 3 (1984): 159–180. Sample studies that illustrate how a Schenkerian approach in Stage 1b may inflect the meanings deduced from tensions with the Schenkerian model include Walter Everett, "Deep-Level Portrayals of Directed and Misdirected Motions in Nineteenth-Century Lyric Song," *Journal of Music Theory* 48 (2004): 25–68 and Charles Burkhart, "Departures from the Norm in Two Songs from Schumann's *Liederkreis*," in Hedi Siegel (ed.), *Schenker Studies* (Cambridge University Press, 1990), 146–164. In the wake of recent interest in neo-Riemannian theory, it is perhaps equally unsurprising that this theory should now serve as a new "explicit method" for Stage 1b. Perhaps the best example to date is David Kopp's *Chromatic Transformations in Nineteenth-Century Music* (Cambridge University Press, 2002), which offers a number of detailed analyses of songs by Schubert – as well as other nineteenth-century composers – using neo-Riemannian theory. Kopp's main focus is on how the musical syntax is elucidated through neo-Riemannian theory, so he deliberately addresses almost exclusively Stage 1b; probing into Stages 2 and 3 was beyond the scope and intention of his study. Compare Germanic studies in which Schenker is largely absent, although notable exceptions include Hellmut Federhofer, "Terzverwandte Akkorde und ihre Funktion in der Harmonik Franz Schuberts," in Otto Brusatti (ed.), *Schubert-Kongress Wien 1978* (Graz: Akademische Druck- und Verlagsanstalt, 1979), 61–70 and Jürgen Blume, "Analyse als Beispiel musiktheoretischer Probleme: Auf der Suche nach der angemessenen Beschreibung chromatischer Harmonik in romantischer Musik," *Musiktheorie* 4 (1989): 37–51.

hierarchical level on which it is understood to operate. For Fink, the surface-level articulation of V–I is vital while large-scale structural patterns seem a lesser concern; for Schenker, the large-scale motion I–V–I is paramount and Schubert's keys – whatever they may be – must be organized within it.[36] In both cases, the logic of Schubert's tonal schemes is articulated through fifth relations, but the harmonic conditions of these two paradigms suggest radically different locations for "hermeneutic windows," which are generally open to meanings at moments of disruption.[37] This being the case, it is imperative to appreciate the full force of the decisions made in choosing a music theory for Stage 1b.

"Auf dem Flusse" is a song in five stanzas. In the first two, the protagonist addresses the stream and observes how still it has become, now that it is covered with ice. As Lewin puts it, Schubert creates for these two stanzas an "icy, immobile E-minor world." In the next two stanzas, the protagonist thinks of his happier past and cuts into the ice the dates of the first and last meetings he shared with his beloved. Schubert sets these "happy, warm E-major memories." Two questions end the poem: the protagonist asks, in E minor, "Mein Herz, in diesem Bache/Erkennst du nun dein Bild?" (My heart, do you now recognize your own image in this brook?). For the second question, the music moves to that troublesome key of G♯ minor: "Ob's unter seiner Rinde/Wohl auch so reissend schwillt?" (Is it, underneath its shell, seething too, and near to bursting?). Schubert then repeats the two questions in E minor.[38]

According to Lewin, the first question makes clear its association with the "icy, immobile E-minor world" of the beginning of the song because it is posed in the same key, namely E minor. The question therefore has a sorrowful answer: like the stream, the protagonist's heart has turned to ice. With what, Lewin asks, is G♯ minor associated? The answer is important from a hermeneutic point of view. As Lewin explains, an understanding of how G♯ minor connects to the main keys of the rest of the song on a structural level will reveal whether Schubert's reading of the second question is as ambivalent as Müller's poem: "Is it, underneath its shell, seething too, and near to bursting?" An association of G♯ minor with the E minor

---

[36] Heinrich Schenker, *Free Composition*, 2 vols., trans. and ed. Ernst Oster (New York: Longman, 1979), 11–12.

[37] Lawrence Kramer introduced the term "hermeneutic windows" in *Music as Cultural Practice, 1800–1900* (Los Angeles and Berkeley: University of California Press, 1990), 1–29. I examine his proposed methodology below.

[38] Lewin, "Image and Background," 135. The translations of Müller's text are Newcomb's; see n. 45.

opening would imply a negative answer to the question, indicating that his feelings for his beloved have gone cold; an association of G♯ minor to the E major section would imply a positive answer, suggesting that the protagonist still yearns for his beloved. If Schubert is to match Müller's ambivalence, then G♯ minor must be tied to both tonics. It is Lewin's prowess as a theorist that allows him to argue in favor of a musical ambivalence.

G♯ minor is most obviously linked to E major as a tonicization of its 3̂. As Lewin writes, "The relation of G♯ minor to E major is clear enough: the G♯ harmony represents iii of E major and . . . the G♯ in the bass at bar 48 can fit very convincingly into a structural arpeggiation of the E-major (!) triad over the bass line of the song as a whole."[39] It is clear from Lewin's language that he is invoking Schenkerian theory here. Yet, this "very convincing fit" of G♯ minor into a structural arpeggiation is precisely the approach that Schenker avoided in his own analysis of this song. Why? As the only large-scale move away from the tonic major or minor in the whole song, and given that large-scale moves are generally assumed to assist in defining home tonics, this particular move poses problems for the home tonic, E minor. E major, the key to which G♯ minor most obviously belongs, is not the home tonic. Hence Lewin's exclamation mark: the unfolding of a major triad threatens the integrity of Schenker's basic tenet of monotonality. Schenker solves this problem by omitting any mention of G♯ minor from his graph altogether. But contrary to what one might assume, this omission takes great effort.

Schenker engineers an enormous arpeggiation in the upper voice to cover the move from E minor to E major and back to E minor, which occupies the first four and a half stanzas of this five-stanza song. This is instead of mixture, the very concept Schenker formulated to accommodate such occasions. It is instructive to explore what an analysis according to his definition of mixture would look like in order to piece together a plausible explanation for why Schenker avoided it.

Example 2.8a is a sketch based on Schenker's graph of mixture in Fig. 28a from *Free Composition*. I have transposed it to E and cast it in the minor to suit the present circumstances. Example 2.8b is a reproduction of Schenker's own graph of "Auf dem Flusse."[40] As Example 2.8a shows, the primary tone above E fluctuates from the minor to the major third and back again, articulating the ABA′ sections of stanzas 1, 3, 5 as annotated in the graph. Why did Schenker avoid this interpretation, given that it even neatly conforms to his proposal that mixture can generate ternary form?[41] A quick

---

[39] Lewin, "Image and Background," 134. The exclamation mark is Lewin's.
[40] Schenker, *Free Composition*, supplement, Fig. 28a.   [41] Schenker, *Free Composition*, 133.

Example 2.8 (a) Sketch of mixture in Schubert, "Auf dem Flusse" in *Winterreise* (D. 911), based on Schenker, *Free Composition*, supplement, Fig. 28a; (b) Graph from Schenker, *Free Composition*, supplement, Fig. 40/2; (c) Placement of Schenker's *Ursatz* in score of "Auf dem Flusse," mm. 53–54

Example 2.9   Opening measures of each section in Schubert, "Auf dem Flusse," mm. 1–6; 22–24; 41–42

glance at the opening of the vocal part of each section shown in Example 2.9 might suggest that Schenker produced this massive upper-voice arpeggiation because he was being sensitive to surface detail: the voice in the first, third and fifth stanzas articulates $\hat{E}$, $\hat{G}\sharp$ and $\hat{B}$ respectively. Those who might normally criticize Schenker for not paying close enough attention to surface detail might congratulate him here for doing so, arguing that his decision to reject mixture in favor of an arpeggiation seems to have been motivated by foreground events.

Unfortunately, any such praise would come too soon. The arpeggiation has a stunning consequence: the *Ursatz* makes an odd appearance in this song. As can be seen from Schenker's graph, it begins in m. 53 and is already over by the first beat of m. 54 (compare the score in Example 2.8c with Example 2.8b). However, quibbling with Schenker on the grounds that the background is puny on the foreground is not recommended. Schenkerians are fond of reminding the uninitiated that such a complaint reveals their ignorance that important events do not necessarily loom large on the foreground.[42] Thus, it seems that, on the one hand, we can neither wholeheartedly praise Schenker for his attention to the surface in the case of the upper-voice arpeggiation nor can we chastise him for ignoring the surface in the case of the *Ursatz*.

There can be little doubt that the G♯ minor passage is the real irritant. Its conspicuous absence from Example 2.8b – the arrow in the example points to where the G♯ should be – begins to tell of the strain Schubert's key puts on Schenker's theoretical principles. Schenker's audacious analytical maneuver with regards to the upper-voice arpeggiation was clearly in response to the problems posed by this harmonic station. As a non-tonic change of key, it constitutes the first large-scale action in the bass in the song. It also has all the necessary qualities to form a bass arpeggiation, as Lewin pointed out.

A bass line that outlines the major triad creates a far greater challenge to Schenker's fundamental principle of *Diatonie* than any arpeggiation in the upper voice ever could. A G♯ in the upper voice is one thing, but a G♯ in the bass is quite another. In other words, if $\hat{1}-\sharp\hat{3}-\hat{5}$ in the upper voice of a minor-keyed piece seems bold for a theorist who is insistent on monotonality, it is nonetheless the lesser of two evils in the face of a potential i–♯iii–V.[43] In actual fact, then, while Schenker does grant the major mode some kind of status through the upper-voice arpeggiation, the terse fundamental structure diverts attention away from the tonicization of G♯ minor. Put this way, the attention to detail represented by the arpeggiation in Example 2.8b is at odds with the suppression of the key of G♯ minor.

It was not, therefore, any dissatisfaction with his own definition of mixture or any desire to elevate the status of E major that led Schenker away from mixture in analyzing this song. Quite the opposite: he wanted to

---

[42] This point is perhaps easily intuited if we compare it to the analogous case of, say, the accented appoggiatura. The dissonant tone may be twice as long as the harmony note, yet the latter is more important, more structural. Similarly, then, the fundamental structure may look like a mere cadence on the surface (as in this case), but in principle it can legitimately rank as structural.

[43] Observe that the elaborations of the bass line in Schenker, *Free Composition*, supplement, Figs. 14–18, are all diatonic *Stufen*; chromaticism may be introduced above the root, as in III♯.

ensure that E major remained subordinate. The striking major-triad arpeggiation in the upper voice does not suggest the first 52 measures are governed by a major key. Schenker is careful to express the "mixture" of modes in the Roman numerals below the stave (see the $I^{\flat 3}$–$I^{\sharp 3}$–$I^{\flat 3}$ in Example 2.8b). With this solution, Schenker successfully maintains his theory of monotonality. That is to say, even though the arpeggiation occupies some 50 measures of the song and is in a major key, it poses no threat to Schenker's notion that the fundamental line and structure must always remain diatonic. It occurs at a lower level than the *Urlinie* (note that the pitches of the arpeggiation are not beamed, but those of the *Urlinie* are).

There is no hint that Schenker's analytical maneuvers are in any way prompted by the text of the song.[44] That being the case, it is clear that the direction of responsibility in Schenker's analysis is towards his theory and not the text. The choices represented in his graph of "Auf dem Flusse" are aimed at containing Schubert's harmony. Schenker domesticates Schubert. The chromatic harmonic activity of this song happens entirely outside of the tones of the background structure. The threat to monotonality is assuaged – E major and its attendant keys take place out of bounds, as it were.[45]

Lewin criticizes Schenker's graph, though for different reasons from those given above. He agrees, however, that the omission of G♯ minor is problematic, especially as it is the key (in both senses of the term) to the meaning of Schubert's setting of "Auf dem Flusse." As we saw earlier, Lewin is perfectly willing to allow the G♯ a place in an E major bass arpeggiation – but only because he has other things in store for the passage. Let's examine

---

[44] Schenker analyzed four of Schubert's songs in *Free Composition* and yet only once did he make any reference to the text. In "Der Schiffer" (D. 694), he remarked that the initial ascent "virtually depicts the breathing ('atme kühl im Licht des Mondes, träume süss im stillen Mute' – 'breathing coolness in the moonlight, dreaming sweetly here in silence')." See *Free Composition*, 46.

[45] Compare the typical scenario, where even if there is a lengthy *Ansteig* (initial ascent), the primary tone and tonic are generally prolonged through more material than is the case here before the structural closure. For a defense of Schenker's position, see Richard Kramer, *Distant Cycles: Schubert and the Conceiving of Song* (Chicago University Press, 1994), 156. Kramer argues that Schenker must have anticipated the objection that the fundamental structure spans a measure, and that his choice is deliberate – especially as the placement of the *Kopfton* was an "altogether consuming issue." As Kramer also points out (p. 157), Anthony Newcomb's criticism of Schubert's graphs paradoxically supports Schenker's choice. Newcomb writes that voice-leading analysis should convey the individuality of a work, which Kramer suggests is the reason Schenker's graph takes the shape it does. For Newcomb's comment, see "Structure and Expression in a Schubert Song: *Noch einmal* Auf dem Flusse *zu hören*," in Walter Frisch (ed.), *Schubert: Critical and Analytical Studies* (Lincoln and London: University of Nebraska Press, 1986), 173, n. 16. While I agree that Schenker conveys the individuality of works in his graphs, in this case the "individuality" of the work also ought to include the passage in G♯ minor; but, as I argue, Schenker suppressed it in the interest of upholding his theory over expressing this aspect of the work.

first, though, how he contemplates the hermeneutic implications of the association of G♯ minor with E major; how he advances from Agawu's Stage 1b to Stage 1c.[46] He writes: "If indeed a *secret* E-major *deep* structure lies *unter der Rinde* of the E-minor *surface* structure, then the poet's heart does indeed preserve its capacity for warmth and the return of a vernal state."[47]

Note his language. There is no question that, in Schenkerian terms, a bass arpeggiation is a sign of a "deep" structure. Yet, why does Lewin cast it as a "secret" one? He draws this conclusion firstly through a hermeneutic metaphor (as Agawu prescribes for Stage 1c) and, secondly, through a bold theoretical maneuver (Stage 1b). In the discussion above, we saw that Lewin was engaged with the world of Schenkerism, where "deep structures" lie at the background and "surface structures" lie at the foreground. Schenker envisioned this space as in Example 2.10, which is Fig. 1 from the original German edition of *Free Composition*. This figure was replaced in subsequent editions, but note how the original's non-diastemmatic nature emphasizes the relationship between levels and their function.[48] The background is diatonic and contains the *Urlinie* and the bass arpeggiation, specified as going through the upper fifth. The middleground binds the foreground to the background through its various levels. The foreground is the place where keys manifest themselves. This conception is maintained in the convention of presenting the background to foreground level from the top to the bottom of a page.

Lewin's reference to "unter der Rinde" in the sentence quoted above draws us back to the poetry. As depicted in Example 2.10, the protagonist in the poem is staring into the stream through the ice, desperate to catch a glimpse of signs of life underneath. We are asked to imagine that E major lurks there too: in other words, the musical deep structure lies under the ice. Note how the topography of these so-called deep structures has shifted: for Schenker, it lies above the foreground or "surface," whereas for Lewin it

---

[46] Lewin, "Image and Background," 134.

[47] Lewin, "Image and Background," 134. Italics mine (except for the German phrase).

[48] The original Fig. 1 appears in *Der freie Satz* (Vienna: Universal Edition, 1935), supplement. Its substitute and more familiar Fig. 1, which is now also the most famous icon associated with Schenker, was introduced in the later edition (Vienna: Universal Edition, 1956), supplement. The conventional layout of Schenker's graphs from background to foreground was showcased, for instance, in Schenker's *Five Graphic Music Analyses* (New York: Dover, 1969). Interestingly, a three-dimensional layout appears in Felix-Eberhard von Cube, *The Book of the Musical Artwork: An Interpretation of the Musical Theories of Heinrich Schenker*, trans. David Neumeyer, George R. Boyd, and Scott Harris (Lewiston, NY: Edwin Mellen Press, 1988), 275. Though impractical, it reveals an attempt to portray the conceptualization of the different levels in what was Schenker's original conception of its dimension, one of depth not height.

Example 2.10 Original Fig. 1 in Schenker, *Der freie Satz* (supplement, 1935) and spatial diagram of surface/depth in Schubert, "Auf dem Flusse"

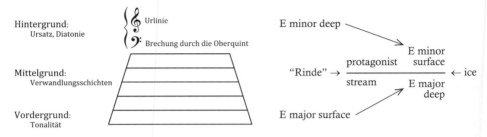

lies below the surface of the ice (compare my spatial drawing to Schenker's trapezoid in Example 2.10).[49] Is this special inversion in the poetic and theoretical imagery the reason this deep structure is "secret"? Or is it secret because Schenker did not opt for it? Or indeed, is it secret in order to keep E major obscured by the ice lest it should usurp E minor as the true key of the song? Given that G♯ minor is more obviously connected to E major than E minor (it does not take Schenkerian analysis to come to this conclusion), it does not seem like much of a secret. But calling it one implies that it is beyond common understanding or can only be known by a few – indeed it can only be revealed through perceptive analysis, for those willing to probe "beneath the surface," like the protagonist. Yet, Lewin also argues that it is possible to conceive of the G♯ as not functioning as iii of E.[50] It can equally be part of E minor. How does Lewin achieve this surprising statement? By switching theoretical allegiance and executing an audacious theoretical move. He returns once more to Stage 1b for more analytical evidence in order to pursue a new line of hermeneutic meaning for G♯ minor.

David Lewin invites Hugo Riemann into the fold, and appeals to both his theory of function and his dualist construction of triads. Dualism enjoyed the premise that all minor triads are generated from the top, and therefore $\hat{D}\sharp$ is considered the root of the triad and $\hat{G}\sharp$ is the "under-fifth" of $\hat{D}\sharp$. Importantly, Lewin's interpretation is aided by the surface of the music: the vocal line hovers around $\hat{B}$s and $\hat{D}\sharp$s and it is, in typical Schubertian fashion, the piano part that completes the unexpected harmony. The

---

[49] Lewin also points to the peculiar use of the word "Rinde." A layer of ice on a stream would usually be called "Decke"; "Rinde" here gives it a metaphorical connection with the cortex ("Rinde") of the heart. Another space which Lewin therefore invokes is inside/outside for the "inner" and "outer" voices in one of his analytical figures, which contain E minor and E major material respectively. This time, the "inner" voice is said to possess "secret" $\hat{G}\natural$s. Spatial images and meaning are important to Lewin; see "Image and Background," 146–8.

[50] Lewin, "Image and Background," 135.

appeal to dualism is neatly justified here.[51] With the importance of $\hat{G}\sharp$ reduced (for it is now an under-fifth rather than a root), Lewin links the triad to the dominant function to which the now all-important $\hat{D}\sharp$ belongs. Instead of reading G$\sharp$ minor as the $\mathcal{T}^+$ or *Leittonwechselklang*, which is Riemann's equivalent to iii of E major, Lewin understands it to be the dominant parallel $(D^+)_p$, or relative of B major. In other words, the first analysis reckons G$\sharp$ minor from the point of the tonic (T), while the second reckons it from the dominant (D).

There can be no doubt that Lewin has performed a truly audacious theoretical move – and one that would have been more obscure to his readers in 1982 than the one that resulted in the so-called secret arpeggiation. Nonetheless, Lewin's reading is not absolutely watertight. Strictly speaking, B major relates to E major, not to E minor whose dominant is the similarly moded B minor. Lewin's symbol, $(D^+)_p$ rather than Riemann's plain symbol D_p, which is the Parallelklang of the dominant, expresses the fact that the dominant is altered to the major mode. Observe in the sentence quoted below that he claims that the *symbol* asserts [the] dominant function and notice that he tucks in a comment about E minor being "structurally prior" rather than a diatonically inherent connection:

That root D$\sharp$ of the asserted $(D+)_p$ functions as the third of a *structurally prior* B-major harmony, a harmony that is in turn the *major dominant* of a *structurally prior* E-minor tonic.[52] (italics mine)

In short, the functional interpretation of the triad is not the convincing part of Lewin's analysis.

To my mind, an ancillary observation that goes with the dualism is the convincing part. As Lewin argues, the dualistic emphasis on $\hat{D}\sharp$ recalls the prominent use of $\hat{D}\sharp$ during the opening A section of the song. At the end of the first phrase, the singer lands on a $\hat{D}\sharp$, which any other composer might have supported by a dominant harmony. Instead Schubert supports it with vii, a D$\sharp$ minor harmony. One $\hat{D}\sharp$ is a fundamental root, the other a dual root. Both appear in the context of sections in E minor and by dint of this are linked to the home tonic, the "icy, immobile E-minor world." Although I have disagreed with Lewin's functional reading, his double reading of G$\sharp$

---

[51] Lewin has brilliantly advocated dualism on a number of occasions, based not on the fact that a triad is minor, as genuine dualists did, but on the presentation of the harmony on the surface of the music. For a number of other examples of surface-level dual presentations of both major and minor triads, see David Lewin, "A Formal Theory of Generalized Tonal Functions," *Journal of Music Theory* 26 (1982): 41–48.

[52] Lewin, "Image and Background," 136.

minor still obtains: on the one hand, G♯ minor connects to E major because diatonic music theory teaches us to understand it as iii of E major and, on the other hand, it connects to E minor because its surface presentation draws attention to the D̂♯, which in turn connects it to the E minor opening of the song.

Lewin's particular analysis, we must remember, was ostensibly carried out in the name of hermeneutics. With G♯ minor "strongly qualified" by this double reading, Lewin finds himself free to argue that Schubert "projects and reinforces his ambivalent reading of the second text question" in the poem.[53] It should be evident that Lewin's quest to draw the conclusion that Schubert matches the ambivalence in Müller's text turns out also to be a quest for music-theoretical paradigms to support it. Lewin's rich understanding of music theory enabled him to achieve this.

Thus we have witnessed Stages 1a, 1b, and 1c in operation: Lewin observed the harmonic data, namely the presence of E minor, E major, and G♯ minor (Stage 1a). He employed two explicit theoretical methods to "reorganize" the data, namely Riemann and Schenker, in order to argue that G♯ minor can be connected to both E minor and E major (Stage 1b). It was the competing interpretations of the harmonies, supported as they are by competing theories, that elicited from Lewin claims of musical meaning (Stage 1c).

Ultimately harmony is most often assumed to harbor the deepest (or, if you like, the most secret) meanings in the enterprise of hermeneutics. Although numerous important studies on Schubert's songs deal with meaning through other parameters, such as motive, phrase and formal structure, meter, mood, rhetoric, style, and accompaniment, by far the most dominant parameter through which connections of meaning between text and music are made is harmony.[54] In light of a comment by Agawu, it is perhaps curious that harmony has attracted the bulk of attention. He has

---

[53] Lewin, "Image and Background," 136. Although I modified Lewin's way of connecting G♯ minor to E major and minor, my findings do not alter his reading of musical meaning.

[54] The literature on these other parameters is too lengthy to mention in full here; the following is therefore necessarily selective. The classic study on motive is Carl Schachter's "Motive and Text in Four Schubert Songs," in David Beach (ed.), *Aspects of Schenkerian Theory* (New Haven: Yale University Press, 1983), 61–76. Schachter's argument on the meaning of 5̂ decorated with its chromatic upper neighbor ♮6̂ in "Der Tod und das Mädchen" has been further developed and applied to *Winterreise* by Walter Everett in "Grief in *Winterreise*: A Schenkerian Perspective," *Music Analysis* 9 (1990): 157–175. For an intriguing reading of motive, phrasing, and formal structure as metaphor for visual imagery, see David B. Greene, "Schubert's 'Winterreise': A Study in the Aesthetics of Mixed Media," *Journal of Aesthetics and Art Criticism* 29 (1970): 181–193. For a particularly sensitive examination of metric displacement and syncopation and their association with the internal animation of a subject and emotional disturbance,

argued in an address to new musicologists that harmony is "probably the least translatable of musical dimensions" when it comes to reading music as a social text.[55] While this was meant to be a caution against making claims of social connections on the basis of observations about harmony, his theory of song analysis nonetheless guides those who wish to get beyond analysis and into the realm of social context precisely to this least translatable dimension. One way to interpret Agawu's contradiction, as well as the vast quantity of literature on harmony and meaning, is to see it as an indication of how enticing the task is. Moreover, the array of approaches exemplified in this literature illustrates just how difficult it is to come to a consensus on how to carry out such a translation.

Nonetheless Agawu's caution is well placed, for the "dictionary" in this precarious translation exercise is that so-called "explicit analytical method" employed in Stage 1b. Not all existing studies appeal to *explicit* methods with the big names, such as Schenker or Riemann. Many rely on what might be termed common-assumption methods, such as reading Schubert's harmonic practice against the expectations of Classical syntax and Classical key schemes, or Roman numeral analyses. Yet even these at one stage had names attached. However, we are not in the habit, for example, of announcing that we shall do a Voglerian or Weberian analysis before launching into Roman numerals.[56] Nor do we credit particular theorists when using the circle of fifths. The point is, however, that the common factor in all these hermeneutic approaches is to establish some kind of norm against which to register Schubert's harmonic adventures. The differences between the two correspond to meaningful moments. Surprisingly few interrogate Schubert harmonic practice in light of his immediate

---

see Yonatan Malin, "Metric Displacement Dissonance and Romantic Longing in the German Lied," *Music Analysis* 25 (2006): 251–288. For a particularly sophisticated study that illustrates the importance of considering mood and figuration in the accompaniment, see Astrid Tschense, *Goethe-Gedichte in Schuberts Vertonungen: Komposition als Textinterpretation* (Hamburg: von Bockel, 2004). Susan Youens remains the gold standard for appealing to the full range of parameters in her readings of Schubert's music. Perhaps her examination of *Winterreise* in *Retracing a Winter's Journey: Schubert's* Winterreise (Ithaca, NY: Cornell University Press, 1991) stands out amongst her books for its specific objective in bringing form, style, meter, tempo, as well as tonality, to bear on the text–music relationship in the course of the cycle.

[55] Kofi Agawu, "Analyzing Music under the New Musicological Regime," *Journal of Musicology* 15 (1997): 305.

[56] Abbé Georg Joseph Vogler was the first to apply Roman numerals to all scale degrees in *Handbuch zur Harmonielehre und für den Generalbaß* (Prague: K. Brath, 1802). Gottfried Weber introduced capitals and lower-case numerals to denote major and minor harmonies in *Versuch einer geordneten Theorie der Tonsetzkunst zum Selbstunterricht mit Anmerkungen für Gelehrtere*, 3 vols. (Mainz: B. Schott, 1817, 1818, 1821).

predecessors,[57] a method whose merits I explore at the end of this chapter. By and large, then, Schubert is measured against notions of music theory.

Analytical models

Earlier I mentioned that some modern scholarship tends toward the "A word will often do it" approach, an approach which focuses mainly on surface-level musico-poetic details, rather than the logic of large-scale "purely musical" harmonic plans. In making this observation, I have in mind such scholars as Richard Böhm, Marie-Agnes Dittrich, Thomas Gerlich, Hermann Hass, Hartmut Krones, Robbert van der Lek, Kristina Muxfeldt, and Susan Youens. Their work is deliberately literary in scope. Their analytical observations often concern Schubert's disturbances of the diatonic equilibrium – whether through a chromatic pitch, dissonant chord, unexpected harmony, or remote modulation – which they regard as expressing the words in the text that they directly underscore. Such details may have large-scale repercussions: a chromatic pitch, especially the first one to appear in a song, often becomes a key later on in the song and is therefore generally seen as a portentous one in the manner first explained through the concepts of a "Romantic detail" or "promissory note" respectively by Kerman and Cone.[58] In an exhaustive study of Schubert's mediant and subdominant relations, major–minor shifts and chromaticism, Marie-Agnes Dittrich carefully reports the words that are stressed through harmonic change.[59] Other approaches have sought to find a semiotics of Schubert's keys and key relations. Akin to the suspicion that Schubert's choice of key for a song was prompted by the general message of the poem

---

[57] Schubert's predecessors are often invoked in discussions of form, melody, and accompaniment. Notable exceptions where their use of harmony is compared are Walter Frisch, "Schubert's *Nähe des Geliebten* (D.162): Transformation of the *Volkston*," in Walter Frisch (ed.), *Schubert: Critical and Analytical Studies* (Lincoln and London: University of Nebraska Press, 1986), 175–199 and Marie-Agnes Dittrich, *Harmonik und Sprachvertonung in Schuberts Liedern* (Hamburg: Karl Dieter Wagner, 1991).

[58] See Joseph Kerman, "A Romantic Detail in Schubert's *Schwanengesang*," *Musical Quarterly* 48 (1962): 36–49 and Edward T. Cone, "Schubert's Promissory Note: An Exercise in Musical Hermeneutics," *19th-Century Music* 5 (1982): 233–241. Both are reprinted in Frisch (ed.), *Schubert: Critical and Analytical Studies*, 48–64 and 13–30 respectively. For an excellent example, see Susan Youens, "Of Dwarves, Perversion, and Patriotism: Schubert's *Der Zwerg*, D. 771," *19th-Century Music* 21 (1997): 177–207. See also Thomas Gerlich, "*Am Meer*: Ein 'romantisches Detail' bei Schubert wiedererwogen," *Perspektiven* 1 (2001): 197–218.

[59] Dittrich, *Harmonik und Sprachvertonung, passim.*

or by Schubert's desire to inflect it with a particular reading,[60] scholars have sought out a particular harmonic move or a peculiar harmony and traced their meaning across Schubert's output.[61] The most comprehensive study in this respect is by Richard Böhm, who produced a database (his term) of generalized semiotics of Schubert's choice of key for a song, as well as for internal modulations and specific harmonies.[62] In addition to meaningful modulations, Schubert is equally capable of rendering the home key strange, as Deborah Stein and Robbert van der Lek have observed.[63] The implication of all these studies is that the shape of Schubert's harmonic structures is driven by the text and they are therefore unlikely to exhibit the logic of "purely musical" design.

Such conclusions are unfortunately often regarded as old-fashioned by champions of music theory. Here we arrive at the tension between text and music or even between those more closely engaged with Schubert's poetry and music theorists. However, it is worth stating emphatically that the attitude that musical design is a product of the text is itself a theoretical statement. Just because it might lead to a lack of systematization does not mean it cannot claim theoretical status. Such a subtle attitude may be found in some early histories of Schubert's music – indeed, in places we no longer think to look. As mentioned in Chapter 1 (and it is worth repeating here), Donald N. Ferguson and Theodore M. Finney explicitly concluded it would be futile to attempt to model a Schubertian song form in the same way that we do instrumental forms. This is not, however, because they gave up on finding "purely musical" harmonic designs but because, as Finney

---

[60] Such a list appears with comments on the range of meanings for each key in John Reed, *The Schubert Song Companion* (Manchester: Mandolin, 1997), 484–494. See also Hermann Hass, *Über die Bedeutung der Harmonik in den Liedern Franz Schuberts: Zugleich ein Beitrag zur Methodik der harmonischen Analyse* (Bonn: H. Bouvier, 1957) and Dittrich, who deals with different affects of mainly the major keys in *Winterreise*, in *Harmonik und Sprachvertonung*, 147–202.

[61] See, for example, Steven Laitz, "The Submediant Complex: Its Musical and Poetic Roles in Schubert's Songs," *Theory and Practice* 21 (1996): 123–166 and Nicholas Temperley, "Schubert and Beethoven's Eight-Six Chord," *19th-Century Music* 5 (1981): 142–154.

[62] Richard Böhm, *Symbolik und Rhetorik im Liedschaffen von Franz Schubert* (Vienna: Böhlau, 2006). For a discussion of the range of parameters Schubert uses, including key, to invoke tragedy, see William Kinderman, "Schubert's Tragic Perspective," in Frisch (ed.), *Schubert: Critical and Analytical Studies*, 65–83. For the argument that the symbolism of Schubert's keys indicates his songs were planned out harmonically, see Hartmut Krones, "Zu Schuberts 'schauerlichen' Werken," 32–40.

[63] Stein illustrates how the tonic at the end of "Erlkönig" is not the same as the one at the opening in "Schubert's *Erlkönig*: Motivic Parallelism and Motivic Transformation," *19th-Century Music* 13 (1989): 145–158. Lek suggests that the home key (C major) of "Daß sie hier gewesen" conceals the depiction of the real tonic F major, in "Zum Verhältnis von Text und Harmonik in Schuberts 'Daß sie hier gewesen,'" *Archiv für Musikwissenschaft* 53 (1996): 124–134.

observed, "No arbitrary attempt is made to carry out a preconceived musical plan"; the art song has no "structural shape that can be subtracted from its materials and viewed as an abstraction," and therefore it is "futile to speak of a 'musical form' for the art song." In other words, each song "makes its own formal laws."[64] Ferguson similarly argued that "the form of the music is constantly created by the text."[65] Two important though nowadays less influential Schubertians, Moritz Bauer and Ernest G. Porter, also both argued that it was "obvious" that Schubert's modulations were a response to the text and that each song is necessarily different.[66] By contrast, Donald Francis Tovey held what might be termed the modern opinion of the "futility of attacking a great composer like Schubert on the *a priori* assumption that the declamation and illustration of words is at variance with the claims of purely musical form."[67]

A "theory-based" approach (to borrow yet another term from Agawu) will demand a "purely musical" logic from the composer, often in addition to a sensitive textual fit.[68] The habit of the music theorist is to systematize the kinds of observations made by Böhm, Dittrich, Bauer, Porter, or Youens. Indeed, the three theorists that I examine below have all sought to model the patterns of Schubert's harmony. They look for architectural designs that are transferable from one song to another. Each fashions a new paradigm or a new set of related paradigms: Thomas Denny finds rising and falling root-interval patterns in Schubert's harmonic stations, Harald Krebs radically modifies Schenker, and Michael Siciliano introduces neo-Riemannian theory.[69] Denny privileges symmetry, Krebs advocates a

---

[64] Finney, *A History of Music*, 430.

[65] See Ferguson, *A History of Musical Thought*, 316. Ferguson's comment was made about "Erlkönig" but would stand for any song.

[66] Moritz Bauer, *Die Lieder Franz Schuberts*, vol. I (Leipzig: Breitkopf & Härtel, 1915), esp. pp. 41–58 and Ernest G. Porter, *Schubert's Song Technique* (London: Dennis Dobson, 1961), esp. pp. 33–45. As Porter makes clear, "There is always such diversity that we can never be sure what turn the melody will take or into what key the harmonies will sprout" (p. 70), but such a statement is not meant to sound the same as complaints that Schubert's harmony is aimless or wandering.

[67] Donald Francis Tovey, "Franz Schubert (1797–1828)," in *The Mainstream of Music and Other Essays*, ed. Hubert J. Foss (Oxford University Press, 1949), 110.

[68] The term theory-based is defined as "technical study that is grounded in an explicit music theory" and Agawu adds "Although no analysis is, in principle, unconstrained by theory, some approaches are more casual than others about making explicit their enabling structures." See Agawu, "Music Analysis versus Musical Hermeneutics," 9. My point in this chapter is that the process of declaring explicit enabling structures has led to a rigid sense of what constitutes a legitimate architectural design, rather than seeing such architectures as dictated by the text and therefore non-transferable from song to song.

[69] See note 15 and Michael Siciliano, "Two Neo-Riemannian Analyses," *College Music Symposium* 45 (2005): 81–107.

conglomeration of complete and partial *Ursätze*, and Siciliano picks out neo-Riemannian cycles. The impetus behind the new paradigms in the case of Denny and Krebs was to explain Schubert's obsession with "directional tonality" or double-tonic complexes between *c.*1813 and 1818. Monotonal approaches clearly will not do precisely because they fail to illuminate the logic behind Schubert's keys. Siciliano's argument for the advantages of neo-Riemannian theory is only coincidentally centered around directional songs, though he argues that consistent patterns of neo-Riemannian transformations "help fill in for the lack of a single tonic."[70]

Denny, Krebs, and Siciliano all envision their paradigms as serving as "explicit analytical methods" precisely in line with Agawu's ambitions for Stage 1b. However, Siciliano deliberately avoids dealing with meaning, while Denny and Krebs do venture, albeit lightly, into hermeneutics.[71] When they do suggest meanings for their harmonic observations, it is the moments where the music is transgressive in relation to their respective theories that elicit the most comments about musical meaning.

Both Denny and Krebs agree that the opening and closing keys in Schubert's songs that begin and end in different keys deserve to be treated as equal tonics. As they point out, this contrasts with Schenker's approach to such pieces. He famously preserved monotonality by introducing the concept of incomplete structures, which means that whatever a piece's opening key, it must still be reckoned in relation to its tonic destination. Such pieces are simply "missing" their opening tonic; they begin, as it were, *in medias res*. Schenker's most famous analysis of this phenomenon has as its subject Chopin's Prelude in A minor, Op. 28 No. 2, which he deemed an incomplete structure that spanned V–I.[72]

As noted by Denny and Krebs, those songs by Schubert that exhibit this phenomenon are usually far too complex to be explained in terms of a single, incomplete background structure as Schenker had proposed.[73] Attempts to describe such songs in terms of a single tonic invariably lead to unwieldy harmonic descriptions. So, for instance, describing "Der

---

[70] Siciliano, "Two Neo-Riemannian Analyses," 92.

[71] Siciliano writes: "These discussions, of course, do not intend to present exhaustive analyses of every aspect of these songs, merely to show how the neo-Riemannian operations can help us understand otherwise problematic harmonic choices. I therefore mostly avoid discussing relations between the text and music." See "Two Neo-Riemannian Analyses," 92, n. 18.

[72] See Schenker, *Free Composition*, supplement, Fig. 110a.3. Other examples beginning in keys other than the dominant of the final destination are shown in the same figure.

[73] Krebs nonetheless argues in "Alternatives to Monotonality," 2–3 that songs that are easily described in one key may reasonably continue to be reckoned monotonally. Denny, "Directional Tonality in Schubert's Lieder," 41–42 disagrees with him on this point.

Alpenjäger" (D. 524) in Roman numerals would yield: ♭III–^{V}/$_{♭III}$–VII♯–
♭VII–^{V}/$_V$–V–I–V–I; or "Ganymed," another particularly adventurous
example, yields: ♭III–♭VII–♭V–VII♯–V–I–V–I. Denny and Krebs rightly
argue that it is far simpler to conceive of such songs in terms of two separate
tonics, with the division between them falling at the point where the
Roman numerals express the most direct relationship to the respective
tonics. The advice to potential analysts is to start with the opening tonic
and apply Roman numerals until things get complicated. Then stop, and
apply Roman numerals in relation to the final tonic. "Der Alpenjäger" is
thus better construed as I–V–♭VI–V in C major, followed by V–I–V–I in A
major and "Ganymed" as I–V–♭III–♭VI in A♭ major, followed by V–I–V–I
in F major. That already looks better.

Both scholars go further than this, however. After carrying out an
exhaustive study of some fifty songs by Schubert that exhibit this trait,
they each produce three basic models to accommodate the three ways in
which they believe Schubert routes his journeys from the opening to the
closing keys. Denny's study was in part a response to Krebs's; however I
shall deal with Denny's first.

Denny's first model represents the formula for songs that begin in one
key and abruptly change to another: $I_a \parallel I_b$; the second represents songs that
go from the first to the last tonic through a prolonged pivot key, as in
$I_a \times I_b$; and the third involves internal keys that behave as harmonic "poles"
to the outer tonics, as in $I_a X_a \parallel X_b I_b$.[74] As can perhaps be immediately
deduced from these models, Denny's focus of attention is on identifying the
main harmonic stations of a given song. If the models are left as just
described, they have the potential, from a purely theoretical viewpoint, to
be meaningless. That is to say, without any limitations on what I_a, I_b, and
the X keys are likely to be, his models say little more than "there may be 2, 3
or 4 keys in a song." Naturally, then, Denny seeks to pin them down
further, to seek patterns. It was presumably gratifying, therefore, that he
could observe that the keys in the first model are always a minor third apart,
related to each other as relative major and minor.[75] There are no exceptions. Denny detects patterns for his other two models as well, but they
prove less predictable. However, they also tend to exhibit third relations,

---

[74] Denny leaves open the possibility that there may be others: the models, he says "outline some of
the ways..." (see "Directional Tonality in Schubert's Lieder," 41). Furthermore, barring a
typing error, it seems he had a fourth model at some stage. On p. 41 the schemas are labeled "3a–
3d," but in the appendix (p. 51) there are only three.

[75] Denny, "Directional Tonality in Schubert's Lieder," 43.

this time between the tonics and X keys, usually in a symmetrical rising and falling relationship (or vice versa).

Even the two songs "Orest auf Tauris" (D. 548) and "Trost" (D. 523) that Denny uses as exemplars for the last two models reveal how problematic it can be to come up with a "purely musical" logic behind Schubert's harmonic design. As shown in Example 2.11a, he summarizes the harmonic trajectory of "Orest auf Tauris," which exemplifies the model I_a X I_b, as follows: the first tonic shifts from E♭ major to E♭ minor, X is G♭ major, which transforms into its minor enharmonic equivalent, F♯ minor, before descending by a major third to the final tonic D major. Note how the interval between the roots of I_a and X forms a rising minor third, while the roots between X and I_b form a descending major third, as also annotated in the example.

The pervasive tonic major/minor relations and thirds invite the application of neo-Riemannian theory. The tonal complexes that occupy Denny's attention translate seamlessly into the core neo-Riemannian transformations P, R, and L. As shown in Example 2.11b, his list of keys in "Orest auf Tauris" (E♭+, E♭−, G♭+, F♯−, D+) involves P, R, P, and L transformations respectively, which suggests a certain tautness in the unfolding of the harmony.[76] As also shown in the example, the combination of transformations means that the song ends a semitone below its starting point.

However, this is not the full story of how the keys unfold in the song, for B major and minor interject between G♭ major and F♯ minor (Example 2.11c). Denny observes their presence but argues that their subdominant function make them subservient to their surrounding keys. Yet by eliminating them from view in the I_a X I_b summary of the song, he gives the impression of a clean harmonic journey through parallel and rising and falling third motions. Whatever the harmonic function of B major and minor, the division of the text supports their inclusion. Mayrhofer's poem is in four stanzas. The first stanza is divided into couplets in E♭ major and E♭ minor; the second stanza is entirely in G♭ major; the third is again divided into couplets – in B major and B minor – and closes in F♯ minor, as an f♯:V^7–i cadence; the fourth stanza is in D major. The diagram in Example 2.11a results from a desire to find a "purely musical" pattern that matches the numerous other double-tonic songs that Denny examined, whereas the diagram in Example 2.11c stems from the structure of the particular text of

---

[76] Plus and minus refer to major and minor respectively. These symbols are customary in neo-Riemannian theory. For clarity of presentation in my musical examples, I use them interchangeably with capital- and lower-case letters for major and minor respectively.

Example 2.11 (a) Denny's harmonic analysis of Schubert, "Orest auf Tauris" (D. 548); (b) transformations lined up with Denny's model; (c) transformations with interjection of B major and minor; (d) common tone $\hat{G}\flat/\hat{F}\sharp$ in all six possible triads

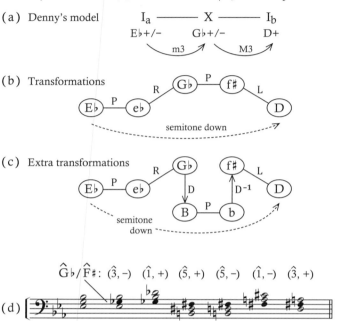

"Orest auf Tauris." To be sure, both diagrams are more precise than a comment such as the one made by John Reed, who writes that within its 54 measures, this song "ranges widely over the hero's emotions, and over the keys."[77] A natural question to ask is whether particular emotions invoke particular keys, or whether the only important factor is that a shift in emotion brings about a shift in key. The former case might produce an illogical unfolding of keys. The latter is more likely to invite music-compositional design, albeit a design peculiar to this song. It is also in this latter sense that one can justly agree with Tovey's argument, stated above, that the declamation and illustration of words need not be at variance with the claims of purely musical form – to which I would only add again that the "purely musical form" will remain peculiar to this song.

Example 2.11d offers another perspective of the diagram presented in Example 2.11c. Each node in the transformation space is represented by its key's tonic triad. Neo-Riemannian theorists most commonly assume a tonal space made up of major and minor triads, an assumption that is

---

[77] Reed, *The Schubert Song Companion*, 351.

not without its theoretical problems. These problems need not detain us here, though I shall hint at some of them in due course. For now, the most striking feature of the set of triads in Example 2.11d is the common tone $\hat{G}\flat/\hat{F}\sharp$ shared by all but the first triad. The separation of the first triad from the rest matches the distinction of the first couplet, which is syntactically a question, from the rest of the poem, which are statements. However, there seems to be nothing significant about the order of the triads in the rest of the song – except to observe that all six possible triads around the single common tone are represented.

Elsewhere I have theorized Schubert's use of presentation of harmony around a single common tone.[78] Given that the phenomenon has now surfaced in so many instances, it will be pertinent to summarize my theoretical findings here. A single pitch may be sounded in a collection of six possible major and minor triads. By adopting + and − to denote major and minor respectively, and by using Schenkerian scale-degree symbols, they may be described as the root of a major and minor triad, the third of a major and minor triad, or the fifth of a major and minor triad, symbolized as follows: $(\hat{1}, +)(\hat{1}, -)(\hat{3}, +)(\hat{3}, -)(\hat{5}, +)(\hat{5}, -)$. Indeed there are no fewer than thirteen transformations available amongst the six triads, and the number of available orderings of the triads is particularly rich.[79] The triads in Example 2.11d exhaust all six possibilities for the common tone $\hat{G}\flat/\hat{F}\sharp$.

The pattern amongst them seems visually somewhat ordered because, as depicted in Example 2.11c, the first move goes up a third (R) and the last move goes down an apparently complementary descending third (L), and the middle of the graph involves a downward fifth (D), followed by an upward fifth (D^{-1}), with a modal shift in the middle (P). Nonetheless, the fact remains that there is little sense of a prevailing diatonic tonal center in the order of keys. That is to say, labeling either the first or the final triad as a tonic would produce precisely the kind of Roman numeral nonsense that Denny was rightly trying to escape. As I have argued elsewhere, this is why I

---

[78] See my "On the Imagination of Tone in Schubert's *Liedesend* (D. 473), *Trost* (D. 523), and *Gretchens Bitte* (D. 564)," in Edward Gollin and Alexander Rehding (eds.), *The Oxford Handbook of Neo-Riemannian Music Theories* (Oxford University Press, in press, 2011).

[79] David Kopp devised a system of 13 transformations through a common tone system that spelled out common tone relations with all three pitches of a C major triad. It yields: I, D, D^{-1}, F, F^{-1}, M, M^{-1}, m, m^{-1}, R, r, P, and S. The table showing their derivation may be found in Kopp, *Chromatic Transformations*, 2. His transformations are explained pp. 165–176. While Kopp's transformations have been criticized for being all-encompassing, my system derives the same transformations, except for Identity, and may be taken as a defense of Kopp's argument, which I argue is paleo-Riemannian. I show how to find each of these transformations among the six triads in Example 10.4 in my "On the Imagination of Tone."

believe it is instead fruitful to think of such works or passages as being "*around* a pitch" rather than "*in* a key."[80] This is one of the ways in which Schubert opens up tonal space.

Admittedly the $\hat{G}\flat/\hat{F}\sharp$ common tone is not salient throughout the song. However, particularly at moments of transition from one key to another, it comes to the fore. The transformation from G♭ major to B major is spelled out by a triadic accompaniment, and the $\hat{G}\flat/\hat{F}\sharp$ is in the top voice of each chord. The shift from B major to B minor occurs underneath a repeated $\hat{F}\sharp$ in the vocal line. Similarly, during the transformation from F♯ minor to D major, the voice concludes its cadences on $\hat{F}\sharp$ for both the F♯ minor cadence at the end of the third stanza and each of the first three cadences in D major in the last stanza. While this song does not focus on this pitch in an entirely obvious way, we have already encountered at least one song that does: "Auf der Donau." It will be recalled that $\hat{E}\flat$ kept appearing in the vocal line, as the common tone in a number of transformations. In the next song under discussion, "Trost" (D. 523), Schubert exploits the common tone in a more audible manner. Schubert also harnesses the order of the triads in such a manner as to create a more diatonically familiar tonal space.

Denny uses "Trost" to exemplify another of his models, I_a–X_a || X_b–I_b. As illustrated in Example 2.12a, the interval between the roots of I_a and X_a is an ascending minor third (G♯ minor to B major) and between the roots of X_b and I_b is a descending minor third (G major to E major). What does the || sign signify? Clearly it suggests some kind of break or rupture. Indeed in another of Denny's models, he makes clear that songs belonging to the model I_a || I_b often have a literal break between the two harmonic spaces; the two keys are often separated by a rest.[81] There is, however, no similar break in the surface of the music in "Trost" (see m. 6 in Example 2.13). It is no less continuous a structure than "Orest auf Tauris," which has no "break" sign in Denny's analysis – perhaps only because, compared to "Trost," it has only one X key, which is a harmonic pole to both tonics. The break in Denny's model and analysis of "Trost" is a vestige of Roman numeral analysis, where X_a relates to the opening tonic and X_b relates to the final one. Meanwhile in order to draw some kind of connection between X_a

---

[80] Clark, "On the Imagination of Tone."

[81] See "Klage" (D. 436), where a rest and a fermata separate the two keys; mentioned in Denny, "Directional Tonality in Schubert's Lieder," 43. Schubert clearly could be indecisive about the degree of abruptness of such a shift. Compare, for example, the four versions of "Geistes-Gruß" (D. 142), where the first and final versions are direct juxtapositions, but the second and third contain a transitional dominant seventh.

Example 2.12 (a) Denny's harmonic analysis of Schubert, "Trost" (D. 523); (b) transformations in "Trost" plotted on LRP cycle; (c) common tone B̂ in LRP cycle

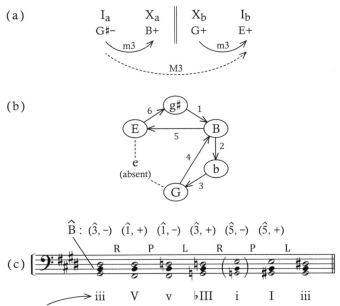

and X_b, Denny is left to explain that X_a "leaps into" X_b and that "the crucial tonal transformation … takes place not between tonics directly, but between their respective secondary keys."[82] There is the beginning of a hermeneutic window here, as the song operates in tension with the demarcations inherent in the model. The one "leaps into" the other only by dint of the ‖ sign that provides a hurdle.

A neo-Riemannian reading sidesteps these problems and underscores the continuity of m. 6 and these two harmonic stations. There is no sudden switch from analyzing keys in the song in relation to one tonic and then another. Instead the neo-Riemannian approach charts the route from I_a to I_b. On closer inspection, the chromatic move from the $\hat{D}\sharp$ to $\hat{D}$ in the vocal line in m. 6 ensures a "maximally smooth" transformation from B major to G major. That is to say, in addition to the four keys mentioned in Example 2.12a, one for each line of poetry, a B minor harmony appears between the middle two. While a direct move from B to G may be denoted by the compound transformation PL, the actual presence of B minor separates it out into P, followed by L. These are "maximally smooth" because both

---

[82] Denny, "Directional Tonality in Schubert's Lieder," 47.

Example 2.13   Schubert, "Trost"

transformations involve the maximum number of common tones (two in the case of triads) and the minimum single displacement (a semitone).[83] If the same were to happen to the final two keys G and E (X_b and I_b in Denny's analysis), then the compound RP would be separated out to R, followed by P – or the sequence G, e, E. In such a case, "Trost" would have cycled systematically through what is known as the LPR cycle, as shown in Example 2.12b. The strophic nature of the poem together with the pattern of repeated lines produce the structure of repeated elements (or repetends) abca bdeb cfgc abca, which provides a strong argument for the cyclic nature of this song.[84] However, as depicted by the arrows in the diagram, "Trost" does not produce a clean sweep around the cycle and, moreover, E minor is absent, as also shown in the example.

In fact, the move from G to E is not direct. The final key is introduced by its dominant B^7 in m. 11. Michael Siciliano, who has analyzed "Trost" using the LPR cycle as model, calls both the B minor of m. 6 and the B^7 of m. 11 "interpolations." The first, as we have already seen, highlights continuity of the cycle, as shown by arrows 2 and 3 in Example 2.12b; the second disrupts it, as shown by arrows 4 and 5, which break the incremental clockwise motion around the cycle. That is to say, in neo-Riemannian terms there is a "break" in the pattern in m. 11. Based on this analysis, Siciliano writes:

The fifth triad of the cycle, e–, is conspicuously absent (indeed, is replaced by the interpolated B^7). This missing triad marks E+ as different from all the others in the cycle. As we travel around the cycle each triad is approached by its immediate predecessor except for E+.[85]

This is how hermeneutic windows are formed. E minor is *conspicuously absent*; E major is *marked*. It is at such disrupted moments that meanings are usually sought – where the analyst moves to the next stage from Stage 1b. Lawrence Kramer has formulated a few "rules of thumb" in a landmark study on hermeneutics, defining the methodology thus:

---

[83] Within a major/minor triadic context, the property of maximal smoothness is unique to the P and L operations, as R satisfies the maximal number of common tones (two) but not the minimal single displacement (because it is a tone, not a semitone). This unique property of P and L lies behind Cohn's development of the hexatonic cycles. See Cohn, "Maximally Smooth Cycles, Hexatonic Systems, and the Analysis of Late-Romantic Triadic Progressions," *Music Analysis* 15 (1996): 9–40.

[84] The line structure given above may be observed in Example 2.13, which provides the full text. Michael Siciliano develops an intricate harmonic argument about the cyclic nature of this strophic song, although without recourse to its text, in "Two Neo-Riemannian Analyses," 101–106.

[85] Siciliano, "Two Neo-Riemannian Analyses," 105.

Hermeneutic windows tend to be located where the object of interpretation appears – or can be made to appear – explicitly problematical. Interpretation takes flight from breaking points, which usually means from points of under or overdetermination: on the one hand, a gap, a lack, a missing connection; on the other, a surplus of pattern, an extra repetition, an excessive connection.[86]

What we see here with Denny and Siciliano is that two systems of analysis bring about a vastly different sense of how the structure of the song unfolds and a vastly different sense of the moment from which interpretation might "take flight" – one theoretical lens suggests a break at m. 6 (Denny), the other at m. 11 (Siciliano). Indeed, Harald Krebs also analyzes this song, offering yet another theoretical perspective. Although he is mainly interested in alternatives to monotonality, "Trost" is one example where he preserves Schenker's notion of incomplete structures. He analyzes it in E major, and there is no break (indeed no Schenkerian "interruption") in the song. For Krebs, the song is threaded together by the *Kopfton* $\hat{B}$ that appears throughout and finally descends in the piano postlude.[87]

As it happens, none of them turn to the poetic text of "Trost" or look for any other extramusical meanings. Thus, while we cannot interrogate the different meanings ascribed to the three different interpretations – for lack of evidence – we can certainly imagine that if each theoretical interpretation were to take its legitimate place in Agawu's Stage 1b and act as a springboard for hermeneutic readings, Stage 1c, each would suggest different "metaphors for these 'purely musical' devices." Hermeneutic windows would appear in the cracks in the musical façade, namely in m. 6 for Denny, m. 11 for Siciliano, and in the extremely delayed *Urlinie* descent and the lack of an opening tonic for Krebs – i.e. the song's "deviances" compared to Schenkerian norms. These three different theoretical conclusions serve to show how fragile hermeneutic windows are and how easily they can migrate from one spot to another. It also reveals that hermeneutics does not depend solely upon the skill of an analyst and his or her ability to draw out details in the music (and text!) but also on the choice of theoretical lens that guides what he or she is likely to detect as a "breaking point" in the music.

Earlier I also suggested that the use of the single common tone and the order of the triads containing it differed in "Trost" in significant ways from those in "Orest auf Tauris." As shown in Example 2.12c, the common tone that unites all of the keys in "Trost" is $\hat{B}$. Indeed, this single common tone has been identified as an important property of the LPR cycle, as has the

---

[86] Kramer, *Music as Cultural Practice*, 12.
[87] Krebs, *Third Relation and Dominant*, 153–154 and "Alternatives to Monotonality," 2.

fact that the voice-leading produces a genuine cycle insofar as the pitch-to-pitch connections from one triad to the next mean that wherever one starts in the cycle, the return to the original triad will be also be at the original octave-level, as illustrated in Example 2.12c.[88] All of the analysts mentioned above consider this pitch important in "Trost," drawn as any listener would be to its salient use in the vocal line during the harmonic shifts in mm. 3–4 and 10–12. It is a pitch that fills in the silences between lines 1 and 2 and lines 3 and 4 of the poem and the corresponding musical phrases (Example 2.13). In each case, the vocalist gets started on lines 2 and 4 too early, befitting the protagonist's impatience to meet death.

An analysis of the song that traces this pitch would inevitably show that between the remaining lines (2 and 3), it is embedded with the texture, rather than being aurally salient. In mm. 6–7, the vocal line highlights the displaced tone rather than the common tone as the harmonies shift. Indeed, although the move is "maximally smooth" in theoretical terms, as we have already observed, its sound quality is not because the single displaced tone is aurally prominent rather than the two common ones. This important distinction in the surface presentation of harmony is all too rarely made by neo-Riemannian theorists.[89] Indeed, such an analysis supports Denny's reading and places the "break" in the pattern set up at the outset of the song once again in this midpoint of the song's text. Nonetheless, it may be fair to conclude that Schubert exploits the common tone differently in "Trost" from "Orest auf Tauris."[90]

It will be recalled from my discussion of "Orest auf Tauris" that the full complement of triads around a single pitch are the six major and minor triads, with the common tone serving as $\hat{1}$, $\hat{3}$, and $\hat{5}$, which in abstract terms I described as $(\hat{1}, +)$ $(\hat{3}, +)$ $(\hat{5}, +)$ and $(\hat{1}, -)$ $(\hat{3}, -)$ $(\hat{5}, -)$. The order of triads in "Orest auf Tauris" did not produce any recognizable diatonic structural architecture, although a quasi-symmetrical pattern was detectable in the set of transformations that contained a complementary pair of thirds on the outside, and pair of falling and rising dominant transformations separated by P. Certainly in "Orest auf Tauris" no dominant key was fashioned out of the collection of triads, and nor did its six triads produce

[88] Richard Cohn, "Neo-Riemannian Operations, Parsimonious Trichords, and their *Tonnetz* Representations," *Journal of Music Theory* 41 (1997): 42–45.

[89] Michael Siciliano is a notable exception, especially for his analyses in "Neo-Riemannian Transformations and the Harmony of Franz Schubert" (PhD thesis: University of Chicago, 2002).

[90] For more on Schubert's salient and embedded use of common tones, as well as a deeper theoretical discussion of these six triads and their origins in Riemann's own thought, see my "On the Imagination of Tone."

the LPR cycle. While it is tempting for a theorist to privilege the discovery of a pattern such as LPR and therefore to measure pieces against it, such a procedure is likely to renew the notion that a work such as "Orest auf Tauris" is somehow disorderly, especially as Siciliano, for example, made the alluring point that the consistent pattern of transformations in the LRP cycle substitutes for the coherence traditionally gained by a single tonic in a musical structure.[91]

To my mind, a more fruitful theoretical approach is to observe the full range of options available to Schubert. These triads could occur in any order, yet cohere through the single common tone. While they can be construed to generate an LPR cycle or they can make use of the available $(\hat{5}, +) \rightarrow (\hat{1}, +)$ or $(\hat{5}, -) \rightarrow (\hat{3}, +) \rightarrow (\hat{1}, +)$ relations in order to stress familiar I–V or i–III–V diatonicism, there is also the opportunity to order them in such a way that opens up new unfamiliar paths in tonal space. The significant difference, then, between "Orest auf Tauris" and "Trost" is that in the case of the former it is by avoiding an ordering of the triads containing an overarching tonic/dominant relation that Schubert opens up tonal space and frees himself of the confines of fundamental bass thinking, while in the case of the latter, Schubert's choice of $\hat{B}$ as the common tone and E as the destination tonic key provides the only configuration of triads that preserves the tonic/dominant axis, as illustrated in Example 2.12c. In short, if diatonicism is sought, then $(\hat{5}, +)$ or $(\hat{5}, -)$ must be assigned the tonic of the collection.[92]

Once Denny had settled on three possible models for Schubert's songs that begin and end in a different key, he sought to pin down the tonal tendencies of each model. The problem is that the moment he did so, his theory has limitations. There is seemingly no way out of this problem, for surely this is the job of any music theorist: to chart tonal spaces and to make sense of them. But a lot is at stake in this delicate theoretical activity, because his theory immediately inflects his perception of Schubert's harmonic practice. Witness the case of "Auf der Donau," the song that Fink also analyzed. Denny concludes that he can fit the song's harmonic stations into the $I_a–X_a \parallel X_b–I_b$ model (the same model as "Trost"), but that – unusually – the two halves of the model form pairs of

[91] Siciliano, "Two Neo-Riemannian Analyses," 92.

[92] The Roman numerals in the example are according to E major as the tonic, as in "Trost." However, either I or i can serve as the tonic to yield a tonic/dominant axis; if the tonic is minor, then obviously bIII in the example should read III and iii becomes ♯iii. As the Roman numerals also illustrate, if all triads are used and E major or E minor as construed as the tonic, then there will still be some chromaticism.

Example 2.14 Denny's harmonic analysis of Schubert, "Auf der Donau"

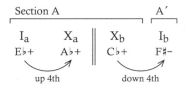

complementary subdominant relationships: E♭ to A♭ and C♭ to F♯ minor (see Example 2.14). As a result, he calls this song "far more complex" than the others he analyzes.[93] But this is really only a product of the fact it does not match his proposed theory – it lies in tension with it. To borrow but reorient the implications of Kramer's words on hermeneutic windows, the object of interpretation *is made to appear* explicitly problematical: with the tonal space of Denny's theory narrowly defined, "Auf der Donau" inevitably appears exceptional. In other words, his deduction about the song's complexity says more about his confidence in his own theoretical formulations than it does necessarily about the song. Indeed, it is worth recalling that when Fink analyzed it, he pointed to the presence of C minor between E♭ and A♭ (remember the offending m. 7). According to Fink, then, "Auf der Donau" does proceed through a series of thirds. Fink's analysis would not solve the problem, though, because his list of keys would not exhibit the property of symmetry Denny is looking for.

Denny's approach burdens song with the need for an overarching harmonic logic, one, moreover, specifically defined by the identity of keys that preferably produce a symmetrical design by root motion – sometimes entirely independently from the poetic form, as in the case of his analysis of "Auf der Donau," where, as illustrated in Example 2.14, I_a, X_a, and X_b are all part of Section A, while I_b articulates the reprise of A′.[94] Schubert's songs can prove difficult to contain in neat symmetries, and he can often suggest more keys in a song than Denny's models permit. Or, to go back a step, it may be possible to discern an overarching logic for some songs, but the assumption that other songs, which do not exhibit one, are somehow more complex or work against the grain of abstract formulae becomes problematic – not least because it generates a particular hermeneutic. For present purposes it should also be noted that the point at which a song ceases to conform to a theory usually marks the beginning of that slippery slope towards hermeneutics. In the case of "Auf der Donau," Denny was

---

[93] Denny, "Directional Tonality in Schubert's Lieder," 47.
[94] Denny, "Directional Tonality in Schubert's Lieder," 47 and 48.

not tempted. But when faced with the apparently even more complex example of "Ganymed" (D. 544), he made that leap.

"Ganymed" is a song that cuts across all of his models. In a certain sense, it has too many keys – a charge Denny does not press, I hasten to add. However, Denny does test the degree to which symmetrical pairs of thirds may be detected in its array of five keys. He spots them between A♭ and C♭ on the one hand and E and C on the other, though this configuration problematically omits the final key from consideration.[95] Unable as Denny is to squeeze "Ganymed" into any of his models, he contemplates another connection between the song's five keys. Indeed, just as his own theoretical enterprise begins to unravel, he seeks assistance from other quarters. Much like David Lewin, he switches theoretical allegiance. Denny invokes Schenker.[96]

The complex of keys in "Ganymed" unfolds beneath, he says, an *Urlinie*. But this is no ordinary *Urlinie*. The thread that joins the keys in "Ganymed" turns out to be an extraordinary turn of Schenkerian events. Denny finds an ascending *Urlinie*, from E♭ to E♮ to F. It is even chromatic. He makes no comment about its unusual behavior (Schenker's final verdict was that an *Urlinie* should always descend and should always be strictly diatonic). Instead, Denny slips seamlessly to another hermeneutic plane and suggests that the *Urlinie* that he identifies "mirrors Ganymed's ascent into the clouds."[97] Let us trace the procedure: it is the song's resistance to his own theory that leads him to Schenker, and it is the song's further resistance to Schenkerian theory that invites this hermeneutic response.

This is a common habit. The tacit assumption is that, if a work is not "in tension" with some paradigm or other, it cannot be meaningful.[98] Points of resistance to norms are generally assumed to be the site of hermeneutic

---

[95] Perhaps this is a remnant of a bias towards Schenker, in which the harmonic background of a work first exhibits a rising interval (a fifth) followed by a falling interval (the same fifth), which forms a "sacred triangle" in the *Bassbrechung*, a topic that will occupy my attention in Chapter 4 of this book. See Schenker, *Free Composition*, supplement, Fig. 7. See also ahead to Lawrence Kramer's analysis (Example 2.16), in which he does find a rising third, followed by a falling one in "Ganymed" – fitting thus the $I_a–X_a \parallel X_b–I_b$ model (A♭–C♭ $\parallel$ A–F).

[96] Having now twice in this chapter drawn attention to a change in theoretical allegiance in the course of analysis (Lewin is the other example), I do not mean to imply that a musical structure should only ever be explained by means of a single theory. Rather, I wish to note that the impulse to shift theoretical positions is usually accompanied by a desire to draw some hermeneutic conclusion that is not accessible through a single method of analysis. Or to put it in terms of Agawu's methodology, the shift in theoretical positions enables new observation in Stage 1b to launch Stage 1c.

[97] Denny, "Directional Tonality in Schubert's Lieder," 46.

[98] An important exception to this assumption is Susan McClary, *Conventional Wisdom: The Content of Musical Form* (Berkeley and Los Angeles: University of California Press, 2000). Her book is a sustained examination of how conventional musical procedures can be meaningful.

windows, which may be prised open to take an analysis from Stage 1b to Stage 1c and beyond. This is why it is so important to scrutinize Stage 1b. The method of analysis chosen to elucidate the technical aspects of the music, even if tailored for the occasion as in the case of Denny's three models, is depended upon by analysts to elicit meaning. It also discourages, if unwittingly, the development of music theory and increasingly sophisticated technical explanation. Musical meaning is all too often assumed to deflate if music theory fills in the gaps, the missing connections, or explains the surplus of pattern etc. The appearance of a breaking point in a diatonic theoretical paradigm may appear normative when viewed through the lens of a chromatic theoretical model. This book aims to expose how an analyst's choice of music theory can shift hermeneutic windows. As suggested already, an object of interpretation can indeed "be *made* to appear explicitly problematic" by one theory, but not another.

Denny's last step in analyzing the music of "Ganymed" corresponds precisely to what Agawu ordered and to what Kramer recommends: he employed an "explicit analytical method," namely Schenkerian analysis, albeit modified. He then reorganized his collected data, itself based on the analytical method he was seeking to formalize (his three models). The discoveries in Stage 1b led him to Stage 1c. He found a metaphor for the odd *Urlinie*.

Krebs also finds meaning in Schenkerian oddities – also on the large-scale level. In his numerous studies of Schubert's double-tonic songs, he questions the most fundamental aspect of Schenkerian theory, namely the insistence that the background level should express a single tonic. He argues that the opening and closing keys each deserve their own background structure.[99] In his article "The Background Level in Some Tonally Deviating Works of Franz Schubert," he explains the variety of ways in which two *Ursätze* may coexist to form a single song. Two triads present themselves at the background level, and each is composed-out, albeit sometimes only partially. He argues that neither triad should be regarded as subsumed by the other (which, at any rate, is the business of monotonality) but that they should stand as equal partners. They form, as he puts it, a "conglomerate."[100]

---

[99] See Krebs, "The Background Level in Some Tonally Deviating Works," 5–18. Another essay by Krebs that also treats the phenomenon but is not exclusively devoted to the works of Schubert is "Alternatives to Monotonality," 1–16. For a detailed discussion on how "unity" is achieved on the foreground when the background is multiple, see his "Tonart und Text in Schuberts Liedern mit abweichenden Schlüssen," 264–271. A related practice, where background structures overlap, is the main focus of "Some Early Examples of Tonal Pairing," 17–33.

[100] Krebs, "The Background Level in Some Tonally Deviating Works," 17.

Of Krebs's three basic configurations or models, one matches Denny's: it involves two complete structures that unfold side by side, but in different keys, as in Denny's $I_a \parallel I_b$. Each structure, therefore, comprises a I–V–I bass line, supporting an *Urlinie* from $\hat{3}$, $\hat{5}$, or $\hat{8}$, as the case may be. The composing-out of each of the two structures is by all other measures standard; the unorthodoxy is that two of them appear in one piece. Another configuration involves at least one incomplete background structure. The opening structure may be incomplete because it is missing its final tonic or the closing structure may be missing its opening tonic. Krebs has found that often only one structure is incomplete but sometimes both are. The final configuration that Krebs considers involves two overlapping rather than successive structures.[101]

The most radical aspect of his approach is that he dispenses with monotonality. In all other respects, Schenker's voice-leading principles function normally. The middle- and foreground levels of these structures may be said to operate in much the same way as other so-called monotonal works. The "deviation" – to use Krebs's word – manifests itself at the point of transition or schism between the two backgrounds.[102]

It is invariably the point at which Schubert's music seems to fracture into different *Ursätze* that Krebs invokes meaning. In successive structures, the shift to a new structure constitutes a "permanent modulation," a nomenclature that distinguishes the need for a new *Ursatz* from other changes in key, which constitute lower-level tonalities ("*Tonalitäten*"). Such permanent modulations are said to illustrate the nineteenth-century concern "with accurate musical representation of texts."[103] In this assessment, we witness the gulf between the location of meaning in modulation for Fink on the one hand and Krebs on the other. Whereas nineteenth-century critics often point to a word here and there that instigates modulation (as we have

---

[101] Occasionally one or more internal keys may also be granted their own, usually incomplete, structure, as in "Der Jüngling und der Tod," which has four not two tonalities; see "Alternatives to Monotonality," 9–11.

[102] In later studies, Krebs also allowed for some additional Schenkerian discrepancies. In "Meeres Stille" (D. 216), for instance, he finds no *Urlinie* descent for one of the structures, yet he firmly considers its C major to be a viable key. Nonetheless, the Schenkerian structures that mark out each of the two keys in any given song always remain discreet and are granted separate graphs, even if they overlap. Indeed, in his latest study Krebs tests the plausibility of a key against Schenker's model. Notwithstanding the stagnant *Urlinie* in "Meeres Stille," an important part of the test is also whether recognizable harmonic progressions are formed by the unfolding harmonies – hence C major is, for him, a viable key after all. See Krebs, "Some Early Examples of Tonal Pairing."

[103] Krebs, "Alternatives to Monotonality," 14. See also Krebs, "Tonart und Text in Schuberts Liedern mit abweichenden Schlüssen," 264–271.

Example 2.15 An abstract representation of the hermeneutic window in Harald Krebs's juxtaposed, incomplete background structures

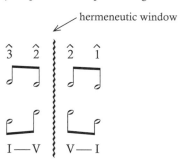

already seen), Krebs points to changes in the direction of the narrative or mood on a more general level that corresponds to the presence of a new background structure. Note therefore the different location of the hermeneutic window in Krebs's analysis of "Ganymed." As illustrated by the abstract diagram in Example 2.15, the song exemplifies Krebs's model of two juxtaposed, incomplete background structures belonging to different keys: the first elaborates the key Ab: I–V–bIII–bVI, the second F: V–I–V–I. As he puts it, the "music appropriately moves from one region into another just as the poem describes Ganymede's move from Earth to Heaven."[104] Clearly it is the disjunction itself between the two structures that is assumed to bear meaning, for the topography of the keys, a descent from Ab to F, is utterly inconvenient: Ganymede presumably does not *descend* into the Heavens.

Harmony and hermeneutics in Schubert's "Ganymed"

Schubert's "Ganymed" has attracted much analytical and hermeneutic attention. Conclusions range in extremes from Richard Capell, who believed the work is a "masterpiece" but that its three main keys Ab, E, and F produce a "rambling key-design," and from Thym and Fehn, who conclude that when "Schubert sets free verse as song ... melody, rhythm, and harmony willy-nilly become forces that shape the text," to Marjorie Hirsch, who argues that the keys follow the drama as many of Schubert's ballades do, and to analytical attempts to find "structural symmetry" in the keys or recognizable portions

---

[104] Krebs, "Alternatives to Monotonality," 14; Krebs puts in his graph the important words that occur at lower-level tonal junctures, 7–8. Interestingly, Krebs's "Tonart und Text" does not contain any Schenkerian analyses and his reading of "Ganymed" is far more detailed; see 267–268. This article additionally addresses in detail the link between harmonic changes and text in "Ballade," "Lied des Orpheus," "Der Pilgrim," "Edone," "Der Wanderer," "Klage," "Auf der Donau," "Die junge Nonne," "Ihr Bild."

of the circle of fifths, as if implicitly to counter Capell's or Thym and Fehn's statement or any other general complaints about Schubert's haphazard designs.[105] Everyone is certainly agreed that the fact that the song begins in A♭ major and ends in F major reflects the shift from Ganymede's earthly existence – wallowing in nature's glistening morning, flowers, grass, morning breeze, misty valleys – to his being carried off to the heavens. The question I shall pursue below is how the multiple tonal areas are analyzed, to what degree analysts have tried to find familiar patterns in its harmonic structure, and how this is understood to lend meaning to the poem.

What better place to scrutinize the dilemma between the apparent need for a logical musical structure in a song and the uncovering of musical meaning than in the work of the scholar who brought to musicology hermeneutics windows and the methodology of detecting them. Lawrence Kramer is also the author of the most sustained and provocative analytical and hermeneutic reading of "Ganymed" in musicology. He has turned to the song on a number of occasions in the course of his career, notably in two studies written over a decade apart, each time employing a different analytical method at Stage 1b. In 1986, his analytical approach looked more like Denny's insofar as he listed the main harmonic stations articulated in the course of the song and found an overarching design in them. In 1997, his approach looked more like Krebs's (and Denny's after he abandoned his own models) insofar as he employed Schenkerian analysis. He was, however, far more radical than Krebs, as he left little of the discipline in Schenker's *Ursatz* intact, but perhaps he is marginally less radical than Denny, for the chromatic *Urlinie* Kramer found is a descending one.[106]

---

[105] Richard Capell, *Schubert's Songs* (London: E. Beun, 1928), 132–133; Jürgen Thym and Ann C. Fehn, "Schubert's Strategies in Setting Free Verse," in Jürgen Thym (ed.), *Of Poetry and Song: Approaches to the Nineteenth-Century Lied* (Rochester, NY: University of Rochester Press, 2010), 278; Marjorie Wing Hirsch, *Schubert's Dramatic Lieder* (Cambridge University Press, 1993), 55; Lawrence Kramer, "The Schubert Lied: Romantic Form and Romantic Consciousness," in Walter Frisch (ed.), *Schubert: Critical and Analytical Studies* (Lincoln and London: University of Nebraska Press, 1986), 229; Timothy Roden, Craig Wright, and Bryan Simms, *Anthology for Music in Western Civilization*, vol. II (Boston: Schirmer Cengage Learning, 2010), 1125.

[106] Lawrence Kramer, "The Schubert Lied," and *Franz Schubert: Sexuality, Subjectivity, Song* (Cambridge University Press, 1998), 123. The foregoing pages on Kramer's analysis of "Ganymed," as well as my own analysis that follows it, are extracted, with revision to suit the present argument, from my "Schubert, Theory, Analysis," *Music Analysis* 21 (2002): 229–238. Indeed, many of the revisions are inspired by his response to my article in Kramer, "Odradek Analysis: Reflections on Musical Ontology," *Music Analysis* 23 (2004): 287–309; certain aspects of my argument have shifted closer to his. I am grateful to Larry for other conversations we have had, which have given me pause for thought over some of the points regarding norms and particulars I made in 2002; nonetheless I remain convinced that oversimplified norms generate hermeneutic windows in problematic ways.

As one would expect, Kramer carefully places analysis into context. Indeed, his book-length study of Schubert's songs was part of an analytical series and was precisely designed to showcase how a contextual analysis should be carried out. In particular, Kramer reminded readers of the importance of treating analysis as a "means, not an end."[107] That is to say, Stages 1a and 1b are a "means" toward the "end" of Stages 2 and 3. The truism that analysis is a "means and not an end" deserves greater scrutiny – not because it should be challenged but because of the one-sided direction towards which analysis is generally held to be responsible. As noted above, the assumption that Stages 1a and b (analysis) are a "means" specifically toward the "end" of Stages 2 and 3 (metaphor and context) exposes an important weakness in accepted habits of doing hermeneutics: there is no stage for addressing the context in which the analytical model in Stage 1b was invented or developed. Yet, as we have seen so far in this chapter, the analytic model is a powerful tool in shaping our sense of the musical fabric and of where hermeneutic windows fit in its façade.

It is striking that in *Franz Schubert: Sexuality, Subjectivity, Song*, Kramer does not explicitly declare his music-theoretical allegiance, though he clearly turns to Schenkerian principles. It is problematic that he does not scrutinize them to the same degree as the literary theories he relies upon. For instance, at an early stage in the argument, he remarks that

Schubert's practice can be understood as an effort to imagine identities that resist, escape, or surmount the regime of the norm. In one sense, this claim is hardly surprising, and needs no elaborate conceptual apparatus to back it; Schubert's predilection for evoking wanderers and other Romantic outcasts, especially in his songs, is a truism.[108]

Yet although he claims that no elaborate literary theoretical backing is necessary in order to understand the subjectivities in Schubert's song texts as deviant, Kramer in fact goes out of his way to provide such a backing, invoking Derrida and Foucault, as well as Freud, Lacan and others, each of whom is dutifully entered in the bibliography and index. By contrast, the critical apparatus employed for his musical interpretations, while recognizable, is hardly discussed. It is striking that the Schenkerian and Roman numeral theoretical models Kramer utilizes are not scrutinized or questioned in any way – nor does either system receive comparable bibliographic support.[109]

---

[107] Kramer, *Franz Schubert*, 7. The series in which Kramer's book appears is the Cambridge Studies in Music Theory and Analysis, edited by Ian Bent.

[108] Kramer, *Franz Schubert*, 2.

[109] For more on this point, illustrated through additional pieces analyzed by Kramer, see my "Schubert, Theory, Analysis," 209–243.

Kramer's reading of "Ganymed" in *Franz Schubert*, thus, relies explicitly on Schenkerian theory to expose where the deviances lie, which are the points where Kramer begins to free himself from its orthodox voice-leading considerations. The song is, according to him, one of those rare Schubertian works "whose emotional tenor is altogether pleasurable," an assessment that appears to contribute to the relaxing of Schenkerian constraints.[110] It is the ultimate absence of a Schenkerian structure (or, for that matter, any identifiable normative framework) in "Ganymed" taken as a whole that most marks the song out as an expression of liberation. In his earlier study, Kramer similarly argued that the breakdown of Classical processes is the quintessential means through which Schubert expresses Goethe's text:

In an effort to capture a moment of supreme ecstasy, *Ganymed* carries presentational independence to a giddy, not to say reckless extreme. The song begins with the most elementary tonic and dominant harmony in A-flat major. By the time it ends, it has evolved into F major by means of a harmonic process that is little more than nonsensical from a Classical standpoint evoked in the opening measures. The melting away of tonal coherence follows closely from an appropriation of Goethe's poem that is both radical and emotionally urgent.[111]

Kramer divides "Ganymed" into three broad sections, which I have annotated on his graph, as reproduced in Example 2.16. The first is itself divided into two (mm. 1–27 and 28–46), roughly covering the two fifth-motions from A♭ major to E♭ major and C♭ major to G♭ major. The second section begins with the enharmonic move from G♭ to F♯ major in m. 46 and ends with the A major/minor shifts in mm. 64–67. The opening of the final section is also defined by a fifth relationship and therefore begins in m. 71 with the C major preparation into F major, whose *Ursatz* starts in m. 75.

Accordingly, these harmonic events create sections of large-scale structures involving "fundamental tonic–dominant relationships in transcendental form."[112] Comparison of this analysis with the one in "The Schubert Lied" helps to understand what is "fundamental" yet "transcendental" about these tonic–dominant relationships. In the earlier article, Kramer emphasizes that the most basic pattern in tonal music is a move away from the tonic to the dominant and a resolution towards it from the dominant: I–V || V–I. He observes that each half of the pattern is actually repeated in "Ganymed," as shown in Example 2.17. Because no two I–V or V–I

---

[110] Kramer, *Franz Schubert*, 128.   [111] Kramer, "The Schubert Lied," 224.
[112] Kramer, *Franz Schubert*, 123.

Example 2.16 Analysis of Schubert, "Ganymed" (D. 544), from Kramer, *Franz Schubert: Sexuality, Subjectivity, Song*, 123

complexes involve the same keys, he calls them a series of "disembodied large-scale cadences" or of "denatured fragment[s] of tonal syntax." They may be fragmentary or disembodied, but, as Kramer maintains, they are ultimately not random. Mediants link the tonic of each pair of cadences: Ab–Cb and A–F (which are stemmed in the second reading, labeled "b," in Kramer's graph in Example 2.16). Taken together, they offer a "new tonal syntax, formed for the moment," in effect replacing the large-scale Classical fifth progression based on a motion of departure and return.[113]

The direction of the mediants – first upwards, then downwards – mirrors the fundamental movement of the overarching Classical progression, but does not contain its strong directional impulse, or lend any sense of

---

[113] Kramer, "The Schubert Lied," 229 and 231.

Example 2.17   Analysis of Schubert, "Ganymed," from Kramer, "The Schubert Lied," 230

```
Section: one                          two          three
         A♭ — E♭                      E♮ — A♮
                  C♭ — G♭ (F♯)                 C — F
         I —— V  I —— V         ‖ V —— I   V — I
```

resolution.[114] By mirroring the Classical procedure, yet without confirming it, these key relationships re-create for Kramer the "movement of transcendence" expressed by Goethe.[115]

Observe again that, in keeping with twentieth-century analytical perspectives, the musical expression of transcendence is said to operate on the large-scale level. The transcendental structure illustrated by Example 2.17 constitutes a "large-scale harmonic drift" or "a kind of sublime nonsense."[116] The "simple" harmony contained within each of the three sections of "Ganymed" helps ground the moment-by-moment level of the song for the listener. In other words, the middle- and foreground follow convention, while the large-scale is novel. Kramer's view is thus similar to Krebs's, whereby the rupture of the tonal paradigm happens at the background level, while the middle- and foreground levels are left intact.

Kramer's discovery of a large-scale pattern goes against the structural expression of the text. In fact, he admits that the "structural symmetry" shown in Example 2.17 "cuts across the divisions of the text," a point which Jürgen Thym and Ann C. Fehn have pursued further.[117] All three scholars agree that Schubert's large-scale musical structure, based on key relations, ignores Goethe's large-scale poetic structure, based on stanza divisions. Goethe's textual divisions of his poem are given below and each line is numbered for reference purposes:

1	Wie im Morgenglanze	
2	Du rings mich anglühst,	
3	Frühling, Geliebter!	
4	Mit tausendfacher Liebeswonne	
5	Sich an mein Herz drängt	Schubert: Herze
6	Deiner ewigen Wärme	

---

[114] Recall the explanation above in n. 95 about Fig. 7 in Schenker's *Free Composition*. I return to this issue in Chapter 3.

[115] Kramer, "The Schubert Lied," 230.

[116] Kramer, "The Schubert Lied," 229 and 231.

[117] Kramer, "The Schubert Lied," 229. Thym and Fehn, "Schubert's Strategies in Setting Free Verse," 277.

7	Heilig Gefühl,	
8	Unendliche Schöne!	
9	Dass ich dich fassen möcht'	
10	In diesen Arm!	
11	Ach, an deinem Busen	
12	Lieg' ich, schmachte,	Schubert: Lieg' ich, und schmachte
13	Und deine Blumen, dein Gras	
14	Drängen sich an mein Herz.	
15	Du kühlst den brennenden	
16	Durst meines Busens,	
17	Lieblicher Morgenwind!	
18	Ruft drein die Nachtigall	
19	Liebend nach mir aus dem Nebeltal.	
20	Ich komm', ich komme!	
21	Wohin? Ach, wohin?	Reichardt/Schubert: Ach wohin, wohin?
22	Hinauf! Hinauf strebt's,	Schubert: Hinauf, strebt's, hinauf!
23	Es schweben die Wolken	
24	Abwärts, die Wolken	
25	Neigen sich der sehnenden Liebe.	
26	Mir! Mir!	
27	In eurem Schoße	
28	Aufwärts!	
29	Umfangend umfangen!	
30	Aufwärts an deinen Busen,	
31	All-liebender Vater!	

According to the interpretation in Example 2.16 (which has precise measure numbers), Kramer's I–V in A♭ spans lines 1–7; the I–V in C♭ major spans lines 8–14. This point is halfway through Kramer's symmetrical structure, which shifts to a V–I in A major/minor spanning lines 18–19. The remaining V–I in F major spans lines 20–31. The lines 15–19, which are missing from this picture of "structural symmetry," are supported by another "disembodied" V–I cadence in B major, which, however, operates at a lower level (see the bracketed [V–I] in Example 2.16). Thym and Fehn bracket Goethe's poem into three main sections: lines 1–8, 9–19, and 20–31, with further subsections based on the articulation of keys. Lines 1–8 in A♭ major are not subdivided; Thym and Feyn thereby ignore the articulation of C♭ major in line 8. Lines 9–14 form a subsection in C♭ major, with an ending in G♭ major; Thym and Feyn thereby assign the articulation of G♭ major at the end of this section a higher status than C♭ major at the end of the previous section. Lines 15–19 form the second subsection (of the second main section) in E major. The final section is subdivided into lines 20–21 in V of F major, and lines 22–31 are in F major. In short, the analysis of Thym and Fehn suggests that Schubert follows Goethe's stanzaic plan for the first stanza, for the second lone couplet, and for the final stanza. Schubert diverges from Goethe's structure in the middle by joining the first lone couplet to the second stanza. Indeed, they question the wisdom of this join, arguing that Schubert's paired setting (lines 9–10 and 11–12 share the same music) "no doubt reduces here some of the richness of the poem."[118]

Yet the question of Schubert's handling of the text is complicated in this particular case – and part of that complication begins with Goethe and has to do with another composer who set this poem. Goethe's poem is in free verse and a case can easily be made that Goethe's own divisions into a stanzaic structure cut across the syntax of the text. Many (but not all!) of the units that Schubert sets up follow the sentence structure, rather than the stanzaic structure, of the text – suggesting that Schubert takes advantage of Goethe's free verse to paint the words or individual syntactic units rather than the broad strokes of the stanzaic structure. Schubert's harmonic structure does not so much cut across the divisions of the text as it is shaped by the syntactic units and key words. Or, to recall once again how Grove put it, "A word will often do it."

As can be seen from the score in Example 2.18, the articulation of A♭ major with a closed arrival on $\hat{1}$ in m. 18 establishes the announcement made in lines 1–3. Only an insistence on keeping E♭ major distinct – because it is the dominant key – forces lines 4–7 or mm. 19–27 to be regarded as a unit. Instead the security of feeling love's thousandfold joy ("Mit tausendfacher Liebeswonne . . .") in the security of the tonic soon gives way to a sumptuous warmth ("Wärme") and unending beauty ("unendliche Schöne") that is depicted through chromatic harmonic shifts. A more detailed analysis is given below, but for now it will simply be observed that it is the surface-level presentation of these harmonies – especially their inversions – that charges them with expressive force. To be sure, lines 9–10 and 11–12 go against Goethe's visual separation of the two statements, but as I argue below Schubert may not have gotten the poem directly from Goethe. He may therefore have assumed that line 9 begins a new longer stanza, beginning again with a statement and excla- mation mark, as in the first stanza. The lack of distinction in the "dich" and "deinem" that Schubert's setting generates – Thym and Fehn argue that

---

[118] Thym and Fehn, "Schubert's Strategies in Setting Free Verse," 274–275.

Example 2.18 Schubert, "Ganymed"

Example 2.18   (cont.)

Example 2.18 (cont.)

Example 2.18   (cont.)

Example 2.18 (cont.)

Example 2.18   (cont.)

these refer to different "Du" – is, however, made up for when A♭ minor colors "deine" in m. 41 and brings back a sonority familiar from m. 25 and the "Du" who provides the sensation of eternal "Wärme."[119] Similarly, if Schubert provides a break between lines 17 and 18 with a piano interlude in mm. 56–61, it suggests a moment of realism. Time passes between morning and night (from "Morgenwind" to "Nachtigall"), as the sound of the wind eclipses into birdsong from m. 59 to m. 60. And harmony shifts too, from root position to first inversion – a subtle, but significant detail in the gradual metamorphosis from A♭ to F major in the course of the whole song. Again, rather than looking for structural shifts, the details seem to be Schubert's harmonic novelty, one I argue was unsettling for such contemporaries as Fink.

From a theoretical point of view, then, a more textually sensitive analytical approach to Schubert's song demands that we go back to first principles. From a methodological point of view, it demands that we question why we believe song as a genre requires an overarching harmonic coherence, especially if it is independent of the text.

Reichardt as background structure, Schubert's foreground

What follows is my own alternative attempt at an analysis of "Ganymed." My account of Schubert's "Ganymed" begins, however, with a setting by someone else. Johann Friedrich Reichardt (1752–1814) published his setting of Goethe's poem in 1809–1811 as part of his *Goethe's Lieder, Oden, Balladen und Romanzen* (volume 2). Although there is no concrete proof that Schubert modeled his setting on Reichardt's, I agree with Kramer that this must have been the case.[120] There are compelling musical reasons, which I shall discuss at greater length than the textual reasons. Suffice it to say here that Schubert's song contains the same textual variants as Reichardt's, as shown in the commentary to line 21 given above on page 117.[121] Although Reichardt, for example, observes the break between lines 10–11, it is possible that Schubert conflated them, believing them to be part of the same stanza, as mentioned above. Schubert exaggerates the short break that Reichardt introduced after the word Herz. Compare Schubert's setting of mm. 46–49

---

[119] Thym and Fehn, "Schubert's Strategies in Setting Free Verse," 274.

[120] Kramer, *Franz Schubert*, 126–127.

[121] Thym and Fehn observe these variants but do not link them to Reichardt. See "Schubert's Strategies in Setting Free Verse," 270.

in Example 2.18 with Reichardt's in m. 17 in Example 2.19. While Reichardt opts for a subtle shift to a new harmony – a perfect L voice-leading transformation if ever there was one – Schubert's accompanist dwells on a longer moment of chromatic tortuousness, also over a pedal, in order to depict Ganymede's burdened heart.

It is such details as these that lead me to argue that Schubert's "deviance" in "Ganymed" is not, after all, on the level of key scheme or musical form but on the level of surface-level syntax and the presentation of harmony. If any "deviance" from monotonal norms is to be detected on the larger level, then in this case it must be viewed as already inscribed onto Goethe's poem by Reichardt, not Schubert. That said, there is little contemporaneous evidence that ending a song in the same key in which it began was in any way taken to be imperative in the tradition that Schubert's inherited.[122]

The immediately obvious musical similarity between Schubert's and Reichardt's settings is precisely in the overall key design: both begin and end in a different key. Reichardt's starts in D major and ends a major third below, in B♭ major, while Schubert's begins in A♭ major and ends a minor third below, in F major. In many ways, the similarities end there, for the manner in which the surface-level harmony is conceived is strikingly different.

The first indication that Reichardt will think his way through the harmonic plan of his song in vertical terms is the chordal figuration that dominates the accompaniment (see Example 2.19). The voice and accompaniment begin simultaneously, and the song settles quickly into a repetitive chordal accompaniment over a long tonic pedal. The F♯ in the voice in the second phrase is supported by a mediant major harmony. Used as a dominant seventh (in an awkward inversion), it sets off a brief circle of fifths that underscores the descent in the vocal line from the ecstatic F♯s to the low C♯ as the protagonist cries euphorically to Nature that his heart is filled with the sensation of Nature's eternal warmth. To conclude this rapturous phrase, Reichardt underscores the sense of endless warmth, heavenly feeling and unending beauty of Nature by avoiding any sense of a cadence in mm. 8–9: under "Schöne" the accompaniment delivers a protracted arrival of the dominant of the dominant at the end of m. 9, which resolves onto a dominant seventh as the voice re-enters in m. 10.

---

[122] For a sobering examination of Brahms's view of tonal unity in contrast to the expression of the text, see John Daverio, "The *Wechsel der Töne* in Brahms's *Schicksalslied*," *Journal of the American Musicological Society* 46 (1993): 84–113.

Example 2.19   Johann Friedrich Reichardt, "Ganymed"

Example 2.19   (cont.)

Example 2.19 (cont.)

Another lengthy pedal closes this section, which resolves into the change of key signature to D minor in m. 14.

The accompaniment momentarily changes figuration. Perhaps in an effort to denote the protagonist listening carefully for a heartbeat as he lies in the bosom of Nature, the dynamic is reduced to *pp* and the bass mimics a faint heartbeat for a few measures. The intensity increases in m. 16, when the accompaniment now consists entirely of eighth notes, as the focus shifts fully to the protagonist's heart. The next piano interlude is no more than a series of repeated chords, yet it contains the first sign of the large-scale move to B♭ major. After the word "Herz," one change of pitch in the accompaniment briefly articulates a B♭ major chord. As mentioned above, the shift is one of the two most minimal triadic moves: it requires only a single semitone move, L. The other minimal shift has already occurred – from tonic major to minor, P. As we have just seen, the move by P from D major to D minor – the latter albeit prepared by its own dominant – accompanied the moment the protagonist realized his wish to clasp Nature in his arms. The subtle surface-level transformation by L from D minor to B♭ major accompanies a shift in focus, when the protagonist addresses Nature directly. The next time the accompanimental figure changes, it underscores another moment of ecstasy and a permanent change of key from D minor to B♭ major. As the protagonist cries out "Ich komm', ich komme! Wohin? Ach wohin?" the answer "Hinauf!" introduces B♭ major.

The harmonic progression at this moment provides a crucial insight into the difference between the harmonic language of Reichardt and that of Schubert. Measure 23 in Reichardt's "Ganymed" prepares the dominant of D minor, which has been the main key since m. 14. After the *ff* dominant chord in the piano in m. 24, Reichardt instructs his performers to pause briefly ("eine kleine Pause"), which increases the surprise of the ensuing B♭ major chord (VI). Reichardt's change of key signature at this point indicates that this is no ordinary deceptive cadence. He does not, in other words, repeat the phrase or organize a resolution to the tonic, although the B♭ harmony in m. 25 strategically has a $\hat{D}$ in the bass. The next harmony in the accompaniment is a dominant seventh of the dominant and – perhaps also strategically – has the $\hat{B}$♭ in the bass. It resolves as it should to the third of F major, which leads to the first cadence in B♭ with the word "Liebe."

Although at this point the style suddenly becomes more operatic (Reichardt was an opera composer), there is little accompaniment following m. 26 for more pragmatic reasons: Reichardt does not need to fill out the harmony to establish B♭ major as a proper key. The $\hat{B}$♭s in the bass in mm. 27–28 help anchor the sound, even though they function as sevenths

Example 2.20 Analysis of Reichardt, "Ganymed" (a) monotonal Roman numeral reading from the opening tonic ("foreground") (b) monotonal Roman numeral reading from the final tonic ("background") (c) reading using transformation theory

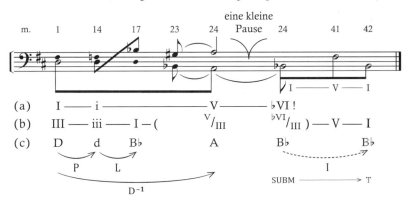

in the dominant of the dominant. Despite the root-position cadence in B♭ major in m. 30 over the word "Liebe," Reichardt takes advantage of the excitement of "Mir!" to reintroduce D̂ in the bass. Again a B♭ major harmony in m. 35 is treated to a first inversion, as if still battling out a finish between B♭ or D. A conclusive finish in B♭ is only achieved in the piano's postlude.

How might the overall tonal structure of Reichardt's "Ganymed" be characterized? In sum, it begins in D major, shifts to D minor and then lands on B♭ major through the dominant of D, as shown in the "foreground" interpretation of the harmony in Example 2.20a. Quite apart from the pervasive chordal accompaniment of the whole song, there is no mistaking that this is a harmonically conceived turn of events. The method by which Reichardt ultimately reaches B♭ is a familiar one, namely the deceptive cadence. It would have been immediately recognizable to his listeners, even if it is subsequently brutally handled. The maneuver is treated unusually because the harmony leading up to the interruption is not immediately repeated in order to end on the tonic instead of the submediant, as it would if it were an ordinary cadential gesture. Rather, Reichardt momentarily suspends the accompaniment, adopting an operatic tone, as he allows B♭ to sink in as the new tonic.

A monotonal reading of this song in the manner advocated by Schenker interprets it through the final tonic and therefore as an incomplete structure starting from the mediant, III–iii–I–($^V/_{III}$–$^{♭VI}/_{III}$)–V–I, as illustrated in Example 2.20b.[123] This is a background-level reading – only possible once

---

[123] This example is modeled on Fig. 110 from *Free Composition*.

Example 2.21 Graphic analysis of important harmonic sonorities in Schubert, "Ganymed" the song is completed. It does not, to my mind, capture a plausible hearing. A more plausible reading (or hearing), in terms of harmonic function, might be called a "foreground" reading, for it describes the functions as the song proceeds, I–i–V–♭VI, as already characterized above (see Example 2.20a). Yet this analysis does not cater for how the listener experiences B♭ major at the end of the song. On its entry, B♭ would be understood as VI in relation to its immediate context of D minor, and ♭VI in relation to the opening tonic major. The function of B♭ gradually changes from submediant to tonic. How might this be symbolized?

Here is where neo-Riemannian transformations are handy. As shown in Example 2.20c, the layer labeled with transformations captures even better this sense of changing functions in the B♭ section – aided as it is by an unconventional use of the symbol I for Identity. The deceptive cadence brings about the sense of the SUBM (Submediant) function for the B♭ major harmony in m. 24. The SUBM becomes T (Tonic) through the I (Identity) transformation, which elegantly explains the shift in function even though no pitches are altered.

Schubert may well have been attracted to Reichardt's setting because of its harmonic plan, but he found an altogether personal way of executing the move from A♭ major to F major. The differences in the syntax between each setting show that Schubert did not think in the same vertical-harmonic sense as Reichardt. Instead Schubert's distinctive compositional style lies in the way his use of pitch drives the structure. We meet in "Ganymed" the same kind of procedure encountered above in "Auf der Donau" and "Selige Welt," where there are prominent voice-leadings suggestive of a particular harmonic move, which, however, are not borne out by Schubert's actual choice of harmony and where a harmonic inflection becomes a new tonicization. Schubert's way of traveling to various keys was primarily by exploiting harmonies related by common tones rather than by virtue of established progressions. In other words, his treatment of pitch – or a kind of non-contrapuntal but highly distilled voice-leading – enabled him to expand harmonic horizons. I would therefore argue that Schubert's large-scale harmonic stations within a song are the structural "result" rather than the "method" by which the composer crafted his harmonic plan.

Example 2.21 shows my own graphic analysis of important harmonic sonorities in Schubert's "Ganymed." Despite its Schenkerian look, it is not intended to be a conventional voice-leading graph. Indeed, instead of highlighting voice-leadings, it highlights the salient pitches in the voice, bass line, and piano interlude, which usher in the harmony from the opening

A♭ major to the final F major. As depicted by the jagged lines next to the beamed A♭ and F, despite a strong start in A♭ major and a strong finish in F major, these keys are never fulfilled in any Schenkerian sense.

From m. 1 to m. 24, the song is centered in A♭ major with the bass rocking back and forth between the tonic and dominant pitches, forming a long and settled section in that key, as observed also by Denny, Krebs, Kramer, Thym and Fehn, and numerous other analysts of this song. A quick glance at my graph is enough to tell that, the moment m. 24 draws to a close, the graph does not abide by Schenkerian principles. Note that throughout Example 2.21, I pay close attention not only to the identity of a harmony or key but also to its presentation: it matters whether it is in root position or an inversion, and it matters which pitches are salient or not in the voice. In what follows I will make a careful distinction between the identity and the presentation of a harmony. By the "identity of a harmony," I mean whether it is A♭ major, A♭ minor et cetera and by the "presentation of a harmony" I mean its appearance on the surface of the music, including such details as a harmony's inversion, which pitch appears in the voice or which pitches are rendered salient in some other way.

I shall aim to show where the principles behind the unfolding of Schubert's harmony differ from the principles of fundamental bass theory. It is unlike either Roman-numeral analysis or Schenkerian theory. Instead of exhibiting the logic of harmonic progression through traditional root motions (as in fundamental bass theory), I shall argue for the importance of the *profile* of Schubert's bass line, which often supplies pitches a fifth apart but not fifth-based harmonies. Or, to put it differently, after staking out a familiar profile in the bass, new harmonic nuances can be introduced. In other instances, I shall argue that a pitch in the voice (or upper voice) guides the harmony, either by providing a traditional-sounding resolution but without the traditional supporting harmony or by remaining on a single pitch around which the harmony turns. From these observations, I will build up a picture of the exits and entrances of Schubert's harmonic spaces, no matter how short or transient they may be. I shall argue, in keeping with my reading of Fink above, that it was Schubert's presentation of harmony that was so novel and that in turn led to his novel structural designs. I shall expose this novelty by comparing Schubert's presentation of harmony in "Ganymed" to Reichardt's.

As already stated, mm. 1–27 are a fairly standard way to establish the tonic. As can be seen in the score in Example 2.18, the bass rocks back and forth between Â♭ and Ê♭, and the harmony between A♭ and E♭. Each phrase in the vocal line is uttered in pairs: mm. 9–11 and 13–15; 19^4–21^2 and

21^4–23^2; 23^4–25^2 and 26–27^2.[124] Even the phrase 16^3–18 may be divided into a pair of gestures for each word "Frühling, Geliebter!" ("spring, my beloved!"), with an extra linking note for the extra syllable in "G*e*liebter!" Although my analytical description of steady harmony and phrases suggests calm, Schubert depicts an ecstatic Ganymede. The voice enters in m. 9, however the piano introduction that precedes it is not a regular 8-measure phrase. Instead, the prelude is a 2+2+2+1 structure, followed by +1, which is a rebeginning in m. 8. The voice therefore opens on the second measure of the piano's accompaniment, rather than the first. Yet because the opening note is an Ê♭, the vocalist makes, as it were, no harmonic faux pas. Ê♭ is a tone common to both the dominant and tonic, so the singer merely enters on the accompanist's dominant. This also gives the sense that Ganymede cries out each phrase *in medias res*, and the rests between each phrase capture his breathless ecstasy.

The accompaniment again takes charge in bringing about a tonicization of E♭ major, starting in m. 19. The voice follows suit. Ganymede is a passive lover here, a point which literary scholars have shown to have important implications for interpreting Ganymede as the feminine object of masculine divine love. He is depicted by Goethe as penetrated by spring and nature; his body and heart are penetrated by spring's warmth, the flowers, and grass. In these measures, Ganymede follows the piano away from A♭ major, as love's thousandfold joy *presses* on his heart ("Mit tausendfacher Liebeswonne / Sich an mein Herze drängt").[125] When Ganymede reflects on the all-loving father's eternal warmth ("deiner ewigen Wärme"), both piano and voice move together to an A♭ minor harmony.

It is the first chromatic moment in the song, caressing the word "Wärme." Despite the change of harmony, the note Ê♭ still lurks in the bass, therefore. Six measures later, after a return to E♭ major in m. 27, the vocal Ĉ♭ that was sung to "Wärme" is tonicized to articulate the word "Schöne" ("beauty") in m. 31. These harmonic shifts are depicted in Example 2.21. In a case of obvious word painting, the words "eternal" and "unending" (in "deiner *ewigen* Wärme" and "*unendliche* Schöne") are elongated, with the latter held in abeyance for a whole measure of D♭ minor, as part of an elaborated ii^6–V^7–I cadence establishing C♭ major. En route to the cadence, there is one more C♮ in m. 29, which appears immediately after the long D♭. It is depicted in my graph in Example 2.21

---

[124] Superscript numbers denote the beat within the measure. No superscript means the voice enters or concludes on the downbeat.

[125] Robert Tobin, *Warm Brothers: Queer Theory and the Age of Goethe* (Philadelphia: University of Pennsylvania Press, 2000), 134–135.

in a manner more salient than might initially be gleaned from the score. As part of an A♭ major (seventh) sonority, it is a brief, yet meaningful, flash of the brightness of the harmony of the opening section – another penetration of nature, if you will. The $\hat{C}♭$ that was introduced as ♭$\hat{3}$ within an A♭ minor triad (m. 25) soon returns and becomes $\hat{1}$ in its new context of C♭ major (m. 31).

We saw precisely this method of modulation in "Selige Welt," and, as it happens, in the same key: it will be recalled that a shift from $\hat{3}$ to ♭$\hat{3}$ was suitably introduced to the words "hin und her" before the music proceeded to a cadence in C♭ major (see Example 2.2). Coincidentally, "Auf der Donau" also modulated to C♭ major through a shift from A♭ major to A♭ minor. Although the entry of the chromatic pitch $\hat{C}♭$ is again prominent in the vocal line before it is tonicized, the pitch I drew out in my earlier discussion of "Auf der Donau" was the recurrence of the pitch $\hat{E}♭$. In that analysis, I was focusing on the pitch that threads all of the harmonies of section A together and which recalls the tonic while the harmonies shift around it. However, salient $\hat{C}♭$s in mm. 13 and 18 prepare for its tonicization in m. 20 (see Example 2.1a).

In "Ganymed," C♭ and G♭^{7} oscillate for some measures to come, the seventh of the latter ensuring that C♭ is heard as a tonic – until, that is, the $\hat{C}♭$ in the voice is supported once again (as in m. 25) by an A♭ minor harmony, this time in root position (m. 41). Again it precipitates the tonicization of a new key, which Schubert brings about by treating G♭ major as tonic rather than dominant, with "Herz" being sung to an open $\hat{G}♭$ in m. 46. During this passage, we are once more reminded about Ganymede's passivity in love, as the all-loving father's flowers and grass again press upon his heart ("deine Blumen, dein Gras drängen sich an mein Herz"). Schubert has the opportunity to use this single pitch as a common tone to shift to a number of different keys, but he chooses to go nowhere. He fleshes out the $\hat{G}♭$ with a major harmony but transforms it into the enharmonic F♯ major. Although hinting at B major (as if C♭ major might return in a new guise), Schubert tonicizes E major.

E major first appears as a first-inversion chord (m. 50). It provides a significant tone in the bass: as observed by Denny, the $\hat{G}♯$ harks back to the $\hat{A}♭$ of the opening key, in the same register (Example 2.21).[126] Moreover, the awkward leap downwards from the $\hat{F}♯$, as well as the awkward spacing of the chord itself, is striking. The new key articulates new appreciations of

---

[126] This E_6 is the inversion Denny commented on. He used it to argue that E major should be considered within the A♭ major tonic because the G♯ sustains the tonic of the first half of the song. See Denny, "Directional Tonality in Schubert's Lieder," 46.

nature: the morning wind ("Morgenwind"), the sound of the nightingale ("Nachtigall"), whose songs are cued in the piano interlude, and the misty valley ("Nebeltal").

Since the music travels immediately from an E major triad to an A major triad (mm. 50–51), another descending fifth seems certain when the next measure uses the same figuration and brings about a dominant-seventh B major chord. Instead Schubert delivers a deceptive cadence, onto a C♯ minor sonority. Unlike Reichardt's odd treatment of the large-scale deceptive cadence, C♯ will not be tonicized. Rather Schubert's is a very ordinary treatment of the progression: the expected E major arrives at the cadence three measures later. Although a piano interlude further tonicizes E major, the voice re-enters on harmonies that are set to move the key elsewhere. In other words, at this point (earlier in the text than in Reichardt's setting) Schubert uses a deceptive cadence but, by comparison, it is a subtle one and, at any rate, not permanent because E major is tonicized instead. Had Schubert remained in E, he would have matched Reichardt's tonal scheme and landed a major third down from the harmonic starting point of the song. Schubert will instead end on F.

He gets there by yet more manipulation of his pitch material (Example 2.21). Between mm. 64 and 67, there is an A major to minor shift, both harmonies of which are in first inversion. This inversion introduces a significant pitch in the bass, $\hat{C}$. A new texture launches a brief bass-line neighbor-note motion to $\hat{B}$ in the bass in mm. 68–70, which supports a B^7–e_4^6 harmony. In the excitement ("ich komm', ich komme!") familiar harmonic progression is ignored, and an L transformation brings about the return to $\hat{C}♯$ in the bass in m. 71 and a C major harmony on the word "ach!" A four-measure pedal on $\hat{C}$ then prepares the cadence to F major. Schubert follows Reichardt's model by reaching his tonal destination in response to the question "wohin?" Ganymede is also ushered up to the clouds.

The secure cadence in F major means that Schubert would not have been required to do much to establish the new key. Settled harmony would not suit the text, however, so in Schubert's setting the harmonic tension continues to mount. Schubert carefully crafts the final section to include a notable amount of F major harmony, but never in a stressed, tonicized root position until near the end of the song, where closure is brought about in stages: by the final exclamation "all-liebender Vater!" first landing on $\hat{2} \atop V$, then on a root-position F major sonority in the piano with the voice on $\hat{3}$ (m. 110), and then by a closed root-position harmony for the final "all-liebender Vater!"

Throughout this section, the presentation of F major – both in terms of the beat it occupies in the measure and its chordal layout – is important to the sense of the music, which tends to intimate rather than assert the harmonic profile. The whole section is filled with repetition of text and modified repetition of the music, the ebb and flow of energy matched by an ascending vocal line as Ganymede strives upwards, and a descending line to depict the clouds – or Zeus, we presume – swooping downwards to seize Ganymede. It is not altogether clear that F major is readily perceptible as the harmonic goal of the piece until the very end, a hearing which Kramer's interpretation rightly stresses. Indeed the final section exhibits touches of the subdominant, and the return of C and F oscillating in the bass in mm. 80–84 and the parallel passage of mm. 95–99 frustrate the sense of V–I rather than articulate it. A rising sequence of cadences dominates mm. 85–92, whose agitated inverted chords will be transformed – but in a way that is no less agitated – when the melodic unfolding is compressed for its parallel return in mm. 101–105 (these passages are aligned in Example 2.21). In this way, Schubert achieves a similar effect to Reichardt, albeit through a different means. In both cases, the final key is established only at the very end of the song, but for Reichardt this happens because he struggles to assert the key of B♭, while for Schubert it happens because he deliberately avoids articulating his final key of F until the very end.

Towards a new theory of Schubert's harmony

As may be evident by now, I would not burden song with the need for an overarching, *a priori* harmonic logic. My graph allows Schubert's harmonic practice – with its implied progressions and exploitation of chordal inversions – to unravel Schenkerian principles. In my reading of Schubert's "Ganymed," it is impossible to pinpoint a single moment that brings the structure from A♭ to F major, especially as there are many intervening keys or harmonic stations. Kramer's Ĝ♭, which is the ♭2̂ in his *Urlinie* and which he therefore regarded as the pivot between the opening and closing harmonies, in my analysis is neither more nor less a point of pivot than the other pitches. In my view, there are no obvious candidates for the transformation of function that summarily exchanges the tonic opening for the tonic ending. Here we catch the first glimpse of Schubert's personal style when unfolding a harmonic structure.

As my analysis of Schubert's "Ganymed" also reveals, the apparent foreground detail of the inversion in which a chord is cast has important structural repercussions. This level of detail is often smoothed over by analysts, especially as, following Rameau's theory of the fundamental bass, the harmony itself rather than its position is understood as most important – witness, for instance, that Kramer provides the root of A major/minor in his graph (Example 2.16). In *Franz Schubert*, Kramer notes that the triads are "all sixth chords, [and] are transitional in another way: their instability portends a new departure." And on their functional role, he observes that "A major becomes A minor, curtailing the fifth-based transitional process of the middle section [of the song] by disqualifying itself as a dominant."[127] For both Denny and Krebs, the A minor harmony is incidental, and therefore it does not feature in either of their deep-level graphs.[128] While Krebs includes the A major to minor shift in its inversion in his foreground graphs (where they form part of a rising scalic motion in the inner voice), the Ĉ♮ is only declared in a *f* dynamic once the full dominant harmony actually sounds in m. 71.

By contrast, my analysis shows that the important feature is that A minor houses the dominant pitch of F major. That is to say, by casting A minor in first inversion, the bass contains the tone that is the dominant of the pitch structure's final destination. When it is first heard, Ĉ is 3̂; after the neighbor-note B̂ in the bass, Ĉ is 1̂. But the perceptible function of an emergent dominant is not in fact gained until just before the cadence into F. The final harmonic destination arrives after a long dominant pedal, without, however, ever dwelling on the actual dominant harmony. The introduction of a tone – whether in the bass or in an upper voice – followed by its tonicization seems to be one procedure that Schubert uses to navigate through keys: large-scale harmonic progression is of lesser concern than giving a pitch the power to direct the harmonic flow.

Example 2.22 contains the pitches that are most decisive in creating the harmonic route through the piece. As mentioned before, the song opens with a lengthy passage oscillating between A♭ major and E♭ major (mm. 1–27). The introduction of Ĉ♭ in the vocal line, which turns A♭, the tonic of the song thus far, into A♭ minor, introduces a tone that will be tonicized a few measures later: 3̂ of A♭ minor thus becomes 1̂ of C♭ major (m. 31). The shift has accompanied Ganymede's admiration of Zeus's warmth and beauty. Similarly the Ĝ♭ introduced in the bass as the seventh of A♭ major in m. 29 is tonicized a measure later as the dominant of C♭ – here Ĝ♭ is first

[127] Kramer, *Schubert*, 122 and 123 respectively. See also "The Schubert Lied," 227.
[128] Denny, "Directional Tonality in Schubert's Lieder," 53 and Krebs, "Alternatives to Monotonality," 7–8.

Example 2.22 Decisive pitches and their change of hue in harmonic route through Schubert, "Ganymed" (a) bass line as roots (b) actual harmonies

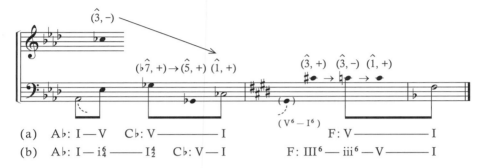

$\hat{7}$, then $\hat{1}$. A reminder of the link between C♭ major and A♭ minor appears in mm. 40–41. The harmony that accompanied Zeus's warmth is now reserved for the word "deine," as Ganymede reveals that Zeus has penetrated his heart. This is also the moment where G♭ begins to assert itself, tonicized as it is in mm. 45–46 ("Herz"). Once tonicized, the tonality moves on, this time by a retention of all common tones: F♯ major, the enharmonic equivalent of G♭ major, is introduced. The tension in the chromatic interlude resolves onto E⁶, the bass ($\hat{G}$♯) of which reactivates the enharmonic equivalent of the opening tonic pitch ($\hat{A}$♭) in the bass but in a new triadic context. The root of E major begins the piano interlude and E major eventually becomes the dominant of the A major to minor shift in mm. 64–67. As already mentioned, their first-inversion format is significant because it introduces $\hat{C}$♮ in the bass, which subsequently serves as the root for the dominant of F major. Again the procedure is that $\hat{C}$ is first $\hat{3}$, then $\hat{1}$. Schubert's practice is gradually revealing itself: he modifies the harmony around a common pitch, which introduces the next key.

Interestingly, once F major arrives there is no more harmonic mutation of this sort; rather, Schubert turns to the resolution of important pitches (which, as my graph additionally shows, invariably articulate important words). The brief homophonic texture which forms the D♭ harmony under "un*end*liche" sets it apart from its immediate context. This D♭ in m. 28 and the $\hat{C}$♯ and $\hat{C}$ of the A major to minor shift in mm. 64–67 remain an issue in the last section. The heightening tension in the words "Mir! Mir! In eurem Schoße aufwärts!," a passage which Schubert sets twice (mm. 85–88 and 100–102), is created by a series of authentic cadences, the first time involving exclusively first-inversion dominant sevenths, the second time root-position chords (the two passages are aligned on the graph in Example 2.21). The changes in harmony, despite a basically similar vocal line, take the song from D minor to F major the first time, but from B♭ major to F major in the second, while resurrecting the alternation between the Ĉ♮ and Ĉ♯. Note how in both cases the pattern established for each phrase is broken on the entrance of "umfangend umfangen!" (mm. 88–89 and 102–103), which certainly leaves one free to interpret the embrace as a rapturous one, especially as both passages are then identical for "aufwärts an deinen Busen" and the beginning of "all-liebender Vater!" (mm. 90–93 and 104–107). Moreover, the second "umfangend umfangen!" increases the tension of the first by including the appoggiatura Ĝ–F̂, an appoggiatura which gains poignancy (and is a remembrance of the dual embrace?) when it appears on the last chord of the piano prelude. There it is coupled with the D̂♭ to Ĉ♮ resolution, itself, one might also presume, a remembrance of "unendliche Schöne!".

Schubert's method, then, is less about composing out functions that assist in a sense of departure and return than it is about navigating a way through the framework set by Reichardt using a kind of domino effect: a pitch inflects a harmony in some way and then becomes the next tonicized event; then a new pitch becomes the focus of attention and is subsequently tonicized, and so on. Example 2.22 indicates the number of times this procedure occurs in "Ganymed."

It is by examining Schubert's "Ganymed" against its compositional model rather than various theoretical models that Schubert's (deviant) procedure becomes most evident. One might say that, in adopting Reichardt's basic harmonic framework, Schubert treats his deviant model as a norm, which in turn forces us to recognize that it is the surface harmonic mechanisms that Schubert recasts. His setting *is* deviant against its model. It offers an entirely new way of reaching a final harmonic destination. In Reichardt's setting the functions of the beginning and ending are clear, even if the final key is uncertain for a moment. I would argue that, in Schubert's setting, the harmonic unfolding is not about mediants representing large-scale dominant-related functions as Kramer suggests, or about a conglomerate of two triads based solely on the opening and closing tonics as Krebs suggests, or about a matrix of keys around the opening tonic or a series of keys under a chromatic *Urlinie* as Denny suggests, but about one key mutating into another throughout the song. Schubert does away with a recognizable overall harmonic progression, which means he does away with the kind of proce-dure that can be captured in the contrapuntal unfolding of either an *Ursatz* or a series of partial *Ursätze*. To be sure, surface-level tonics and dominants help articulate the gradual changes, but the overall effect is one of harmonic metamorphosis rather than a series of functional relationships.

From this analysis of the song, it should be evident that listing the keys in a Schubert song tells but a fraction of the harmonic story, and certainly trying to find meaning in a pattern of such a list is a distraction. Instead Schubert navigates through his keys through harmonic mutation, implying but often avoiding recognizable harmonic progressions. As illustrated in Example 2.22, Schubert achieves this by conceiving a given pitch as having the potential to serve as $\hat{1}, \hat{3}, \hat{5}$, or $\hat{7}$ in a chordal context, making a network of major and minor triads and (in this case also) dominant-seventh chords.[129] One minute a pitch might be $\hat{3}$, the next $\hat{1}$; between the two there is obviously a change of harmony. If one imagines a V^7–I cadence, it has three contrapuntal components, as Rameau described it: the bass V goes to I, the leading tone rises to the tonic, and the seventh descends to the third. Schubert often decouples these strands from their expected harmonic context. For example, an apparent leading tone to tonic $(\hat{7}-\hat{8})$ prominently placed in the voice may not be accompanied by the expected V–I harmony in the piano. Or a seventh descending to the third may be pronounced in the melody, but again one or other of the pitches may be supported by a harmony other than the dominant or tonic chord. Similarly, a bass line that outlines tonic and dominant pitches might be fleshed out by some harmony other than an actual tonic and dominant.[130] For this reason, the harmonic annotations labeled (a) in Example 2.22 interpret the bass line "as if" their tonic/dominant groupings produce tonic/dominant harmonies in the keys suggested. The harmonic annotations labeled (b) are, by contrast, the actual harmonies.

It is precisely these kinds of maneuvers – or harmonic dishonesty, if you will – that disconcerted Fink. They no doubt unsettled Goethe too. Indeed, Schubert presented and dedicated his setting of "Ganymed" to Goethe, but the gesture was famously met with a stunning silence from the poet. Perhaps Schubert was naïve in thinking that the best way to impress the poet with his new genre of "truly expressive song" was to transform a musical setting of one of Goethe's closest friends and to render music as immediately expressive as the text.

---

[129] If dissonances are included, then the possibilities for the chordal context of any given common tone are wide open. Schubert's frequent use of common tones in both consonant and dissonant contexts serves as a good argument for following David Kopp's lead (in *Chromatic Transformations*, passim) and including dissonances, a measure for which he was criticized by Richard Bass in "Review of David Kopp, *Chromatic Transformations in Nineteenth-Century Music*," *Music Theory Online*, 10:1 (2004).

[130] I shall elaborate further on the theoretical implications of these observations about Schubert's manipulation of pitch in Chapter 3, where similar procedures may be found in the lyrical themes in his sonata forms.

We can also neatly return to Lewin and his comment that a song takes as its "structural premise ... [the] musical syntax, as it was understood at the time." In adopting Reichardt's overall structure for his setting, Schubert seems precisely to concentrate on transforming Classical syntax, and for us to understand him, it seems advisable to take Reichardt's setting as Schubert's background structure, rather than Schenker's *Ursatz*. In this way, we too can focus less on *which* keys Schubert visited or on whether he fulfills Schenkerian structural conditions and focus instead on *how* he reached his keys. By the same token, theorists who have catalogued the meaning of Schubert's modulations by key – through either scale-degree (*Stufen*) or function theory – need additionally to observe how the key is treated on the surface of the music. Not all A♭ majors are alike, and not all moves from there to C♭ major sound alike, as we have witnessed in the case of "Ganymed," "Selige Welt," and "Auf der Donau." The same harmonic move can engender opposite meanings, depending on how it is handled.[131] Thus, although these songs share a progression from A♭ major to A♭ minor to C♭ major, and "Selige Welt" and "Ganymed" are especially close because their A sections are based on it, the point I wish to emphasize is that it is the *technique* that Schubert reuses, not the structure. Indeed, the rest of these songs unfold differently from one another. Although this chapter has focused on harmony, a broader study would necessarily add the equally expressive roles of piano figuration, topics, phrase rhythm, dynamics et cetera.

Schubert's treatment of pitch allowed him to turn on a dime, as it were. He could change harmonic course for any aspect of the text, so as to emphasize a word, highlight a shift in mood or follow any turn the text might take. Examining Schubert's most adventurous harmonic structures in relation to existing theoretical paradigms will certainly illuminate all the ways in which Schubert doesn't follow them. *E contra* the desire on the part of modern theorists to find the musical design behind Schubert's harmonies in the songs (the instrumental music is another matter) is, to my mind, a misplaced one – even if motivated by the rightly placed desire to rescue Schubert from the reputation of rambling, disordered modulation. A lack of an overarching design that makes purely musical sense need not be synonymous with lack of intent.

---

[131] The move from, for instance, a C major triad to an A♭ major triad could emphasize the common tone and make the move sound smooth or it could emphasize the displaced pitches, in which case it will sound harsher. For a Schenkerian expression of this voice-leading phenomenon, see David Bretherton, "The Poetics of Schubert's Song Forms" (DPhil. thesis, University of Oxford, 2008); see also n. 88 and n. 89 above.

As we saw earlier, Ferguson, Finney, Bauer, and Porter argued that Schubert composed each song anew, each structure made for the moment, made to reflect the text. His compositional fecundity – or prowess, if you will – enabled him to rise to the challenge of the aesthetic values of his illustrious contemporary Herder. The philosopher invented the term "urwürsig" (meaning "growing from scratch"), which has been applied to Schubert's use of through-composition – a form readily acknowledged as a response to the text.[132] *Urwürsigkeit*, I would argue, ought equally to apply to the harmony.

Earlier I hinted that instrumental music is different. Here, I refer to and agree with Moritz Bauer, who astutely remarked almost a century ago that the duties of harmonic design are different in Schubert's songs and instrumental music, and they arise for different reasons.[133] Schubert's setting of "An die Musik" (D. 547) will serve to explain the point. It is an exquisitely simple strophic song – an apparent throwback to the "Volkslied." From a harmonic standpoint, it is remarkably tame. All cadences are in the tonic, except the penultimate one, which is in the relative minor. There is no mixture, no sudden or remote modulations. Why didn't Schubert show off his harmonic capabilities? As an ode to *music* – and not to the *poetry* or even *himself* as a composer! – Schubert seems to have depicted an idealized music. It is the very music that any conservative critic would admire. In contrast to this, the harmonic adventures found in his other songs are expressions of the *text*.

While new paradigms were being sought for the songs in the 1980s, new paradigms to cater for Schubert's instrumental music – notably his sonata forms – have been far slower to emerge. In the rest of this book, I contend that Schubert's exploration of harmony in the sonata forms was, to be sure, also expressive but, more important, Schubert was necessarily constrained by large-scale formal concerns. I argue the opposite intuition to the one that may be traced in modern Schubert studies: new paradigms of transferable harmonic large-scale structures are unnecessary for the songs but are imperative for the sonata forms. In other words, instrumental music – or at least, "organized" instrumental music, such as sonata, ternary, binary and rondo forms as opposed to fantasies, preludes et cetera – requires a balance of harmonic design that song does not demand.

---

[132] Richard Taruskin, *The Oxford History of Western Music: The Nineteenth Century*, vol. III (New York: Oxford University Press, 2005), 146.
[133] Moritz Bauer, *Die Lieder Franz Schuberts*, 41–42.

And this provides a cautionary tale to Agawu's Stage 1b: to be sure, invoking canonical techniques of analysis in the analysis of song seems like a good idea. Music theory is, after all, supposed to be the very thing that helps us to explain music. However, the power of music theory to shed light on musical meaning cannot be taken for granted, for what we have witnessed in the work of Lewin, Denny, Krebs, Siciliano, and Kramer and indeed in my own, is that hermeneutic windows themselves can be just as elusive as the meaning that supposedly lies beyond them. In song, music and text are brought tantalizingly close together, and Schubert, so his friends confidently claimed, was the greatest painter of words. That ought at least to give us room for optimism about our chances of understanding his musical meaning. In closing, I can, however, assure readers of one thing: in painting those words, Schubert didn't always paint the picture of music theory as we currently know it.

| Music theory and the musicological imagination: perceptions of Schubert's sonata form

Harmony and hermeneutics

The first movement of the Piano Sonata in B♭ Major (D. 960) is one of the most analyzed movements in Schubert's instrumental repertoire. Its fascinating array of keys and special effects has inspired both technical and narrative analytical accounts, as well as drawn scholars to the sketches in order to seek solutions to analytical problems. It was even used recently as a case study to test a new theoretical paradigm.[1]

The main aspects of the movement that have drawn attention are: the trill in measure 8; the ABA' structure of the first thematic area, whose midsection is in the remote key of G♭ major; the move to F♯ minor for the secondary theme (or thematic transition, as some have labeled it); the entry

---

[1] The sonata served as the case study for Richard Cohn's theory of hexatonic cycles in his "As Wonderful as Star Clusters: Instruments for Gazing at Tonality in Schubert," *19th-Century Music* 22 (1999): 213–232. While the literature on the sonata is too vast to mention in full here, other important transformational analyses include David Kopp, *Chromatic Transformations in Nineteenth-Century Music* (Cambridge University Press, 2002), 29–32 and 189–190, and Fred Lerdahl, *Tonal Pitch Space* (Oxford University Press, 2001), 114–115. For an excellent diatonic account, see Richard Taruskin in *The Oxford History of Western Music: The Nineteenth Century*, vol. III (New York: Oxford University Press, 2005), 96–100. The more extensive narrative studies include Byron Almén, *A Theory of Musical Narrative* (Indiana University Press, 2006), 139–161; Charles Fisk, "What Schubert's Last Sonata Might Hold," in Jenefer Robinson (ed.), *Music and Meaning* (Ithaca, NY, and London: Cornell University Press, 1997), 179–200; Charles Fisk, *Returning Cycles: Contexts for the Interpretation of Schubert's Impromptus and Last Sonatas* (Berkeley: University of California Press, 2001); Peter Pesic, "Schubert's Dream," *19th-Century Music* 23 (1999): 136–144; and Nina Noeske, "Schubert, das Erhabene und die letzte Sonate D. 960 – oder: Die Frage nach dem Subjekt," *Schubert: Perspektiven* 7 (2007): 22–36. Important Schenkerian approaches to the sonata may be found in Xavier Hascher, *Schubert: La forme sonate et son évolution* (New York: Peter Lang, 1996), 199–201 and Deborah Kessler, "Motive and Motivation in Schubert's Three-Key Expositions," in L. Poundie Burstein and David Gagné (eds.), *Structure and Meaning in Tonal Music: Festschrift in Honor of Carl Schachter* (Hillsdale, NY: Pendragon Press, 2006), 259–276. For a study that combines analysis, sketch study, and musical meaning in an especially insightful way, see Nicholas Marston, "Schubert's Homecoming," *Journal of the Royal Musical Association* 125 (2000): 248–270. Other important analyses that rely on sketch material include Hans-Joachim Hinrichsen, *Untersuchungen zur Entwicklung der Sonatenform in der Instrumentalmusik Franz Schuberts* (Tutzing: Hans Schneider, 1994), 333–335. Joseph N. Straus examines the discourse on the sonata from the perspective of the burgeoning field of disability studies in "Normalizing the Abnormal: Disability in Music and Music Theory," *Journal of the American Musicological Society* 59 (2006): 113–184.

of C♯ minor at the beginning of the development; the preemptive return of the first thematic material at the end of the development in another miniature ABA′ structure (supported by D minor, B♭ major, and D minor); and the recomposition of the first thematic material in the recapitulation.

The sonata starts with a threefold statement of the opening theme in B♭ major, G♭ major, and B♭ major, making up the ABA′ format that Felix Salzer identified as so characteristic of Schubert's opening themes and overall lyric impulse.[2] The low menacing trill is famous for intruding on the otherwise serene quality of the passage. In this regard, the main Ĝ♭ pitch of the trill is seen as "not merely a coloristic element, but a seemingly portentous one."[3] This turns out to mean two things: it demands a technical explanation but it also invites extramusical description. On a technical level, the trill's Ĝ♭, which settles on an F̂, is generally agreed to generate the two large-scale remote harmonic stations in the exposition, first to G♭ major (mm. 20–35) and then to the enharmonic F♯ minor (mm. 48–80).[4] Both remote harmonic stations reflect the outcome of the trill insofar as they settle on an F̂ afterwards: G♭ major goes to a second-inversion B♭ major harmony within the first thematic complex and F♯ minor goes to F major for the closing section. The chromatic pitch may therefore be said to prepare the later appearance of G♭ major and F♯ minor, in the manner of a "promissory note" (Cone) or "Romantic detail" (Kerman).[5]

On a narrative level, the trill has variously been heard as "ghostly," "distant thunder," a "mysterious sonority," a "stranger," a "mysterious, impressive, cryptic, Romantic gesture" or, as Charles Fisk decisively put it, "from wherever the theme may come, the trill comes from somewhere else."[6] The trill's consistent characterization as an intruder or as isolated from the rest of the

---

[2] Felix Salzer, "Die Sonatenform bei Franz Schubert," *Studien zur Musikwissenschaft* 15 (1928): 98–100.

[3] Fisk, *Returning Cycles*, 241.

[4] F♯ minor is not as prominent as my measure numbers would suggest: already by m. 58, A major is suggested, and other harmonies ensue; m. 80 is the beginning of the closing section. Regarding the famous trill, one leading commentator has argued that its generative force is not nearly as significant as the dyad {A, B♭}, which is "ubiquitous but rhetorically latent" and therefore has attracted less attention. See Cohn, "As Wonderful as Star Clusters," 219, 222, 226, and 230.

[5] Edward T. Cone, "Schubert's Promissory Note: An Exercise in Musical Hermeneutics," in Walter Frisch (ed.), *Schubert: Critical and Analytical Studies* (Lincoln and London: University of Nebraska Press, 1986), 13–30 and Joseph Kerman, "A Romantic Detail in Schubert's Schwanengesang," in *Schubert: Critical and Analytical Studies*, 48–64.

[6] The citations refer respectively to Taruskin, *Oxford History of Western Music*, 97; Donald Francis Tovey, "Franz Schubert (1797–1828)," in Hubert J. Foss (ed.), *The Mainstream of Music and Other Essays* (Oxford University Press, 1949), 119; Charles Rosen, *Sonata Forms*, rev. edn. (New York: W. W. Norton, 1988), 261; Pesic, "Schubert's Dream," 139; Kerman, "A Romantic Detail," 59; and Fisk, "What Schubert's Last Sonata Might Hold," 179.

theme has led scholars to look to nineteenth-century notions of alienation and wandering to interpret the meaning of the large-scale harmonic consequences of the trill in the sonata. In a remarkable coincidence, two scholars in particular, Charles Fisk and Peter Pesic, relate the harmonic scheme of the first movement to a literary fantasy that Schubert wrote on July 3, 1822, which his brother Ferdinand later entitled "Mein Traum" ("My Dream").[7] These studies provide us with a golden opportunity to examine a general consensus on how connections are made between harmonic analysis and extramusical meaning – or how, in other words, music theory guides the musicological imagination.

The tale tells in the first person of a son's banishment from home by his father after he refused to enjoy the "delicious dishes" of a feast with his family. Forced to wander for years, he returns upon the news of his mother's death and looks upon her corpse and watches her coffin being lowered into the ground. The son is welcomed back home until banished for a second time, this time for not being able to conceal his revulsion for his father's "favourite garden." During the second episode of wandering, he hears news of a maiden who had died and finds his father at the graveside. The tale ends with the reconciliation of the father and the son.

The son's activities during the first episode of wandering seem characteristically Romantic: he is consumed by conflicting feelings of "greatest grief" and "greatest love." His activities during the second banishment seem especially Schubertian. He again feels a conflict between pain and love, but this time expresses it in song: "For many and many a year I sang songs. Whenever I attempted to sing of love, it turned to pain. And again, when I tried to sing of pain, it turned to love."[8]

---

[7] Both studies were published around the same time and neither writer seems to have been aware of the other's recourse to "Mein Traum" (see Pesic, "Schubert's Dream" and Fisk, *Returning Cycles*). It could, of course, be argued that the coincidence is not so remarkable, especially as much of Schubert's instrumental music would have made a good candidate for the analogies with the tale. Indeed Fisk draws parallels with other works, but D. 960 attracts by far his most sustained effort. To shore up the connection with wandering and alienation, both scholars find connections between the sonata and one of Schubert's songs in order to draw out further narrative meaning from the harmony – Fisk links the sonata to "Der Wanderer" (D. 489) through a melodic quotation and the shared key of C♯ minor, whereas Pesic engages "Der Neugierige" from *Die schöne Müllerin* (D. 795) through a parallel harmonic gesture. A translation of "Mein Traum" may be found in Otto Erich Deutsch (ed.), *Schubert: A Documentary Biography*, trans. Eric Blom (London: J. M. Dent, 1946), 226–228.

[8] There has been much speculation about the significance and circumstances of the composition of this story. Early biographies suggested it was the result of a party game; see Maurice J. E. Brown, "Schubert's Dream," *Monthly Musical Record* 83 (1953): 39–43 and *Schubert: A Critical Biography* (New York: St. Martin's Press, 1966), 114–116, and John Reed, *Schubert* (London: The Master Musicians, 1987), 94. The latest detailed biography, however, suggests it may have been

Pesic and Fisk are both interested in the banishment, wandering, and reconciliation motives in this miniature tale. They personify the harmonic plan of Schubert's sonata and imagine a protagonist journeying through its structure, somewhat analogously to the son of "Mein Traum" who experiences banishments and homecomings. Their language is evocative and entirely spurred on by the theoretical premises of their musical analyses. Their purpose is to show that the home and remote keys in the first movement of the sonata unravel in a manner that the tale is purported to elucidate. Pesic claims to recognize in the tale an ABA′ form on the basis of the familial bliss at the beginning and end, and the contrasting array of sentiments and conditions in the middle.[9] A ternary design is surely questionable, given that the plot involves a "double-banishment" (as Pesic puts it) and two returns to "home," features that more readily suggest the rondo structure proposed by Fisk.[10] At any rate, their point was not to match structure for structure the tale and the sonata, nor were they suggesting that the tale is meant to serve as a program for the sonata. Instead they argue that the tale acts as a kind of general hermeneutic document for the sonata's harmonic proclivities.[11]

Example 3.1 contains the main harmonic events they discuss, and the annotations summarize their narrative readings.[12] The happy opening is interpreted by Fisk as representing the "opening chorus" and by Pesic as the "'feast' of untroubled 'family music.'" The trill, as we have already seen, is "portentous," or a "stranger to parallel the dreamer, the prodigal son on whom the story turns" or "the dreamer's divergence [which] alters or disrupts the simple beginning and draws it to wander."[13] Both writers link it

opium-induced prose; see Elizabeth Norman McKay, *Franz Schubert: A Biography* (Oxford: Clarendon Press, 1996), 126–129. For psychological interpretations, see Maynard Solomon, "Franz Schubert's 'My Dream,'" *American Imago* 38 (1981): 137–154 and Andreas Mayer, "Der psychoanalytische Schubert," *Schubert durch die Brille* 9 (1992): 7–31.

[9] Pesic, "Schubert's Dream," 137.

[10] Fisk, *Returning Cycles*, 10.

[11] Pesic, "Schubert's Dream," 137 and 139 n. 11. This recalls Scott Burnham's clarification of nineteenth-century narratives surrounding Beethoven's *Eroica*: "we must not for a moment think that the symphony is about these narratives, for it is precisely the other way round: these narratives are about the symphony"; see Burnham, *Beethoven Hero* (Princeton University Press, 1995), 25.

[12] Fisk's annotations come from his own chart, *Returning Cycles*, 254–255; an identical chart appears in his "What Schubert's Last Sonata Might Hold," 180, which, as will be discussed later, is a narrative reading based solely on his analysis and without recourse to Schubert's "Mein Traum." Pesic's phrases are extracted from his "Schubert's Dream," *passim*. There are different traditions in the labeling of the section in F♯ minor: for some it is a transition (Fisk), for others a second theme (Pesic). I shall call it a second theme. I call the section in F major the "closing," while Fisk and others see it as the secondary theme, undoubtedly because it is in the dominant.

[13] Pesic, "Schubert's Dream," 139 and 138.

Example 3.1 Main harmonic events in Schubert, Piano Sonata in B♭ Major (D. 960), first movement, and their narrative meaning according to Charles Fisk and Peter Pesic. Based on Fisk's table in *Returning Cycles*, 254–255

Exposition			Development		Recapitulation
① [theme]	②	ⓒⓛ	①	①	①
A B A′		:		A B A′	A B A′
B♭ G♭ B♭	f♯	F	c♯	d B♭ d	B♭ G♭/f♯ B♭
HOME	BANISH-MENT # 1	RETURN HOME	BANISH-MENT # 2 (Fisk)	BANISHMENT # 2 (Pesic)	RECONCILIATION

to the protagonist of Schubert's tale, and both understand its chromaticism – that is, its foreignness to the tonic's major mode – as drawing the harmony to venture away from "home." As the pitch in m. 8 becomes a key in mm. 19–35 – ♭$\hat{6}$ becomes ♭VI – the protagonist "individuates himself through the trill" for the "first, charmed exploration of the G♭-major territory."[14]

Although the sonata has reached a distant harmonic territory by m. 19, neither commentator was tempted to speak of it as the protagonist's first banishment from home. Another parameter comes into play here, guiding their interpretations. In formal terms, we are still within the first thematic complex – still presumably stationed "at home." This chromaticism is therefore taken to symbolize the protagonist's growing discomfort at home, rather than his ejection from it. Perhaps melody is another parameter that influences their reading: the protagonist is still, as it were, singing the opening melody – indeed even from the same starting pitch, though the rest is altered to fit within its new triadic context (compare the interval structure of the melodies in mm. 1–2 and 19–20 in Example 3.2; S means semitone, T means tone).

Pesic says very little about the return to B♭ major that closes the first thematic area, but Fisk draws particular attention to it, and especially to its open-endedness. Rather than closing with a cadence in the tonic, it goes straight into F♯ minor and launches the next formal section of the exposition. It is as if, having experienced G♭ major, the protagonist

cannot take part any longer in a B♭-major cadence. Instead he is drawn back into the territory of the G♭ itself, which has suddenly turned darkly minor. Like the protagonist of "Mein Traum," he is cast out – not for rejecting his father's garden of

---

[14] Fisk, *Returning Cycles*, 242.

Example 3.2 Schubert, Piano Sonata in B♭ Major, first movement (a) mm. 1–9 and (b) 19–27

delights, but for already venturing into his own – and he begins to search and to wander.[15]

The chief images to remember from this quotation are that the protagonist is "cast out" into a remote key and begins to "search" and "wander" away from the home diatonic key. Both scholars concur that the next passage in F♯ minor marks the first "banishment" of the protagonist, and therefore parallels the first episode of exile and wandering in the tale.[16] They are not alone in their view: Charles Rosen, for example, considers it a "magnificent

---

[15] Fisk, *Returning Cycles*, 242.

[16] Pesic, "Schubert's Dream," 140 and Fisk, *Returning Cycles*, 242.

detour" before the structural dominant.[17] F♯ minor supports new thematic material, and some analysts have suggested it qualifies as a second theme, while others have termed it a "transitional theme" – presumably because this movement would otherwise have no transition. Whatever its thematic label, the shift in mode from G♭ major to F♯ minor might at first seem a rather subtle harmonic change for the pivotal claim that F♯ minor represents banishment, whereas G♭ major did not. However, typical readings of the key according to diatonic theory support their narrative. There are important technical details in the relationship between B♭ major and F♯ minor, which both scholars point out, that facilitate their interpretation of the latter key as "exiled" from the former: F♯ minor is as remote as Schubert could make a submediant relationship. It has no tones in common with the tonic.

A number of scholars have been struck by the strange aural effect engendered by this key relation; the diatonic nomenclature, "enharmonic equivalent of the flat submediant minor," makes it sound particularly distant. Pesic and Fisk call it a "disturbing tonal region" and "darkly minor" respectively, while Richard Taruskin argues that "it has the quality of a mirage, or a will-o'-the-wisp," which he suggests has as much to do with the diminished-seventh appoggiatura through which it appears and disappears as with the key itself.[18] For similar reasons, Susan Wollenberg hears the arrival of F♯ minor as "pure enigma," even though it can be "logically derived from what has preceded it."[19] Adorno considered it an example of Schubert's characteristic "sudden, nondevelopmental modulations [that] occlude daylight like camera shutters."[20] When the same key relation recurs between the end of the exposition and the beginning of the development section, Ernst Kurth heard it as "a magnificent display in sentiment and color of genuine Romantic magic" and Richard Kramer as "audacious," "unorthodox," and "breath-taking."[21]

Richard Cohn has persuasively argued that the diatonic characterization of F♯ minor as "an enharmonically respelled minor inflection of the triad on the flattened submediant degree pays the price of revealing the descriptive clumsiness of a diatonic model of this chord. Worse yet, it reveals the

---

[17] Rosen, *Sonata Forms*, 261.

[18] Pesic, "Schubert's Dream," 140, Fisk, *Returning Cycles*, 242, and Taruskin, *The Oxford History of Western Music*, 100.

[19] Susan Wollenberg, "Schubert's Transitions," in Brian Newbould (ed.), *Schubert Studies* (Ashgate: Aldershot, 1998), 21.

[20] Theodor W. Adorno, "Schubert (1928)," trans. Jonathan Dunsby and Beate Perrey, *19th-Century Music* 29 (2005): 12.

[21] Quoted in Cohn, "As Wonderful as Star Clusters," 218.

model's explanatory inadequacy."[22] The price paid has precisely to do with
the discourse of aimlessness, wandering, and even flaws that surround
Schubert's music. To cite one pertinent example, Fisk had attached a
narrative of his own invention to the first movement of the Sonata in B♭
Major a couple of years before writing the study under discussion. Based
purely on a diatonic analysis, he came up with a "psychological scenario" of
the sonata, namely a narrative of an outsider protagonist wishing for inclusion, and he labeled F♯ minor "banishment of protagonist."[23] In his later
study, the tale simply confirms his narrative and harmonic intuition. Many –
besides Pesic – would likely agree with his choice of metaphors. As Jeffrey
Perry emphatically stated: "Schubert's music is the music of a wanderer."[24]

In one of the most far-reaching reassessments of Schubert's harmony,
Cohn understood his hexatonic model to offer a systematic account of
those Schubertian moments traditionally seen as tonally "indeterminate,"
"arbitrary," "aimless," and "puzzling."[25] His cycles were precisely designed
to clarify the logic behind the harmonies that Fisk and Pesic take to
represent wandering and banishment, to illuminate the modulations that
Adorno says occlude daylight, and to expose the trade secrets behind what
Kurth views as Romantic magic.

Cohn's interest in the hexatonic cycles stems from his fascination with
the properties of the core transformations available amongst major and
minor triads with minimum pitch displacement and maximum common
tone retension. These conditions yield only three transformations, P, L, R,
which have been described earlier in this book. From C major, the first
corresponds to the parallel tonic, the second to the mediant minor, and
the third to the relative minor. Put this way, the latter two transformations
are diatonic – the first brings about the diatonic mediant, the second goes
to the familiar relative key. However, neo-Riemannian models are generally
intended to explain chromatic mediants, which are not well served by
diatonic theory. Thus, it is by combining P with L or R, as in LP or PL
and RP or PR, that chromatic mediants are produced. To illustrate how this
works, we may take C major as our starting point: LP produces E+ and PL

---

[22] Cohn, "As Wonderful as Star Clusters," 218.

[23] Fisk, "What Schubert's Last Sonata Might Hold," 180 and 199.

[24] Jeffrey Perry, "The Wanderer's Many Returns: Schubert's Variations Reconsidered," *Journal of Musicology* 19 (2002): 374. Other notable linkings of Schubert's music with metaphors of wandering include William Kinderman, "Wandering Archetypes in Schubert's Instrumental Music," *19th-Century Music* 21 (1997): 208–222; Harald Krebs, "Wandern und Heimkehr: Zentrifugale und Zentripetale Tendenzen in Schuberts Frühen Liedern," *Musiktheorie* 13 (1998): 111–122; and Nicholas Marston, "Schubert's Homecoming."

[25] Cohn, "As Wonderful as Star Clusters," 213, 214, and 231.

produces A♭ major; RP produces A major and PR produces E♭ major. Cohn's hexatonic cycles focus on the L and P combination as a cyclic subset of the LPR transformations. His interest in these stems from their unique property: L and P, unlike R, both involve a single semitone displacement (sometimes called SSD for short).

Indeed, the hexatonic cycle spells out the incremental SSD moves from triad to triad, which, as shown in the topmost cycle of the cylinder in Example 1 of the Introduction to this book, goes through C+, C−, A♭+, A♭−, E+, E−, C+ or PLPLPL. This clockwise direction around the cycle emphasizes repeated ♭VI moves for which Schubert and numerous other nineteenth-century composers are so famous. The tonic cycle for the Sonata in B♭ Major may also be found in the Introduction's Example 1. As can be plainly seen from the diagram, F♯ minor is on the opposite side of the cycle to B♭ major; it is the "hexatonic pole."[26]

Cohn's theory has disconcerted many scholars. Most notably, in the issue of *19th-Century Music* following the publication of Cohn's analysis, Fisk responded that he would not be using Cohn's theory any time soon. He objected to Cohn's "economical" designations, arguing that they "may have the effect of making even the most extraordinary progressions in Schubert seem ordinary – or at least, in some aspects, normative."[27] He prefers instead the diatonic framework's "awkward designations" for Schubert's chromatic keys, citing in particular the relationship of F♯ minor to B♭ major. The "enharmonically respelled minor triad on the lower sixth degree" is, to him, more helpful to hermeneutics than Cohn's designation "polar key of the tonic" which, Fisk says "obscures" the "drama" that he finds inherent in the diatonic description.[28]

Indeed Cohn himself hinted that his theory of hexatonic cycles challenges the status quo of the discourse and aesthetic judgement associated with Schubert's music since the early nineteenth century: "The method [the hexatonic model], to the extent that it furnishes satisfactory systematic contexts for these passages, problematizes such attributions [of aimlessness etc.] and *ipso facto*, the aesthetic or ethical judgments or *Zeitgeist* resonances to which they give rise."[29] In short, Cohn believes his new music theory has the capacity to shift our perception of what Schubert's music means. A systematic analytical description is unlikely to bring to mind metaphors

---

[26] The hexatonic model is laid out in Cohn, "Maximally Smooth Cycles, Hexatonic Systems, and the Analysis of Late-Romantic Triadic Progressions," *Music Analysis* 15 (1996): 9–40.

[27] Fisk, "Comment & Chronicle," 301. Fisk's criticism of Cohn, followed by the latter's response, appears in "Comment & Chronicle," *19th-Century Music* 23 (2000): 301–304.

[28] Fisk, "Comment & Chronicle," 302.   [29] Cohn, "As Wonderful as Star Clusters," 214.

of aimlessness, enigma, magic, or even somnambulism. Or indeed, with tonal map in hand, the wanderer protagonist in the B♭ Sonata is all too likely to make his way home.

This raises a new point to my discussion in Chapter 2 about the power that music theory wields in shaping musical hermeneutics. When nineteenth-century critics could not make sense of Schubert's harmonic architecture, they concluded that his intuition had misguided him into illogical digressions. While the metaphors of wandering, enigma, mirage, will-o'-the-wisp, and magic all seem strikingly close to the accusations of nineteenth-century critics, Fisk and all the other scholars mentioned in the previous paragraphs embrace the reversal of the nineteenth-century critical and aesthetic judgement of Schubert's music. They celebrate, rather than condemn, Schubert's harmonic practice. His music is not *really* aimless or wandering or enigmatic, but is carefully constructed to sound that way.

Cohn reveals this careful construction, at least as exhibited in the first movement of the B♭ Sonata. The problem, thus, is not so much with Cohn's theory as with attitudes towards theorizing Schubert's harmony. The problem has to do with the perennial belief that intuition may yield to analysis, but analysis does not lead to intuition. And this, I believe, explains the reluctance of many Schubert scholars to embrace Cohn's theory of hexatonic cycles – in contrast to scholars analyzing other composers who have not been saddled with a reception history of intuition, clairvoyance, or somnambulism. Nonetheless, there are ways in which Cohn is right and yet overstates the capacity for his theory to alter perceptions of musical meaning. In order to illuminate what I mean by this last claim, I need to conclude my examination of Pesic's and Fisk's hermeneutic analyses of the B♭ Sonata, and to survey quickly the meanings they draw out of the rest of the movement.

As with all of Schubert's three-keyed expositions in a major key, this one ends in the dominant, F major. Belonging as it so clearly does to the realm of the "home" tonic, the moment seems ready made for an interpretation that links this section to the protagonist's first return home after the mother's death, as told in "Mein Traum." Fisk therefore chooses to characterize it as a "quest for inclusion," while Pesic suggests that

the mysterious cloud around G♭ has dispersed, leaving us with a calm and simple second theme. This simplicity recalls the warm "family singing" of the initial theme ... After the shadow of F♯ minor, this simplicity comes as a relief, a reassurance that nothing terrible has happened and that we can return to the untroubled warmth with which we began.[30]

[30] Fisk, *Returning Cycles*, 254 and Pesic, "Schubert's Dream," 140.

According to these readings, the bulk of the tale has been represented within the exposition. Remaining in the tale are the second banishment and final reconciliation; remaining in the sonata are the lengthy development and recapitulation. The harmonic adventure of the development and return to the tonic of the recapitulation both seem good fits for a banishment and reconciliation. However, the latter certainly seems to depend more on the abstract notion that recapitulations bring everything back to the tonic in a kind of tonal reconciliation than it does on the Schubertian habit of including non-tonic adventures in his recapitulations (the story would have to read that the protagonist was reconciled with his father, but was never entirely happy or settled at home). Indeed, such lack of attention to the details of the recapitulation is symptomatic of the scholarly habit of considering recapitulations the "et cetera" of musical form, whose outcome is more or less formulaic. In Schubert's sonata forms, recapitulations are far from formulaic, though certain patterns emerge and even become predictable.[31]

The only difference between Pesic's and Fisk's reading of how the tale maps onto the music is in their choices of key for the second banishment. Fisk places it at the very opening of the development (in C♯ minor); Pesic puts it at the very end (in D minor). There is, however, a similar logic to their choices. Both keys support statements of the first theme, both recast the major mode of the theme into the minor, and both function as some kind of submediant.

Fisk's interpretation has the advantage that the harmonic relationship of the second banishment exactly replicates the first, albeit transposed up a fifth. The progression to C♯ minor from F major therefore functions again "as if suddenly taking the protagonist back into exile" and, once there, its presentation of the first thematic material represents a "memory and reflection in exile."[32] This reading beautifully takes care of both the parallel harmonic move and the fact that we now hear the opening lyrical theme (the first banishment, it will be recalled, involved new thematic material). Indeed it is hard not to be tempted, as Fisk was, by the parallel between the opening of the development and the protagonist's singing while in exile,

---

[31] Important exceptions to the general scholarly trend mentioned above are Hascher and Hinrichsen, who both give careful and fairly exhaustive consideration to Schubert's recapitulations. See Hascher, *Schubert: la forme sonate* and Hinrichsen, *Untersuchungen* and "Die Sonatenform im Spätwerk Franz Schuberts," *Archiv für Musikwissenschaft* 45 (1988): 16–49.

[32] Fisk, *Returning Cycles*, 247 and 254. In addition to the key's relationship with its surrounding harmonies, there are external reasons for assuming such a meaning: "Der Wanderer" (D. 489) opens in C♯ minor; for an expanded list of other associations of C♯ minor and wandering, see Harald Krebs, review of Fisk's *Returning Cycles* in *Music Theory Spectrum* 25 (2003): 390.

especially as the major-key lyrical theme is now recast in the minor: "What musical pattern could correspond more perfectly to the singing-in-exile of 'Mein Traum' – to its pain turning to love, and its love to pain?"[33]

Pesic also argues that the harmonic move of the second banishment duplicates the first, though he has a convoluted way of demonstrating it. His argument hinges on finding a pattern of "sixths" in Schubert's array of keys, a pattern that unfortunately confuses harmonic moves to the sub-mediant with moves by the interval of a sixth. The slip perhaps prompted his idiosyncratic nomenclature for chains of descending thirds, which he incorrectly calls "circles of *sixths*." At any rate, important to Pesic's narra-tive reading is that similar rotations of "sixths," by which he means cycles of major thirds, have similar meanings. Pesic argues that the second banish-ment in the sonata is a submediant move from the first one: D minor "marks the second move around what I call the 'circle of sixths'; it parallels the second banishment [in the tale]." It can hardly escape notice that Pesic's analysis is a thinly disguised version of Cohn's hexatonic cycles.[34]

The point to be drawn from these narrative readings of the Sonata in B♭ Major is that extramusical meaning is understood to be primarily encoded in the harmony – and that music theory plays a vital role in unlocking the harmonic code. That is to say, diatonic or closely related keys represent home and reconciliation, while chromatic or remote keys represent exile or banishment. This observation seems uncontroversial enough, perhaps even banal. Indeed such interpretations of tonal space have a strong pedigree: witness their invention in Joseph Riepel, who anthropomorphized the six most common diatonic keys according to the social and economic status of people on a farm, involving therefore a master (C major), overseer (G major), head maid (A minor), day laborer (F major), chambermaid

---

[33] Fisk, *Returning Cycles*, 256.

[34] Pesic, "Schubert's Dream," 140–141. Pesic's analysis is marred in several places by similar slips between scale steps and intervals: he writes: "Although these examples sometime use melodic thirds, for simplicity I shall call them sequences of sixths, since each stage in the sequence can be expressed harmonically as ♭VI of the preceding stage" (p. 142). Nonetheless, his basic argument (that Schubert's chains of major thirds deserve greater attention) is a cogent one. He analyzes the cycle F♯ minor – D minor – B♭ major as ♭vi–♭vi/♭vi–♭VI/♭vi/♭vi. Strictly speaking, an interpretation of these compound submediant harmonic moves within a diatonic framework, but assuming enharmonic equivalence, yields: ♭vi–vi/♭vi–VI/vi/♭vi. That is to say D minor in relation to F♯ minor is strictly vi, not ♭vi, and B♭ major in relation to D minor is VI. Cohn's hexatonic model bypasses these very problems, labeling the transformations between harmonies, rather than the harmonies themselves in light of *Stufen* and mode. In place of Pesic's labels, one might, following Cohn, use one of three taxonomies starting from B♭: PLP–LP–L or H–LP–L or T_3–T_2–T_1.

(E minor), and errand girl (D minor).[35] Put this way (even if we modernize Riepel's social group), harmonic theory seems a very blunt instrument. Nonetheless we often turn to characterizations of keys, based on their distance from the tonic, and from there devise extramusical narratives.

The Sonata in B♭ Major contains a number of instances where such prescribed theoretical meanings are problematized by a key's presentation on the surface of the music – not least the tonic itself. There are no fewer than three instances where the tonic B♭ major does not sound like a tonic; it does not embody the "home" key. Neither of the returns to B♭ major sounds like a tonic in the ABA′ statements in the exposition and recapitulation. In the case of the exposition, the second inversion lends B♭ a dominant feel. In the case of the recapitulation, Nicholas Marston has shown in a brilliant analysis of surface detail that the harmonic preparation into the root-position B♭ major turns it into a flattened submediant. With this harmony no longer expressing the default tonic function, Marston interprets it as an uncanny homecoming, transformed as it is from a tonic "into something rich and strange."[36]

B♭ major is also rendered strange when it appears in the middle section of the miniature ABA′ section at the end of the development. Encased within two statements of the first theme in D minor, it again functions as a submediant. Tovey remarked that a lesser composer would have used this B♭ as the real recapitulation "and think himself clever," as if the key's default status as tonic would be enough to do the trick.[37] As Fisk points out, there are other, more aurally immediate features to explain why this moment would unquestionably be heard as a false reprise: the melody is up an octave and the accompaniment all happens above middle C. The passage therefore "feels more like the song of the exiled protagonist, the lonely wanderer, than like the theme in its more choral, more angelic initial form. The texture, too, is soloistic, like that of the second strain's first, still angelic occurrence," and it is "more like a memory than a true return to the opening phrase."[38] Pesic hears the passage similarly: "Its return in this

---

[35] Riepel's theory of tonal space appears in *Grundregeln zur Tonordnung insgemein* (1755). For a quick summary of various social power relations inscribed in tonal spaces, see Brian Hyer, "Tonality," in Thomas Christensen (ed.), *Cambridge History of Music Theory* (Cambridge University Press, 2002), 731. Hyer has also astutely observed that even the apparently less affective language of formalism is "social in basis."

[36] See Marston, "Schubert's Homecoming," 257–264. For other examples of tonic illusions in Schubert's music, see L. Poundie Burstein, "Devil's Castles and Schubert's Strange Tonic Allusions," *Theory and Practice* 27 (2002): 69–84.

[37] Tovey, "Franz Schubert," 119.

[38] Fisk, *Returning Cycles*, 252 and "What Schubert's Last Sonata Might Hold," 193.

way has a beautiful irreality, as if one were seeing double: the tonic returned at last, and yet not the tonic."[39]

These instances illustrate that no theory of key relations supplies ready-made answers to musical meaning: even the tonic may not at times seem like the "home" key. Surface-level details have the capacity to undermine the default position of any theory's definition of tonal space. In Schubert's music, the details always count.

Yet it was undoubtedly the general habit of assuming that harmonic theory prescribes default meanings for key relations that accounts for why Fisk reacted so swiftly and strongly to Cohn's invention of a new theory of tonal space, and his application of it to the Piano Sonata in B♭ Major. Fisk worries that, if Cohn's theory were to catch on, cherished narratives surrounding Schubert's music might no longer register as appropriate. Indeed, the emergence of awkward descriptions according to the diatonic system implies that the harmony is "out of bounds" in relation to the inner harmonic field, a technical observation that leads Fisk seamlessly to interpret the section as representing the "banishment of the protagonist"; similarly, the arrival of the conventional dominant at the end of the exposition, as a key close to "home," leads Fisk to speak of the protagonist's "quest for reinclusion."[40] As we can see, analytical nomenclature is a potent force in hermeneutics. Cohn's designations are evidently too clinical for Fisk to generate the kind of narrative he envisioned for the movement. Thus, while Cohn had heralded his theory as a new instrument – like a sophisticated telescope – that allows a fresh look at Schubert's harmonic procedures, Fisk insisted he would continue to use his more modest binoculars of diatonic theory. With music theory frozen in time, hermeneutics would be saved.

However, it so happens that Cohn's theoretical explanation of the F♯ minor passage can still support a reading of banishment. As the hexatonic pole to B♭ major, F♯ minor is the farthest transformation within the cycle. The fact that it has no tones in common with the tonic is the very gauge of its distance, given that the hexatonic model is based on how displaced and common tones are handled. Moreover, in an article that scans the literature from Gesualdo to Monteverdi, Haydn, Schubert, Wagner, Grieg, Strauss, Sibelius, Puccini, Ravel, and Schoenberg for uses of hexatonic poles, Cohn has convincingly shown that composers associated the progression with death, magic, and hell's spirits, and that in the nineteenth century it signified the uncanny. The consistency of these readings seems to support Fisk's interpretation of banishment, although Cohn's history of associations

---

[39] Pesic, "Schubert's Dream," 141.   [40] Fisk, *Returning Cycles*, 254.

might suggest an even more sinister reading behind the move to F♯ minor.[41] Although Cohn's hexatonic system organizes the triadic data in such a radically different way from traditional diatonic theory, the perception of Schubert's harmony is not in this case altered out of all recognition, as Fisk claims. It remains distant, but the distance is "measured" differently – namely by semitone displacements rather than scale steps.

The same cannot be said, however, for Cohn's superimposition of the tonic, dominant, and subdominant functions onto three of the four cycles (the four cycles in question may be found in Example 1 of the Introduction to this book).[42] Cohn's model, as specifically exemplified in his article on Schubert, reckons B♭ major, G♭ major, F♯ minor, and D minor all to belong to a single, tonic cycle, and F major and C♯ minor to belong to another, dominant cycle. In one theoretical stroke, the movement seems threaded together; harmonies belong; they have their place. How, one might legitimately ask, can one speak of alienation and wandering in the wake of such an analysis? How, ultimately, are we to decide what the music means?

In short, the difference of opinion between Fisk and Cohn is about the status of music theory. It problematizes the accepted methodology of hermeneutics and the assumption that tonal space dictates narratives. An important point may be made to assuage Fisk's anxiety, however. Schubert's music – or any other music, for that matter – does not lose its meaning in the wake of clearer theoretical explanation. As we shall see in the course of this chapter, the suspicion that this might be the case pervades the literature on Schubert. The assumption that nebulous-sounding music must be explained nebulously, and that precise-sounding music must be explained with precision is a fallacy. Indeed, most scholars nowadays are at pains to point out that the dream-like quality of Schubert's music is the result of careful calculation, and I shall point to many instances of this claim in this chapter. The job of the music theorist, surely, is to explain that careful calculation. While diatonic theory is certainly conducive to

---

[41] Cohn, "Uncanny Resemblances: Tonal Signification in the Freudian Age," *Journal of the American Musicological Society* 57 (2004): 285–323.

[42] This is not the most compelling aspect of Cohn's model, as applied to Schubert's music. Cohn writes in a footnote (Cohn, "As Wonderful as Star Clusters," 219 n. 20): "the notion of 'region' suggested here generalizes Riemann's harmonic functions in the spirit of Ernö Lendvai's 'axis tonality,' but along different lines. Lendvai focuses on the functional equivalence of pitch-classes related by minor third, where the regions of fig. 4 [in Cohn's article] suggest functional equivalence between harmonies whose roots are related by major third." Indeed. But even a forgiving skeptic might be alarmed to find that opinions about something as apparently fundamental as functions could diverge so drastically, yet invite so little comment. Lendvai's theory is explained in *Béla Bartók: An Analysis of His Music* (London: Kahn & Averill, 1971).

metaphors of wandering and somnambulism in the case of the B♭ Sonata, a more systematized account of the attributes of Schubert's sound world will not suddenly make the music sound "purposeful" or "awake."

And this brings me back to the material of Chapter 1, for the stifled condition of music theory in Schubert studies owes much to the belief that the sound of Schubert's music (and especially its harmonic design) represents how it was composed and how it should be absorbed in performance and interpreted. This may seem an alarming statement given the sheer quantity of analytical studies that have called for new perspectives on Schubert's sonata forms over the past century.[43] But the persistence of diatonic thinking within Schubert scholarship despite an equally persistent call – often within the same study – for Schubert's music to be understood "on its own terms" is a contradiction that will occupy my attention throughout the rest of this chapter.

The Schubertian, or the non-Beethovenian

In a seminal article published in 1978 on Schubert's String Quartet in G Major (D. 887), Carl Dahlhaus called for a redefinition of sonata form, acknowledging, as many had before him (and as many have again since), that Schubert's practice exhibits a distinctive formal dynamic. He argued that the standard theory of sonata form, shaped as it was according to Beethoven's practice, is not equipped to analyze Schubert's music. Explicitly influenced by Theodor Adorno's perspective on Mahler and August Halm's on Bruckner, he identified Schubert's sonata form type as "lyric-epic," in contrast to Beethoven's, which he saw as "dramatic-dialectic."[44] In the

---

[43] This chapter will examine many of these, so I will forgo additional citation here.

[44] Dahlhaus's article originally appeared as "Die Sonatenform bei Schubert: Der erste Satz des G-dur Quartetts D887," *Musica* 32 (1978): 125–130. I shall refer to its translation: "Sonata Form in Schubert: The First Movement of the G-Major String Quartet, op. 161 (D. 887)," trans. Thilo Reinhard, in Walter Frisch (ed.), *Schubert: Critical and Analytical Studies* (Lincoln and London: University of Nebraska Press, 1986), 1–12. Schumann was perhaps the first to champion Schubert's treatment of sonata form as worthy in its own right. For an excellent overview of how Schumann developed this opinion, see John Daverio, *Robert Schumann: Herald of a "New Poetic Age"* (Oxford University Press, 1997), 43–54. As we saw in Chapter 1, however, Schubert's biographers Kreissle and Grove shared the prevailing view of Schubert's instrumental works at the time: they were perplexed by his large-scale forms and considered them flawed. In addition to being influenced by Adorno and Halm, Dahlhaus may have seen his essay as overturning Salzer's and perhaps even Hans Gal's view that Schubert's lyricism was incompatible with the essential dramatic, goal-oriented quality of sonata form; see Salzer, "Die Sonatenform bei Franz Schubert," 125 and Hans Gal, *Franz Schubert and the Essence of Melody* (London: Victor Gollancz Ltd., 1974), 103 and 111–115.

course of his close analysis of the first movement of Schubert's G Major String Quartet, he identified numerous Schubertian features, most notably the variation cycles that make up the thematic groups and the ubiquitous quality of reminiscence.

Also in 1978, James Webster produced an encyclopedic study of over forty sonata form movements by Schubert, with the aim of uncovering the full range of Schubertian formal traits. He looked at every corner of the form: how Schubert closes the first thematic units; what key relationships obtain between the ends of the transitions and the beginnings of secondary thematic groups; how expositions close; how developments are structured; what strategies Schubert employs for recapitulations. Contrary to what many had deduced before him, Webster declared that Schubert's principles of sonata form are "logical" and "subtle."[45] In 1978, Schubert's sonata form was thus poised to come into its own.

However, neither Dahlhaus nor Webster fully managed to achieve a new Schubertian definition of form, despite their important insights into his formal habits. Even as Webster admitted that Schubert had an "aversion to the dominant," he adopted the Schenkerian method – in which the dominant could not be more vital – in order to elucidate Schubert's treatment of form.[46] Schubert's non-dominant salient harmonies are shown as middleground to the dominant's background, as is standard practice in Schenkerian interpretations. Schubert's most glorious moments therefore lurk in the shadow of the *Ursatz*, paying the price that Cohn refers to, namely re-inscribing the idea that his music is full of digressions and unrestrained lyricism. Similarly for Dahlhaus, as we shall see at greater length here. He set out to elucidate Schubert's particular handling of variation technique and musical representation of memory. However, a close reading of the article reveals not so much a definition of Schubert's idiosyncracies as Dahlhaus's own obsession with that quintessential Beethovenian trait of motivic development. Midway through the article, he expresses "surprise" at the complexity of the motivic relations in Schubert's work. Surprise turns to praise, as, in the end, he concludes that the complex web of motives "vindicates" Schubert's strategy of form.[47]

Every section of the quartet's first movement comes under Dahlhaus's scrutiny, from the motivic construction of the first and second thematic areas in the exposition, to the large-scale thematic and harmonic processes of the development, to the reshaping of the material in the recapitulation.

---

[45] Webster, "Schubert's Sonata Form," 35.   [46] Webster, "Schubert's Sonata Form," 22.
[47] Dahlhaus, "Sonata Form in Schubert," 7 and 12.

Each section is compared to what Beethoven would do: how he would generate his themes, how he would offset their character yet link their essentials, how he would shape his development and recapitulation sections. By isolating those aspects in Schubert's quartet that Dahlhaus thought properly corresponded to the principle of sonata form (nay, to Beethoven's practice), Dahlhaus identified in the fallout the lyric-epic qualities that make the quartet Schubertian – a strategy that means that the Schubertian consistently emerges as the non-Beethovenian.

Dahlhaus argues that the first thematic group "obeys the rule of sonata form" insofar as it divides into four sections with the recognizable functions of antecedent (mm. 15–23), consequent (mm. 24–32), elaboration (mm. 33–53) and transition (mm. 54–63).[48] The introduction (mm. 1–14) is not recognizably structured, an observation which is crucial to an intuition he has about how Schubert generates the quality of reminiscence – a point to which I shall return. By contrast, Walter Frisch has since identified a sentence structure in the introduction, albeit one that is highly transformed. He too invokes Beethoven – with the added clout of music theory. Frisch hears Schubert's sentence structure as transformed from the Beethovenian model of the Sonata in F Minor, Op. 2, No. 1, as immortalized by Arnold Schoenberg's theory. Specifically, Schubert's phrase structure is a reminiscence of the abstract structural formula.[49]

Dahlhaus shared Frisch's ambition to view the opening introduction of the quartet as thematic, but, by contrast, he had thought it necessary to abandon the Beethovenian notion of a theme as a structural entity, as in the sentence. He replaced it with the notion of "thematic configuration" ("thematische Konfiguration"), meaning a theme made of a "multitude of elements." This did not mean he abandoned Beethoven in defining the Schubertian, however: this new definition of theme also has its model in Beethoven – conveniently in one of his theme and variations.[50]

In Classical variation form, a relatively melodic "theme," presented in a clear binary or rounded binary form, invites elaboration through various ornamental figurations and new accompaniment patterns in the variations. As Dahlhaus (and Beethoven himself) pointed out, Beethoven's Piano

---

[48] Dahlhaus, "Sonata Form in Schubert," 2.

[49] Walter Frisch, "'You Must Remember This': Memory and Structure in Schubert's String Quartet in G major, D. 887," *Musical Quarterly* 84 (2000): 584–585. Schoenberg's analysis of Beethoven's sentence structure appears in *Fundamentals of Musical Composition*, ed. Gerald Strang and Leonard Stein (London: Faber and Faber, 1967), 20–24.

[50] Dahlhaus explored the concept of "thematic configuration" in Op. 35 and the *Eroica* symphony, as well as Opp. 31, No. 2 and 59, No. 3, in "Beethovens 'Neuer Weg,'" *Jahrbuch des Staatlichen Instituts für Musikforschung Preußischer Kulturbesitz* (Berlin, 1975): 46–62.

Example 3.3 The major–minor shift, dotted-rhythm, and descending half-step motives in Schubert, String Quartet in G Major (D. 887), first movement, mm. 1–5

Variations, Op. 35, depart from the standard variation technique.[51] Later coined the "Eroica" Variations for their reuse in the Third Symphony's finale, Op. 35 has as its "theme" a melody, a bass, and a harmonic-metrical gesture, which are presented one after the other at the outset of the work. Multiple run-throughs of the binary structure gradually reveal that these different strands work together in a complex whole. Once all elements of the theme are finally stated together, they are once again parsed out for the ensuing variations.

According to Dahlhaus, Schubert's presentation of the motivic material in the String Quartet in G Major is similar. There are three motivic elements, each presented in succession within the first five measures of the movement. As shown in Example 3.3, there is a major–minor shift, a dotted-rhythmic pattern, and a descending half step.[52] It is questionable whether taking this kind of motivic approach to Schubert's music is either fair or necessary. Schubert is hardly known for constructing his music through intricate motivic means (just as, for example, Mozart was less

---

[51] Dahlhaus, "Sonata Form in Schubert," 4 and 9.

[52] Dahlhaus, "Sonata Form in Schubert," 4–5. These are the measures that Frisch called the "basic idea" of the sentence structure. Strictly speaking a "b.i" (to use William Caplin's terminology) should consist of one idea (hence its name) and only two measures. Although it is clearly repeated in the dominant, which is another hallmark of the sentence structure, the presence of a "multitude of elements" is presumably what prevented Dahlhaus from analyzing the introduction through a Schoenbergian lens as Frisch did; see Caplin, *Classical Form: A Theory of Formal Functions for the Instrumental Music of Haydn, Mozart, and Beethoven* (Oxford University Press, 1998), 9–12.

motivically minded than Haydn). Persisting with this approach speaks more to Dahlhaus's assumption that motivic work is the essential constitution of sonata form composition than it does to his commitment to redefine Schubert's sonata form from the bottom up. Nonetheless Schubert survives this particular scrutiny: Dahlhaus declares that the three elements develop in "a musical chain of logic" that permeates not only the first group but the whole movement, a process which, as mentioned earlier, "vindicates" Schubert's form.[53]

Despite a purposeful unfolding of material, the apparently teleological elements mingle with the epic, which in Dahlhaus's estimation prevents Schubert's music from being goal-oriented. That is to say, some teleological energy is aroused through the tight fabric of the motivic ideas. However, Dahlhaus explains that they are largely "devoid" of forward drive because they often function as reminiscences and occur in variation cycles.[54] Beethoven's "dramatic-dialectic" practice mixes logic with pathos, defined respectively as motivic-thematic generation and the energy of forward-driving development.[55] Dahlhaus points out how easy it is to assume that these two ingredients are inextricably linked. They are in fact separable, he wants us to know. While Schubert's music employs a perceptible "logic" of motivic-thematic generation, it lacks the "pathos" or energy that presses it forward. Beethoven's music presses *ahead*, proceeding from earlier to later events. Schubert's music depends on *remembrance*, which "turns from later events back to earlier ones."[56] Of course, the music unfolds in each case in the same direction – from beginning to end – but Beethoven's music is understood in a forward direction, while Schubert's music is understood to reflect back. I shall interrogate these observations shortly – especially as they have been taken up in recent scholarship – but first I shall scrutinize further Dahlhaus's views about Schubert's variation technique.

The four sections (antecedent, consequent, elaboration, transition) within the first thematic group and the four repetitions of the theme within the secondary group relate to each other as variations – but, Dahlhaus felt compelled to add, in a manner wholly different from that attained by Beethoven a few years earlier in the self-proclaimed "completely new way"

---

[53] Dahlhaus, "Sonata Form in Schubert," 6 and 2.

[54] Dahlhaus, "Sonata Form in Schubert," 6–9. See also Dahlhaus, *Nineteenth-Century Music*, trans. J. Bradford Robinson (Berkeley and Los Angeles: University of California Press, 1989), 153, where he similarly concludes that the opening lied-like melody of the *Unfinished* Symphony "strikes a lyric tone . . . which invites the listener to dally and which is inconsistent in equal measure with both the dramatic and the monumental side of Beethoven's symphonic style."

[55] Dahlhaus, "Sonata Form in Schubert," 7.   [56] Dahlhaus, "Sonata Form in Schubert," 8.

of his "Eroica" Variations.[57] Again, we seem poised to learn how Schubert was distinctive in his treatment of variations, but the real question remains: why does Dahlhaus bring Op. 35 into the discussion at all? To be sure, Beethoven is often credited with transcending what is generally assumed to be the inherently non-organic nature of theme and variations, non-organic because of their closed and repetitive form.[58] This "new way" inspired him to create other monumental sets of variations that exhibit his characteristic irreversible teleological trajectory, the most notable example of which is none other than the reworking of Op. 35 for the finale of the *Eroica* Symphony. But why compare Schubert's practice to a novel Beethovenian one?

At first blush, it may seem that, in limiting himself to a comparison of Schubert's music with a set of Beethoven's piano variations, Dahlhaus was making a concession, anticipating accusations of unfairness were he to hold Schubert's quartet up to a symphony – particularly *that* symphony. Yet Dahlhaus intended no concession here. It was undeniably the declaration of the "new way" that drew him to Op. 35. To be sure, by the time Schubert wrote his quartet, a teleological approach to variation had been pioneered by Beethoven and was therefore available to Schubert, but Dahlhaus seems to have dodged the most obvious point of comparison. Just prior to comparing Schubert to Beethoven's variation technique, he had restored Schubert into a tradition of sonata form composition by pointing out that his variation-cycle construction of the quartet's first and second themes followed the variation-*cum*-sonata techniques of his predecessors and had a future in Brahms and Mahler. In this historical narrative, Beethoven is construed as the odd one out, diverging from the historical trend to which Schubert, arguably, not only belonged, but to which he so obviously made an important contribution. Instead, by raising Beethoven's Op. 35, Dahlhaus traps Schubert (like everyone else) in a binary opposition with Beethoven. In Dahlhaus's preferred narrative, Schubert's variation tradition (and everyone else's) "deviates substantially from the evolutionary path dictated by Beethoven."[59]

---

[57] Dahlhaus, "Sonata Form in Schubert," 4. Hans Gal also attempted to articulate the difference between Beethoven's and Schubert's approach to variations by pointing to the former's preference for the term "*Veränderungen*," which suggests transformations of a theme, compared to Schubert's intensification of a theme that remains largely unchanged. See Hans Gal, *Franz Schubert and the Essence of Melody*, 56.

[58] For a particularly elegant analysis of the thread that makes Op. 74's slow movement organic, see also Nicholas Marston, "Analysing Variations: The Finale of Beethoven's String Quartet op. 74," *Music Analysis* 8 (1989): 303–324.

[59] Dahlhaus, "Sonata Form in Schubert," 4. As Dahlhaus's endorsement of the "twin styles" demonstrates, he was deeply committed to this narrative; see *Nineteenth-Century Music*, 8–15 and

Information in the article about the specific characteristics of Schubert's variation technique is scant. What Dahlhaus did have to say, however, seems to have been inspired by Adorno's anniversary essay on Schubert or possibly by A. B. Marx. Although Dahlhaus did not mention either, his reading resonates with Adorno's image of a wanderer going around in circles in a barren landscape and of variations cast in different harmonic stations so that the themes may be illuminated in different "atmospheric perspectives."[60] Marx similarly defined variation as "a succession of repetitions of a *Liedsatz* (*theme*) in constantly altered presentations – the consideration of the same idea from different perspectives, its application in a different sense."[61] Adorno additionally spoke of an "ex-centric construction of that landscape, in which every point is equally close to the center, [and] reveals itself to the wanderer walking round it with no actual progress."[62] Dahlhaus rephrases these ideas. According to him, Schubert draws "circles, ever expanding circles, around the theme," which "resembles a commentary 'meandering' about the theme, illuminating it from different sides."[63]

These cyclical qualities are particularly noticeable in the second thematic group of the first movement of the G Major String Quartet, which seems to form a genuine harmonic circle. The transition ends with an F♯ major chord, and the ensuing statements of the theme are in D major and B♭ major. Another transition revisits the F♯ major chord before the final statement is sounded once again in D major. The harmonic trajectory F♯–D–B♭–F♯–D forms a hexatonic cycle.

The fourfold repetition of the theme is precisely the kind of non-economical Schubertian habit that led early critics to regard Schubert's music as flawed. Yet Adorno made a remarkably obvious point: given Schubert's fertile melodic invention, he could so easily have conjured up endless different tunes instead of repeating himself. The repetition must therefore be deliberate. According to Adorno, then, the point of Schubert's repetitions is precisely to encounter "repeated features in new lighting":

"Franz Schubert und das 'Zeitalter Beethovens und Rossinis,'" in *Franz Schubert: Jahre der Krise, 1818–1823*, eds. Werner Aderhold, Walther Dürr, and Walburga Litschauer (Kassel: Bärenreiter, 1985), 22–28. On the fate of Schubert in relation to the twin styles of Beethoven and Rossini, see my "Beethoven and Rossini in the Reception of Schubert," *The Age of Beethoven and Rossini*, ed. Nicholas Mathew and Benjamin Walton (Cambridge University Press, in press).

[60] Compare Dahlhaus, "Sonata Form in Schubert," 2 and 9 to Adorno, "Schubert," 10–11.

[61] A. B. Marx, *Musical Form in the Age of Beethoven: Selected Writings on Theory and Method*, ed. and trans. Scott G. Burnham (Cambridge University Press, 1997), 86. Italics original.

[62] Adorno, "Schubert," 10.

[63] Dahlhaus compares Schubert and Beethoven in this respect in "Sonata Form in Schubert," 2.

It would be insane to explain this recurrence [of themes] as some kind of fixation in this musician who could have found hundreds of other themes in his almost excessively trumpeted melodic treasure chest; the wanderer encounters these repeated features in new lighting – they are timeless and appear to be disconnected, isolated. This scenario concerns not only the repeated use of the same theme in different pieces, but in actual fact the very make-up of Schubertian form.[64]

Standard definitions of sonata form are not suited to Adorno's insight. They emphasize expediency. According to such definitions, there seems little structural point to either the four statements of the secondary theme or the presence of B♭ major and D major after a statement of the theme had already been placed in the dominant.

Small wonder that Tovey concluded that the first movement of the String Quartet in G Major was full of "redundancies and diffuseness" or, as we saw in Chapter 1, that Mason used it as an example of Schubert's "flabbiness" of musical design.[65] The problem is particularly acute for Schenkerians, as the arrival of the dominant $\hat{2}$ during the first statement of the secondary theme completes the "task of the exposition," rendering the ensuing statements structurally unnecessary. Beach, Burstein, Hascher, Salzer, and Webster all place the structural dominant at the first statement of the theme.[66] The material after it spins off into a cycle of thirds (Beach) or the two dominants house a "diversion" or "purple patch" in ♭VI, although the cycle of thirds is also noted (Hascher, Webster, and Salzer). Or, in a unique analysis by Burstein, the final repetition of D major closes a I–III#3–V–I arpeggiation in D major, although this means that the thematic statement in B♭ is conspicuously absent at this structural level.[67]

---

[64] Adorno, "Schubert," 10. Tovey made the opposite point: while he admired Schubert's "masterly" means of bringing the unexpected keys of his second themes round to the expected key, he criticized Schubert's new themes. It would be better if Schubert were to "stick to the main themes and not dissipate energy on a multitude of new ones." Tovey, "Franz Schubert," 121–122.

[65] Tovey, "Franz Schubert" 119. See also Chapter 1.

[66] David Beach, "Modal Mixture and Schubert's Harmonic Practice," *Journal of Music Theory* 42 (1998): 98 and "Schubert's Experiments with Sonata Form: Formal-Tonal Design versus Underlying Structure," *Music Theory Spectrum* 15 (1993): 17, L. Poundie Burstein, "Lyricism, Structure, and Gender in Schubert's G Major String Quartet," *Musical Quarterly* 81 (1997): 51–63, Hascher, *Schubert: La forme sonate*, 162, Salzer, "Die Sonatenform bei Franz Schubert," 99, and Webster, "Schubert's Sonata Form," 21. I will revisit these readings of this movement of the quartet in Chapter 4. A fuller explanation of the role of the dominant as part of the "task of the exposition" is also given in Chapter 4.

[67] Visual representations of these analyses are given in Example 4.27. Burstein's unique approach may be viewed in Example 3.8c.

By explaining Schubert's propensity to repeat as "variation," Dahlhaus does at least seem to have succeeded in relieving such passages from implications of needless or "vain" (Tovey's word) repetitions.[68] Yet he does not succeed in making them purposeful either. He cannot ascertain why Schubert stopped the repetitions when he did, except to concede that the music must stop "somewhere," and only then because Schubert's self-indulgent, apparently involuntary repetitions must give way to the essential business of sonata form.[69] Dahlhaus does not even, for example, attempt to raise the practical point that the four variations serve to give each member of the quartet an opportunity to play the tune.

The notion of the involuntary relates to that thread of criticism which, as we saw in Chapter 1, has to do with the long tradition of seeing Schubert as a somnambulist or clairvoyant. Dahlhaus meets the problem of the involuntary again in the development: its "excessive length" breaks off the "largely limitless continuation" of the principal theme "*as if by chance*, not because a goal has been reached" (italics mine).[70] Accordingly, Schubert's music possesses an "element of the involuntary," an element entirely compatible with the composer's penchant for the "sensuous," for "timelessness," and for "endless lingering."[71] "*As if by chance*" is an important qualifier here, especially given the impression of Schubert's "involuntary" compositional process discussed in Chapter 1. It should be noted that Dahlhaus makes the important point (perhaps also inspired by Adorno) that Schubert's *music* possesses the element of the involuntary, not (also) Schubert himself: the involuntary is a matter of perception, not of compositional process. Indeed, he specifies that the compositional act involves the exact opposite to the aural effect: "What appears as involuntary occurrence nevertheless represents the outward manifestation of precise calculation; there is no question of unreflective composing."[72] But Dahlhaus does not tell us what this precise calculation is. He does not even attempt the task. Instead, after making this statement, Dahlhaus's article ends. Why end there?

---

[68] Tovey, "Franz Schubert," 122.

[69] See Dahlhaus, "Sonata Form in Schubert," 1 and 11.

[70] Dahlhaus, "Sonata Form in Schubert," 10.

[71] Dahlhaus, "Sonata Form in Schubert," 2, 7, and 8.

[72] Dahlhaus, "Sonata Form in Schubert," 12. Again there is a faint echo here of Adorno's article in Dahlhaus's. Adorno argued that the nineteenth-century transformation of Schubert's character into a "repulsive specimen of petit bourgeois sentimentality" led to a problematic musical hermeneutics, whereby either Schubert's compositional method or his psyche were regarded as reproduced in the material of the music. See Adorno, "Schubert," 8 and 10. On this topic, see also Esteban Buch, "Adorno's 'Schubert': From the Critique of the Garden Gnome to the Defense of Atonalism," *19th-Century Music* 29 (2005): 25–30.

Here we come to the crux of the analytical problem: Schubert's greatest Romantic statement – the creation of a music that projects intuition rather than reason, spontaneity rather than labor – reduces his analysts to silence. In fact, Dahlhaus was twice silenced. Perhaps it seems a contradiction to theorize the mechanics of intuition and spontaneity. The other time he pointed to the impression of the involuntary in Schubert's music was with regard to his motivic returns: the motivic "link between the themes is not deliberately brought about; it simply happens."[73] He does not explain how Schubert "calculates" this effect either. Instead, he makes this statement, and immediately changes the subject.

The involuntary is also the cornerstone of Dahlhaus's theory of Schubert's musical representation of reminiscence. On close inspection, this too suffers a lack of explanation, although Dahlhaus is careful to point out where to find it. Dahlhaus generally understood the nature of "remembrance" literally: one must hear something in the music more than once, so that later instances recall earlier ones.[74] Again, this means he defines reminiscence in Beethovenian motivic terms. He points to two examples in the String Quartet in G Major.

The first is cunningly phrased. Notice how subtly Dahlhaus proposes that the music harks back to previous events, rather than pressing ahead in a Beethovenian motivic manner:

When Schubert has the rhythm of the subsidiary theme (bar 65) emerge gradually during the principal group (bars 2, 34, 43, and 51), nothing prevents us from speaking of "contrasting derivation."[75]

Read Example 3.4 backwards, from right to left (not necessarily linearly so), in accordance with the first part of Dahlhaus's sentence, which mentions m. 65 first and then claims it emerges from its previous incarnations. This is

---

[73] Dahlhaus, "Sonata Form in Schubert," 8–9.

[74] An observation that Dahlhaus made about the opening five measures of the String Quartet in G Major puts into relief the usual confines he had in mind for Schubert's portrayal of memory. In these measures, the three elements that make up the introduction (see Example 3.3) are "related in the way that images of recollection overlap with one another." See Dahlhaus, "Sonata Form in Schubert," 9. This idea of what it feels like to remember – as opposed to pointing to specific memories – has been a fruitful line of inquiry in recent studies of memory. See especially Scott Burnham, "Schubert and the Sound of Memory," *Musical Quarterly* 84 (2000): 655–663.

[75] Dahlhaus, "Sonata Form in Schubert," 8. The sentence reads as follows in the original (p. 128): "Wenn Schubert in der Exposition des G-dur-Quartetts den Rhythmus des Seitenthemas (T. 65) im Hauptsatz allmählich entstehen läßt (T. 2, 34, 43 und 51), so hindert nichts, von 'kontrastierender Ableitung' zu sprechen." It should come as no surprise that the theoretical apparatus mentioned in this sentence – Arnold Schmitz's theory of "contrasting derivation" – was developed for Beethoven's music.

Example 3.4 Motivic reminiscence, according to Carl Dahlhaus, in Schubert, String Quartet in G Major, first movement, mm. 2, 34, 43, 51, 65

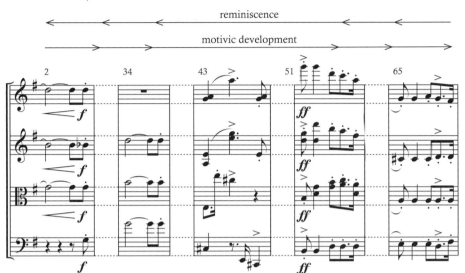

how one might experience the recognition of something from the past in a present moment. Now read Example 3.4 again, this time in the usual way, from left to right, to see how the rhythmic motive develops over the course of the first thematic group, transition, and secondary theme, gradually *becoming* the figure in mm. 51 and 65.

Dahlhaus's motivic detective work is brilliant, but for anyone interested in listening, what guides the ear to listen to m. 65 as dwelling on previous material? What, in other words, allowed Dahlhaus – and others who have followed his cue – to call a transformed motive "motivic development" in Beethoven's case, but "reminiscence" in Schubert's? Dahlhaus provides no answer in this case, but he hints at one in his second example.

The second example involves a threefold (and again modified) repetition of the descending half-step figure, which, according to Dahlhaus, sometimes possesses the qualities of motivic growth and sometimes those of remembrance. Again, what distinguishes these roles? After much detailed analysis (and for Dahlhaus's readers much reading between the lines), the distinction depends on whether or not the motive serves a structural purpose. The motive's first appearance is structural: it forms the lament bass in the first theme, $\hat{G}-\hat{F}\sharp/\hat{F}\natural-\hat{E}/\hat{E}\flat-\hat{D}$ (see Example 3.5), and projects the harmonic sequence, $G-D_6-F-C_6-E^\flat-G_4^6$. The motive's second incarnation is also structural. It appears in the transition, as a rising

Example 3.5 Extension of half-step motive (in Example 3.3) as a chromatic lament bass in first theme in Schubert, String Quartet in G Major, first movement, mm. 15–21

Example 3.6 Appearance of half-step motive in transition in Schubert, String Quartet in G Major, first movement, mm. 54–59

sequence $\hat{G}-\hat{F}\sharp/\hat{A}-\hat{G}\sharp/\hat{B}-\hat{A}\sharp$ (Example 3.6). It controls the harmonic sequence that brings about the F♯ major harmony, which announces the second theme.[76] Both serve a structural purpose, and therefore "press ahead" in a Beethovenian manner.

---

[76] Dahlhaus, "Sonata Form in Schubert," 2 and 6.

Example 3.7 Appearance of half-step motive in secondary theme in Schubert, String Quartet in G Major, first movement (a) in exposition mm. 64–69; (b) in recapitulation mm. 343–348

The next appearance, in the second theme, constitutes the reminiscence. Specifically, it recalls the contour of the motive of the opening theme, insofar as it also descends chromatically through a fourth from D̂ to Â, as shown in Example 3.7a. It does nothing to guide the harmonic framework. Lest one should spot the re-voicing of the motive in the recapitulation (Example 3.7b) and assume its presence in the bass would endow it with structural purpose, Dahlhaus points out that its role is one of "lyrical counterpoint."[77] In other words, despite starting in the bass, it does not

---

[77] Dahlhaus, "Sonata Form in Schubert," 8.

guide the underlying harmonic progression, and therefore it too constitutes a reminiscence. At best, one can conclude that, according to Dahlhaus, a moment is a memory if it can be shown in analytical terms to be non-structural.

Memory and the lyric impulse

The concept of memory has been a vital thread in scholarship since the time of Dahlhaus's study. In an introduction to a series of essays on the topic, Walter Frisch justified its importance by arguing that "the vocabulary of memory offers a plausible alternative" to the "language developed for analyzing the music of Schubert's great 'other,' Beethoven."[78] To be sure, the vocabulary of memory is a compelling one. But note that the proposal involves substituting a language that *explains* the workings of Beethoven's music for one that *describes* Schubert's. This results in the kinds of claims I pointed to earlier, where Schubert's skewed sentence structure at the opening of the G Major String Quartet is taken to "recall" the Beethovenian phrase that has become the theoretical model of the phrase type. Schubert, thus, "remembers" abstract formal models.[79] Similarly, standard motivic analyses are carried out but are dressed in the new vocabulary of memory, as in the case of the following: "the theme of the adagio *derives from (or, better, remembers)* the motive first introduced . . . near the beginning of the movement" (italics mine).[80]

One study that is particularly helpful in revealing the technical details behind Schubert's expressions of memory is a study that focuses not so much on memory, but on lyricism. Su Yin Mak examines the traits of Romantic lyric poetry and defines their relevance to Schubert's music: lyric poetry often contains intensely personal accounts of a particular moment; it often explores such moments from different perspectives, and spotlights extreme emotions associated with them. It voices contemplation, reflection, introspection, musing, meditation, reverie, et cetera, which gives an air of stopping the flow of time or even timelessness or looking back. This is why lyricism and memory are so closely aligned. Structurally and

---

[78] Frisch, "Memory and Schubert's Instrumental Music," *Musical Quarterly* 84 (2000): 581.

[79] Frisch, "'You Must Remember This'," 584.

[80] Fisk, "Schubert Recollects Himself: The Piano Sonata in C Minor, D. 958," *Musical Quarterly* 84 (2000): 649.

syntactically, lyricism favors juxtaposition, repetition, chiasmus, and para-
taxis over development, narrative, and hypotaxis.[81]

Yet the problem – again – is that, however astutely Mak identifies the
range of technical devices that constitute lyricism, she reverts to Schenkerian
analysis to illustrate her point. Schenkerian analysis is not suited to capture
such devices: it downplays repetition in an effort to summarize structural
content, and it seeks *Urlinien* and *Bassbrechungen* that go somewhere, that
move on. Schenker could not be a more inappropriate port of call to convey
the important insights she made in her otherwise groundbreaking study.

All of the lyric qualities mentioned by Mak may be identified in the
second theme of Schubert's String Quartet in G Major, and I venture to say
that these are responsible for the reminiscence Dahlhaus was hearing.
To illustrate how radically unsuited the aesthetic agenda of Schenkerian
analysis is to portray these qualities, I shall examine first some analyses by
Schenkerians, including some who themselves wrote about the paratactic
and lyric in this quartet, and I then shall offer my own analysis.

Xavier Hascher's analysis of this second theme shows a descending
$\hat{5}$-line, from an overall $\hat{2}$ (Example 3.8a), which is perhaps the most standard Schenkerian interpretation of second themes in the dominant key in
sonata form.[82] Burstein and Beach take a more unusual approach to the
Urlinie, accommodating the more idiosyncratic details in Schubert's score:
both portray the theme as controlled by $\hat{3}$ ($\hat{F}\sharp$) of D major, which stems
from the unusual arrival of VII at the end of the transition.[83] As can also be

---

[81] For a particularly insightful account of lyricism as it pertains to Schubert's music, see Su Yin
Mak, "Schubert's Sonata Forms and the Poetics of the Lyric," *Journal of Musicology* 23 (2006):
263–306. Hascher also discusses the paratactic in *Schubert: La forme sonate*, 51. On
motionlessness and the sense of pastness in Schubert, see Beth Shamgar, "Schubert's Classic
Legacy: Some Thoughts on Exposition-Recap. Form," *Journal of Musicology* 18 (2001): 150–169
and John Daverio, "'One More Beautiful Memory of Schubert': Schumann's Critique of the
Impromptus, D. 935," *Musical Quarterly*, 84 (2000): 604–618.

[82] None of the large-scale graphs in Hascher's book, *Schubert: La forme sonate*, contain measure
numbers; the graph of the quartet is on p. 162. I have deduced measure numbers on the
following assumption: $\hat{5}$ is the neighbor-note in m. 65, $\hat{4}$ is presumably the $\hat{G}$ in mm. 67–68, $\hat{3}$
may be the return of the $\hat{F}\sharp$ in m. 68 or, more likely, the $\hat{F}\sharp$ an octave higher over D major in
mm. 75–76, with the $\hat{E}$ and $\hat{D}$ marking the V–I close of the second theme in m. 77. Webster's
analysis of this movement also shows a $\hat{2}$ support for the secondary theme; his graph is deep
middleground and shows no further detail, "Schubert's Sonata Form," 21.

[83] Burstein, Example 3, in "Lyricism, Structure, and Gender," 55 and Beach, Figure 11, in "Modal
Mixture and Schubert's Harmonic Practice," 98 and Beach, Example 12, in "Schubert's
Experiments with Sonata Form," 17. It should be noted that Burstein argues that Schubert's lyric
impulse derives from the underlying levels of structure rather than from the foreground. Even
though I focus in this chapter on the surface level, I am not arguing the opposite of Burstein's
point: rather the surface *also* exhibits paratactic qualities. My large-scale interpretations of the
paratactic in Schubert may be found in Chapter 4.

Example 3.8 Analysis of exposition of Schubert, String Quartet in G Major, first movement from (a) Hascher, *Schubert: La forme sonate*, 162; (b) Beach, "Schubert's Experiments with Sonata Form," 17; (c) Burstein, "Lyricism, Structure, and Gender," 55

seen by comparing Examples 3.8b and 3.8c to Beach's 1998 graph, Beach gives greater prominence to Ĝ than Burstein, who inverts the surface salience of pitches in his analysis – a not uncommon (and perfectly legitimate!) Schenkerian habit. Hascher's and Burstein's bass lines suggest that there is nothing particularly unusual in Schubert's presentation of D major. By contrast, Beach shows the second theme as part of a large-scale descending tetrachord – $\hat{G}-\hat{F}\sharp-\hat{E}-\hat{D}$ – which he considers a major-key response to the minor-key descending tetrachord found at the opening of the movement (and identified by Dahlhaus in the lament bass).

Hascher's analysis of the second theme is the most conventional, Burstein's draws out Schubert's lyrical handling of large-scale harmonic structure, and Beach's analysis is a truly brilliant Schenkerian reading insofar as he ties the structure together in a manner no other analyst has achieved. In particular, he provides a contrapuntal-harmonic explanation for the peculiar F♯ major arrival at the end of the transition, for the peculiar appearance of A major in second inversion, and for the late arrival of D major in the second theme. Nonetheless, I would argue that his analysis draws out the hypotactic construction of the theme at the expense of the paratactic. In short, Beach, Burstein, and Hascher all succeed in capturing Schubert's second theme in elegant Schenkerian graphs. What their method does not – indeed, cannot – capture, however, is the static, repetitive, non-syntactical aspects of Schubert's sound world.

Let us, then, examine the lyric traits, as defined by Mak, in the second theme of the quartet. First among these is the way the entry of the theme is staged as a juxtaposition (see Example 3.9). It is a hallmark of Schubert's sonata forms that his second themes are introduced through abrupt modulation.[84] In this case, the transition ends in the remote key of F♯ major, emphasized with a *ffz* marking and followed by the pregnant pause so commonly associated with this juncture in sonata form. The generic signals, to borrow from Hepokoski's and Darcy's conception of form, are standard: there is a strong arrival of a *ffz* major chord at the end of the transition, followed by a characteristic silence, followed by a secondary theme.[85] Up to this point the gestures are familiar, but the harmony is unfamiliar. As shown in Example 3.9, the upbeat–downbeat gesture suggests $\hat{7}-\hat{8}$, as if the key is still G major. It is as if chord VII is being treated like a leading-tone. However, this will be Schubert's skewed means of landing on $\hat{G}$ as the seventh (marked $\hat{7}$ in the example) of an A major seventh harmony. The main harmonic trajectory of the second theme itself

[84] The kinds of modulations that Gottfried Wilhelm Fink complained about in the songs (see Chapter 2) resurface between the end of the transitions and beginning of the second themes in Schubert's sonata forms. For a general discussion of these, see Webster, "Schubert's Sonata Form," 22–24 and Susan Wollenberg, "Schubert's Transitions."

[85] James Hepokoski and Warren Darcy, *Elements of Sonata Theory: Norms, Types, and Deformations in the Late-Eighteenth-Century Sonata* (Oxford University Press, 2006), 34.

Example 3.9 Schubert, String Quartet in G Major, first movement, mm. 54–77

Example 3.9 (cont.)

is also familiar. It begins with a dominant harmony, A major, and ends with a tonic harmony, D major. But, as it turns out, its presentation is unfamiliar (it is neither V^7–I nor even V^6_5–I, but V^4_3–I).

The second theme is "in D major," as all analysts concur. Yet there is disagreement as to where D major starts to be prolonged (to phrase it in Schenkerian terms). Hascher and Burstein argue that a D major prolongation begins at the end of m. 65, although their opinions vary as to whether $\hat{A}$ or $\hat{F}\sharp$ launches the middleground *Urlinie* (see Examples 3.8a and 3.8c). I agree with Beach, who argues that D major arrives only at the end of the second theme (Example 3.8b). Such a scheme – whether used by Mozart

(K. 545), Beethoven (Op. 2, No. 1), or Brahms (Op. 99), to cite some famous examples in the analytical literature – invariably lends the second theme a sense of pressing ahead, as it strives towards the articulation of its key. As just mentioned, Schubert's theme even starts with a dominant seventh (m. 65), cadencing only at the very end (mm. 75–77). Given such a compelling progression from dominant to tonic (in D major), it is rather significant that Schubert manages to obviate the apparently innate forward-driving quality of the progression. This is one important characteristic of Schubert's lyric quality.

Schubert's theme comprises much rhythmic, melodic, and harmonic repetition. As can be seen in Example 3.9, the rhythm that Dahlhaus identified as a reminiscence in m. 65 permeates the second theme. Every measure is based on it. In terms of pitch material, over half of the melody hovers between Ĝ and Ê, seemingly stuck in a rut of conjunct motion (mm. 65–71). Examination of a rejected version of the melody in Schubert's manuscript indicates that m. 72 was originally conceived to begin yet again on Ĝ, as shown in the extra stave in measure 72 of Example 3.9. Schubert changed his mind, only to create a melody stuck on a new set of repeated pitches in mm. 72–74.[86] Relief from this pitch rumination or contemplation or meditation (to use words associated with the lyric) is finally found in the modest melodic leaps at the (also repeated) cadences in mm. 74–77.

The harmonies of the second theme include (in order): F♯ major, A major, D major, A major, A minor, E minor, B major, E minor, and a repetition of F♯ major, A major, D major, A major, A minor, E minor, before shifting to G major, F♯ major, and finally the cadence from A major to D major. While it is possible to find adjacent fifth-relations in the list above, the harmonic flow does not suggest standard chord progressions. Indeed, a Roman numeral analysis of these chords seems forced, although there are some laudable, if necessarily impractical, attempts in the literature (see again the analyses in Example 3.8).[87] Instead, consider this passage as a paratactic arrangement of

---

[86] The manuscript is available for consultation at www.schubert-online.at. The cello statement was originally in D major (which in the final version is in B♭ major, mm. 109ff.) and is crossed out on fol. 4r of the autograph. The repetition of the Ĝ in the equivalent place to m. 72 mentioned above is in this crossed-out version. A full discussion of Schubert's autograph and its structural implications is to be found in Hinrichsen, *Untersuchungen zur Entwicklung der Sonatenform*, 209–219.

[87] See Burstein, Example 3, in "Lyricism, Structure, and Gender," 55 and compare Beach, Figure 11, in "Modal Mixture and Schubert's Harmonic Practice," 98. Perhaps for this reason, Beach's earlier analysis included only the broadest motion III♯–V$_3^4$–V$_3^5$–I. See Beach, Example 12, in "Schubert's Experiments with Sonata Form," 17.

harmonic sonorities, which unfold through an exploration of the pitch content and possible color-effects of the harmonies, rather than being guided by conventional fundamental bass progressions. How does their paratactic nature work?

As already indicated, the downbeats in mm. 65–71 are mostly $\hat{G}$s and twice $\hat{E}$s. These pitches are always "harmony notes" insofar as they belong to the harmonies beneath them. This is not to say, however, that they are always equally consonant. The first $\hat{G}$, as already observed, belongs to an A^4_3 chord and is thus the $\hat{7}$ of its harmony; the ensuing $\hat{E}$ also belongs to an A major triad, this time in root position. The harmony has not changed, but – crucially – its presentation has: the chord in second inversion with a dissonance has become a root-position closed triad with no dissonance. They sound palpably different; the harmonic hue has changed. Next, the melody moves upwards by step – from whence it came. When $\hat{G}$ sounds again, the harmony has changed; $\hat{G}$ is now a consonance, a $\hat{3}$ of E minor. It retains the same profile when it returns in the next measure. Because of the nature and succession of chords, their harmonic function seems also to shift. That is to say, thanks to its normal usage in common practice, A^4_3 emits a dominant function, and by association so does the A^5_3 that follows it. However, after the arrival of the root-position E minor, A major loses its power and E minor seems unable to comply as a (cadential) supertonic. Instead it seems solely to provide a new harmonic and modal setting for the recurring downbeat $\hat{G}$s. The first three measures of the theme repeat their respective downbeats, and just as the ear settles into the repeat, the fourth measure breaks it. As mentioned above, $\hat{G}$ was originally meant to come back yet again, this time transformed into $\hat{1}$ of G major. Nonetheless the final version $\hat{G}$ as $\hat{1}$ is hardly camouflaged despite being in an inner voice. In the course of the theme, the pitch has been dissonant, consonant, and tonicized; it has been $\hat{7}$, $\hat{3}$, and $\hat{1}$.

The point to take from this observation is that each time $\hat{G}$ re-emerges, it has a different quality to it. Adorno's comment about Schubert's variations presenting a theme in different harmonic hues applies here to a single pitch. This also explains why this passage is not about harmonic progression in the conventional sense; it is not steered by a bass line or driven by the fifth-progression logic of fundamental bass. Instead, Schubert makes use of common-practice harmonic vocabulary but presents it differently, and makes it sound elusive. As we saw in some of his songs in Chapter 2, he attends to repeated pitch material, repositioning it within different triads or chords. In this case, he is oddly obsessed with the movement's tonic pitch, $\hat{G}$, at a place in the musical form where the music is meant to venture elsewhere. The technique generates the sense of reminiscence, as an important pitch of the past is recast within the present harmonic context. Moreover, the other repetitions – of rhythm and phrase material – and the rumination of the harmony all point to familiar activities of memory.

This kind of pitch repetition, as well as instances where Schubert recasts melodic fragments into new harmonic contexts, is evident in many other passages where scholars have invoked memory. A clear example where Schubert recasts a melody into a new modal context may be found in the Sonata in B♭ Major, examined at the outset of this chapter. As mentioned there, Fisk hears the return of the first (lyrical) theme in C♯ minor at the opening of the development as a "memory in exile." He argues that the remoteness of the key and the shift to the minor mode create the effect of memory. I would instead argue that this is another – and particularly striking – example of how Schubert recasts pitch material in a new harmonic light (to use Adorno's phrase again). The opening pitches of the first theme in the context of the tonic major key are given in Example 3.2. As annotated in the example, the first few pitches of the melody in B♭ major are $\hat{1}-\hat{1}-\hat{7}-\hat{1}-\hat{2}-\hat{3}$; their interval pattern is SSTT (S refers to semitone; T to tone). The return of the theme in the development (Example 3.10) is not a mere transposition and inflection of the passage into C♯ minor. Instead, the melody is repeated using the same interval pattern SSTT, but it now sits within the upper third of the triadic harmony as $\hat{3}-\hat{3}-\hat{2}-\hat{3}-\hat{4}-\hat{5}$. Crucial to the sound effect is that the opening intervallic content of the melody is identical. The "shift in perspective," or "change of light," is brought about by recasting the melody within the upper third of the minor triad, rather than lingering around the lower third of the major triad as it does in the exposition.

My final example is perhaps one of the most breathtaking examples of pitch repetition in Schubert's output. The passage is the second theme of

Example 3.10 Opening measures of the first theme in the development of Schubert, Piano Sonata in B♭ Major, first movement, mm. 117–119

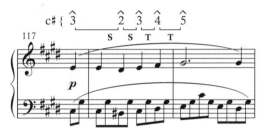

Example 3.11 Schubert, String Quintet in C Major (D. 956), first movement, mm. 57–79

Example 3.11 (cont.)

the String Quintet in C Major (D. 956) (Example 3.11). It is ostensibly in
Eb major, although there is no authentic cadence to ground it.[88] This hazy
key definition is not, to my ears at least, the reason it seems like a
reminiscence. Building on an observation by John Gingerich, Burnham
attributes the "sound of memory" to the obsessive presence of the pitch Ĝ
in the melody. The "ever-renewed G changes hue at every turn," and Eb
major "seems to list to one side, towards its mediant." It is "perched at an

---

[88] Due to the lack of cadence, Webster considers the theme a "lyrical transition" and a "gigantic
floating pivot chord" in "Schubert's Sonata Form," 29. Rosen disagrees on account of the return
to the tonic in m. 71, see *Sonata Forms*, 258.

odd angle," just as memories "will always be obliquely angled to our present experience."[89]

This brings to mind Tovey's idea that Schubert's works with unorthodox harmonic progressions are like paintings with competing vantage points, as if "the tower was drawn from below but the man on the top of it was drawn from the roof."[90] Whereas Classical harmony involves a single key, like a single vanishing point in a unified picture, Schubert's more adventurous works seem to shift perspective. Tovey's reference to star clusters seems to be getting at the same thing. Instead of the traditional "solar system" of Classical harmony, as Momigny characterized the gravitational pull of central tonic and the orbiting closely related keys, Schubert's tonality is "as wonderful as star clusters."[91] These clusters, whether open or globular, have a common gravitational bond but to the observer no single eyepiece of a telescope view will resolve all the stars.

Rather than characterizing the second theme in the String Quintet as *in* E♭ major but listing towards its mediant – or even hovering around E♭ major because the key is never established through an authentic cadence – I prefer to characterize the passage as *around* the $\hat{G}$. As shown in Example 3.11, the $\hat{G}$ shifts in hue from $(\hat{3}, +)$ to $(\hat{1}, +)$ back to $(\hat{3}, +)$ to $(\hat{5}, +)$ to $(\hat{1}, +)$ as it resonates within all the possible major triads, E♭ major, C major, and G major. This $\hat{G}$ strikes the ear even before the second theme begins, for the expected grand pause after the cadence at the end of the transition is filled in with a lone $\hat{G}$ in mm. 58–59. Though it is a $(\hat{1}, +)$ because it belongs to the G major triad, it functions as a $\hat{5}$ or V of C major. There are, thus, multiple layers through which a pitch may be analyzed.

Memory is so often invoked in Schubert's remote modulations, where Schubert is best known for his lyric impulse. It seems to me, however, that neither remoteness nor lyricism are the only cues. Again, it is the presentation of the material on the surface that counts. In the case of the Piano Sonata in B♭ Major, it is the fact that an identical-sounding melody reappears but couched within minor sonorities. In the case of the String Quintet in C Major, it is the fact that the expected dominant pitch appears in the secondary theme but couched in all of the possible major triadic sonorities. In the case of the String Quartet in G Major, the second theme,

---

[89] Scott Burnham, "Schubert and the Sound of Memory," 662 and John Gingerich, "Remembrance and Consciousness in Schubert's C-Major String Quintet, D.956," *Musical Quarterly* 84 (2000): 620–621.

[90] Tovey, "Tonality in Schubert," in Hubert J. Foss (ed.), *The Mainstream of Music and Other Essays* (Oxford University Press, 1949), 134. Tovey was quoting Mark Twain.

[91] Tovey, "Tonality in Schubert," 159.

according to most scholarly conclusions, is first sounded in the dominant key because keys are defined by cadences. Yet the details that count are, firstly, the fact that most of the theme is spent elsewhere harmonically, as D major is only asserted as a cadence at the very end of the thematic unit, and, secondly, the emphasis on the pitch $\hat{G}$, which both harks back to the opening tonic and colors it with new harmonic hues. As we shall see in the next section, a similar treatment of pitch may be discerned in the Symphony No. 8 in B Minor (*Unfinished*, D. 759), but its musical meaning is interpreted through the lens of sexuality.

Once more, Schubert's biography

We have already witnessed in Chapter 1 of this book the role that Schubert's biography – in the form of his purported clairvoyance and physical appearance – played in the nineteenth-century reception of his creative output. The habit of reading Schubert in his work was not only a nineteenth-century phenomenon. Well-known modern attempts include Hugh Macdonald's argument that Schubert's musical outbursts stem from his "volcanic temper" or Edward T. Cone's view that Schubert's music from 1822 onwards was infused with a sense of desolation and dread.[92]

Interestingly, this habit of linking "the man and the music" only came under real scrutiny – or, rather, attack – in the wake of debates about Schubert's possible homosexuality and its manifestation in the music. Maynard Solomon, who first raised the issue explicitly in print, was cautious about making such a link: "We may never uncover the traces of Schubert's character within the music."[93] Susan McClary, who did more to publicize the issue, stood accused of claiming a direct link between Schubert's homosexuality and his music. However, responses to her work are marred by hearsay: her paper delivered at the annual Schubertiade at the 92nd Street Y in 1991 rapidly became the most talked-about – yet clearly the least read – paper in musicology in the 1990s.[94] While perhaps it

---

[92] Hugh Macdonald, "Schubert's Volcanic Temper," *Musical Times* 119 (1978): 949–952 and Edward T. Cone, "Schubert's Promissory Note: An Exercise in Musical Hermeneutics," in Walter Frisch (ed.), *Schubert: Critical and Analytical Studies* (Lincoln and London: University of Nebraska Press, 1986), 28.

[93] Maynard Solomon, "Franz Schubert and the Peacocks of Benvenuto Cellini," *19th-Century Music*, 12 (1989): 206.

[94] By way of anecdote, I recall as a graduate student participating in numerous graduate student roundtable discussions on the topic, yet the newsletter existence of a transcript of the spoken version was rarely mentioned: the published version (which is modified from the 92nd Street

did not help that in one written forum in 1993 (before the publication of her article in *Queering the Pitch*) she referred to her own paper as "my talk linking Schubert's sexuality and his music,"[95] in both the delivered paper and its subsequent published version she was as sensitive as everyone else who weighed in on the issue to the distinction between Schubert's personality and his artistic persona – hence her portrayal of his music as a "*construction* of subjectivity" (my italics). For all the debate and, in some cases, deplorable remarks made by those who were unable even to contemplate the possibility of Schubert's homosexuality, McClary's main point is incontrovertible: Schubert's music depicts a markedly different version of masculinity from the prevailing norm of masculinity – a "norm" which, incidentally, is equally a construction.

In her reading of Schubert's harmony and form, McClary was accused of essentialism – of taking Schubert's propensity for third relations and idiosyncratic loosening of forms as an expression of this alternative masculine subjectivity. Webster cautioned that Beethoven also used third relations, while Agawu suggested that making such connections "can seem forced, even laughable."[96] The point, however, is that Beethoven's third relations cannot be mistaken for Schubert's, and vice versa. Their presentation on the surface is radically different. Beethoven takes all necessary steps to ensure that, for example, the prominent third relations in the Piano Sonata in C Major (*Waldstein*) Op. 53 are prepared with plenty of dominant to maintain that teleological, normative appeal. Schubert takes all necessary steps to ensure that his prominent third relations do not. In short, it is the details that count.

In her article, McClary finds an altogether more imaginative means of capturing the distinctive quality of Schubertian subjectivity in her harmonic analysis than in her formal analysis. The latter relies on the common habit of viewing Schubert's personal statements as digressions from the norm. By contrast, the subtlety of her claims about Schubert's harmonic vocabulary have been missed in the debate. She observes that in order for Schubert to

---

Y version, and it's worth comparing the two versions) did not appear until 1994. Although I was fortunate to be in a group of graduate students ready to embrace McClary's ideas, I nonetheless found reading McClary's work a revelation compared to what everyone *thought* it said. The spoken version is still available at: *Gay/Lesbian Study Group Newsletter* 2, no. 1 (April 1991): 8–14, online at www.ams-lgbtq.org. The final published version is "Constructions of Subjectivity in Schubert's Music," in Philip Brett, Elizabeth Wood, and Gary C. Thomas (eds.), *Queering the Pitch: The New Gay and Lesbian Musicology* (New York: Routledge, 1994), 205–233.

[95] Susan McClary, "Music and Sexuality: On the Steblin/Solomon Debate," *19th-Century Music* 17 (1993): 84.

[96] See Agawu, "Schubert's Sexuality: A Prescription for Analysis," *19th-Century Music* 17 (1993): 82 and Webster, "Music, Pathology, Sexuality, Beethoven, Schubert," *19th-Century Music* 17 (1993): 92–93.

create a sound world that represents an alternative male subjectivity, he had to "rework virtually every parameter of his musical language," which was "not easy to accomplish, either conceptually or technically." Crucially, she also maintains that it "had to be constructed painstakingly from the stuff of standard tonality."[97] I shall comment first on her (less inventive) reading of formal matters before turning to aspects of harmony.

McClary sees the modification of sonata form, particularly once it had become notionally standardized, as a mark of a composer's personal expression. She uses Mozart to make her point, arguing that he "began to inflect his movements in such a way as to introduce subjective expression into the more objective formal plan of sonata" and that he "worked at striking a balance between the goal-oriented narratives that propel his pieces and the lyrical passages that suggest depth, sensitivity, interiority."[98] There is a clear sense here of a distinction between the active and the expressive aspects of structure, in much the same way that Dahlhaus suggests that the variation elements do not actively participate in the "pathos" or energy of the structure, or that Fisk and Pesic suggest that non-structural keys represent exile. Needless to say, Schubert tipped that balance in favor of the subjective, rendering the distinction between the active and the expressive components of form even starker.

The extended lyrical passage that most qualifies for such an expressive reading in the *Unfinished* Symphony is the second theme of the first movement. As part of what McClary identifies as a "victim narrative," the second theme is the "vulnerable lyrical subject, which is doomed to be quashed."[99] There is, of course, nothing unusual about having a contrasting lyrical theme in the exposition. As McClary explains in *Feminine Endings*, the narrative of sonata form hinges on the "tonic protagonist" subjugating the material occupying the secondary formal position.[100] The point in her essay on the *Unfinished* Symphony is that, unlike standard movements, Schubert's lyrical passage "invites the listener to identify with a subject that stands in the subordinate position, rather than with the opening complex."[101] As McClary reports, Hanslick identified with it in just this way. In reviewing the first performance in 1865, he remarked that upon hearing the second theme, "every heart rejoices, as if Schubert were standing alive in our midst after a long separation."[102]

---

[97] McClary, "Constructions of Subjectivity," 222–223.
[98] McClary, "Constructions of Subjectivity," 212.
[99] McClary, "Constructions of Subjectivity," 225.
[100] McClary, *Feminine Endings: Music, Gender, and Sexuality* (University of Minnesota Press, 1991), 12–17 and more specifically 15–16.
[101] McClary, "Constructions of Subjectivity," 225.
[102] McClary, "Constructions of Subjectivity," 225.

If Schubert himself seems to echo through the G major cello theme, he makes himself vulnerable to the trappings of lyricism. Because it is not in a standard key, Richard Taruskin argues that "the whole of the second theme, for all that it is the longest sustained span in the movement so far, could be snipped right out with no loss of tonal coherence. It is an island of repose."[103] He made the same kind of comment with regards to a passage in the Symphony No. 9 in C Major (*Great*, D. 944), which had fifths lurking nearby to maintain tonal coherence. However, the G major of the second theme is the only contrasting key in this exposition. Snipping out the material from the B major that ends the transition (m. 38) to the unison B̂s at the end of the second theme (m. 104) may produce a seamless join, but it leaves only a seven-measure link – in the tonic, no less – back to the repeat of the exposition. Without the second theme, the exposition has no secondary key whatsoever.

While in Taruskin's hands Schubert's lyric theme in a non-structural key is "quashed" by a structural scalpel, McClary means that second themes generally give way to the tonic in recapitulations. Perhaps here positioning Schubert as part of a "subculture" more so than an "alternative culture" led her to downplay the fact that Schubert's recapitulation does something different: the submediant theme reappears in the mediant, not in the usual tonic. The opportunity was missed here (and is one I take up in Chapter 4) to claim that this movement engages with a paradigm of tonal space that was gaining ground in nineteenth-century sonata forms.

Such an opportunity was not missed with respect to the harmony of the second movement. From the very opening (Example 3.12), this movement is harmonically unconventional, as McClary points out:

each of several moments within the opening theme becomes a pretext for deflection and exploration: the passage drifts through time by means of casual, always pleasurable pivots that entice the E-major theme variously to C♯ minor, G major, E minor, and then – without warning or fanfare – back to E major.

This is *not* how one ordinarily establishes one's first key area. In a Beethovenian world, such a passage would sound vulnerable, its tonal identity not safely anchored; and its ambiguity would probably precipitate a crisis, thereby justifying the violence needed to put things right again. Yet Schubert's opening section provokes no anxiety (at least not within the music itself – critics are another matter): it invites us to forgo the security of a centred, stable tonality and, instead, to experience – and even *enjoy* – a flexible sense of self.[104]

---

[103] Taruskin, *Oxford History of Western Music*, 110.

[104] McClary, "Constructions of Subjectivity," 215. If the key sequence in the first paragraph cited above is to match the order in the piece, it should read E major, C♯ minor, E minor, G major.

Example 3.12 Schubert, Symphony No. 8 in B Minor (*Unfinished*, D. 759), second movement, mm. 1–32

Example 3.12 (cont.)

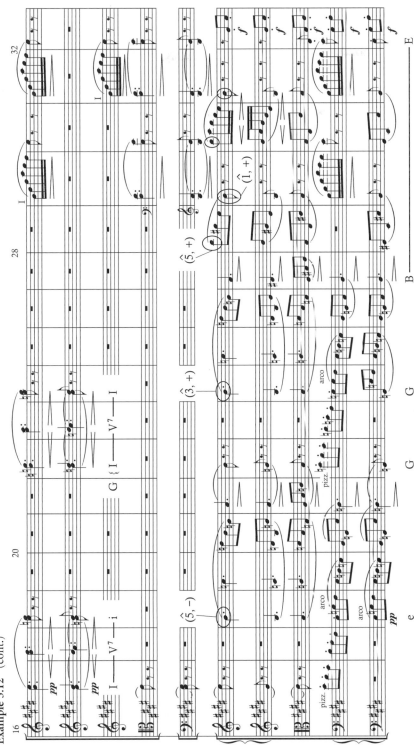

Notwithstanding the fact that it is a second movement, the main point McClary raises here is that the opening of Schubert's movement operates differently from normal openings, which usually set about establishing their tonic key. It is third relations above and below the tonic key that catch her attention. They are identifiably Schubertian. Although Beethoven also makes plenty of use of third relations, there is no mistaking the sound world of the two composers. In an article about subjectivity, McClary's language here is deliberate. She describes the effects that Schubert's music has on his listeners: his thirds are to be "experienced" and "enjoyed," and they are "casual, always pleasurable pivots." Note that there is no call at this point for Schubert's harmony to be rationalized, no call, that is, for a music-theoretical explanation.

Later in her article, however, McClary does offer an insightful – and, for the would-be music theorist, promising – description of Schubert's harmonic procedure. She focuses on *how* he pushes harmonic conventions to "the limits of comprehensibility":

Instead of choosing secondary keys that reinforce the boundaries of his tonic triad, Schubert utilizes every pitch of the chromatic scale as the pivot for at least one common-tone deflection. The tonic always rematerializes, but never as the result of a crisis. On some level, centred key identity almost ceases to matter, as Schubert frames chromatic mutation and wandering as sensually gratifying.[105]

There are a number of theoretical points to observe in this brief statement. According to McClary, Schubert is unconventional in his choice of keys and in the means by which he reaches them. Instead of using either the dominant or the relative major, which reinforce the overall key, all keys are open to him because every pitch of the chromatic scale is eligible to launch the music into a new key. McClary implies, therefore, that Schubert replaces conventional secondary keys with other keys. His *modus operandi* is to bring in a new key through "common-tone deflection."[106]

With little modification, her point about every pitch of the chromatic scale serving as a "deflection" could be systematized to produce the kinds of relationships defined by neo-Riemannian theorists, transformations of major and minor triads whose content exhausts the chromatic scale, and which are obtained through a careful balance of common tones and single

---

[105] McClary, "Constructions of Subjectivity," 223.

[106] It is unclear what McClary means by "at least one common-tone deflection." "Common-tone deflection" seems an oxymoron, as a pitch is either a common tone or a displaced pitch. I expect she means that there is "at least one displaced pitch between harmonies and the remaining pitches are common tones." For the sake of clarity in the discussion that follows, I have separated out common tones, which are shared pitches, from "deflections," which are displaced pitches.

pitch "displacements." Neo-Riemannian theorists have been primarily interested in cycles, cycles in which the "tonic" or starting point rematerializes.[107] McClary's description suggests a more liberal system than theirs, even if she too points to a tonic or starting point that "always rematerializes." In her account, key juxtapositions are not systematized into cycles, but are "flexible," and the tonic returns after "trying out" various keys.

On closer inspection, the passage McClary describes is harmonically far richer and more stable than she suggests. As annotated in Example 3.12, the bassoons and horns, followed by the flutes and oboes, outline a $I-V^7-I$ cadence at the beginning of each phrase, twice in E major (mm. 1–3 and 7–9), once in E minor (mm. 16–18) and finally in G major (mm. 22–24). McClary argues that the tonal identity of this passage is "not safely anchored." It is, I would argue, precisely because Schubert *does* anchor each phrase with a straightforward cadence that he can proceed to venture from key to key. Moreover, the insistent note B̂, which begins each melodic phrase in the violins, further serves as a kind of anchor because it belongs to each of the main keys established by the cadences in the bassoons and horns and flutes and oboes (see Examples 3.13a and 3.13c.) Around these points of stability, Schubert "mutates," to use McClary's word, from one harmony to the next, mostly using common tones as shown in Example 3.13b.

To my mind, it is these features that generate the "sensuous" – or indeed "hedonist" – quality McClary talks about.[108] Schubert replaces the idea of staking out a tonal area with tonics and dominants, as was the operating procedure in the Classical period, with a system based around a common tone as anchor. This example is almost dualistic in conception, with the anchor being the fifth of the tonic key. I refer here to the dualist conception that the minor triad was generated from the fifth. This is a theory of the origin of the minor triad, whereas David Lewin brilliantly applied the concept to moments in musical works where the surface-level presentation of any harmony is from the top.[109] I use the single common tone in an even

[107] Schubert's music is plotted against various cycles in Michael Siciliano, "Neo-Riemannian Transformations and the Harmony of Franz Schubert" (PhD thesis, University of Chicago, 2002). Although one advantage of these cycles to neo-Riemannian theorists is that they do not presuppose hierarchy, in a tonal system that adopts them, the cycles do indeed explain how a tonic rematerializes.

[108] See Webster, "Music, Pathology," 92 on the hedonist quality in Schubert's music. On the assumption that definitions of "gay" are fluid, see Ruth A. Solie, review of *Queering the Pitch: The New Gay and Lesbian Musicology*, in *Journal of the American Musicological Society* 48 (1995): 311–323.

[109] David Lewin, "A Formal Theory of Generalized Tonal Functions," *Journal of Music Theory* 26 (1982): 41–48. Lewin's Riemannian solution to the logic and meaning of the G♯ minor key in "Auf dem Flusse" discussed in Chapter 2 is another example of the analytical application of this principle.

Example 3.13 Schubert, *Unfinished* Symphony, mm. 1–32 (a) melodic tone analysis; (b) common-tone analysis; (c) harmonic structure

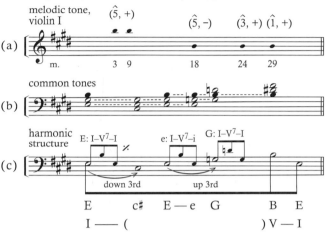

broader sense. It binds a series of harmonies together, from the top, middle, or bottom of a triad. We have now come across this phenomenon in a number of pieces: the Ê♭ in "Auf der Donau," the Ĝ♭/F̂♯ in "Orest auf Tauris," the B̂ in "Trost" (Chapter 2), the Ĝ in the second theme of the String Quartet in G Major and the Ĝ in the second theme of the String Quintet in C Major. A single pitch can belong to many keys or harmonies that are both diatonically and chromatically related to the "home" key (or main key of a section), and it can be the focal point around which the harmonies turn. As I put it in Chapter 2, instead of presenting such themes "*in* a key," Schubert presents them "*around* a pitch."

The opening of the second movement of the *Unfinished* Symphony adopts precisely the same interpretation of the common tone B̂ as found in "Trost." That is to say, among the six potential triads around B̂, only the use of B̂ as $(\hat{5}, +)$ for the tonic key will yield a tonic/dominant relationship among the triads. By contrast, the ordering in the second theme of the String Quintet in C Major, where Ĝ was $(\hat{3}, +)(\hat{5}, +)(\hat{1}, +)$ within a framework of E♭ major, obviates the tonic/dominant relationship.

My discussion of common tones has been almost exclusively triadic. However, as the first sonority in the second theme of the String Quartet in G Major suggests, there is no reason to restrict the corpus of sonorities to major and minor triads.[110] Dissonances could be introduced into the theoretical framework, as in the $\hat{7}$ within the dominant seventh which

---

[110] My reason for doing so in my article "On the Imagination of Tone" was that Riemann had done so in the theoretical study I was examining.

opens the second theme of the quartet. The presence of dissonances adds a new dimension to the number of pitches in a chordal entity, but it also introduces the issue of resolution or avoided resolutions into the equation. That is to say, if the $\hat{7}$ is resolved in its ensuing harmony, then clearly the common tone is no longer present. If however the common tone remains in the ensuing harmony, then normative contrapuntal resolution has been avoided.

This issue is not entirely new to the instances of Schubert's use of common tones that we have encountered in this book. Recall the case of $\hat{C}\flat/\hat{B}\natural$ in "Selige Welt." As shown in Example 2.3, the common tone served as $\hat{3}$ of A♭ minor, $\hat{1}$ of C♭ major, $\hat{3}$ of G major, and $\hat{5}$ of E minor. When, however, in m. 16 the $\hat{B}\natural$ in the upper voice of the piano became the leading note in the progression V^7–i in C minor, it demanded resolution (see the score in Example 2.2). As my analytical graph in Example 2.3 shows, the end of the tonal exploration around this pitch comes to an end when it is resolved to $\hat{C}$.

When analyzing Schubert, it is not enough, then, to label the keys or harmonies of a passage from the bottom using Roman numerals, and to find in the awkward labels Schubert's expansions of tonal space. Nor is it enough to use neo-Riemannian labels even though they ostensibly denote which pitches shift and which are retained between harmonies. Rather, it is important to demonstrate how the harmony is presented on the surface of the music. A single common tone may bring his harmonic exploration together, and each time we hear the pitch, its new harmonic context will change its quality. In the technical terms described above, $\hat{B}$ changes hue from $(\hat{5}, +)$ to $(\hat{5}, -)$ to $(\hat{3}, +)$ to $(\hat{1}, +)$ within the first 32 measures, as shown in Examples 3.12 and 3.13a. Each sonority is articulated by a cadence at the beginning of each phrase, but the sonorities themselves explore new tonal spaces of E major, E minor, G major, within a larger-scale *Bassbrechung* that encases them all, as shown in Example 3.13c. The passage sounds palpably different if one hears it as McClary describes, by listening out for the fluid harmonic changes of key or pleasurable pivots, rather than the way I have described it by listening out for the repeated $\hat{B}$, around which the harmonies turn.

Resisting analysis, embracing trance

In an article on Stravinsky, Taruskin highlights the role of Schubert's use of thirds in the development of octatonicism and whole-tone tonality. As part of a historical study he undertook in order to resolve the question of whether or not the octatonic collection in particular was fundamental to the harmonic language of Stravinsky's pre-serial works, Taruskin observes a direct connection between the composers of what he argues are the incipient and the crystallized phases of octatonicism.[111] In 1906, Stravinsky played through a four-hand version of Schubert's *Great* Symphony, with Rimsky-Korsakov's wife. Vasilii Yastrebtsev, a witness to the occasion, recorded a remark made by Rimsky-Korsakov, who was also present. He apparently said that Schubert was "the first composer in whom one can meet such bold and unexpected modulations. Before Schubert there was no such thing."[112] We are not specifically told which modulations he had in mind, but Taruskin speculates that he probably meant the mediant progressions.

As Taruskin observes, Schubert's thirds appear on all structural levels, expanding Classical tonality along both diatonic and chromatic lines. He interprets their structural significance as follows: at the lowest level they are "fleeting" chords, but at increasingly larger levels they may constitute progressions, underpin the thematic areas of the form, or provide links between different movements. Of particular interest to Taruskin are those mediants that form complete chains of thirds because he believes they constitute the early origin of both octatonicism and whole-tone tonality. These scales arise when rotations of either minor or major thirds (respectively) are filled in with passing notes.[113] As he observes, such chains of thirds were mostly only fragmentary during their nascency in the music of the early Romantics, whereas their appearance in later music was more complete, more pervasive, and more structural. Taruskin's attitude to the thirds in the *Great* Symphony serves his historical point: despite the prominent use of thirds – including even a fully formed hexatonic cycle – none of them forms an active ingredient in the large-scale structure. He writes:

---

[111] Richard Taruskin, "Chernomor to Kashchei: Harmonic Sorcery, or, Stravinsky's 'Angle,'" *Journal of the American Musicological Society* 38 (1985): 78.

[112] For a fuller discussion of this citation and the circumstances under which it was made, see Taruskin, "Stravinsky's 'Angle,'" 79.

[113] Neo-Riemannian theorists are interested in these same cycles. While cycles comprising minor thirds are known as "octatonic," those comprising major thirds are known as "hexatonic" rather than whole-tonal. These labels express different ways of construing their pitch material: neo-Riemannian theorists focus on the pitch material of all the major and minor triads within a single cycle. In the case of the minor-third cycle, these make up the same octatonic collection as the scale that Taruskin derives from inserting passing tones between the roots of the triads. The same does not obtain with the major-third cycle, whose triadic pitch content produces a "hexatonic" collection (set class 6–20) while Taruskin's scalar procedure produces a whole-tone scale.

A *locus classicus* of novel third relations . . . occurs in the Great Symphony during the codetta of the first movement . . . The boxed material [reproduced as Example 3.14] shows a complete circle of major thirds *inserted* within a circle of fifths. Seen within its overall context, this circle of thirds, which achieves closure after only three progressions, has to be classified as *nonfunctional* in the sense that it could be *removed* without disturbing the coherence of the fifth-related successions that bind the passage together and connect it with the rest of the movement. But of course the really memorable music in this section of the movement is contained precisely within the box. And especially memorable is the A-flat-minor episode (the famous trombone solo) that shows up in our analysis simply as a *digression within a digression*. It is precisely the *remoteness* of the progression that appeals, not its logic, although its logic is certainly demonstrable. The circle of thirds is *an island of mysterious repose* that *interrupts* the forward thrust of the fifths progression. Its quality of time is *static* rather than active. It calls out to the passing moment, "Stop, stay awhile, thou art so fair!"[114] (italics mine)

Taruskin's view is clear: the "really memorable" music in this passage, supported as it is by thirds, is "inserted," "nonfunctional," "removable," "digressive," "remote," "static," but – with a Faustian edge – "so fair." It is evident from this analysis that, despite emphasizing that these thirds are novel, the emphasis of the analysis is on how they are subordinate to the fifths.[115]

Taruskin republished his analysis of the *Great* Symphony a decade later in *Stravinsky and the Russian Traditions: A Biography of the Works through* Mavra. The passage cited above is reproduced unchanged, but for one significant addition which he even placed in quotation marks:

. . . Seen within its overall context this circle of thirds, which achieves closure after only three progressions, has to be classified as a "prolongation" – nonfunctional in the sense that it could be removed without disturbing the coherence of the fifth-related successions that bind the passage together and connect it with the rest of the movement. . .[116]

---

[114] Taruskin, "Stravinsky's 'Angle,'" 81.

[115] Thirds are also prominent elsewhere in this movement, most notably between the first and second thematic areas in the exposition and recapitulation. However, these were not part of Taruskin's study because they do not involve circles of thirds, for the tonal structure is as follows: the exposition starts in the tonic, C major, for its first thematic area and ventures to the mediant minor, E minor, for the second. G major begins the codetta and launches the trombone passage mentioned by Taruskin. The recapitulation starts in the tonic but the second theme begins in the tonic minor, C minor, and modulates down a third to the submediant minor, A minor, before returning to the tonic major, C major.

[116] Richard Taruskin, *Stravinsky and the Russian Traditions: A Biography of the Works through Mavra* (Berkeley and Los Angeles: University of California Press, 1996) vol. I, 256.

Example 3.14 Harmonic reduction of Schubert, Symphony No. 9 in C Major (*Great*, D. 944), first movement, mm. 181–240, from Taruskin, "Stravinsky's 'Angle,'" 81

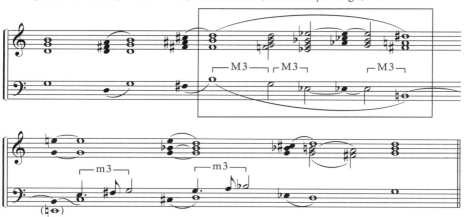

The added word "prolongation" endorses Taruskin's reading with a ringing Schenkerian term, and the allegiance to a theory that espouses the exclusive structural power of fifth relations is made explicit. In buttressing his analysis using this tradition, Taruskin underscores further his continued allegiance to diatonic theory, at the expense of showcasing Schubert's thirds.

Indeed, this perspective perpetuates the analyses of Tovey and Hans Gal. Tovey contended that after the second theme reaches its normative dominant, Schubert wanders away from it, producing a digression:

> This glorious theme [i.e. the second theme in E minor] veers round towards the *normal* key of the dominant, G major; whence however it *wanders away* into the most wonderful of all Schubert's unorthodox *digressions*, a *locus classicus* for the imaginative use of trombones in a pianissimo. (italics mine)[117]

However, he also saw novelty in the passage: it "is so masterly in design as well as in poetic power that *it is far more like a new art-form than a failure to execute an old one*" (italics mine).[118]

Hans Gal's view of mm. 174–240 of the first movement of the *Great* Symphony also is reflected in Taruskin's analysis. These measures could be cut "without altering a single note, and no gap would be noticeable," wrote Gal – a thought that may also have inspired Taruskin's similar comment on the second theme of the *Unfinished* Symphony mentioned above.

---

[117] Tovey, *Essays in Musical Analysis*, vol. I: *Symphonies* (London: Oxford University Press, 1946), 206.
[118] Tovey, *Essays in Musical Analysis*, vol. I, 207.

Schubert's first performers and numerous nineteenth-century critics might have welcomed Gal's cut, though Gal himself is clear that he was not making an editorial suggestion, a point which he makes more forcefully than Taruskin did after him: to remove those measures "would only cripple the movement by removing its most beautiful episode." In words recalled by Taruskin, Gal writes that the trombone solo possesses a "mysterious grandeur" that relies on the remoteness of the key: it is "a call from another world [that] intrudes on the bright, serene scene of the first movement. A flat minor, a key from the opposite end of the tonal spectrum, is a symbol of this distance."[119]

Taruskin returned yet again to the codetta of the *Great* Symphony in *The Oxford History of Western Music*, although this time he placed his analysis in a different historical context. No longer staged as a precursor to the musical language of late nineteenth-century Russians, the passage now epitomizes "aria time" or the Romantic obsession with generating "musical trance" through remote modulations, which "imping[es] on the progress of a more extended musical argument."[120] He clarifies what this means by comparing Beethoven's and Schubert's approaches to sonata form: we expect a "single-minded, overarching trajectory through struggle to the inevitable victory" from Beethoven, but Schubert "is likely to entice us – and entrance us – with islands of mysterious repose amid the hurly-burly, interrupting the forward thrust of the circle of fifths and calling out with Faust to the passing moment, 'Stop, stay awhile!'" Echoing the earlier incarnations of his analysis, he offers a new analytical synopsis, as follows:

The passage [in the *Great* Symphony] between the B-minor triad in measure 185 and the dominant seventh on B in measure 212 amounts to a sequence of flat submediants, creating a closed circle (enclosed in a box) that *could be excised from the analytical chart* without disturbing the coherence of the surrounding circle of fifths that gives the codetta its tonally functional import. But of course the really memorable and affecting music is contained precisely within the box. Most memorable of all is the Ab-minor episode, rendered uncanny by the virtually unprecedented use of a solo trombone. It shows up in the analysis simply as a digression within a digression.

Again, it is the remoteness of the progression that appeals to the imagination, and its attendant static quality of time, rather than its logic – even though ... the logic of even the most remote connections can easily be demonstrated, and their relationship to the active harmonic ingredients easily understood. Moreover, and

[119] Gal, *Franz Schubert and the Essence of Melody*, 125–126.
[120] Taruskin, *Oxford History of Western Music*, 94.

somewhat perversely if one insists on measuring Schubert's procedures by a Beethovenian standard of efficiency, the actual running time of the different harmonic areas and individual chords seems as if by design to vary inversely with their functional caliber.[121] (italics mine)

Note how Taruskin this time specifies that the circle of thirds could be "excised from the *analytical chart*." There is no confusion here: the removal of such harmonies is a statement about music theory, not a solution to irritations of Schubertian length.

Yet Taruskin's attitude to music theory remains curious. In all cases in which he analyzes this passage, he points out that the logic of these remote digressions is easily (!) demonstrated but ultimately irrelevant. In the *Oxford History of Western Music*, Taruskin is even more insistent on this point than in his previous studies, arguing that an appreciation of Schubert's remote harmonies *depends* on setting that logic aside. In addition to the comments on the *Great* Symphony, he offers a lengthy and particularly insightful analysis of Schubert's Impromptu in E♭ major, Op. 90, No. 2. He similarly concludes that its remote key, B minor, "can be traced logically, and is therefore intelligible, but its distance, not the logic of its description, is what registers. *The logic, while demonstrable, is beside the point. To insist on demonstrating it works against the intended effect*" (italics mine).[122] For the record, this is the same key relation as that battled out by Fisk and Cohn in the Piano Sonata in B♭ Major: it is the enharmonic equivalent of the flat submediant minor, or a hexatonic pole. But theorizing Schubert's remote keys is easy, says Taruskin. This comment was not intended to encourage us all to do it. Analyzing, we are instead told, is the wrong response to this music – or at least it won't do anything to enhance the listening experience. This kind of music should not provide its listeners with the urge to rush into action to produce a Hoffmanesque critique about its inner workings. The implication here is that Beethoven's music, on the other hand, rightly sent theorists and critics scurrying to their desks to pen detailed critiques, as well as treatises on musical form and harmonic syntax.

The variety of responses we have encountered in this chapter towards Schubert's sound world explains a great deal about the fate of the reception of Schubert's music. As Adorno, Dahlhaus, and McClary have all agreed, Schubert's music sounds involuntary but was not created that way. In Chapter 1, we saw that Schubert's contemporaries and subsequent

---

[121] Taruskin, *Oxford History of Western Music*, 95–96.
[122] Taruskin, *Oxford History of Western Music*, 89.

nineteenth-century critics were, however, precisely under the illusion that it had been. While I have argued that Adorno, Dahlhaus, and McClary do not go far enough in exposing the technical devices behind Schubert's "carefully calculated" sound world, many of Schubert's tricks of the trade are, by contrast, elegantly revealed in Taruskin's textbook. Readers of the *Oxford History of Western Music* learn how Schubert used not only flat submediants but also Neapolitan, augmented sixth, and diminished chords to navigate his way through a vastly expanded tonal space. Indeed, in the first of Taruskin's studies cited here, he concluded that "circles of thirds offered composers an alternate course of harmonic navigation that bypassed the circle of fifths," and he predicted that a "large chapter in the as-yet-unwritten history of nineteenth-century harmony will show how composers increasingly availed themselves of these new harmonic paths that tended to short-circuit the traditional key system."[123] Indeed, in the final study examined here, from *The Oxford History of Western Music*, Taruskin wrote much of that missing chapter of nineteenth-century harmony. But for him, analyzing such passages, though easily accomplished, is as much a digression as the harmonies themselves. The message for student readers is "don't try this at home."

For all of the effort that Taruskin exerts in explaining how Schubert constructs his tonal space, the end result is no different from the following comment made by Walter Raymond Spalding nearly a century ago:

[In Schubert's chamber music] we do not look for architectonic power – we must admit, in fact, at the risk of seeming ungracious, that Schubert is diffuse at times – but our senses are so enthralled by the imaginative freedom and by the splendor of color, that all purely intellectual judgment is suspended. The magician works his wonders; it is for us to enjoy.[124]

According also to Spalding, Schubert's music is to be consumed in awe, not in technical analysis.

I remain unconvinced that closing one's mind to Schubert's technical devices is best for the ears. Take the audience of a magician by way of analogy. To be sure, one can delight in seeing a rabbit appear from a hat, and, after a certain age, we know that anyone who thinks it is actually "magic" is deluded. The inquisitive amongst us will surely wonder how it is done. Do those who find out fail to appreciate the show? No. They begin

---

[123] Taruskin, "Stravinsky's 'Angle,'" 80.

[124] Walter Raymond Spalding, *Music: An Art and a Language* (Boston: Arthur P. Schmidt Co., 1920), 166. Spalding's comment was referring to the Piano Trios (D. 898 and D. 929), Quartet in A minor (D. 804), Quartet in D minor (D. 810), and Quintet in C Major (D. 956).

instead to appreciate the mastery required to create the optical illusion. So with Schubert. The well-informed listener can appreciate how the aural illusion is carried out – the illusion of effortlessness, of somnambulism, of trance, of exile, and of memory; the illusion, in other words, of apparently magical harmonic effects.

From excursion to structure, from chaos to circle

Neo-Riemannian theorists have also eagerly attempted to fill in the lacuna left by that as-yet-unwritten history of nineteenth-century harmony. The cycles of major and minor thirds, which interested Taruskin for the development of whole-tone and octatonic scales, have been an important concern of neo-Riemannian theorists. We saw at the opening of this chapter how Richard Cohn applied his hexatonic model – made up of cycles of major thirds – to Schubert's Piano Sonata in B♭ Major. As we saw, Fisk read the non-structural harmonies as symbolizing the protagonist's wanderings in exile. Cohn's theory transformed such moments from excursion to structure, from chaos to circle. It took a separate, exhaustive study of the history of the hexatonic pole – not just from the nineteenth century, but from Gesualdo to Schoenberg – to establish that composers (of vocal music) employ the move to signal the uncanny. It should come as no surprise, therefore, that, when the move appears in instrumental music, it has invited descriptions such as mysterious, eerie, otherworldly, and ghostly. Yet this does not mean that the theoretical explanation needs to match the sound, or that we need to be kept in the dark.

On the contrary, the perceptions of Schubert's sonata forms that we have encountered in this chapter, with their moments of exile, banishment, memory, alternative subjectivities, and mysterious islands of repose, illustrate the urgent need for music theory to catch up with the musicological imagination. In this chapter, I demonstrated how Schubert exploits common tones to open up tonal space on a surface level, that is, within a thematic unit. His exploration of harmonic sonorities united by a common tone may either reinforce the tonic/dominant axis or undermine it. In Chapter 4, I shall examine Schubert's constant reinvention of large-scale tonalities and shall scrutinize the theoretical habits of the twentieth century in generalizing large-scale harmonic schemas.

The greatest problem for late twentieth- and twenty-first-century Anglo-American scholars in particular is that we have inherited a particularly restrictive – albeit powerful – system of tonal analysis: Schenkerian theory.

Whether one is specifically trained as a Schenkerian or not, knowledge of the structural focus on the tonic and dominant is inescapable. Schubert's harmonic adventures – whether diatonic or chromatic – are therefore almost certain to be considered digressive, middleground obstacles on the way to the necessary harmonic goals of the dominant and ultimately the closing tonic. As Taruskin explicitly stated (and as everyone who has encountered Schubert has observed), "if one insists on measuring Schubert's procedures by a Beethovenian standard of efficiency, the actual running time of the different harmonic areas and individual chords seems as if by design to vary inversely with their functional caliber."[125] One way of demonstrating this inversion is to elevate these middle- and foreground harmonic excursions to the level of structure, as Cohn has done – in other words, to explore how Schubert turns the Classical paradigm upside down and inside out.

It is with this latter perspective in mind that I turn to my next chapter. It is a critique of music theory. It primarily addresses the habits of thought that have been absorbed through the geometrical modeling of tonal space. I focus on the theoretical repercussions of Schenker's "sacred triangle" and the advantages and disadvantages of neo-Riemannian theory's focus on cycles of recurrent transformations. These geometries have tended to privilege symmetrical or recurring representations of tonal space, yet diatonicism (and even Schubert's version of chromaticism) is fundamentally asymmetrical. In Chapter 4, I focus on Schubert's idiosyncratic use of every degree of the scale other than the tonic and dominant, and also on his use of modal mixture. I narrow down the works I analyze to those sonata forms which use these degrees as large-scale harmonic stations in such a way as to suggest symmetry. At the same time, these apparent symmetries lay bare the fundamental asymmetry of diatonicism and the problems of designing beautiful geometries of tonal space.

---

[125] Taruskin, *Oxford History of Western Music*, 96. Note again the "as if by design" – surely a vestige of that suspicion that Schubert's designs might have happened by accident.

A sonata is a metaphorical representation of a perfect human action. It is a narrative "action" because it drives through a vectored sequence of energized events toward a clearly determined, graspable goal, the ESC [essential structural closure]. It is "perfect" because (unless artificially blocked from achieving the goal) it typically accomplishes the task elegantly, proportionally, and completely.

A sonata is a linear journey of tonal realization, onto which might be mapped any number of concrete metaphors of human experience. Since a central component of the sonata genre is its built-in teleological drive – pushing forward to accomplish a generically predetermined goal – the sonata invites an interpretation as a musically narrative genre.[1]

Astonishing words for 2006. They come from the latest addition to theories of sonata form, namely Hepokoski's and Darcy's *Elements of Sonata Theory: Norms, Types, and Deformations in the Late-Eighteenth-Century Sonata*. As can be seen from the above two paragraphs, the norm according to Sonata Theory remains a one-sided masculinist view of "human experience," which, moreover, is characterized as the "perfect" human experience. While the authors promised to provide a fresh perspective on sonata form, they reassert the privileged teleological, masculine paradigm that has been the subject of sustained feminist critique.[2] Why are we still being presented with an apparently old-style version of sonata form?

The novelty in the approach of Hepokoski and Darcy lies in the emphasis they place on musical hermeneutics. Few sonata forms – or rather few sonata forms worth discussing – attain this "perfection." Even the great works of Haydn, Mozart, and Beethoven, whose works form the main corpus of their analyses, fall from grace, as it were. Passages where "conventions" are not met are described as "deformations," "wrong," "signs of decay," "failures," and so on. Meanwhile, Hepokoski and Darcy reinforce the norm by speaking of

---

[1] James Hepokoski and Warren Darcy, *Elements of Sonata Theory: Norms, Types, and Deformations in the Late-Eighteenth-Century Sonata* (Oxford University Press, 2006), 252 and 251 respectively.

[2] The fountainhead of this critique may be found in Susan McClary, *Feminine Endings: Music, Gender, and Sexuality* (University of Minnesota Press, 1991), 13–16.

conventions as the "acceptable" procedures. Composers may, for example, arrive at the "wrong key" at the end of the transition, and then resume the secondary theme in an "acceptable key," only to omit the "essential structural closure" and turn the movement into "sonata failure." Despite these negative-sounding words, Hepokoski and Darcy insist that a "failure" is a prized hermeneutic moment. These are not intended to be catastrophic but wondrous failures – moments of awe-inspiring creativity against the generic norm. In other words, Sonata Theory endorses the analytical and hermeneutic procedure we have witnessed in the readings of Schubert's sonata forms in Chapter 3: it encourages a focus on deviant pieces over conventional ones, draws attention to how composers thwart generic expectations, and emphasizes how non-normative moments invite extramusical explanation. As I demonstrated in Chapters 2 and 3, it is easier to see how deviant moments demand extra-musical explanation as opposed to moments that do not defy convention. For this reason, the choice and characterization of the norm is crucially important. As indicated in previous chapters, the most common impulse is to define a norm in the most basic generic sense in order that Schubert may remain special.

It cannot escape notice that the above two paragraphs capture the same norm that Hubert Parry had in mind when he wrote the following brutal assessment of Schubert a century ago:

[Schubert] had no great talent for self-criticism, and the least possible feeling for abstract design, and balance, and order . . . In instrumental music he was liable to plunge recklessly, and to let design take its chance.[3]

He was always uncertain in the management and control of design . . . Of all great composers Schubert is the one who depends most on the actual attractiveness of his musical ideas and his musical personality; . . . his works of the sonata order are often obviously redundant and imperfect in design and bear cutting without much injury.[4]

Parry's remarks are fairly standard for the turn of the twentieth century. They stem from a confident feeling of what abstract design, balance, and order constitute. He invokes a norm – a sense of how music ought to go – in order to judge where Schubert went wrong, where he was "imperfect." Parry targets the composer's sonata forms in particular, which, after a few judicious editorial cuts, could be brought into line with expected – nay, "perfect" – formal standards.

[3] Hubert Parry, *The Evolution of the Art of Music* (London: Kegan Paul, Trench, Trubner, & Co. Ltd., 1897), 287–288.

[4] Hubert Parry, *Summary of the History and Development of Mediæval and Modern European Music* (London: Novello and Company, 1904), 75.

Although Hepokoski and Darcy assert that non-normative moments are to be prized and must invite exegesis, the language they use throughout their treatise to characterize anomalies comes perilously close to Parry's. Hepokoski and Darcy encourage readers to apply their theory to Schubert. But how is even the most well-intentioned hermeneut supposed to leap from an analysis that speaks of "wrong keys," "modal failure," "sonata failure" to a hermeneutics of celebration for breaking the norm – especially in Schubert's case? How indeed is one supposed to distinguish between their language of "deformation," "fail- ure" or "wrong" harmonic turns and the language of nineteenth-century critics, who also called Schubert's music "flawed"? Despite numerous attempts to assure readers that they do not mean these terms negatively, the history of negative appraisals of Schubert's music runs so deep that it seems insincere to adorn Schubert with praise in light of an analytical language that suggests the opposite.[5] Nonetheless, at its core, there is a real difference between Parry on the one hand and Hepokoski and Darcy on the other. For Parry, norms are disciplining forces to be followed, for Hepokoski and Darcy they are a generic set of conventions that composers are meant to negotiate.

This chapter will offer a critique of norms and how we press them into service for the purposes of musical analysis. I shall consider both harmonic and thematic formal models of sonata form, focusing further on Sonata Theory and in particular on Schenker's theory of sonata form and the latter-day assimilation of *Formenlehre* into Schenkerian practice. I shall also consider neo-Riemannian models of tonal space, particularly as relevant to Schubert's idiosyncratic use of thirds. Each of these lines of inquiry could take up a book in itself. Thus, I have necessarily had to make choices in order to limit the current discussion. The chapter will examine Schubert's use of each degree of the scale other than the tonic and dominant – again an expansive topic that requires delimitation. This approach is inspired by Tovey's examination of each scale degree and how they relate as keys to the

---

[5] The number of pages on which the words listed in the above paragraph appear in Hepokoski and Darcy, *Elements of Sonata Theory* are too numerous to cite here. For example, on a cursory count, the word "wrong" (used in connection with the generic expectation of a key or of the placement of an action-space) is mentioned on over fifty pages. It sometimes appears in quotation marks (scare quotes?), sometimes not: note, for example, "wrong key" appears in quotation marks for the heading on p. 237 but not on p. 178 (compare these in their Table of Contents). Their so-called technical term "deformation" receives an 8-page explanation in an appendix on how the term is not intended to carry with it any associations of disability or anything negative (pp. 614–621). Given its consequences for their own negative language in describing composers' "deformations," it seems even they are not immune from its connotations, as lessons from feminist, queer, and disability studies might have predicted. Indeed, this problem pervades their text: given that their treatise focuses on musical instances where composers break the norm, there is hardly a positive adjective in the book.

tonic in "Tonality in Schubert," although I focus exclusively on how Schubert exploits these keys as large-scale harmonic stations in the expositions and recapitulations of his sonata forms. My exclusion of development sections is deliberate and also follows Tovey's lead. As he remarked, "Probably the most fundamental rule for operations in large-scale tonality is that key-relation is a function of form. It is no use citing passages from the course of a wandering development to prove that a composer regards a key as related to his tonic: the function of development is contrast, not tonic relation."[6] I am interested in Schubert's conceptualization of tonal space with respect to how keys relate to a tonic center.

I am specifically interested in how Schubert created obvious harmonic symmetries to define musical form. I focus on the appearance of the subdominant at the point of thematic recapitulation, the use of diatonic and chromatic mediants and submediants that offset each other in the secondary themes of expositions and recapitulations, Schubert's use of the supertonic and "subtonic" as a potential harmonic pairing, and the structural consequences of parallel major/minor equivalence.

I am aware of the numerous other – non-symmetrical – ways in which Schubert uses these harmonies. My choice in favor of symmetrical patterns is governed by my desire to critique longstanding habits in the history of music theory, which has witnessed the configuration of tonal space in impressive symmetrical geometries. It may at first blush seem more logical to approach such a critique using Schubert's *asymmetrical* harmonic forms; however, as will become evident throughout this chapter, Schubert's *symmetrical* forms cut to the very heart of the problems in the history of symmetrical or intervallically recurrent configurations of tonal space. As we shall see, the diatonic framework from which Schubert worked is not always conducive to the kinds of geometries of recurrent root-moves developed in the nineteenth century or to the cyclic geometries that sparked neo-Riemannian theory. In addition to scrutinizing geometries well known in neo-Riemannian theory, I shall examine a less well-known geometry that is fundamental to Schenkerian theory. It has never seriously been scrutinized because of the apparent mysticism attached to it: Schenker's "sacred triangle." Similarly, I shall examine a geometry in Sonata Theory which underpins its teleological status. In short, I am interested in turning the tables: instead of using existing theoretical systems to analyze Schubert's music, I shall use Schubert's music in order to analyze existing theoretical systems.

---

[6] Donald Francis Tovey, "Tonality in Schubert," in Hubert J. Foss (ed.), *The Mainstream of Music and Other Essays* (Oxford University Press, 1949), 145.

The dynamic of sonata form: a view from music theory

In his *Harmony* treatise of 1906, Schenker assumed that the normative large-scale harmonic stations in musical form would follow nature's course. The norm need not be strict, however. While a structure might be expected to unfold through either the dominant or relative major, depending on whether it stems from a major or a minor tonic, he considered it possible for composers to replace normative harmonies with other keys:

Art would not be free art, however, if it insisted always and under all circumstances on a development of a composition in major toward the fifth and of a composition in minor toward the third. Both in the progression of steps, as they complete a single thematic complex, and in a succession of keys, as they produce the total of the content, we therefore find deviations from the development toward the fifth or the third.[7]

In this passage, we see that Schenker introduces a distinction between the "normative" inclinations of harmonic form and the freedom in compositional practice. "Deviations" ("Abweichungen"), as he called them, from the expected keys are welcome. Schenker goes on to explain how deviation may work in sonata form, or indeed in other forms. Note how he insists that only a "layman" would take the harmonic norm to define the quality of form:

[the layman] speaks of a "sonata form," a "symphonic form," etc., as if, eg., all sonatas were the same merely because their harmonic development often moves from the tonic to the dominant, etc. Instead of recognizing in this a feature of Nature, which cannot be rejected by any genius but can at most be *replaced at certain times by modifying surrogates*; instead of understanding that Nature must penetrate all forms of music – be they sonatas or waltzes, symphonies or potpourris – the layman will mistake the command of Nature for a quality of form! (italics mine)[8]

Schenker saw the danger that belief in strict formal models could exert on aesthetic judgement: indeed, he is speaking to the Hubert Parrys of the world. It is clear that Schenker felt that all other keys – whether the subdominant or all shades of thirds and seconds – may replace or may act as surrogates for the so-called natural keys, and he provided numerous examples from the music of Beethoven, Schubert, Mendelssohn, and Brahms.[9] Schenker's attitude towards substitute keys also reveals his attitude toward thematic elements in the definition of form. In *Harmony*, he

---

[7] Schenker, *Harmony*, trans. Elisabeth Mann Borgese, ed. Oswald Jonas (Cambridge, MA: MIT Press, 1973), 248.

[8] Schenker, *Harmony*, 250.   [9] The examples may be found in Schenker, *Harmony*, 246–249.

still aligned himself with *Formenlehre*, for the only way to identify the presence of a substitute key is to think in thematic terms, as he explicitly does in the first passage quoted above.

By the time Schenker put *Free Composition* together, he himself may be said to "mistake the command of Nature for a quality of form" – or perhaps he changed his mind over who was mistaken. In *Free Composition*, his "surrogate keys" are no longer surrogate at all, for they *displace* rather than *replace* natural harmonies.

A comparison of his analyses of the first movement of Mozart's Piano Sonata in C Major (K. 545) in *Der Tonwille* and *Free Composition* illustrates this point. The sonata is famous for its recapitulation of the first theme in the subdominant; the tonic reappears only with the arrival of the second theme. In *Harmony*, Schenker would undoubtedly have considered the reappearance of the first theme as the start of the recapitulation, and its subdominant key as a surrogate for the tonic. He analyzed the movement in just this way as late as 1923, in an essay in *Tonwille*, referring to the "brilliant stroke of the recapitulation, which places at its head the key of the subdominant!"[10] When he returned to the movement in *Free Composition*, however, the subdominant was instead interpreted as delaying the onset of the recapitulation, which had for Schenker come to be inextricably associated with the retaking of the primary tone and tonic (Example 4.1).

The phenomenon behind Schenker's shift in thinking is a geometric shape of mystical importance: a sacred triangle. As Schenker explains, the *Bassbrechung* of the *Ursatz* is made up of two parts – unlike the *Urlinie* or fundamental line, which is "indivisible." As shown in Example 4.2, the bass arpeggiation contains a rising and a falling fifth, which are labeled (1) and (2) in the example. For Schenker there is only one imaginable order in which these two fifths can appear. The ascending fifth takes precedence over its descending counterpart, owing to the direction of the overtone series, where nature always comes ahead of artifice. The configurations shown in Example 4.3, which reverse the order of the natural and artificial direction of the fifth and therefore bring about a I–IV–I and V–I–V structure respectively, are "out of the question," as Schenker emphatically states in the accompanying prose volume of *Free Composition*.[11] Note especially that

---

[10] Schenker, *Der Tonwille: Pamphlets in Witness of the Immutable Laws of Music, Offered to a New Generation of Youth*, vol. I, ed. William Drabkin (Oxford University Press, 2004); see the chapter "Mozart Sonata in C Major, K. 545," trans. Joseph Lubben, 156.

[11] Schenker, *Free Composition*, trans. and ed. Ernst Oster (New York: Longman, 1979), vol. I, 14.

Example 4.1 Schenker's analysis of Mozart, Piano Sonata in C Major (K. 545), first movement, from *Free Composition*, supplement, Fig. 47/1

Example 4.2 The "sacred triangle" from Schenker, *Free Composition*, supplement, Fig. 7

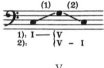

Example 4.3 From Schenker, *Free Composition*, supplement, Figs. 6.4 and 6.5

his strict view of the direction and order of fifths eliminates the possibility of the subdominant ever featuring in the background.

As is typical for Schenker and also for tonal theory generally, these opening remarks in *Free Composition* are all illustrated through the major mode, but they are intended to pertain to the minor as well. This leads to some inconsistencies concerning his attitude towards fifths and thirds, an inconsistency that is present as early as the *Harmony* treatise. Sometimes he equates fifths and thirds as "natural progressions," as he does in *Harmony* when he discusses progressions by second, which are the only ones that are categorically "artificial." Elsewhere he exalts fifths above thirds, heralding "the natural law of the dominant."[12] As he explains in the course of his derivation of the major–minor system, the major triad and the move to the dominant stem from a unique balance that art maintains with nature's overtone series. The major triad and the dominant or fifth as interval are therefore the only

---

[12] Schenker, *Harmony*, 236 and 247.

rudiments the artist can truly recognize in and take from nature. The minor system is an imitation of the natural one – thus making it "natural" in behavior but "artificial" in creation. Its propensity for the relative major is a sign of its ultimate attraction to nature: in imitation of nature's major system, it ought to seek out its own dominant, following the path of the undeniably natural interval of the fifth; but given that its diatonic dominant is a *minor* triad, it instead scouts out a major triad, hence minor's predilection for the relative major.[13] In *Free Composition*, the *Bassbrechung* in the minor mode visits the mediant but it must still attain the fifth to be complete.

In *Free Composition*, Schenker immortalizes the only legitimate bass line, shown in Example 4.2, with the following advice and exclamations:

May the musician always carry in his heart the image of the bass arpeggiation! Let this triangle be sacred to him! Creating, interpreting – may he bear it always in the ear and eye![14]

Interestingly, it is only in Ernst Oster's English translation that this observation about the geometry of the bass was afforded a section unto itself (section 19). In the German edition (1935 and 1956), it is a continuation of section 18 on the division of the bass arpeggiation into two parts. As the passage above accurately translates, Schenker asks that the triangle be held sacred to the artist. The title given to the new section in the translation – "The Sacred Triangle" – endows the triangle itself with sacredness.

The very first sonata form Schubert ever wrote plunged in precisely the direction forbidden by Schenker (Example 4.4a). Composed on June 29, 1811, the Overture for String Quintet in C Minor (D. 8) contains three discrete thematic units in C minor, A♭ major, and F minor respectively. The exposition ends by briefly revisiting the secondary unit in F major. There is no development. The recapitulation responds with each thematic unit respectively in C major, G major, and G minor, before closing in C minor. As shown in Example 4.4a, Schubert's structure heads first in the downward direction, toward the subdominant, and then in the upward direction, toward the dominant, in the recapitulation. The example illustrates below the stave how the sacred triangle is broken up.

Of course, knowing that the Schenker of *Free Composition* does not consider the salience of a key or harmony to be indicative of its structural importance, order can be quickly restored in the Overture. Schubert's

---

[13] For more on Schenker's derivation of the major–minor system, see my "Schenker's Mysterious Five," *19th-Century Music* 23 (1999): 84–102.

[14] Schenker, *Free Composition*, 15.

Example 4.4   (a) Descending fifth (1) before ascending fifth (2) in the harmonic architecture of the thematic units in the exposition and recapitulation of Schubert, Overture for String Quintet in C Minor (D. 8); (b) Schenkerian reinterpretation of (a), preserving the sacred triangle

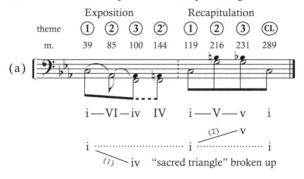

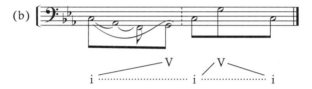

harmonic plan can easily be reinstated into the Schenkerian sacred triangle. Just before the return of the recapitulation in C minor, there is a brief preparatory dominant. In a perfectly routine analytical gesture, it can serve as the structural dominant. As we shall see shortly, it falls in the standard place for a minor-key sonata form. While Schubert may not have made much of his retransitional dominants – rarely giving them the weight that Beethoven bestowed on them – Schenker can fortify them. If, as shown in Example 4.4b, we attach the arpeggiation down to the subdominant to the dominant of the retransition, then the sacred triangle can once again be carried in the eye and ear – despite the fact that it appears below the initial tonic in range.

In this chapter, I have other things in store for the eye and ear. Using a methodology that may be coined "what you see/hear is what you get," I explore the theoretical consequences of taking salience as an indication of structural level, rather than a key's or harmony's generic contrapuntal function within diatonic common practice. Issues that have arisen already in this book come to the fore in this chapter. Recall Example 2.7, where a long section in A♭ major in "Die Allmacht" returns to the home tonic C major after a brief dominant preparation. In contrapuntal terms, A♭ major is the ornamental key and the dominant and tonic are hierarchically superior, as illustrated by the Schenkerian reading given in Example 2.7a. Example 2.7b interprets the key relations according to their weight on the surface of the music. Schubert showcases the large-scale move from A♭ to C, labeled LP in the example. In this analysis, the dominant is a surface-level dominant preparation for C major. Similarly recall "Selige Welt," where all the articulated keys in the song are third relations, each with their own surface-level preparatory dominant harmonies. In Schenkerian terms, the third relations are all surface-level elaborations between the tonic/dominant arpeggiations of the interrupted structure of the song's ABA' form. As was shown in Example 2.5, the two structural dominants appear in mm. 17 and 20. Although each of them plays a mere cadential role in the music and one of them is even a pivot pitch that hovers between $\hat{3}$ of C minor and $\hat{5}$ of A♭ major, for Schenkerians they serve as the all-important structural dominants.

These are but two examples of what Taruskin observed about such analytical treatments of Schubert's harmony: "somewhat perversely if one insists on measuring Schubert's procedures by a Beethovenian standard of efficiency, the actual running time of the different harmonic areas and individual chords seems as if by design to vary inversely with their functional caliber."[15] My interest in this chapter is to witness what happens to the sacred triangle if we revert to Schenker's earlier conception of form, where a range of keys may substitute for the so-called natural or conventional keys of the dominant and relative major in secondary themes in the exposition or of the tonic in the first and second themes in the recapitulation.

Given that much of this chapter will critique Schenker's mature conception of sonata form, it is necessary to rehearse here Schenker's view of the distribution of the points of the sacred triangle within sonata form. In order to accommodate Schubert's paratactic sonata-form practice, my analytical approach also dispenses with a trademark geometry of Hepokoski's and Darcy's Sonata Theory. However, it will also be clear that there are many other ways in which our approaches align.

In *Free Composition*, Schenker retains the exposition, development, and recapitulation sections, but assigns them new tasks compared to the "conventional" or *Formenlehre* theory found in *Harmony*. No longer was it relevant to scout out first and second themes, transitions, and closing sections in order to make sense of their keys and motivic connections. Rather, each of the three main sections is defined by its specific harmonic-contrapuntal task(s).

---

[15] Taruskin, *Oxford History of Western Music*, 96. This passage was also mentioned in Chapter 3.

The first task of any exposition is to achieve the primary tone, which may be $\hat{3}$, $\hat{5}$ or $\hat{8}$ and which may be stated immediately or approached through an initial ascent or preliminary arpeggiation. Schenker concentrates firstly on matters pertaining to $\hat{3}$- and $\hat{5}$-lines, leaving $\hat{8}$-lines mostly out of the picture at this stage.[16] For a sonata form in a major key, it is "imperative" that the primary tone looks forward to the next important task of the exposition, which is the appearance of $\hat{2}$. Schenker focuses on the journey from $\underset{\text{I}}{\hat{3}}$ to $\underset{\text{V}}{\hat{2}}$ in order to address the preparation of the latter in the transition (to use a "conventional" term). So, $\underset{\text{V}}{\hat{2}}$ may either follow directly from the prolonged $\hat{3}$ or come after auxiliary harmonies that tonicize $\underset{\text{I}}{\text{II}}$, which is Schenker's label for V of V. The location of thematic complexes is not hard to spot in this discussion. In thematic terms, the auxiliary harmony produces a V–I relationship between the end of the transition and the new key of the secondary theme. For Schenker, this represents the preferred generic approach, a preference that may be gleaned from the greater effort he exerts to justify transitions that end on the dominant. He argues that "the great masters are not to be criticized when they allow the $\hat{3}$ to move directly to the $\hat{2}$; for this procedure is very much in accord with the sonata form, that is, with the division that is basic to it."[17] The implication, of course, is that many might be poised to criticize pieces without an auxiliary harmony, but Schenker points to none other than the first movement of Mozart's Piano Sonata in C Major (K. 545) as a worthy example of one (see Example 4.1 above). In fact, he could have selected almost any of Mozart's piano sonatas in a major key, for Mozart favored the bifocal close.[18] Compared to Schenker, Hepokoski and Darcy reverse the generic status of these two medial caesura (MC) procedures. Mozart's favorite habit, which they label I:HC MC, is the first-level default and considered suitable for shorter pieces, while V:HC MC is the next option and is suitable for longer pieces. Their labels refer to a transition whose medial caesura is launched by a half cadence in the tonic key (I:HC) or dominant key (V:HC) respectively.[19]

---

[16] The primary tone $\hat{3}$ is the most common in major movements and $\hat{5}$ is more common for minor movements in sonata form. $\hat{8}$ is the least common primary tone.

[17] Schenker, *Free Composition*, 134.

[18] Robert Winter, "The Bifocal Close and the Evolution of the Viennese Classical Style," *Journal of the American Musicological Society* 42 (1989): 275–337.

[19] Hepokoski and Darcy, *Elements of Sonata Theory*, 24–25.

Part of the reason that Schenker goes to such additional lengths in clarifying that transitions which land on the dominant are acceptable is that they raise the issue of the correct placement of the structural $\hat{2}$. Although thematic presentation is not meant to matter, the structural dominant is not the $\hat{2}$ at the end of the transition but the one that begins the secondary thematic area; hence the clear distinction in levels of the two dominants in the exposition of Example 4.1.[20] While Schenker repeatedly implored his readers to ignore so-called conventional sections of sonata form, clearly these sections do implicitly facilitate the articulation of the structure.

The arrival of $\hat{2}$ fulfills the basic requirement of the exposition of movements in a major key. Expositions in a minor key, which most commonly make use of $\hat{5}$ as their primary tone, fulfill their basic requirement with the arrival of $\hat{3}$. This necessarily means that the development sections of major- and minor-keyed movements serve different purposes. In the case of the former, the development prolongs $\hat{2}$, and its main duty is to eliminate any chromaticism, which usually involves eliminating the leading tone of the dominant key by incorporating a lower-seventh in the dominant in the final moments of the development, creating a V^{8-7} motion.[21] By contrast, the development of minor-key movements must achieve the motion to the dominant major, $\hat{2}$.

The recapitulation requires a return to the main key, which occurs after the interruption. It entails a retake of the primary tone in the case of $\hat{5}$- or $\hat{3}$-lines; $\hat{8}$-lines are a special case.[22] The task of the recapitulation

Example 4.5 (a) Temporal representation of Schenker's sacred triangle and (b) representation of sacred triangle in an interrupted structure

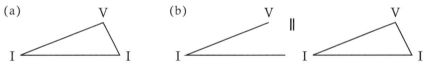

[20] Schenker's graph and the placement of the two $\hat{2}$ may be compared to the score of the end of the transition and beginning of the second theme, which is given below in Example 4.23.

[21] This last point is crucial to Schenker's mature view of the subdominant recapitulation, as we shall see shortly.

[22] Schenker, *Free Composition*, 137. Schenker's placement of the interruption sign ‖ in his graphs is inconsistent in *Free Composition*. Sometimes it appears just before the retake of the primary tone (as I have characterized it in the main text above), but sometimes it appears before the development is completed. This issue need not detain us here, but the nuances that these differences potentially express deserve further investigation. For matters pertaining to the division of the $\hat{8}$-line, see Schenker, *Free Composition*, 33–34 and 40. His Figs. 27a and b show that the task of the exposition of an $\hat{8}$-line structure is to reach $\hat{5}$ rather than $\hat{2}$. (It is interesting that Fig. 27b never shows up again as a model for $\hat{8}$-lines in *Free Composition*.)

Example 4.6 From Schenker, *Free Composition*, supplement, Fig. 14

in all cases is to reach $\hat{1}$. Although this marks the point of closure in the movement, it does not necessary mean that the music stops: once the final $\hat{1}$ has been reached, a coda may follow.

In real music and in real time, Schenker's sacred triangle is never the symmetrical isosceles shape presented in Example 4.2. It may be imagined to be more like Example 4.5, which depicts the peak of the *Ursatz*'s dominant arriving at the end of the piece. The steady incline of this stretched-out triangle captures the rising tension of the events striving towards the goal of the final tonic: "The *goal* and the course to the goal are primary. Content comes afterward: without a goal there can be no content. In the art of music, as in life, motion toward the goal encounters obstacles, reverses, disappointments, and involves great distances, detours, expansions, interpolations, and, in short, retardations of all kinds."[23] In the case of sonata form, there are two attempts to reach the apex of the triangle, as depicted on the right-hand side of Example 4.5. The first occupies the space of the exposition and development, and the journey to the apex is revisited in the recapitulation, albeit through different thematic material. However stretched-out the triangle may be in musical time through digressive harmonies between the rising tonic and dominant, one aspect of the geometry is immutable: its altitude remains unchanged: it always measures a fifth above the tonic.

Schenker provides no fewer than four sets of figures on how the space between the opening tonic and dominant may be filled in, and how the different *Urlinien* interact with the bass line.[24] Example 4.6 reproduces the first such figure, which contains only the bass line. Each of the other three figures is similarly divided into six sections, which are further divided into various subsections. The figures are seemingly exhaustive. Yet only *Stufen* II, III, and IV are represented. Missing from consideration are VI and VII. Their absence begins to tell the story of just how sacred Schenker's triangle was to him. To include these two *Stufen* would destroy the visual impression of the bass arpeggiation being contained within this sacred triangle. VI and VII appear "out of bounds" of the tonic/dominant tonal space, as shown in Example 4.7.

---

[23] Schenker, *Free Composition*, 5. Observe the similarity between this oft-quoted statement by Schenker and Hepokoski's and Darcy's characterization of sonata form quoted at the outset of this chapter.

[24] Schenker, *Free Composition*, supplement, Figs. 14–16 and 18.

Example 4.7   Position of submediant and seventh degree in relation to the sacred triangle

$$\text{I} — (\text{VI}) - \text{V} - \text{I} \qquad \text{I} — (\text{VII}) - \text{V} - \text{I}$$

Example 4.8   Schenker's analysis of Chopin, Étude, Op. 10, No. 8, from *Free Composition*, supplement, Fig. 7b

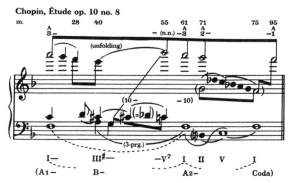

In the depths of *Free Composition* Schenker does explore VII unfolding to V, but consideration of VI–V is notably absent.[25] There is, of course, a simple contrapuntal explanation for the omission. Parallel fifths occur when $\hat{3}$ moves to $\hat{2}$ over VI–V (the move from $\flat\hat{3}$ to $\hat{2}$ over a $\flat$VI–V has the same problem). However, even when other harmonies intervene between VI and V, Schenker prefers to downplay the submediant. Witness the case of his analysis of Chopin's Étude, Op. 10, No. 8. The beamed mediant, III$^\sharp$, in Example 4.8 is a visual distraction away from the submediant immediately before it. Schenker's graph indicates that the B section of the ternary form in Chopin's Étude begins in III$^\sharp$. The overall tonal plan of the A and B sections is I–III$^\sharp$–V^7, a fifth-space (followed by another, notwithstanding Schenker's placement of the dominant below the tonic in this case). In fact, an analysis of the surface thematic material reveals that the B section starts with the D minor immediately before it, notated as a flagged note and as still part of the A section. Therefore, Schenker's III$^\sharp$ is in fact a V/vi.

---

[25] Schenker, *Free Composition*, 89–90.

This observation must be credited to the eagle eye of Charles J. Smith, whose patience in comparing hundreds of Schenker's graphs with *Formenlehre* analyses of the scores was rewarded by finding numerous examples like this – of curious discrepancies between form and structure in Schenker's writings.[26] Why the aversion to starting the section in the submediant? I am convinced that the graph's proximity to Schenker's explanation of the sacred triangle provides important clues to his solution: VI lies outside the sacred tonal space of the triangle, and thus he emphasized III instead. I am equally convinced that this also explains the lack of analyses in *Free Composition* of sonata-form movements with salient submediant moves – an otherwise curious lacuna given how prevalent they are in the literature. Ernst Oster, the translator and editor of the English edition of *Free Composition*, calls for greater attention to sonata forms with large-scale mediant and submediant moves in his elaborate footnote to Schenker's section on sonata form.[27]

The Sonata Theory of Hepokoski and Darcy also has a geometry, an arc, that is treated as "sacred," though it is not explicitly labeled as such. The graphic representation of the "generic layout of sonata form" is reproduced in Example 4.9. It illustrates the first theme (P) going upward to the second theme (S), which is generically in the dominant or relative major. The transition (TR) is shown to work its way to the medial caesura (MC), which we have already seen is generically triggered either by I: HC or V: HC, although these options are not specified on the graph. The apostrophe (') represents the silence or "caesura" commonly found between TR and S in Classical music. The closing section (C) is separated from S, but shown generically to continue in the same key. EEC refers to the "essential expositional closure" which is one of the trademarks of their theory. Its corresponding moment in the recapitulation is labeled ESC, meaning "essential structural closure." Securing the ESC is the "central generic task of the sonata," as can be read in the small print below the recapitulation in Example 4.9. The "final cadence" at the end of the exposition and recapitulation, as well as the "V as chord" just before the recapitulation are cadences of lesser articulative importance. The differences between the points of

---

[26] Charles J. Smith, "Musical Form and Fundamental Structure: An Investigation of Schenker's *Formenlehre*," *Music Analysis* 15 (1996): 191–297. He resketches Fig. 7b on p. 222.

[27] Ernst Oster's comments appear in Schenker, *Free Composition*, 139–141. Hellmut Federhofer has pursued the study of third relations in Schubert from a Schenkerian perspective, concluding that they elaborate the tonic-to-dominant space. See Federhofer, "Terzverwandte Akkorde und ihre Funktion in der Harmonik Franz Schuberts," in Otto Brusatti (ed.), *Schubert-Kongress Wien 1978* (Graz: Akademische Druck- und Verlagsanstalt, 1979), 61–70.

Example 4.9 Generic layout of sonata form, from Hepokoski and Darcy, *The Elements of Sonata Theory*, 16

The entire structure: the Essential Sonata Trajectory (to the ESC)

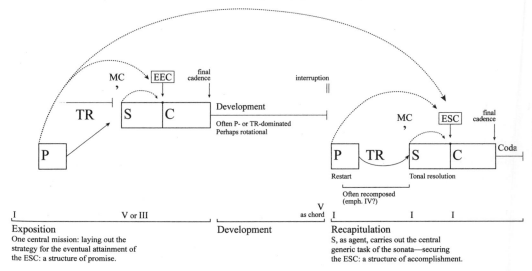

articulation in a generic sonata form according to Sonata Theory and Schenker are evident here. In a major mode, the beginning of S, which usually articulates $\hat{2}$, is crucial for Schenker, not the EEC at the end of it. In a minor mode, the "V as chord" is likely to be the structural dominant, if no other dominant is present. (We witnessed just this scenario in Schubert's Overture for String Quintet, Example 4.4b). In both modes, the "final cadence" just before the coda is Schenker's structural closure and not the ESC cadence.

Both theories share the commitment to teleology. The "essential sonata trajectory (to the ESC)" is illustrated in Hepokoski's and Darcy's graph by the arc of the dotted arrow. This arc is not dissimilar to the rising and falling direction of the sacred triangle – although, by contrast, Hepokoski and Darcy are not insistent on a journey through the fifth. They are, however, insistent on the arc's journey from P in the exposition (hereafter P_{EXP}) to the ESC, conferring on the latter tonal resolution in the tonic. Without it, a sonata risks "failure." Their large-scale arc is no different in concept to Schenker's sacred triangle, for it ensures a certain quality and dynamic of form, and its absence leads to various levels of "failure."[28]

---

[28] A missing or unsecured PAC (perfect authentic cadence) at EEC or ESC leads to "failed expositions" and "failed recapitulations" respectively; see Hepokoski and Darcy, *Sonata Theory*, 177–179 and 245–247.

By contrast, the advantage of Sonata Theory is that, for example, an S_{EXP} in the submediant could be graphed below the level of the tonic P_{EXP}, and it could be separated from C_{EXP}, which might appear in another key. Schubert's sonata forms, which show considerable tonal flexibility for S, often with C in a different key, can have these distinctions clearly depicted. However, it seems to me prudent to dispense with all of the forward-driving arrows in order to accommodate Schubert's non-teleological dynamic of form. Maintaining the arcs from P→EEC and S→EEC upholds the accepted wisdom that Schubert's remote modulations are "digressions" or interruptions away from the main business of sonata form. My discussion of Schubert's sonata forms in the rest of this chapter explores a paratactic perception of the form.

Schubert's expansion of tonal space mainly involved testing the generic expectations of the harmony connected with the MC, providing new harmonic stations for S, and exploring non-tonic Ps in the recapitulation. He also explored new ways to fill in the silence between TR and S with harmonically suggestive pitches. I shall assess Schubert's large-scale architecture of tonal space in a paratactic sense by associating each formal component of the exposition with its counterpart in the recapitulation, P with P, TR with TR, MC' with MC', S with S, and C with C.[29] My approach shares many resonances with Hans-Joachim Hinrichsen's method of comparing expositions and recapitulations in Schubert's late works.[30] In the harmonic stations of P, S, and C, Schubert explored possible architectures of every possible *Stufen*, including some chromatic ones. I turn now to an illustration of his tonal spaces, beginning with Schubert's use of the subdominant recapitulation.

The subdominant and the repetition of the fifth-space

The subdominant recapitulation has the reputation for being the lazy composer's sonata-form option. Its I–V ‖ IV–I harmonic architecture permits a literal repetition of the exposition, transposed down a fifth to form the recapitulation. In practice, however, few composers exploit its labor-saving potential; most make changes of some sort, however small or

---

[29] In the analyses, I adopt no Sonata Theory labels as analytical tools, except MC', which I take to include the cadence at the end of the transition, and I use the apostrophe to denote the characteristic silence. I use other symbols only to comment on Hepokoski's and Darcy's theory.

[30] Hans-Joachim Hinrichsen, "Die Sonatenform im Spätwerk Franz Schuberts," *Archiv für Musikwissenschaft* 45 (1988): 16–49.

apparently insignificant. Nonetheless, this form is frowned upon because it is mechanical. Charles Rosen, for example, went so far as to call it "a kind of degenerate recapitulation."[31] Tovey argued that "In works like the *Forellen-quintett* Schubert was exhausted by the effort of his grand expositions and fell back with relief upon a mere copyist's task by way of recapitulation. This was wrong."[32]

When analyzing even the most repetitious subdominant recapitulations, few analysts merely transpose their harmonic analysis of the exposition down a fifth, and consider their work for the recapitulation done. It seems analysts work harder than the composer! This is especially the case in Schenkerian theory, where, as we have seen, the harmonic-contrapuntal definition of sonata form relies on the return of the tonic key for the articulation of a proper recapitulation. In other words, a Schenkerian interpretation of the form suggests a level of formal sophistication that belies the apparent mechanical nature of its formal construction.

Schenker's exemplar was the first movement of Mozart's Piano Sonata in C Major mentioned earlier. The changes in the recapitulation involve a modified transition and elongated secondary theme, neither of which make it into Schenker's graph. In *Free Composition*, he represented the subdominant with a black, stemmed note (Example 4.1). As the graph also shows, he considered it still part of the development. The recapitulation begins with the reappearance of the tonic, which, given the absence of measure numbers, we are left to presume starts with the secondary thematic material.

If according to the Schenker of *Der Tonwille* the subdominant recapitulation was a "brilliant stroke" on Mozart's part, then the interpretation of it in *Free Composition* was a "brilliant stroke" on Schenker's part. It preserves the "sacred triangle" and exemplifies the schism he fostered between thematic and harmonic definitions of form. Moreover, it beautifully shores up his claims for the task of the development. As we saw above, its task in a major-key sonata is to eliminate the chromaticism generated by the tonicization of the dominant in the exposition. Normally, this requires no more than the introduction of the seventh in the dominant seventh: $\hat{F}\sharp$ cedes to $\hat{F}\natural$, as shown in the graph. In the case of Mozart's sonata, the subdominant harmony, F major, is composed out from this seventh, $\hat{F}$, in the dominant seventh. This event is therefore a dissonance on an upper

---

[31] Rosen, *Sonata Forms*, rev. edn. (New York: W. W. Norton, 1988), 288.

[32] Tovey, "Franz Schubert (1797–1828)," in *The Mainstream of Music and Other Essays*, ed. Hubert J. Foss (Oxford University Press, 1949), 118.

level and a consonance on the lower level, which also supports Schenker's view that keys are surface-level phenomena, as depicted in the trapezoid in Example 2.10. What makes this structure unusual, then, is not its subdominant recapitulation (for even to call it such would require taking thematic material into account, something a strict late-practice Schenkerian should not do) but the transformation of the seventh into a consonant harmony at the end of the development. Rarely is a seventh itself prolonged in the manner it is here.

Schenker's graph has drawn much criticism from Schenkerians – although not for the principles behind his treatment of the subdominant. The exploration of numerous alternatives to Schenker's graph are more a critique of what happens *after* the subdominant. The main criticism has little impact on Schenkerian interpretations of Schubert's Piano Quintet in A Major (*Trout*, D. 667), which is the work I discuss below. Schenker's retaking of the primary tone $\hat{3}$ in Example 4.1 is seen as problematic because Mozart's secondary theme has no root-position tonic harmony with which to support it. The first suitable root position does not occur until the end, in fact where the final $\hat{1}$ appears.[33] The second thematic complex in the *Trout* Quintet does provide a root-position tonic, so portraying the retake of the fundamental structure is unproblematic.

The other criticism, which has broader ramifications, including for Schubert, is the observation that the dominant reappears at the end of the transition, after the first theme's subdominant. Schenkerians have argued that Schenker's incomplete neighbor note, $\hat{F}$, in Example 4.1 should read as a complete neighbor note, going back to $\hat{G}$. They have therefore modified slightly Schenker's interpretation of the subdominant by treating it not as the consonant support of a V^7, but as a neighbor-note consonant support within the prolonged dominant. However, this only goes to embed the subdominant more deeply into the development.[34] David Beach, for example, follows this modification in the analysis of Schubert's *Trout* Quintet, while Xavier Hascher does not. However, the main thrust of

---

[33] John Snyder has therefore suggested that Mozart's sonata movement is better regarded as an uninterrupted structure; see "Schenker and the First Movement of Mozart's Sonata K. 545: An Uninterrupted Sonata-Form Movement?" *Theory and Practice* 16 (1991): 51–78.

[34] See Edward Laufer, who proposes a "different [lower-level] order of interruption," in "Revised Sketch of Mozart, K. 545/I and Commentary." Laufer's sketch appears as an appendix to Gordon Sly, "Schubert's Innovations in Sonata Form: Compositional Logic and Structural Interpretation," *Journal of Music Theory* 45 (2001): 144–150. See also Eric Wen, "A Response to Gordon Sly and Edward Laufer: An Alternative Interpretation of the First Movement of Mozart's K. 545," *Journal of Music Theory* 46 (2002): 364–368.

Schenker's concept of the underlying structure remains essentially the same in both of their analyses.[35]

The *Trout* Quintet has one of the few subdominant recapitulations amongst the many in Schubert's output in which he almost literally transposes the exposition. He shortens the recapitulation by omitting the exposition's mm. 1–24 and 100–113. The absence of these passages in the recapitulation are of varying interest depending on the analyst's theoretical apparatus.

Mm. 1–24 and 25–50 cover roughly the same ground. The recapitulation, which begins at m. 210, corresponds to the material from m. 25 onwards. Schenker generally dispenses with repetitions, and thus a Schenkerian is likely to graph only mm. 1–24 and ignore mm. 25–50. However, one crucial difference between the two passages is their respective endings. The former leads to a tonic cadence (m. 24–25), the latter to an emphatic *fz* subdominant harmony, which is followed by a rest for further emphasis (m. 50). In light of the subdominant recapitulation, this striking moment is a hint of things to come – a characteristic hint, for this is classic Schubert. Schubert frequently prepares harmonic events with a promissory note or chord, which, as in this case, need not always be chromatic as are more famous promissory gestures. The recapitulation, thus, contains only the passage that goes to the subdominant (now the subdominant of the subdominant).

The omission of mm. 100–113 is again of little interest to a Schenkerian but has important consequences for Sonata Theory. S_{EXP} ends with two perfect authentic cadences (PACs) in mm. 99–100 and 113–114, which therefore problematicize the choice of the EEC cadence under Hepokoski's and Darcy's rules of thumb. By contrast, the recapitulation collapses the two PACs into one, skipping from V in m. 99 to I in m. 114. The ESC is therefore more clear-cut than the EEC. Such happy circumstances are often exploited by analysts to bolster claims for the validity of one theory over another.

The first movement of the *Trout* Quintet contains three themes, but, unusually for Schubert, they are not configured into a three-keyed exposition. Instead the first theme is in the tonic and the other two are squarely in the dominant. Although the exposition showcases a generic harmonic trajectory, it is a rare assertion of convention for a composer usually thought to possess an "aversion to the dominant."[36] The transition also

---

[35] David Beach, "Schubert's Experiments with Sonata Form: Formal-Tonal Design versus Underlying Structure," *Music Theory Spectrum* 15 (1993): 12 and Xavier Hascher, *Schubert: La forme sonate et son évolution* (New York: Peter Lang, 1996), 126–127.

[36] James Webster, "Schubert's Sonata Form and Brahms's First Maturity (I)," *19th-Century Music* 2 (1978): 22.

ends conventionally, albeit without the typical gesture of an *f* cadence followed by a caesura. The second theme is instead launched seamlessly with a PAC in m. 64 and is therefore distinguished only by a softening of the dynamics to *p*. There is no mistaking the entry of the third theme, even though again there is no conventional announcement of it through an *f* cadence and pregnant pause. Instead, it too begins in m. 84 with a PAC and is distinguished by a reduction in texture to the piano playing solo. Both themes also end with a clear PAC, a feature which prompts the main discrepancy between the graphs of Beach and Hascher, and which raises interesting problems unique to Sonata Theory. The problem with Schubert is usually finding clear cadences to establish a key; here we have too many.

Both Beach and Hascher are in agreement that the thematic material in the subdominant is a "recapitulation," rather than still part of the development. Nonetheless return of the tonic still articulates the second half of the underlying structure. Their emphasis on the difference between the articulation of form on the level of design versus underlying structure has been part of a welcome revival of aspects of *Formenlehre* in Schenkerian theory. However, the strategy further cements the schism between harmonic and thematic design.[37] Indeed, it creates a tension in this structure that goes against the general perception that a subdominant recapitulation loosens the teleological energy of normative sonata forms.

Analyzing the form through the lens of Sonata Theory has the same effect due to the emphasis placed on the $P_{EXP} \rightarrow ESC$ arc as the formal goal of all sonata form movements. Despite the obvious advantages of including the subdominant recapitulation as a "second-level default option" in Sonata Theory, the subdominant has no palpable impact on the main harmonic argument of the movement because the arc bypasses the recapitulation's primary theme (P_{RECAP}). Indeed, the subdominant – or any other key, including the tonic, for that matter – plays little role in this overall journey.

Transformation theory may be of some assistance in capturing the dynamic of the subdominant recapitulation. Instead of giving the impression that such a recapitulation nonetheless possesses a teleological drive towards the tonic or final structural cadence, transformation theory wonderfully captures the repeated trajectory of exposition and recapitulation. The movement may be characterized as a pair of D^{-1} transformations from

---

[37] Beach contemplated two possible interpretations of the *Trout*, but preferred the interrupted one because it shows clearly the distinction between the thematic design and the underlying division of the structure and the subdominant return is shown as a variant of the norm. See "Schubert's Experiments with Sonata Form," 13.

I–V and IV–I, whereby the recapitulation undergoes a wholescale D transformation of the exposition, as illustrated in Example 4.10a.[38] Such a straightforward analysis deliberately deflates the complexity of the Schenkerian and Sonata Theory approaches, in order to reveal the simplicity of the form. My analysis captures the essence of the construction or compositional process of the form, and showcases its paratactic quality. We can also see clearly how the so-called sacred triangle has disintegrated. As shown in Example 4.10a, the first angle of the triangle is intact, but instead of preserving the impression that Schubert's *Trout* Quintet comprises a rising and falling structural fifth, by subsuming the subdominant into the dominant, my diagram of tonal space draws attention to the pair of rising fifths. Similarly, instead of preserving the arc motion to the ESC goal, Example 4.10a emphasizes how the tonic at the outset is the source of the transformation, whereas the tonic at the end emerges from the transformation.

That said, Schubert's *Trout* Quintet, taken as a whole, suggests that there may be some truth to Schenker's sense of structural satisfaction in works that open *up* through a *rising* harmonic motion and close *down* through a *descending* one. The overall dynamic of the tonal space in the first movement of the *Trout* Quintet appropriately opens up the space, with the pair of rising fifths shown in Example 4.10a. The work is not over after the

Example 4.10 Transformations and tonal space in Schubert, *Trout* Quintet (D. 667)
(a) first movement; (b) finale

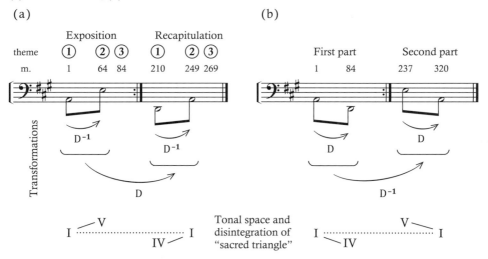

[38] I am following Brian Hyer here (who in turn was following David Lewin) in taking the D
     transformation to be a downward fifth, and the inverse D^{-1} to be the upward one. See Hyer,
     "Reimag(in)ing Riemann," *Journal of Music Theory* 39 (1995): 101–138.

first movement – even if analytical fascination more often than not ends there. The finale is an equally repetitious form, also involving block transposition. The movement is in two symmetrical halves, divided by a double-bar with a repeat of the first section. The second half is a direct transposition of the first, with a few adjustments in register. This time, each half spans *downward*, closing fifths, I–IV and V–I, shown as a pair of D transformations in Example 4.10b. The whole structure is generated through a block D^{-1} transformation, as also illustrated in the example. The finale therefore provides a suitable gesture for closure of the whole work: it traverses the same tonal space as the first movement, but in the reverse order and direction. This is but one of many instances where Schubert reverses transformations that are generally regarded as teleological in orientation. Such syntactical reversals are part of his paratactic outlook on tonal space and musical form. Moreover, these two movements of the *Trout* Quintet are a beautiful example of the vast scale on which Schubert controls his tonal space.

Thinking in these terms has a profound effect on the Schenkerian model in particular. Firstly, and most controversially, the subdominant has to be granted a structural status. As I have illustrated elsewhere, a crucial motivating factor for the exclusion of the subdominant in the background goes far beyond the simple fact that Schenker wanted only the tonic and dominant in the background. It stems from his derivation of the major/minor system outlined in *Harmony*. In order to derive the major scale, Schenker argued that nature unfolds an infinite series of fifth projections, which the artist abbreviates at the fifth projection based on the "mysterious postulate of the number five." This yields C, G, D, A, E, B – all *Stufen* of the C major scale except the subdominant, F. Only by retracing one's steps through the fifth progressions and overshooting the tonic in the "artificial" or non-natural direction does the artist gain the subdominant. The subdominant is therefore a harmony of "extraneous character."[39]

Schenker's treatment of the subdominant in *Free Composition* is a logical outcome of this idea, and the sacred triangle is another manifestation of it. It is safe to say that nowadays such derivations have ceased to impress us, and thus we need not heed their outcomes. In other words, there is no logical reason why the *Ursatz* needs preserving in its current state.[40] To be

---

[39] Schenker, *Harmony*, 38–44 and see also my "Schenker's Mysterious Five," 91–92. The minor scale is derived in imitation of the major scale, the details of which need not detain us here.

[40] Indeed Schenkerians who wish to preserve the conditions of the *Ursatz* and Schenker's other principles must necessarily adopt an axiomatic approach, as for example Matthew Brown has demonstrated in *Explaining Tonality: Schenkerian Theory and Beyond* (Rochester, NY: Rochester University Press, 2005).

sure, the graphs in Example 4.10 are not Schenkerian despite their notational look, but my purpose is to explore ways in which a thematically defined approach to tonal space may usefully exert pressure on Schenkerian theory and coalesce into a new way of thinking about (sonata form) background structures.

The mediant and submediant, and the repositioning of the fifth-space

Schubert is legendary for his use of third relations. We saw in the previous chapter how he uses them to produce cyclic chains, as in the codetta of the first movement of the Symphony No. 9 in C Major (*Great*, D. 944) and the second thematic complex of the String Quartet in G Major. We also saw how they may oscillate above and below a tonic, as in the opening of the second movement of the Symphony No. 8 in B Minor (*Unfinished*, D. 759), or provide a contrasting harmonic station within a thematic complex, as in the B section of the ABA′ first thematic area in the Piano Sonata in B♭. Third relations are also Schubert's most common choice for his remote secondary themes. All of the movements studied in the previous chapter are examples. Moreover, in Chapter 2, we saw that thirds are prevalent in the songs, both as internal keys and especially as double-tonic complexes in many early songs.

Contrary to my argument on the songs, where I claimed that seeking abstract, purely musical harmonic patterns should be resisted, I shall argue the opposite case for Schubert's sonata forms. Indeed, it is something of an irony that scholars have sought patterns in the songs, where the text is clearly a guiding factor in harmonic choice, but have been slower to seek the formal logic of the instrumental music and instead have turned to narratives to explain their idiosyncratic harmonic architecture. Of course, I do not mean to imply that instrumental music is not narrative; I merely point out that the exploration of narratives and new vocabularies has come at the expense of new technical analyses or the development of new paradigms for Schubert's instrumental music.

When Schubert inherited sonata form, he inherited a form that was pretty much defined – not by theorists, but through usage. It must have been clear to him what expositions, developments, and recapitulations do. He undoubtedly knew that major-key movements have the greatest tendency to modulate to the dominant and minor-key movements to the mediant in the exposition. He was undoubtedly aware that developments

explore various keys and generally end in the dominant; and that recapitulations restate material, generally in the tonic. Contrary to the beliefs of
Schubert's early commentators, including even his friends, it was unlikely
to be out of an absence of knowledge that Schubert avoided such conventions. The problem – and it has been a persistent one – has been in finding a
theoretical framework to explain the dynamic of Schubert's sonata forms.

David Kopp has recently challenged the assumption that Schenker invariably
regarded thirds as phenomena of the middleground and foreground, but not
background. He points to some graphs in *Free Composition* in which he claims
that Schenker assigned them a background status. Unfortunately, however, his
conclusions are based on a misreading of details in Schenker's notation. In a
way, Kopp was trying to lend historical support to his theoretical claim that
chromatic and diatonic third relations deserve structural status, and he was
aiming to share some of the credit for his claim with Schenker. Schenker
deserves no such credit. In looking at Figs. 30a, 102/6, 130/4a and 130/4b in
Free Composition, which all prolong the tonic through some kind of submediant, Kopp observes that the *Urlinie* and bass pitches in the submediants all
share the same open-notehead notation as the tonic/dominant material of the
background. It is worth revisiting these graphs, in order to highlight the fact
that, if we wish to see chromatic and diatonic third relations enjoy independent
structural status, conventional Schenkerian theory will not get us there.[41]

Specifically, Kopp argues that Fig. 130/4a is a "background sketch" that
"makes clear the deep structural significance of this [lower] relative
mediant." In the case of Fig. 30a (reproduced as Example 4.11), he argues
that Schenker does not "relegate" the chromatic lower flat mediant to the
middleground as expected, and that "surprisingly, he includes its fifth, Cb,
in the *Urlinie*, necessitating temporary chromatic alteration of the C♮.
Schenker indicates this Cb *at the same level* as the C♮ which surrounds it,
as an open note bearing the $\hat{3}$ symbol" (my italics).[42]

And finally, concerning Fig. 102/6, he states his opinion most strongly:

Remarkably, he [Schenker] accommodates chromatic motion in the *Urlinie* itself,
connecting the fifth of the LFM [lower flat mediant], Fb, as a whole note to the F♮ of
the *Urlinie*, also a whole note (although he does not actually apply the symbol b$\hat{3}$ to the
Fb), rather than simply assigning it as E♮ to an inner voice, an easy alternative. In this

---

[41] I have only reproduced Fig. 30a (Example 4.11) in the discussion that follows. The other graphs
examined by Kopp may be consulted in David Kopp, *Chromatic Transformations in Nineteenth-
Century Music* (Cambridge University Press, 2002), 114–115 or in Schenker, *Free Composition*,
supplement.

[42] Kopp, *Chromatic Transformations*, 113 and 116.

Example 4.11   From Schenker, *Free Composition*, supplement, Fig. 30a

Chopin, Mazurka op. 17 no. 3

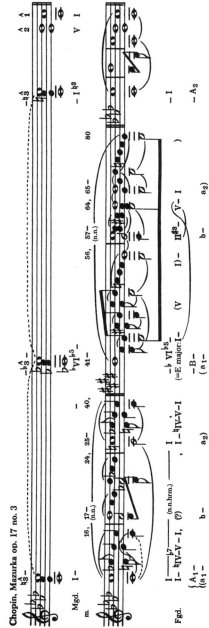

example, then, Schenker has allowed chromatic pitches into both the principal bass arpeggiation and the *Urlinie*. This is what it takes to accommodate a structural lower flat mediant, and despite the risk of straining the limits of his analytical theory, Schenker, at least *in this incontrovertible case*, felt obliged to faithfully reflect the obvious. In sonata form pieces, such a background structure is improbable.[43] (my italics)

While such a background is indeed improbable in sonata form, the case is far from incontrovertible, as Kopp claims. Schenker intended all of these to be middleground events.

Schenker does not only portray levels through noteheads. In each of these figures, the slurs and dashes around the scale degrees of the *Urlinie*, the Roman numerals, and formal labels indicate the parenthetical nature of the third relations. Indeed, in the case of Fig. 30a (Example 4.11), the abbreviation for middleground, "Mgd.," even appears in the bottom left-hand corner of the upper stave. Moreover, Schenker clarifies in the main text that "The examples in Fig. 30 refer to Fig. 28a."[44] In other words, he understands the mixture in Fig. 30a no differently from the mixture that arises from the parallel major and minor harmonies shown in Fig. 28a (reproduced here as Example 4.12). Observe the beams in Example 4.12 and imagine them superimposed onto Example 4.11. Schenker usually omits beams in extended graphs, but had he included them, he would have beamed the *Kopfton* to the closing $\hat{2}-\hat{1}$ and the opening tonic to the closing V–I.[45] Moreover these latter figures belong in the section on mixture "of the first [i.e. middleground] order," where Schenker also clarifies that "in the fundamental structure, the fundamental line remains strictly diatonic."[46] Even the diatonic submediant in Fig. 130/4, which poses no threat to the fundamental structure's diatonicism, cannot belong to it:

---

[43] Kopp, *Chromatic Transformations*, 114–116. In a footnote (p. 116, n. 19) to this passage, Kopp further emphasizes that the background status of the lower flat mediant is "clear and unmistakable."

[44] Schenker, *Free Composition*, 41. The abbreviation "Mgd." in Fig. 30a is not present in the equivalent graph in the German edition (1956). I expect that Ernst Oster had a hand in this clarification. Kopp reproduces the graph from the English edition.

[45] If one turns the page to Fig. 30b (which is also meant to be modeled on Fig. 28a), the beams of the *Ursatz* are located only at the end of the structure. Meanwhile in the immediately following synopsis of the same graph, all of the pitches, including the mixture, are beamed together. However, the solid and dotted slurs again make clear the lower status of the mixture. (Fig. 30b so happens to be a graph of a piece by Schubert, Waltz, Op. 9, No. 2.) In this respect, the closing dominant in Schenker, *Free Composition*, supplement, Fig. 102/6 (not reproduced here), is also deceptive. It is a black notehead but is not meant to signal a lower-level event. It should be a white notehead, and again, if beams were added, the opening *Kopfton* and tonic would be connected to the concluding $\hat{2}-\hat{1}$ and V–I. However, Schenker is not even consistent in the way he beams.

[46] Schenker, *Free Composition*, 40.

Example 4.12   From Schenker, *Free Composition*, supplement, Fig. 28a

Schenker graphs a synopsis of Figs. 130/4a and 130/4b as Fig. 153/2, where only the final $\hat{3}-\hat{2}-\hat{1}$ *Urlinie* descent is beamed, clearly illustrating that the submediant is not part of the background.

In sum, orthodox Schenkerian analysis does not support Kopp's main claim that diatonic and chromatic thirds hold a background status. Given their prominent use in the nineteenth century, I am in agreement with Kopp (and other neo-Riemannian theorists) that they deserve such a status. It is beyond the scope of the present study to draw out the distinction between Kopp's approach to neo-Riemannian networks and the work of others, such as Cohn and Siciliano (whose theories we have seen in Chapters 2 and 3). Perhaps the most pertinent distinction for the present discussion, however, is that the latter both focus on cycles of thirds in Schubert, whereas Kopp does not. Cohn's analysis of the sonata form of the Piano Sonata in B♭ Major, for example, scrutinized Schubert's thirds in relation to his hexatonic model, which worked well in that case. I do not consider cycles in the material below because they are not appropriate for the large-scale mediants I examine. However, when useful, I use LPR transformations rather than Kopp's nomenclature.

Schubert's first ever sonata form, the Overture for String Quintet in C minor (D. 8), seems to have been specifically modeled on Luigi Cherubini's Overture to *Faniska*.[47] For this reason, I shall analyze Schubert's harmonic strategy against Cherubini's, much like I did in Chapter 2 with Schubert's and Reichardt's settings of "Ganymed." The motivic and textural aspects of the model are thinly veiled, but even at this young age Schubert recasts Cherubini's harmonic plan in auspicious ways.

Cherubini's exposition goes from F major to A♭ major for its first and second themes. Generically speaking, this is an unconventional move: instead of the expected dominant, Cherubini borrows from the minor mode and replaces the dominant with the flattened mediant. One might expect Schubert to follow suit, especially as such modal mixture became one of his hallmarks. Schubert's response to Cherubini's structure is

---

[47] Martin Chusid, "Schubert's Overture for String Quintet and Cherubini's Overture to *Faniska*," *Journal of the American Musicological Society* 15 (1962): 78–84.

telling. His Overture starts in C minor and goes to A♭ major, followed by another discrete thematic unit in F minor, as illustrated earlier in Example 4.4(a). Schubert transforms the structure into his own, and already there are telltale signs of his characteristic means of expanding tonal space.

Firstly, it is significant that Schubert's first pre-compositional decision was to change Cherubini's tonic from a major to a minor one. But if he had matched this with a modulation up a third, he would have turned Cherubini's unconventional I–♭III into a conventional i–III. Thus, secondly, it is equally significant that the first move Schubert ever made away from a minor tonic in sonata form was towards a *lower* third relation. Schubert was already thinking in oppositional terms: while Cherubini's third relation went upwards, Schubert's would go downwards. His responding to an upper mediant with a lower one turns out to be essential to the oppositional third-relations I investigate in this section. While Schubert's first sonata form responds to the harmony in another work in an oppositional manner, his later works would contain oppositional thirds within a single movement.

The finale of the Piano Sonata in A Minor (D. 784), composed much later, in 1823, contains an intriguing pair of oppositional thirds. In order to grasp their structural effect, it is necessary to start with an examination of the first movement. Indeed, in these two outer movements, Schubert plays with two strategies of creating a fifth-space. The exposition of the first movement does not trace the usual path for minor-key sonatas by going through the mediant. Instead Schubert jumps straight from the tonic of the first theme to the dominant for the second. While this is not unheard of in minor-key sonata forms, such a harmonic trajectory is nevertheless relatively uncommon. The frank tonic–dominant polarity of this exposition opens up the harmonic fifth-space immediately and in so doing contrasts with the strategy adopted in the finale.

As illustrated in Example 4.13a, the finale is perhaps most easily understood as a rondo form: $AB_1AB_2CAB_3 + \text{CLOSING}$. It is highly repetitious: each of the A sections is identical, save for the adjustment to its tail end in order that the transition may bring about a different key each time for the B sections. Similarly, the B sections are all identical, save for the fact that they are transposed into different keys. The interesting point here is that Schubert gains the fifth-space within the form by using the mediant and submediant as an oppositional pair – placing the opposition explored between his and Cherubini's thirds into a single movement. He opts for the unusual move first: A minor first goes to F major for B_1 (i–VI).

Example 4.13   Schubert, Piano Sonata in A Minor (D. 784) (a) harmonic and formal outline of finale; (b) sacred triangle on its side

(a)   (b)

Taking only AB$_1$ into consideration, all the components are there for the material so far to serve as an exposition of a sonata form. However, instead of putting in a double-bar line and repeat after the B$_1$ in m. 79, Schubert repeats his "exposition" in an unusual manner, as shown in Example 4.13a: he writes it out in full and recomposes it so that the second hearing goes from the tonic, A minor, to the mediant, C major (i–III), which creates a third relation in the other direction. In this case, the structural argument is only apparent once both parts of the exposition (or AB$_1$ + AB$_2$ of the sonata-rondo form) have been heard. Schubert replaces the direct move to the dominant, as in the exposition of the first movement, with an indirect fifth between the two mediants (Example 4.13b).

It is important to note that these mediant keys arrive with little dominant preparation, despite the presence of a clear transition section. They are not, therefore, presented as harmonic goals in the traditional manner. The motion is not *from* the tonic *to* the submediant; nor, on the second hearing, is it *from* the tonic *to* the mediant. Rather, these mediants emerge and are "endpoints" (as in, they are the apex and the trough) in a harmonic space insofar as they carry the harmonic range of the structure. What this means in theoretical terms is that for Schubert the tonic is no longer a harmonic pole; instead it is an axis. Now literally a tonal *center*, the tonic is in the *middle* of the structure. Schubert's is a gradual, leisurely opening up of tonal space, which adds up to a full fifth relation *around* the tonic, not *from* it. Schubert has, as it were, placed Schenker's sacred triangle on its side, as conveyed in Example 4.13b. The fifth-space around the tonic is resolved tonally with the appearance of B₃ in the tonic. To be sure, the use of third relations in B sections of rondos is not uncommon in other composers; however, they are not usually "resolved" through a third repetition of the B section in the tonic.

Schubert also explored the accumulated fifth-space in a number of other minor-mode movements. The first movement of the Sonata for Violin and Piano in G Minor (D. 408) is one such example. Its exposition contains three discrete thematic units in the tonic, mediant, and submediant. As shown in Example 4.14, the fifth-space is again attained gradually around the tonic. The recapitulation responds by reversing the order of the third relations, again resulting in a fifth-space, as shown in the example. Schubert's recapitulation of the two secondary themes is not designed to resolve the tonal space of the exposition – instead they explore it further, through a non-teleological, paratactic strategy. That is to say, Schubert's keys are reversible: mediant followed by submediant becomes submediant followed by mediant. The closing section brings about tonal closure, though it hardly has the quality of a hard-won ESC or closure of the *Ursatz*. Rather, it feels like an addendum, a "mere" closure – as if part of a palindrome, where the entire tonal structure is retrogradable and the end is also the beginning.

This kind of paratactic structural thinking can shed light on one of the most famous examples of large-scale thirds: the first movement of the *Unfinished* Symphony. The usual mediant relation is replaced by the

Example 4.14 Harmonic architecture of the themes in the exposition and recapitulation of Sonata for Violin and Piano in G Minor (D. 408), first movement

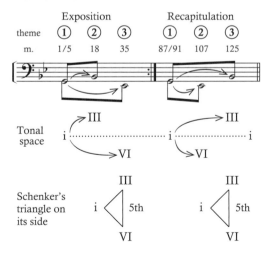

submediant in the exposition, only for the mediant to be found – unex-pectedly – in the recapitulation. As shown in Example 4.15a, both mediants – G major and D major – are diatonic to the opening tonic, which means that their roots are a major and minor third from the tonic respectively. In this case, the tonal fifth-space is not gained within the exposition, as in the other examples, but across the whole movement. This also means that, as with the Violin and Piano Sonata, the secondary theme in the recapitulation does not provide tonal resolution – rather, it continues to open up the tonal space, a practice of many nineteenth-century sonata forms. Schubert's idea seems to be to expand the harmonic range of the secondary thematic material, first in one direction, then in the other. But the expansion stops at an important point: the distance between the diatonic mediant and the diatonic submediant is a perfect fifth.

This kind of gradual expansion corresponds to a strategy that Rosen has argued may be found in Schubert's songs: the range of the voice expands first in one direction, then in the other; the starting point is in the middle.[48] Indeed the melody played by the lower strings at the opening of the *Unfinished* Symphony adopts this strategy, a melodic strategy which Schubert translates into a harmonic strategy. As with the other examples analyzed above, the fifth is displaced: it straddles the tonic and does not stem from it. Once again the sacred triangle is on its side (Example 4.15a). Such a reading relies on a spatial rather than linear connection among the harmonic stations in a sonata form.

Another Schubertian fingerprint is crucial to the relaxed dynamic of the movement. The submediant in the exposition arrives with minimal dominant preparation. That is not to say that the transition does not possess some verve. Quite the opposite: almost everything about its grand gestures is conventional: the energy and dynamic level increase and the cadence at the end of the transition lands on a *fz* tutti chord. Harmonically, however, the transition has gotten nowhere, for it ends in B minor. The ensuing G major of the luscious second theme is often highlighted for its abruptness.[49] Its abrupt entry belies the efficient voice-leading – an L transformation – which involves only a single semitone displacement from $\hat{F}\sharp$ to $\hat{G}$. Observe in Example 4.16 how the clarinets retain the common tones, generating continuity. Despite the minimal change in pitch to generate the new tonic triad, the perceptible change in

---

[48] Charles Rosen, *Frontiers of Meaning: Three Informal Lectures on Music* (New York: Hill and Wang, 1994), 72–126.

[49] Webster, "Schubert's Sonata Form," 23.

Example 4.15 Schubert, *Unfinished* Symphony, first movement
(a) harmonic outline of thematic material in exposition and recapitulation,
with a diagram of tonal space and sacred triangle on its side; (b) tonal space
of statements of first theme in exposition, development, and recapitulation,
with a diagram of sacred triangle upside down

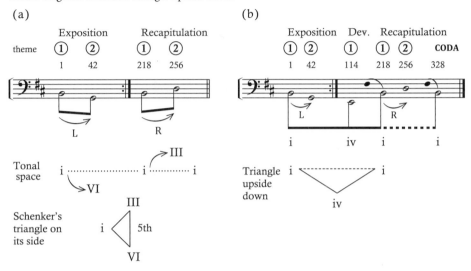

the sound world of the second theme comes from the shift from the
minor-mode first theme to the major-mode second theme.

There is also an important Schubertian feature between the end of the
transition and the start of the second theme. Schubert substitutes sound for
the conventional silence of the MC' (Example 4.16). The "caesura-fill" (to
use Hepokoski's and Darcy's term) is a dominant preparation to the new
key – precisely the harmony normally expected before the silence.
Although, as shown in Example 4.17, Schubert's decision to end the
transition in the tonic emphasizes the third relation or L transformation,
he nonetheless slips in a dominant preparation. He extracts the common-
tone $\hat{D}$ in the horns, a pitch which transforms from $\hat{3}$ of B minor to $\hat{5}$ of G
major to serve – by the thinnest possible thread – as the dominant preparation for the new key (see Example 4.17).

In keeping with generic expectation, the transition of the recapitulation
is recomposed. It even heads towards the dominant of B minor, as if to
effect a conventional tonal resolution to the tonic. However, the necessary
raised leading note is never forthcoming. Instead Schubert once more
draws out the common tone, as depicted in Example 4.17: $\hat{A}$ as $\hat{3}$ of F♯
minor becomes $\hat{5}$ of D major. The R transformation of B minor (first
theme) and D major (second theme) is not so immediately perceptible

Example 4.16 End of transition, medial caesura, and beginning of the second theme in the exposition of Schubert, *Unfinished* Symphony, first movement

Example 4.17 Analysis of harmony that triggers medial caesura-fill and the beginning of the second theme in the exposition and recapitulation of Schubert, *Unfinished* Symphony, first movement

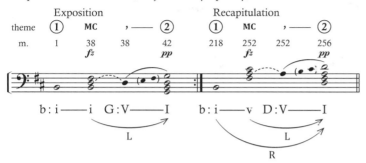

because they are not juxtaposed, as in the exposition. The alterations to the recapitulation's transition are therefore not so much to redirect the harmony towards closure as to ensure a parallel with the exposition. In each case, the large-scale relation is a diatonic third – L in the exposition and R in the recapitulation – and the role of the dominant preparation for the new keys is minimized.

In these analyses, I have focused almost exclusively on expositions and recapitulations for reasons given above. When Ernst Oster analyzed the harmonic scheme of the *Unfinished* Symphony in a footnote in *Free Composition*, he pointed out that the development section completes the descending arpeggiation of the exposition and finally reaches the structural dominant before the recapitulation: i–VI–iv–V.[50] Thus, although I have argued that the tonal space occupied by the first and second themes in the exposition and recapitulation equates to a fifth around the tonic, the music does, of course, go on. My analyses of Schubert's tonal space are based on key relations from the tonic and thematic associations between expositions and recapitulations. This is, I argue, part of the paratactic quality of Schubertian form. His self-contained, closed thematic units are often abruptly articulated and therefore somewhat unrelated to their immediate neighboring units. This encourages the perception of Schubert's forms as discontinuous and excisable (hence Taruskin's drastic excision of the whole of the second theme in the *Unfinished* Symphony, as described in Chapter 3). Instead of ordering Schubert's keys sequentially and seaming them together, I argue that their connection is elsewhere. Schubert's memorable thematic material whose brightness or darkness shifts through transpositions enables long-term or

---

[50] Schenker, *Free Composition*, 140.

"spatial" connections to be drawn – aurally, as well as analytically. Although Tovey excluded keys in development sections (and I have followed suit) because they provide no insight into how keys relate to the overall tonic, the opening key of the development is one possible exception, especially when underpinning a substantial statement of the first thematic unit. By extension therefore (and as an aside to my discussion of Schubert's third relations), if my reading were to include the subdominant appearance of the first theme at the beginning of the development section in the *Unfinished* Symphony, it would yield yet another permutation of Schenker's sacred triangle – one that is upside down, as conveyed in Example 4.15b. That is to say, the large-scale harmonic association among the three appearances of the first theme in the exposition, development, and recapitulation also spans a fifth, i–iv–i – producing one of the forbidden structures Schenker depicted in Example 4.3.

To read the prominent use of the mediant and submediant in a work such as the first movement of the *Unfinished* Symphony in terms of the Schenkerian paradigm (or, for that matter, the "norm") is to miss how Schubert creates a sense of "non-teleology" and how he diminishes the role of the tonic/dominant axis and shifts it to a new fifth-based space. In a Schenkerian – or any other linear – reading, Schubert's thirds either get lost as middleground expansions or are assessed as obstacles to conventional harmonic goals. It also misses how Schubert uses the oppositional pairing of upper and lower mediants to show the fifth relationship in a new light.

To be sure, other composers make use of thirds to create the same overall key structure. However, as Schenker illustrates in two works by Beethoven and Brahms, a heavily weighted auxiliary cadence is crucial to the entry of the mediants in the *Waldstein* Piano Sonata and a forward-driving incomplete transference drives the secondary theme to its release in an A minor middleground tonic in Brahms's Cello Sonata in F Major, Op. 99.[51] They use extensive dominant preparation to maintain a sense of teleological drive. By comparison Schubert's dominant preparations are vastly under-played, intensifying the sense of the "trance-like" or magical appearances of third relations.[52] Schubert thus emphasizes the non-teleological potential of third relations and does not seek to compensate for their non-teleological status in the manner achieved by Beethoven and Brahms.

---

[51] Schenker, *Free Composition*, 135 and *Free Composition*, supplement, Fig. 110, d2.

[52] See my "Terzverwandtschaft in der 'Unvollendeten' von Schubert und der 'Waldstein-Sonate' von Beethoven: Kennzeichen des 19. Jahrhunderts und theoretisches Problem," *Schubert durch die Brille* 20 (1998): 123–130. Some of the comments above may be taken as a response to Hellmut Federhofer's reply to my article; see Federhofer, "Terz- und Quintverwandtschaft in der Harmonik Schuberts: Eine Replik," *Schubert durch die Brille* 21 (1998): 157–161.

I have thus far mentioned examples of movements in minor keys. Schubert's treatment of third relations in major-key sonata form movements suggests additional aspects of generic expectation are at play in his compositional decisions. While the same dynamic often obtains – whereby the direct fifth relation of the exposition is replaced by thirds orbiting the tonic – the diatonic mediants around a major tonic produce minor secondary keys. Moreover, Schubert's major-key expositions invariably end in the dominant after the remote modulation, adding another key to the tonal space. The *Great* Symphony and the String Quintet in C Major (D. 956) provide a useful illustration of the harmonic issues at stake in major-key forms.

The *Great* Symphony's transition into the second theme is strikingly similar to that of the *Unfinished* Symphony. As shown in Example 4.18, the cadence at the end of the transition lands in C major in m. 130. Thus for all the pomp and circumstance, the harmony has gone nowhere. The characteristic silence is again filled in – this time by repeated $\hat{C}$s in the strings, until the last two beats before the entry of the second theme. The dominant, B major, passes by in a split second before E minor enters. The harmonic transformation between the first and second themes is L, with a momentary dominant preparation falling within the conventional silence (see Example 4.19).

The diatonic L transformation means that the second theme is in a minor key. Generically, second themes are always in a major key, whether the overall tonic is major or minor. This striking difference in the harmonic hue of the thematic material perhaps accounts for Schubert's decisions in the recapitulation. The theme is not immediately introduced in the concomitant A minor, but rather in C minor. While the strategy of the recapitulation's transition is also the same as that in the *Unfinished* Symphony insofar as it veers towards the dominant, the fact that the dominant of C major produces a major key encourages a different outcome. As shown in Examples 4.19 and 4.20, the recapitulation does not contain a direct transposition of the transition's cadence, caesura-fill, and opening of the second theme, as it was for the *Unfinished* Symphony shown in Example 4.17. With the conventional dominant preparation already in place, Schubert makes no final harmonic adjustments in m. 439 to bring about a third relation in the *Great* Symphony. Instead a tonic resolution ensues upon the arrival of the secondary theme. However, the repetitions of the secondary theme enable each possible expectation to be played out: C minor satisfies the generic expectation that the material of the second theme will return at

Example 4.18   End of transition, medial caesura, and the beginning of the second theme in the exposition of Schubert, *Great* Symphony, first movement

Example 4.19 Analysis of harmony that triggers medial caesura-fill
and beginning of the second theme in the exposition and
recapitulation of Schubert, *Great* Symphony, first movement

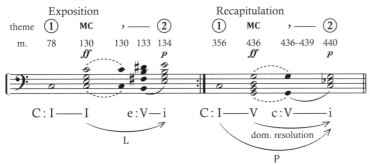

the tonic level and be modally matched; A minor satisfies the expectation that material in the recapitulation will be transposed down a fifth;
C major satisfies the norm that secondary keys are at the tonic level and
generically always major.

None of Schubert's major-key sonata forms showcase diatonic third
relations in the exposition and recapitulation in as frank a formula as
witnessed in his minor-key forms. They do, however, when Schubert alters
them chromatically in order to obtain major-mode secondary themes.
Unlike Beethoven, who altered the diatonic thirds into mediant and submediant majors in order to maintain the convention that second themes
are major (such as in the *Waldstein* Sonata), Schubert prefers to introduce
chromatic roots to obtain modal convention – hence his propensity for
flattened mediants and submediants. Witness the String Quintet in C
Major, whose fifth-space between the second themes is housed by E♭ and
A♭ major. Such a chromatic balance for secondary themes is particularly
prevalent in Schubert's overtures. For example, in both the Overture in the
Italian Style in D Major (D. 590) and the Overture to the Singspiel
Zwillingsbruder (D. 647), which is also in D major, the exposition goes to
F major and is balanced by the flattened submediant, B♭ major.

In major-key sonata forms, Schubert's thirds have generally been
regarded as massive parenthetical statements, especially because they
occur between lengthy thematic statements in the tonic and dominant.
Additionally in the case of the String Quintet, the mediants are chromatically remote and, as we saw in Chapter 3, not established through authentic
cadences, which further encourages their subjugation to fifth-relations.
Moreover, behind Schubert's apparently colorful expansions of tonal
space lies block transposition by fifth, which often leads to the same kind

Example 4.20   End of transition, medial caesura, and the beginning of the second theme in the recapitulation of Schubert, *Great* Symphony, first movement

of disparaging comments about compositional laziness as the subdominant recapitulation. The block transposition in the String Quintet, for example, begins as early as with material from the first theme (m. 33 onwards), producing a C–F–A♭–C recapitulatory strategy.

Yet there are surface-level matters of greater importance than such a general harmonic overview. As mentioned in the previous chapter, the second theme of the String Quintet is anchored by the pitch Ĝ in the melody, rather than by any authentic cadences in E♭ major. The harmonies in the secondary area therefore revolve around Ĝ, including all possible major-mode harmonies, namely E♭, C, and G majors – in keeping with the convention that second themes are in the major mode. The chromaticism in this exposition stems from a diatonic entity, and from a conventional move to the dominant, albeit transformed into a single anchoring pitch, Ĝ, from which Schubert opens up tonal space. The transposition down a fifth means the recapitulation's anchoring pitch is appropriately the conventional Ĉ.

The fact that Schubert invariably closes his major-key expositions in the dominant also requires comment. The usual analytical convention is to see the dominant as the arrival of the generic harmonic goal after a harmonic detour, despite the fact that it generally serves as a closing or codetta section – a kind of cadential afterthought. When Schubert deviates from the path of the relative major in the case of a minor-key sonata form, no such equivalent statements are made when the relative major finally arrives. In other words, no analyst would say of the first movement of the *Unfinished* Symphony that Schubert deviates from the conventional path of the exposition only to arrive finally at the relative major in the recapitulation. To be sure, the main reason for this is that the cachet enjoyed by the dominant is not shared by any other harmony. Moreover, Schenkerian analysis does not place any store on distinguishing between a dominant that supports a theme versus a dominant that supports cadential closure. An analytical system that does make such a distinction makes possible the view that the thematic/harmonic articulations perform a central role in a movement's tonal space and closures perform a *separate*, yet equally important role. The importance of this perspective is more evident in the case of the *Great* Symphony than in the String Quintet in C Major because the former does not involve block transposition: the secondary thematic complex is engaging with its tonal role of opening up tonal space and the closing section (or codetta, as Taruskin called it) is engaging with its tonal role of articulating ends, conclusions, and resolutions.[53] Unusually in the

---

[53] For a similar argument regarding the separation of the dominant from the main tonal argument of the rest of the exposition, see Hali Fieldman, "Schubert's *Quartettsatz* and Sonata Form's New Way," *Journal of Musicological Research* 21 (2002): 99–146.

case of the *Great* Symphony, the secondary theme engages in both resolution (in the statements in C minor and major) and the opening up of tonal space (the statement of A minor).

In the structures examined thus far in this chapter, Schubert opens up tonal space through the most straightforward and commonly practiced transpositions. These structures gain their elegance of tonal opposition through fifth transpositions. The remaining *Stufen* offer different structural challenges, which I shall now explore.

The supertonic and subtonic, and the problem of the fifth-space

The supertonic and seventh (or subtonic) degrees are the remaining scale-steps available in the diatonic system. Based on my preceding examination of the subdominant recapitulation and the pairing of the mediant and submediant in secondary themes, one might expect a trend – that Schubert might construe the supertonic and subtonic into a parallel transposition of keys or into an oppositional pair; or indeed that something else significant might happen to reposition the fifth-space of Schenker's sacred triangle. Instead, Schubert's treatment of these two harmonies on the large scale points to the limits of a diatonically symmetrical expansion of tonal space within the formal architecture of sonata form. When Schubert places a large-scale thematic complex in the supertonic or subtonic, he uses only one or the other as a harmonic station, but never both within a single sonata-form movement. This limitation not only reveals important information about the inherent properties of these key relations but also allows us to understand more deeply the properties which made the other structures discussed in this chapter attractive to Schubert.

To appreciate the principles at work in Schubert's compositional decisions, it is necessary to go into theoretical detail. The supertonic and subtonic have unique properties compared to the other scale degrees discussed so far. In the discussion that follows, I will assume C major and C minor as my theoretical models, and thus any harmonies mentioned should be assumed to belong to those two specific scales. Within the minor mode, I shall assume the natural minor scale as my theoretical basis.

In the major mode, the tonic, dominant, and subdominant triads are all major, while the mediant and submediant triads are minor. Conversely, in the minor mode, the tonic, dominant, and subdominant triads are all minor, while the mediant and submediant triads are major (and, as any student of harmony exercises will recall, the major dominant is achieved by raising the leading note).

On a large-scale level, the use of the subdominant recapitulation, as in I–V ‖ IV–I, means material remains in the same mode when transposed. Similarly, the transposition by fifth of the mediant to submediant – or vice versa – retains the same mode. As we saw in the previous section, the *diatonic* mediant and submediant keys of the Piano Sonata in A Minor, the Violin and Piano Sonata in G Minor, and the *Unfinished* Symphony are all major, while they are minor in the *Great* Symphony. In other words, the diatonic secondary keys of a minor tonic conveniently produce major keys, which are generically normative for second themes. In the case of the *Great* Symphony, whose tonic is major, its secondary themes are generically unusual insofar as they are minor. While Schubert's use of chromatic mediants – ♭III and ♭VI – in major-key movements introduces chromaticism, they do at least produce the generically expected mode for secondary themes. In short, the tonic, dominant, and subdominant complex and the mediant and submediant complex offer modal consistency, which is convenient for thematic transposition. Additionally, each of these complexes can easily be construed into fifth relations, another important and practical trait when designing the tonal architecture of thematic units.

The supertonics and subtonics of the major and minor modes are untidy in this respect. In the major mode, the diatonic triads available on the second and seventh degrees of the scale are ii (D minor) and vii° (diminished triad on $\hat{B}$) respectively. In the minor mode, they are ii° (diminished triad on $\hat{D}$) and VII (B♭ major) respectively. Obviously, chromatic adjustment is required in order to turn the diminished triads into usable keys. Minimally, ii° and vii° can be turned into a minor triad, by raising their diminished fifth by a semitone, or they can be turned into a major triad, by lowering their respective "roots." The advantage of the former is that, in a major key, ii and vii are thereby modally matched, allowing for a simple transposition of thematic material. The option of transforming vii° into ♭VII means that the key is no longer modally matched with its counterpart, ii. Moreover, its usage entails large-scale modal mixture insofar as the key would be understood to be "borrowed" from the minor mode. Similarly, in the case of the minor mode, the transformation of ii° into ii means that the pair of keys ii and VII are not modally matched, for which reason ♭II could be regarded as a practical solution.

For these reasons, the second and seventh degrees pose a compositional challenge. The two harmonies are riddled with problems of balance, and balance is key to the structures examined in this chapter. They share none of the luxuries of the built-in elegant patterning of the other two types of structures examined so far in this chapter. Quite apart from the modal and transpositional issues outlined above, neither are good contrasts for a formal section, as Tovey once remarked.[54] They are difficult to establish as independent tonics, and are therefore better suited to the harmonic movement of a transition or development section. In sum, their range from the tonic is narrow (a mere step from the tonic and a third from each other), their modes are often conflicting, and they share no common tones with the tonic – and potentially share too many common tones with each other.

These theoretical and practical considerations highlight the importance of the interval of the fifth in the other structures investigated in this chapter. The use of both the supertonic and the subtonic within a single structure is the least attractive structural option. A work whose main structural argument counterbalances a secondary theme in, say, ii in the exposition and vii in the recapitulation (or vice versa) would occupy too little tonal space. Placing each harmony a seventh away from the tonic – that is, the supertonic below the tonic and the seventh degree above it – would increase the range, but would not solve the problem of functional tonal space. Moreover, the conglomeration of the tonic, supertonic, and seventh degree cannot be construed to create a fifth anywhere. It is undoubtedly for these reasons that Schubert never developed a sonata form structure around these two harmonic stations in relation to an overall tonic.[55] Certainly a structure that starts I–ii and ends with vii–I (or vice versa: I–vii; ii–I) would allow for Schubert's habit of block transposition, though adjustments would have to be made for the tone and semitone in the stepwise motion. That Schubert did not use them as a pair in a frank way in any sonata form is as likely to suggest that he was aware of the theoretical problems that I have highlighted as it is to suggest that he did not think of generating such a structure.

These problems did not stop Schubert from facing the compositional challenge of using at least one of the two keys on a large scale within a single movement – and of exploiting their precarious tonal tendencies. Very early

---

[54] Tovey, "Tonality in Schubert," 141. Much as I have suggested above, Tovey considers the supertonic and seventh as "converse" keys and regards their instability as arising from the need to alter their diminished chords into a "common chord" – by which he means major or minor triads (p. 135). At the same time, he declared "There are no forbidden modulations," so he does not exclude the possibility of employing them (p. 142). Schenker also argues that VII can be chromatically altered in *Free Composition*, 90.

[55] The only work I know of where Schubert makes explicit structural use of ii and ♭VII is No. 14 of the *Wiener Damenländler*, Op. 67 (D. 734).

in his career, he experimented with presenting the secondary theme of his String Quartet in B♭ Major (D. 36) in the supertonic (C major) and with presenting the powerful recapitulation of the String Quartet in D Major (D. 94) in ♭VII (C major). Later in his career, he seems to have preferred the subtonic. The piano duet *Lebensstürme* in A Minor (D. 947) and the Piano Sonata in C major (*Reliquie*, D. 840) both feature the seventh degree in the secondary theme of their expositions (A♭ major and B minor respectively).[56] The *Reliquie* Sonata additionally recapitulates its first theme in B major. The harmonically enigmatic String Quartet in C Minor (*Quartettsatz*, D. 703), which is also famous for omitting the first thematic material in the recapitulation, recapitulates with the secondary theme in VII (B♭ major). No particular large-scale key pattern is immediately evident in any of these movements.

On closer inspection, however, two of these pieces seem to make something of their counterpart harmony. The *Quartettsatz* contains striking uses of D♭ throughout the movement, a Neapolitan or Phrygian counterpart to VII. The *Reliquie* Sonata, by contrast, is intriguing due to a glaring omission: it sets up a supertonic (D minor) response to the exposition's subtonic (B minor) second theme. But at the last minute Schubert thwarts its entrance – the avoidance is telling. Examining the tonal architectures of the two movements more closely will illustrate some of the issues raised by Schubert's choice of tonalities.

The *Quartettsatz* contains a motley of keys, whereby the logic behind the architectural tonal scheme is difficult to fathom. The harmonic trajectory of the exposition is familiar enough to students of Schubert: C minor, A♭ major, G major. By contrast, the recapitulation is enigmatic: it not only begins with the second theme, but the key is B♭ major (VII); an abbreviated first theme reappears in the tonic as the coda. VII is treated locally as the dominant of the mediant, such that the second iteration of the second theme falls to E♭ major after, as it were, a dominant preparation (the double statement of the second theme in the exposition is, by contrast, completely in A♭ major). The G major closing material of the exposition is transposed down a fifth to C major, following convention. The movement ends in the minor with the opening material serving as the coda.

Hascher has come up with an ingenious Schenkerian solution in order to argue that this movement is an interrupted sonata form structure despite

---

[56] Brian Newbould cites these keys in the *Lebensstürme* and *Reliquie* Sonata as evidence of Schubert's greater harmonic freedom than Beethoven; see *Schubert: The Music and the Man* (Berkeley and Los Angeles: University of California Press, 1997), 393.

its anomalies (Example 4.21). Radically, his analysis shows that the recapitulation begins with E♭ major, not with B♭. With B♭ major now part of the
development, his reading provides another example of oppositional
mediant and submediant harmonies between secondary themes of the
exposition and recapitulation. Yet he rightly points out that there is no
difference whatsoever between the presentations of thematic material of the
B♭ major and E♭ major sections of the second theme. The listener, we are
told, can only expect to realize this "a posteriori."[57] Why does B♭ major
remain part of the development? And why is E♭ major the recapitulation?
Only under these circumstances can the *Urlinie* remain intact, with its
concomitant notion of interruption and the retaking of the primary tone
that characterizes sonata form. Contrary to Webster, Hascher has found
enough vestiges of the Schenkerian sonata form (interruption and retaking
of primary tone) to call this movement a sonata form.[58]

Example 4.21   From Hascher, *Schubert: La forme sonate*, 189–190

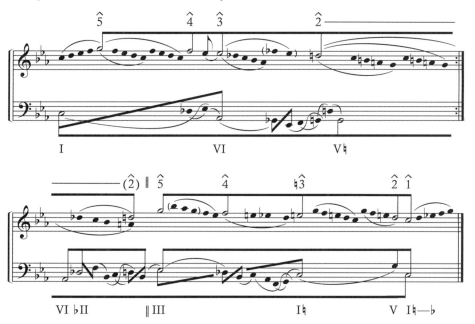

[57] Hascher, *Schubert: La forme sonate*, 189.
[58] While the exposition follows identifiable attributes of sonata form, Webster concludes "the
     movement as a whole is not in sonata form"; see Webster, "Schubert's Sonata Form," 26.

According to Hascher, the structural $\hat{2}(\hat{D})$ starts in the exposition over a conventional dominant support, and is supported at the end of the development by VII (B♭ major), as shown in Example 4.21. Unusual perhaps, but Schenker describes such cases in *Free Composition*.[59] This ingenious solution enables Hascher to argue that there is a standard retaking of the *Kopfton* $\hat{5}(\hat{G})$ in the recapitulation, even if its harmonic support is the utterly non-standard relative major (E♭ major) instead of the tonic (C minor).

To be sure, this reading goes against the grain of what many Schenkerians have seen as a problem with some of Schenker's own interpretations of the retaking of primary tones. Recall the debate generated by the retaking of $\hat{3}$ in Mozart's Piano Sonata in C Major (K. 545), which is seen as problematic because it is supported by a first-inversion rather than a root-position tonic. Certainly, if an inversion is considered insufficient support, then a mediant must be even more insufficient. Yet others might agree with Hascher that extraordinary circumstances call for extraordinary solutions.[60] Others still, however, argue that there is no chance that this structure is uninterrupted, given both the lack of tonic and the skewed thematic rotation.[61] However one looks at it, the result is a blurred recapitulation, and the *Quartettsatz* is Schubert's most radical example of "l'ambiguïté structurelle entourant le commencement de la reéxposition" (structural ambiguity over the beginning of the recapitulation). Hascher argues that this musical structure is a reflection of Schubert's so-called "crisis years."[62] The real crisis, however, lies in the inability of Schenker's contrapuntal system to analyze B♭ major as a "beginning" in this context.

We are therefore still left with the task of explaining the thematic return in B♭ as the recapitulation's tonal beginning. Thinking in terms of oppositional harmonic architecture, the harmonic station VII in the recapitulation suggests we should look for some kind of supertonic in the exposition. No theme is devoted to it. However, it could be argued that the constant reappearance of D♭ chords throughout the movement provides an omnipresent counterpart to VII. The D♭ chord first appears in m. 9, as a *ffz* first-inversion climax, ♭II⁶, after a crescendo from the otherwise whispering opening. The chord also stands out because it is the first harmonic simultaneity of the movement, even fleshed out by double stops in the inner strings. Schubert draws attention to it in terms of harmonic content,

---

[59] Schenker, *Free Composition*, 136–137.
[60] This is essentially the message in Charles J. Smith, "Musical Form and Fundamental Structure."
[61] Webster, "Schubert's Sonata Form," 26.   [62] Hascher, *Schubert: La forme sonate*, 188–191.

dynamics, contour, and texture. As Hali Fieldman has observed, its disruptive force is meant to be heard and it calls attention to itself as a truly Schubertian version of a *Grundgestalt*.[63] Looking elsewhere in the movement, Db also brings about the secondary key, Ab major. In mm. 23–24, the bII[6] turns into IV[6] of Ab major, generating a "quick transition" that Susan Wollenberg hears as yet another example of Schubert's "poetic transitions."[64] As she also observes, $\hat{D}b$ is strongly emphasized within the Ab theme. An important part of its "strangeness," according to Fieldman, is its role in the plagal cadence in measures 32–34, which closes the first phrase of the second theme.[65] Whereas Schubert's second themes can often be nostalgic for the opening tonic (witness the reappearance of C major in m. 71 in the second theme of the String Quintet in C Major), in the *Quartettsatz* the secondary theme is nostalgic for the Db harmony.[66] It is fitting, therefore, that the second theme should set out in Bb major in the recapitulation, acknowledging the role of Db in the exposition. The split of the second theme into Bb and Eb thus could be read as counterbalancing both the omnipresent Neapolitan and the Ab major of the exposition's second theme.

This kind of analysis raises as many questions as it answers. Unlike the other movements studied in this chapter, the *Quartettsatz* suggests no immediately logical or symmetrical overarching tonal form. It not only breaks with the idea of "rotation" – another generic staple of Sonata Theory – it defies convincing explanation in terms of a comparison of the recapitulation with the exposition.[67] Indeed it breaks up the kind of symmetrical relationship enjoyed between the first and second themes and the second themes and closing sections expressed in the other structures examined in this chapter. Yet, in this respect, it shares many qualities with other enigmatic and apparently unstructured architectural designs of many of Schubert's sonata forms. Although many have argued the logic behind the design lies in the lament-bass at the outset of the movement, which governs the harmonic-contrapuntal structure of the movement writ large, the keys

---

[63] Fieldman, "Schubert's *Quartettsatz*," 118–120 and 123. See especially p. 118 n. 41 for her explanation of how Schubert's *Grundgestalten* are often commonplace harmonic devices that conventional theories would regard as "nothing special." Yet, Schubert turns them into "events" that shape a work, often by calling attention to them or by making them strange. See also her dissertation "The *Grundgestalt* and Schubert's Sonata Forms" (PhD thesis, University of Michigan, 1996) for her detailed argument of this phenomenon.

[64] Susan Wollenberg, "Schubert's Poetic Transitions," in Xavier Hascher (ed.), *Le style instrumental de Schubert: sources, analyse, évolution* (Paris: Sorbonne, 2007), 271.

[65] Fieldman, "Schubert's *Quartettsatz*," 124.

[66] Wollenberg, "Schubert's Poetic Transitions," 272–273.

[67] "Rotation" refers to the generic expectation that themes established in the exposition will appear in the same order later in the work, including in the development and recapitulation.

and thematic design seem tailored to create a fractured sense of tonal space.[68]

In the case of the *Reliquie* Sonata, it is perhaps more possible to trace how Schubert negotiated the relative relations between the first and second themes and the second theme and closing (or P and S; S and C, in Sonata Theory terms), when recapitulating a set of relations that do not readily lend themselves to block transposition. Example 4.22 begins with m. 43 of the *Reliquie* Sonata, where the flow of the modulating sequence of the transition is interrupted by the arrival of the dominant triad G major. If Schubert had borrowed a page from Mozart and employed a bifocal close here, then he could have considered his work of the transition done. Indeed, Schubert's gestures in Example 4.22 even look like a page from Mozart, with the build-up of the transition to the cadence that triggers the MC, followed by a two-measure "vamp" before the entry of the secondary theme (compare the extract from Mozart's Piano Sonata in C Major in Example 4.23, which crucially contains the Classical caesura between the end of the transition and the beginning of the second theme, an airspace that Schubert is fond of filling in, as we have already seen).[69] As shown in Example 4.22, from m. 45 onwards, Schubert exaggerates G major, melodically outlining it in a closed position, $\hat{1}-\hat{3}-\hat{5}$. By introducing a $\hat{7}$ and $\flat\hat{9}$ in the next two measures, Schubert declares that he has other harmonic adventures in mind.

Schubert refashions the Classical (read: Mozartian) model of the bifocal close and the generic gestures associated with the end of the transition and beginning of the second theme. He again fills in the Classical caesura after the transition's final cadence. As in so many other of his works (we have already witnessed this in the *Unfinished* and *Great* Symphonies, for example), the would-be airspace contains the dominant to the destination key of the secondary area. Turning the previous dominant ninth into an augmented sixth function, the bass line in the *Reliquie* Sonata moves further afield to $\hat{F}\sharp$ in m. 51. Schubert then turns the $\hat{7}$ and $\flat\hat{9}$ into enharmonic appoggiaturas that coalesce onto a six-four on F$\sharp$. A simple cadence in m. 52 – still the fill-in for the caesura – prepares B minor. With its simple arpeggios and accompaniment, Schubert could not have made B minor any clearer as the new tonic of this section.

The second theme does not, however, end in B minor. Instead the tail end of the fourth utterance of the theme gravitates to G major in mm. 69–71, a simple maximal common-tone L transformation. Despite being the

[68] David Beach, "Harmony and Linear Progression in Schubert's Music," *Journal of Music Theory* 38 (1994): 13–17 and Su Yin Mak, "Schubert's Sonata Forms and the Poetics of the Lyric," *Journal of Musicology* 23 (2006): 294–298.

[69] Hepokoski and Darcy, *Sonata Theory*, 106.

Example 4.22 End of transition and beginning of second theme in exposition of Schubert, Piano Sonata in C Major (*Reliquie*, D. 840), first movement, mm. 43–58

Example 4.23 End of transition, medial caesura, and introduction to second theme in Mozart, Piano Sonata in C Major (K. 545), first movement, mm. 10–15; compare Example 4.22

dominant, this G major is hardly stable; nor does it maintain the glow of its major-mode status against the relative darkness of the minor-mode secondary theme: a lengthy sequential passage travels through D minor, C minor, B♭ major, and finally back to G major before the second theme is stated again in G major in m. 86. Convention has it that this G is the goal of the exposition and Webster and Hascher, for example, both read B minor as Schenker would, namely in relation to the dominant, as iii of V (compare their analyses with Example 4.7).[70]

For three-key expositions, Schubert's simplest method of recapitulation is to provide a block transposition down a fifth, so that the movement neatly ends in the tonic. Such a maneuver in the case of the *Reliquie* Sonata would bring about E minor for the secondary area and C major for the closing. Schubert does not choose this option. Instead the concomitant place for the entry of the secondary key suggests he had in mind to go to D minor. Example 4.24 picks up at the spot in the recapitulation parallel to the beginning of Example 4.22. Schubert's transition now outlines an E-major ninth chord. An exact replica of the exposition would bring about G♯ minor in m. 210. However, Schubert alters the harmony in m. 208 to prepare instead for D minor, which would have been the recapitulation's ii to the exposition's vii. But Schubert seems uninterested in generating a B minor/D minor opposition for his second theme. At the last minute, he adds five measures to bring in the second theme in A minor. For all the compositional effort and extra measures, Schubert could have gone straight to A minor from his E^9 chord.

As Richard Kramer argues, Schubert is playing at some "*jeu*" of expectations in these passages.[71] However, I hear the game differently from Kramer. There are multiple layers of expectations being thwarted in this recapitulation. Firstly, a listener attuned to what happened to the dominant ninth in the exposition will assume the dominant ninth in the recapitulation is also destined to be treated as an augmented sixth. He or she would therefore no longer expect a resolution onto A major or minor, but rather a resolution onto to G♯. However, Schubert heads straight to an Â in the bass in m. 208, only to make this chord itself a dominant ninth (with an appoggiatura). It settles onto D minor in m. 210, the oppositional key to B minor. In m. 210, we are back on track for the entry of the second theme. However, Schubert is not ready to settle in a new key yet. Instead he goes to A minor – the very destination that the original dominant ninth chord in

---

[70] Webster, "Schubert's Sonata Form," 28, Hascher, *Schubert: La forme sonate*, 192.
[71] "The Hedgehog: Of Fragments Finished and Unfinished," *19th-Century Music* 21 (1997): 142.

Example 4.24   End of transition and beginning of second theme in recapitulation of Schubert, *Reliquie* Piano Sonata in C Major, first movement; compare Example 4.22

mm. 200–207 set up. The set-up *for* A minor and the *avoidance of* D minor are important theoretical statements.

Why might Schubert opt for A minor instead of pairing the second theme with the supertonic? To borrow an important question from Kramer: do we hear these harmonic stations as inevitable next steps in the harmonic plotting of the work?[72] Or, to put it in terms of Sonata Theory, what are the generic expectations of a recapitulation in light of an exposition that goes C–b–G? The simplest answer is C–e–C on the basis that first themes usually recapitulate in the tonic and that Schubert's

---

[72] Kramer, "The Hedgehog," 142.

Example 4.25 Harmonic architecture of the themes in the exposition and recapitulation of Schubert, *Reliquie* Piano Sonata in C Major, first movement

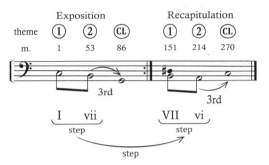

simplest recapitulations tend to transpose the secondary material along with the closing material down a fifth. However, we already know that the second theme and closing do not follow this scheme but instead go a–C. With hindsight, we may deduce that perhaps A minor is there because it creates another kind of opposition using third relations: the unfolding of the downward third in the exposition from B minor to G major in the exposition is answered by an upward third from A minor to C major in the recapitulation, as annotated in Example 4.25. These are like the shifting vantage points mentioned in Tovey's treatise on Schubert's tonality: Schubert approaches the dominant from above and the tonic from below.[73] Another important factor in Schubert's architectural designs is control of the relationship between the keys of the first and second themes. The non-tonic recapitulation of the first theme also has something to do with the choice of A minor for the secondary theme. Indeed, the only harmonic outcomes that are a generic given in Schubert's major-key sonata forms are the dominant at the end of the exposition and the tonic at the end of the recapitulation. The choice of secondary key in the exposition and the approach to the final tonic via a potential non-tonic first and second theme in the recapitulation are highly negotiable. In the case of the *Reliquie* Sonata, the relationship between the first and second themes turns out to be the consistent element in the exposition and recapitulation, leading to a non-tonic recapitulation.

After 24 measures of a dominant pedal on F♯ major, the recapitulation bursts in in B major (m. 150), and flirts with B minor shortly thereafter (m. 163). The overall harmonic profile of the first and second thematic units in the exposition and recapitulation are: C major to B minor; B major to A minor. While the exposition reaches its second theme by step, so too

---

[73] Tovey, "Tonality in Schubert," 134.

does the recapitulation – bringing about a non-tonic recapitulation. Schubert seems to be aiming for diatonic roots, hence the semitone move C–b is adjusted to a move by tone B–a. Given also the fact that the diatonic triad on the seventh degree in major is vii°, Schubert opted for both minor and major tonalities. As an important nineteenth-century harmony textbook once put it, since modulation to new keys is a powerful means of creating variety, a composer should not return to the same remote key in the same mode within a single movement.[74] Had Schubert opted for B major in both cases, he would have constructed a situation where both the secondary theme in the exposition and the first theme in the recapitulation appear in the same remote key. However, John Taylor's compositional advice did not exclude the possibility of returning to different modes of the same remote tonic, as Schubert does with B minor and major.

It is hard – if not impossible – to answer Kramer's question with a resounding yes in the case of the *Reliquie* Sonata. The fact that Schubert so obviously steered clear of a symmetrical ii and vii pairing when the opportunity to do so was available suggests a dissatisfaction with the kind of architecture that would have resulted from such a scheme. When listening to this movement, any ear is likely to be struck by Schubert's roving harmonies, and by the unaccustomed harmonic color of the minor-keyed second themes. One can hear Schubert rooting around, as it were, for new *Stufen* with which to support a new architectural structure. Yet the harmonic solution in the *Reliquie* Sonata, C–b; B–a, is elegant: it provides stepwise motion from the first to second theme in each of the exposition and recapitulation and it provides modally matched themes – although Schubert rewrites the first theme to such a degree that analysts dispute the exact point of recapitulation.[75]

The kind of analytical attention to questions of tonal balance *around* the tonic or *away from* and *back to* the tonic addressed in this section, as well as the attention given to generic expectations on both the surface and the large-scale harmonic levels, is an approach that could be suited to numerous other sonata structures where order is not immediately obvious. After the fact, one can make some sense out of the paired stepwise motion

---

[74] John Taylor, *The Student's Text-book of the Science of Music* (London: George Philip and Son, 1876), 290. Tovey cites this rule of thumb but without giving the source of the treatise in "Tonality in Schubert," 145.

[75] Daniel Coren and Irene Girton, for example, argue that this movement is a subdominant recapitulation, which starts in m. 168; see Coren, "Ambiguity in Schubert's Recapitulations," *Musical Quarterly* 60 (1974): 570 and Girton, "Promises Fulfilled: Neighbour Notes in Some Late Works of Schubert," in Xavier Hascher (ed.), *Le style instrumental de Schubert: sources, analyse, évolution* (Paris: Sorbonne, 2007), 98. The 24 measures of F♯ major convince me (and others) that this is a dominant preparation for a far more unusual recapitulation in B major.

between the first and second themes and the thirds between the second theme and closing sections. Interestingly, Schubert's exploration of tonal space is confined to *Stufen* that are diatonic to C major. I turn next to Schubert's exploration of chromaticism, which he achieved through the equal treatment of the parallel major and minor keys.

The parallel major and minor, and the expansion of tonal space

In a chapter on harmonic opposition and symmetries among the *Stufen* of the major and minor keys, there is one final opposition implicit in a tonal system that consists of two modes: the opposition between the parallel major and minor. Indeed, as Webster has observed, the expanded system of tonal relations in Schubert's sonata forms stems from the composer's assumption that major and minor may serve as equally valid representations of the tonic.

Although I end this chapter with an exploration of major/minor equivalence, we have already witnessed its consequences in previous sections and chapters. The assumption of their equivalence is the impetus behind many of the chromaticisms already encountered in this book – most notably, Schubert's propensity for setting the second themes of major-key movements in the flattened mediant or flattened submediant. These remote relations are borrowed from the minor mode. Examples we have already come across include the flattened mediant in the exposition of the String Quintet in C Major and the flattened submediant in the Piano Sonata in B♭ Major. Of these two, only the String Quintet offsets the exposition's second theme with its counterpart, ♭VI, in the recapitulation. Again, thus, the second themes are stated a fifth apart, balanced on either side of the tonic – Schenker's sacred triangle is once again on its side.[76] Although the harmonies are themselves chromatic in relation to their tonic, they are anchored to each other through the fundamental diatonic force of the perfect fifth. Schubert never, for example, pairs an exposition theme in the diatonic mediant *Stufe*, III or iii, with a corresponding recapitulation theme built on a chromatic *Stufe*, ♭VI or ♭vi (or vice versa).[77]

---

[76] Compare Hascher's Schenkerian model of ♭III and ♭VI, where such a linear reading interprets ♭III as part of a rising arpeggiation and ♭VI as an expansion of the tonic, in *Schubert: La forme sonate*, 172–173.

[77] Note, by contrast, that Schoenberg does explore such spaces in his Third String Quartet, Op. 30, which Martha M. Hyde has convincingly demonstrated is a deep imitation of Schubert's String Quartet in A Minor (D. 804) in "Neoclassic and Anachronistic Impulses in Twentieth-Century Music," *Music Theory Spectrum* 18 (1996): 223–235.

Rather than analyze how Schubert employs chromatic keys as harmonic stations, my purpose in this section is to investigate the implications of the use of parallel tonics in one of its most famous incarnations. According to Webster, the quintessential example of this phenomenon in a sonata form is the String Quartet in G Major (D. 887), with its striking shifts from the parallel major to minor and minor to major at the openings of the exposition and recapitulation respectively, and the oscillation between the two tonics at the end of the first movement. The finale also fluctuates between the two parallel tonics.[78] In the discussion that follows, I explore further the large-scale structural consequence of this major/minor equivalence in the String Quartet's first movement.

Schenkerian theory is unable to express major and minor as equivalent in a single structure. As acknowledged in my discussion of "Auf dem Flusse" in Chapter 2 and of Kopp's interpretation of Schenker's representation of modal mixture through chromatic submediants earlier in this chapter, Schenker assumes that one mode colors the other. They cannot be equal, as is made clear by the following statement in *Free Composition*: "In the fundamental structure, the fundamental line remains strictly diatonic. At the first level, however, it can contain a *mixture* of the major and the minor third."[79] This statement is incompatible with the observation frequently made about Schubert's equal treatment of major and minor tonics.

The exposition of the String Quartet presents a perfect example to see mixture differently. This new perspective again reveals how Schubert achieves something novel through an inventive application of convention. G major and minor are equal partners on a structural level not only on account of the oscillation between the parallel tonics, as Webster observes, but because, as I will demonstrate, Schubert grants them equal structural expression in the second thematic complex of the exposition. By convention, expositions of major-key movements tend to go from the tonic to dominant and those of minor-key movements go from the tonic to relative major and sometimes onto the dominant. Schubert includes both arpeggiations within a single exposition, and through this means expresses their equal structural weight.

As shown in Example 4.26a, the first two statements of the second theme may be said to "complete the task of the exposition" for G major. The subsequent statement of the second theme in B♭ major is a manifestation of

78 James Webster, "Sonata Form," in *New Grove Dictionary of Music and Musicians*, vol. XXIII, ed. Stanley Sadie and John Tyrrell (London: Macmillan Publishers Ltd, 2001), 695–696.

79 Schenker, *Free Composition*, 40. Italics in original.

the minor aspect of this movement. As shown in Example 4.26b, the third and fourth statements supply the typical arpeggiation for G minor, although, as explained above, it is usually the task of the development to reach the structural dominant, while the exposition only reaches the relative major. Both G major and G minor are equally active in this exposition. They cannot, of course, sound at the same time because of diatonic constraints; they appear, therefore, in turns in temporal order. Both arpeggiations are utterly conventional. Unconventional, however, is the fact that they appear together in one exposition, as illustrated in Example 4.26c.

To understand them in this way requires imagining the structure of the exposition in spatial and not linear terms. In linear terms, the movement does indeed begin with a G major chord that switches immediately to G minor, and the second theme appears in two different keys, D major and B♭ major, with a further statement in D major. Other scholars have interpreted them linearly, either by explaining B♭ major as the flattened submediant within the secondary tonic, D major, as illustrated on the left in Example 4.27, or by including the F♯ major harmony at the end of the transition and connecting each key to the next in a circle of thirds or a complete "hexatonic cycle," as illustrated on the right in Example 4.27.[80] In my spatial

Example 4.26 Analysis of the exposition of Schubert, String Quartet in G Major (D. 887), first movement (a) arpeggiation of major constituents; (b) arpeggiation of minor constituents; (c) combined major and minor arpeggiations

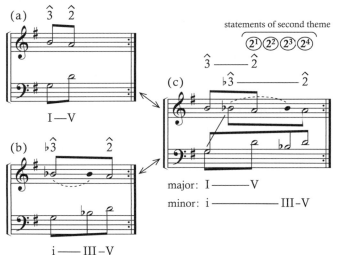

[80] See Chapter 3 for detailed discussion of analyses of the secondary theme by other scholars.

Example 4.27 The two chief Schenkerian intepretations of the
exposition of Schubert, String Quartet in G Major

reading, the elements belonging to the major side and to the minor side of
the structure are extracted separately. Appropriately, each mode is attached
to two statements of the theme, which reinforces the sense of equality.
Importantly, the final dominant is another variation of the theme rather
than being a closing section with distinct material. Each of the four
variations serves a structural purpose.

Compare the critical assessments of Tovey and Webster, who interpreted
the movement linearly and concluded that it has "an enormous (and very
redundant) exposition," and that the recapitulation is "mercifully shorn of
its remote-key statement of the theme and the second transition."[81] When,
as I suggest, the exposition is understood to express both major and minor
on an equal structural level, it even seems appropriate that the exposition
turns out to be "enormous," for it must express two main structures and
not just one. My interpretation therefore gives a unique purpose to
Schubert's repetitions.

The exposition of the String Quartet finds itself dominant-heavy. This has
important repercussions for how Schubert balances the harmonies of the
exposition in the recapitulation. It is balanced by the subdominant in the
recapitulation, where there are two statements of the theme in C major,
followed by a final one in the tonic G major (Example 4.28). Rosen has
pointed out that most recapitulations include some subdominant in the
recapitulation to balance the large-scale dominant in the exposition.
Schubert's use of the subdominant in this movement is much more marked
than its use in the sonata-form movements that Rosen talks about, where it
usually appears shortly after the recapitulation and only to play a passing
function.[82] As we saw earlier in the String Quintet, Schubert often maneuvers a subdominant-space as early as during the first theme, after which the
rest of the recapitulation can play out as a block transposition – a mode of
transposition for which Schubert is famous and often indicted for laziness.

---

[81] Tovey, "Tonality in Schubert," 143 and Webster, "Schubert's Sonata Form," 34.
[82] For the use of the passing subdominant in the recapitulation, see Rosen, *Sonata Forms*.

Example 4.28 Dominant/subdominant opposition in the harmonic architecture of the themes in exposition and recapitulation of Schubert, String Quartet in G Major

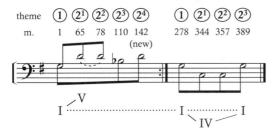

In other words, it is a procedure that serves as a crucial means through which Schubert can maintain the relationships amongst the keys of his expositions in his recapitulations.[83] In the G-Major Quartet, the subdominant is delayed until the secondary thematic complex and appears for two entire statements of it – however, block transposition does not immediately explain the D–D–Bb–D versus C–C–G structure of the respective secondary areas. That is to say, the overall plan of keys in the secondary area of the exposition is not preserved in the recapitulation. Instead, Schubert introduces another frank opposition between the upper and lower dominants (dominant and subdominant), carefully located in the same thematic material.

Schubert's autograph manuscript is enlightening in this respect, and allows for a rare glimpse into the composer's compositional thought process. It also lends some credence to Webster's suggestion that Schubert's exploitation of the subdominant is an important means through which the key relations of the exposition are maintained in the recapitulation.

In the autograph, the bottom stave of fol. 1v and the top two and a half staves of 4r are crossed out. They used to be connected by material on an intermittent folio, which Schubert discarded and which is now lost.[84] Schubert replaced this single, discarded folio with two folios of material (now numbered fols. 2r–3v). The crossed-out material that remains in the autograph is just enough to deduce Schubert's original concept of the exposition. What is left suggests that Schubert originally had in mind a

---

[83] Webster, "Schubert's Sonata Form," 33–34.

[84] The autograph is available at www.schubert-online.at. Hans-Joachim Hinrichsen reconstructs the original conception of the movement in *Untersuchungen zur Entwicklung der Sonatenform in der Instrumentalmusik Franz Schuberts* (Tutzing: Hans Schneider, 1994), 210–218. My analysis of this movement is indebted to Hinrichsen's reconstruction.

block transposition, at least so far as the harmonic framework of the secondary thematic statements is concerned. The first passage of crossed-out material ends exactly where the transition ends, poised for the entry of the secondary theme on the following recto folio, 2r. The original crossed-out version of the transition ends in B major, a fifth below the final version in F♯ major. This suggests that the ensuing secondary theme would have been in G major. Although this is a highly unconventional key choice, it should be recalled that the cadence in G major would only have appeared at the very end of the thirteen-measure theme, and the theme begins with a dominant, giving a hint of conventionality. Nonetheless this is an extra-ordinary first thought. A comparison of the number of folios it took for Schubert to write out the corresponding passage in the recapitulation suggests that there would have been two statements of the theme before the repetition in D major, which is crossed out on fol. 4r. On this basis, the thematic complex of the exposition would likely have followed a G–G–D harmonic formula, corresponding to the recapitulation's C–C–G. The original conception of this movement involves block transposition and confirms Webster's suspicion that Schubert's "antipathy to the dominant" often means that he "hates to leave the tonic in the Classical manner."[85]

If Schubert narrowly escaped producing an extraordinary piece of evidence concerning his reluctance to leave the tonic, of greater interest to my present discussion is that Schubert escaped it through a fifth transposition – a fifth transposition that is more conceptual than actual. That is to say, the surface-level details of the themes are not transposed replicas. In keeping with the observation that Schubert's four thematic statements in the exposition are more variations than repetitions, in the recapitulation Schubert provides new variations for all but the second statement. Theme 2^1 in the recapitulation is similar but not identical to theme 2^1 in the exposition; both themes 2^2 are identical; and the texture of the accompaniment of theme 2^3 in the recapitulation is similar to the inner-voice accompaniment of theme 2^4 of the exposition but the cello is more lyrical. Assuming that the final and missing versions of themes 2^1 and 2^2 in the exposition were the same, then Schubert's revision of the original exposition G–G–D to D–D–B♭–D involved more work than a simple fifth-transposition and the insertion of a new statement in B♭ major. Using superscripts to denote the corresponding versions of thematic variations, the revisions were not from G^1–G^2–D^3 to D^1–D^2–$B\flat^{NEW}$–D^3 but from G^1–G^2–D^3 to D^1–D^2–$B\flat^3$–D^{NEW}. The revision therefore began as another

[85] Webster, "Schubert's Sonata Form," 24.

instance of Schubert's predilection in his late works for block transposition,[86] but instead of taking the easy option and inserting a new statement in B♭ major to offset the monotony of three consecutive statements in the dominant, Schubert crossed out the cello statement in D major (as can be seen on fol. 4r in the manuscript), transposed it down a third to B♭ major, and then composed a new variation in D major.

As the compositional process reveals in the case of the String Quartet, the recapitulation was originally the result of a block transposition by fifth of a highly unusual set of key relations in the exposition. The conventional opening to the secondary theme was the result of a subsequent fifth-transposition of the first two statements of the theme. The outcome is a structure that opposes the fifth above the tonic with a fifth below it. The third relation, B♭ major, was not an insertion between statements in the dominant but was the result of a deliberate transposition of material previously in the conventional dominant. The final statement in D major was the newly composed afterthought.

And this is an apt observation with which to end this chapter. Existing analytical paradigms encourage the view that the dominant is structural and that remote modulations are digressive insertions. Schubert is often criticized for generating his recapitulations through mechanical block transposition by fifth. Yet transposition by fifth is the most common transposition performed by any composer of sonata forms (most sonata forms are in a major key and the dominant of the exposition appears in the tonic in the recapitulation). When Mozart employs the bifocal close that technically requires no recomposition at all and only requires the transposition of the secondary theme and closing to finish off a movement, few charge him with laziness – perhaps because Mozart rarely exploits the formula and instead adds in a few artistic, structurally unnecessary changes. Similarly, Beethoven's secondary and closing themes are usually mere transpositions, but his lengthy added codas do not suggest a strategy of shying away from expending compositional effort.

Yet what we have witnessed in this chapter is that Schubert often arrived at novel tonal spaces by thinking in fifths. I agree with the view of

---

[86] Hans-Joachim Hinrichsen, "Die Sonatenform im Spätwerk Franz Schuberts," *passim*. See also his harmonic comparison of the exposition and recapitulation of the Quartet in G major (p. 33), in which the fourth statement of the second theme is lined up with the third statement of the recapitulation. While this is a logical analysis stemming from a study on Schubert's fifth transpositions, Hinrichsen's subsequent study of Schubert's compositional process in *Untersuchungen zur Entwicklung der Sonatenform* suggests, as I have explained above, that the third statement of the recapitulation owes its origins to the third statement of the exposition, which is now in B♭ major, but was originally in D major.

Hepokoski and Darcy that a transposition down a fifth from a non-dominant secondary theme is not a resolution because it appears a fifth below its original statement. The whole point of such a theme is "its persistent 'alienation' from the tonic."[87] Transposition by fifth – in both the upward and downward directions – became a primary means through which Schubert opened up tonal space in both his expositions and reca-pitulations. This thinking governed the subdominant recapitulation and the oppositional thirds in both major- and minor-key sonata forms. It even lies behind the conventional opening of the secondary theme of the String Quartet in G Major, as well as the key relations of the recapitulation – even though the final structure does not reveal this fact. When as a consequence of these fifth transpositions Schubert needed harmonic variety for the exposition, he presumably felt that the addition of a remote modulation was in order. B♭ major, the most conventional key belonging to G minor, was the logical choice.

Schubert also rethought the role of the dominant in other ways, as in the case of the String Quintet in C Major. While on one level the harmonic point of departure of its second theme, E♭ major, is an unstable coloration of the tonic, the harmonic exploration within it is anchored by conven-tional expectation: the fifth degree. It is, however, treated as a melodic rather than a harmonic entity – $\hat{G}$, not G. If in all of these cases the fifth continues to play a structuring role in Schubert's harmonic architectures, albeit through new frames of reference, perhaps the greatest irony of all for a composer famed for his predilection for third relations is the composi-tional problems served up by seconds and sevenths. One might expect Schubert to have been lured by the fact that these keys generate third relations with each other. Yet the obstacle to using them in a large-scale tonal architecture may well have been that they cannot be construed in such a way that recasts the fifth. In the structures we have examined with a large-scale use of the seventh degree, Schubert replaced the balance gained through the fifth with other transpositions that retain certain key relations of the exposition or that reach the tonic from below, where the dominant had been reached from above.

I remarked at the outset of this chapter that I would limit my consid-eration to structures that exhibit some form of opposition of *Stufen* around a tonic center or opposition between major/minor tonics. If there is a single principle that governs all of these structures, it is the *diatonic* force behind Schubert's exploration of symmetrical tonal space when a tonic is still in

---

[87] Hepokoski and Darcy, *Sonata Theory*, 245.

force. This is perhaps a surprising statement to make about a composer so noted for chromaticism. What is meant by this conclusion is that Schubert's key relations surround a central tonic in *Stufen* that are diatonically (rather than intervallically) equidistant from the tonic: a perfect fifth above and below the tonic in the case of the dominant and subdominant; a major third above and a minor third below a major tonic; and a minor third above and a major third below a minor tonic. Although it may seem a contradiction in terms, diatonically equidistant *Stufen* also prevail in the case of chromatic mediants around a tonic center. In the case of ♭III and ♭VI around a major tonic, the mediants reflect the third relations of the tonic minor and are therefore a minor third above and a major third below the tonic. In addition to exploring novel diatonic and chromatic key relations, Schubert also explored new modal hues for secondary themes by setting them in the minor mode rather than the conventional major. This feature surfaces in major-key works and stemmed either from the use of *diatonic* thirds (iii or vi, as opposed to rendering them chromatically as III or VI) or by maintaining the *diatonic* "root" of the diminished seventh and rendering it into a minor chord (vii° becomes vii). An examination of how Schubert's choice of key relations in the exposition and recapitulation balance each other or are replicated through transposition deflates the sense of complexity that transpires from a Schenkerian approach that sees the thematic units of Schubert's harmonic stations in tension with the conventional underlying structure of sonata form. Tovey remarked of Schubert's formal devices: "All his structural devices seem so absurdly simple, when pointed out, that only the cumulative effect of their number, variety, and efficiency will suffice to undo the injuries that our understanding of Schubert's art has suffered from over-emphasis on his incapacity to theorize in words, and from academic ignorance of the nature of musical art-forms on a large-scale."[88] While Tovey was countering the harsh criticisms of Schubert's forms by such figures as Hubert Parry and Henry Heathcote Statham, there is, I believe, merit in explaining Schubert's exploration of tonal space in the simplest, most straightforward terms possible and in explaining their number and variety through multiple paradigms of tonal space, rather than through the single, linear lens of the I–V–I *Ursatz* or as digressions of various default levels towards an ESC cadence.

---

[88] Tovey, "Franz Schubert," 132.

Epilogue

I opened this book with an examination of a watercolor by Kupelwieser (see Introduction, Plate 1) and used the cylinder shape of the kaleidoscope and the wheel of the draisine in order to speak of a clash between hexatonic and diatonic perspectives of Schubert's music. In closing this book, I want to draw attention to a third, much fainter object in Kupelwieser's painting, which serves as a metaphor to draw the strands of this book together.

Dangling from Schubert's left wrist is his schoolmaster's cane – no doubt included in the picture because it is an effective visual means of identifying Schubert's profession at the time. Schubert was widely reported to have hated teaching, and he left the profession as soon as he could. The cane also symbolizes discipline, order, obedience, and learning. The question of whether these traits are present or absent in Schubert's music is the central matter of debate that runs throughout Schubert's reception.

As we have seen, Schubert's close friends came up with the idea that Schubert was a clairvoyant in order to explain his overwhelming productivity and the depth of his compositional wisdom despite his apparent lack of learning. To Schubert's critics, the harmonic digressions, endless repetitions, and unconventional forms that arose from this mode of composition came across as undisciplined and disorderly. If they found themselves able to concede that Schubert often reached formal perfection with respect to his songs, they nonetheless proclaimed that song is not the learned genre from which coveted places in the history of musical genius are granted.

Much scholarly critique of the twentieth and twenty-first centuries has been occupied with overturning the strict definitions of what constitutes discipline, order, obedience, and learning. As many argue, the impression that Schubert's music lacks these qualities is generated by looking at Schubert through the wrong – invariably Beethovenian – lenses. Yet despite this clear recognition that Schubert needs to be considered in his own terms, few have risen to the challenge of devising a Schubertian lens through which to peer at his music. The problem, as I have articulated it, lies with the sheer force of music theory in shaping our ways of understanding music.

In the past few decades, the discipline of musicology has undergone significant re-evaluation of its methodologies. Perhaps the insistence that the results of music analysis are placed in broader historical contexts counts as a shift in methodology of the greatest seismic proportions. Schubert even held center stage during part of this debate, as scholars addressed the question of the degree to which (or even whether or not) biography can play a role in the understanding of a composer's music. If music theorists have wisely embraced these new contextual frameworks, this book asserts that the methodologies of music theory itself have remained remarkably unchanged.

To be sure, since Schubert's own time and especially in recent times, a litany of new theoretical models has been devised precisely to cater for Schubert's favorite harmonic moves. Indeed, between the invention of the circle of fifths and the cylinder of hexatonic cycles, which I imagined clashing in Kupelwieser's watercolor, numerous other geometries of tonal space have also been invented. They each represent a different vista on the discipline and order of tonal space. Some, as we have seen, privilege the fifth relation and relative major and minor, such as the circle of fifths, others privilege the fifth relation, parallel major and minor, and the major-third relation, as in Cohn's cylinder. Others still dispense with the fifth relation altogether and privilege the parallel major and minor and both major- and minor-third relations, as in the LPR cycle that has cropped up during the course of this study. Put bluntly, music theory is the disciplining of key relations into circles, triangles, toruses, grids, and other multidimensional geometries of recurring harmonic relations. The quest for new maps of tonal space is associated with the belief that, if only the right diagram could be found, the code to harmonic logic and even harmonic possibility would be cracked.[1]

While there are some stunning moments of alignment between these geometries of tonal space and Schubert's harmonic practice, my book has focused on songs and sonata forms that do not align with them. Indeed, most scholars are attracted to works where there is a tension between music theory and practice, especially as such schisms invite hermeneutics. There is thus nothing new or alarming in my gravitation towards pieces by Schubert that exhibit tensions with music theory. The difference – and it is a major difference – is that instead of following conventional habits of reading Schubert against models of music theory, I use Schubert to question the

---

[1] For the strongest recent statement of this view, see Dmitri Tymoczko, "The Geometry of Musical Chords," *Science* 313, no. 5,783 (2006): 72–74.

theoretical assumptions in the models. To put it again, the main question that has motivated this book is: what might music theory look like if Schubert's music were taken as the laboratory for constructing music theory? My purpose has not been to replace existing theory with a new paradigm but rather to work towards a distinctly Schubertian paradigm, one that analyzes Schubert through Schubertian rather than Beethovenian or Classical or other lenses that skew the Schubertian project.

Through my analyses of some early double-tonic songs in Chapter 2, lyrical passages in the instrumental music in Chapter 3, and large-scale tonal spaces in the sonata forms in Chapter 4, I offer some new directions for my vision of a Schubertian music theory. With respect to the songs, I show how Schubert manipulates familiar contrapuntal motions in order to create fresh harmonic progressions. When Rameau developed his proto-typical V_7–I cadence, he laid the foundations for the procrustean bed of harmonic motion. The prototype comprises three crucial components: the fifth in the bass, the leading tone resolving to the tonic, the seventh falling to the third. As I show, Schubert often takes these familiar contrapuntal motions and presents them in new light. He is most likely to present either a strong fifth in the bass or an emphatic leading tone to tonic in the voice, only to couch one or other of its pitches in a new harmony. For example, he might harmonize $\hat{B}$–$\hat{C}$ in the upper voice with E major and C major chords respectively. In so doing, I argue that Schubert opens up tonal space by recontexualizing a conventional gesture.

Another mechanism through which I show that Schubert opens up tonal space is pitch repetition. Each time the same pitch is reiterated, Schubert may place it in a different triadic or chordal context. For any given pitch, Schubert has six possible major and minor triads from which to choose – and there are more harmonic possibilities if dissonances are brought into the equation. I demonstrate Schubert's use of this technique both in the songs and in some famous passages from the instrumental music. The six triads that arise from a single common tone can be construed into a single unique order that generates the LPR cycle or one that reinforces the conventional tonic/dominant axis. As one might expect, the former order has been of great interest to music theorists, for it produces a beautiful pattern. Often Schubert is tempted by the pattern, but he also exploits other constellations of the collection. As I argue, these serve as a powerful mechanism through which Schubert obviates both the tonic/dominant axis and conventional theoretical designs.

Similarly, my approach to Schubert's large-scale key relations in the sonata forms portrays how Schubert broke away from Classical tradition in a way far more striking than simply expanding or digressing from its harmonic model. I differ fundamentally from the view that Schubert's (remote) modulations were sparked by his "aversion to the dominant."[2] My analyses show instead how Schubert opened up tonal space by rethinking and repositioning the familiar fifth-relation. Fifth transposition is perhaps the most common routine for any composer of sonata forms. Most sonata-form movements are in the major key. In their generic format, the conventional dominant in the exposition will be transposed by fifth to the tonic. A hot debate has recently ignited over whether or not this procedure constitutes the sonata *principle*.[3] However that debate may ultimately be settled, the fact remains that composers were most in the habit of fifth transposition. I argue that this familiar transposition lies behind Schubert's exploration of new tonal spaces in some of his most famous sonata forms, and it lies behind the limits of his exploration of certain harmonic stations.

What I would like the reader to take away from this book is that the analytical paradigms that have long been used for explaining, interpreting, and thinking about music might in fact be no more than a pedigreed habit of thought. Indeed, Schubert's music seems to offer us the opportunity to explode many assumptions about the normative and prescriptive pretentions of music theory. In short, while Beethoven's music was certainly the vehicle through which much tonal theory was shaped, it seems that his contemporary, Schubert, is the ideal vehicle through which it can be questioned.

---

[2] James Webster, "Schubert's Sonata Form and Brahms's First Maturity (I)," *19th-Century Music* 2 (1978): 22.

[3] James Hepokoski and Warren Darcy, *Elements of Sonata Theory: Norms, Types, and Deformations in the Late-Eighteenth-Century Sonata* (Oxford University Press 2006), 242–245.

Bibliography

Adorno, Theodor W., "Schubert (1928)," trans. Jonathan Dunsby and Beate Perrey, *19th-Century Music* 29 (2005): 7–14.

Agawu, Kofi, "Analyzing Music under the New Musicological Regime," *Journal of Musicology* 15 (1997): 297–307.

"Music Analysis versus Musical Hermeneutics," *American Journal of Semiotics* 13 (1996): 9–24.

"Schubert's Sexuality: A Prescription for Analysis," *19th-Century Music* 17 (1993): 79–82.

"Structural 'Highpoints' in Schumann's *Dichterliebe*," *Music Analysis* 3 (1984): 159–180.

"Theory and Practice in the Analysis of the Nineteenth-Century *Lied*," *Music Analysis* 11 (1992): 3–36.

Almén, Byron, *A Theory of Musical Narrative* (Indiana University Press, 2006).

Anon., "Am I a Genius?" *The Critic* 8, no. 192 (1887): 120.

"Manliness in Music," *The Musical Times and Singing Class Circular* 30, no. 558 (1889): 460–461.

review of Henry Heathcote Statham, *My Thoughts on Music and Musicians*, in *The Musical Times and Singing Class Circular* 33, no. 587 (1892): 44–45.

Bass, Richard, review of David Kopp, *Chromatic Transformations in Nineteenth-Century Music*, in *Music Theory Online*, 10:1 (2004).

Bauer, Moritz, *Die Lieder Franz Schuberts*, vol. I (Leipzig: Breitkopf & Härtel, 1915).

Beach, David, "Harmony and Linear Progression in Schubert's Music," *Journal of Music Theory* 38 (1994): 1–20.

"Modal Mixture and Schubert's Harmonic Practice," *Journal of Music Theory* 42 (1998): 73–100.

"Schubert's Experiments with Sonata Form: Formal-Tonal Design versus Underlying Structure," *Music Theory Spectrum* 15 (1993): 1–18.

Bent, Ian (ed.), *Musical Analysis in the Nineteenth Century,* vol. 2: *Hermeneutic Approaches* (Cambridge University Press, 1994).

Blume, Jürgen, "Analyse als Beispiel musiktheoretischer Probleme: Auf der Suche nach der angemessenen Beschreibung chromatischer Harmonik in romantischer Musik," *Musiktheorie* 4 (1989): 37–51.

Böhm, Richard, *Symbolik und Rhetorik im Liedschaffen von Franz Schubert* (Vienna: Böhlau, 2006).

Bretherton, David, "The Poetics of Schubert's Song Forms" (DPhil. thesis, University of Oxford, 2008).

Dürr, Walther, "'Ausweichungen ohne Sinn, Ordnung und Zweck' – Zu Tonart und Tonalität bei Schubert," in Erich Wolfgang Partsch (ed.), *Franz Schubert– Der Forschrittliche? Analysen–Perspektiven–Fakten* (Tutzing: Hans Schneider, 1989), 73–104.

"Entwurf – Ausarbeitung – Revision: Zur Arbeitsweise Schuberts am Beispiel des Liedes *Der Unglückliche* (D. 713)," *Die Musikforschung* 44 (1991): 221–236.

"Schubert and Johann Michael Vogl: A Reappraisal," *19th-Century Music* 3 (1979): 126–40.

Everett, Walter, "Deep-Level Portrayals of Directed and Misdirected Motions in Nineteenth-Century Lyric Song," *Journal of Music Theory* 48 (2004): 25–68.

"Grief in *Winterreise*: A Schenkerian Perspective," *Music Analysis* 9 (1990): 157–175.

Federhofer, Hellmut, "Terz- und Quintverwandtschaft in der Harmonik Schuberts: Eine Replik," *Schubert durch die Brille* 21 (1998): 157–161.

"Terzverwandte Akkorde und ihre Funktion in der Harmonik Franz Schuberts," in Otto Brusatti (ed.), *Schubert-Kongress Wien 1978* (Graz: Akademische Druck- und Verlagsanstalt, 1979), 61–70.

Ferguson, Donald N., *A History of Musical Thought* (New York: F. S. Crofts & Co., 1935).

Fieldman, Hali, "Schubert's *Quartettsatz* and Sonata Form's New Way," *Journal of Musicological Research* 21 (2002): 99–146.

"The *Grundgestalt* and Schubert's Sonata Forms" (PhD thesis, University of Michigan, 1996).

Finck, Henry Theophilus, *Chopin and Other Musical Essays* (New York: C. Scribner's Sons, 1889).

Fink, Gottfried Wilhelm, *Der neumusikalische Lehrjammer, oder Beleuchtung der Schrift: Die alte Musiklehre im Streit mit unserer Zeit* (Leipzig: Mayer and Wigand, 1842).

Finney, Theodore M., *A History of Music* (New York: Harcourt, Brace and Company, 1935).

Fisk, Charles, "Comment & Chronicle," *19th-Century Music* 23 (2000): 301–304.

Returning Cycles: Contexts for the Interpretation of Schubert's Impromptus and Last Sonatas (Berkeley and Los Angeles: University of California Press, 2001).

"Schubert Recollects Himself: The Piano Sonata in C Minor, D. 958," *Musical Quarterly* 84 (2000): 635–654.

"What Schubert's Last Sonata Might Hold," in Jenefer Robinson (ed.), *Music and Meaning* (Ithaca, NY: Cornell University Press, 1997), 179–200.

Flothuis, Marius, "Schubert Revises Schubert," in Eva Badura-Skoda and Peter Branscombe (eds.), *Schubert Studies: Problems of Style and Chronology* (Cambridge University Press, 1982), 61–84.

Ford, Walter A. J., "Song," in *Encyclopedia Britannica: A Dictionary of Arts, Sciences, Literature and General Information*, 11th edn. (New York: Encyclopaedia Britannica Company, 1911), vol. XXV, 400–413.

Forster, E. M., *Howards End* (New York: Alfred A. Knopf, 1921).

Frisch, Walter, "Schubert's *Nähe des Geliebten* (D. 162): Transformation of the *Volkston*," in Walter Frisch (ed.), *Schubert: Critical and Analytical Studies* (Lincoln and London: University of Nebraska Press, 1986), 175–199.

"'You Must Remember This': Memory and Structure in Schubert's String Quartet in G major, D. 887," *Musical Quarterly* 84 (2000): 582–603.

Gal, Hans, *Franz Schubert and the Essence of Melody* (London: Victor Gollancz Ltd., 1974).

Georgiades, Thrasybulos G., *Schubert: Musik und Lyrik* (Göttingen: Vandenhoeck and Ruprecht, 1967).

Gerlich, Thomas, "*Am Meer*: Ein 'romantisches Detail' bei Schubert wiedererwogen," *Perspektiven* 1 (2001): 197–218.

Gibbs, Christopher H., "'Poor Schubert': Images and Legends of the Composer," in Christopher H. Gibbs (ed.), *The Cambridge Companion to Schubert* (Cambridge University Press, 1997), 36–55.

The Life of Schubert (Cambridge University Press, 2000).

Gilman, Lawrence, "Music of the Month: Songs of a Rustic Angel," *North American Review* 213 (1921): 844–848.

Gingerich, John, "Remembrance and Consciousness in Schubert's C-Major String Quintet, D.956," *Musical Quarterly* 84 (2000): 619–634.

Girton, Irene, "Promises Fulfilled: Neighbour Notes in Some Late Works of Schubert," in Xavier Hascher (ed.), *Le style instrumental de Schubert: sources, analyse, évolution* (Paris: Sorbonne, 2007), 93–100.

Gorer, Richard, "Cecil Gray," *Music Review* 12 (1951): 307–308.

Gramit, David, "Constructing a Victorian Schubert: Music, Biography, and Cultural Values," *19th-Century Music* 17 (1993): 65–78.

Gray, Cecil, *Carlo Gesualdo: Prince of Venosa, Musician and Murderer* (London: Kegan Paul, Trench, Trubner, 1926).

The History of Music (London and New York: Kegan Paul, Trench, Trubner, & Co. Ltd., 1928).

Greene, David B., "Schubert's 'Winterreise': A Study in the Aesthetics of Mixed Media," *Journal of Aesthetics and Art Criticism* 29 (1970): 181–193.

Grove, George, *Beethoven, Schubert, Mendelssohn*, ed. Eric Blum (London: Macmillan, 1951).

"Schubert," in *Grove's Dictionary of Music and Musicians*, ed. J. A. Fuller Maitland (London: Macmillan, 1908), 280–335.

Hadow, W. H., *The Oxford History of Music,* vol. V: *The Viennese Period* (Oxford: Clarendon Press, 1904).

Hascher, Xavier, *Schubert: La forme sonate et son évolution* (New York: Peter Lang, 1996).

Hass, Hermann, *Über die Bedeutung der Harmonik in den Liedern Franz Schuberts: Zugleich ein Beitrag zur Methodik der harmonischen Analyse* (Bonn: H. Bouvier, 1957).

Heinichen, Johann David, *Neu erfundene und gründliche Anweisung* (Hamburg: Benjamin Schiller, 1711).

Hepokoski, James and Warren Darcy, *Elements of Sonata Theory: Norms, Types, and Deformations in the Late-Eighteenth-Century Sonata* (Oxford University Press, 2006).

Hilmar, Ernst and Margret Jestremski (eds.), *Schubert-Lexikon* (Graz, Austria: Akademische Druck- u. Verlagsanstalt, 1997).

Hinrichsen, Hans-Joachim, "Die Sonatenform im Spätwerk Franz Schuberts," *Archiv für Musikwissenschaft* 45 (1988): 16–49.

    Untersuchungen zur Entwicklung der Sonatenform in der Instrumentalmusik Franz Schuberts (Tutzing: Hans Schneider, 1994).

Hirsch, Marjorie Wing, *Schubert's Dramatic Lieder* (Cambridge University Press, 1993).

Hutchings, Arthur, *Schubert* (London: J. M. Dent, 1945).

    Schubert, rev. edn. (London: J. M. Dent, 1973).

Hyde, Martha M., "Neoclassic and Anachronistic Impulses in Twentieth-Century Music," *Music Theory Spectrum* 18 (1996): 200–235.

Hyer, Brian, "Reimag(in)ing Riemann," *Journal of Music Theory* 39 (1995): 101–138.

    "Tonality," in Thomas Christensen (ed.), *Cambridge History of Music Theory* (Cambridge University Press, 2002), 726–752.

Jensen, Claudia R., "A Theoretical Work of Late Seventeenth-Century Muscovy: Nikolai Diletskii's *Grammatika* and the Earliest Circle of Fifths," *Journal of the American Musicological Society* 45 (1992): 305–331.

Kerman, Joseph, "A Romantic Detail in Schubert's *Schwanengesang*," in Walter Frisch (ed.), *Schubert: Critical and Analytical Studies* (Lincoln and London: University of Nebraska Press, 1986), 48–64.

    "How We Got into Analysis, and How to Get Out," *Critical Inquiry* 7 (1980): 311–331.

    "The State of Academic Music Criticism," in Kingsley Price (ed.), *On Criticizing Music: Five Philosophical Perspectives* (Baltimore: Johns Hopkins University Press, 1981), 38–54.

    Write All These Down: Essays on Music (Berkeley and Los Angeles: University of California Press, 1994).

Kessler, Deborah, "Motive and Motivation in Schubert's Three-Key Expositions," in L. Poundie Burstein and David Gagné (eds.), *Structure and Meaning in Tonal Music: Festschrift in Honor of Carl Schachter* (Hillsdale, NY: Pendragon Press, 2006), 259–276.

Kinderman, William, "Schubert's Tragic Perspective," in Walter Frisch (ed.), *Schubert: Critical and Analytical Studies* (Lincoln and London: University of Nebraska Press, 1986), 65–83.

    "Wandering Archetypes in Schubert's Instrumental Music," *19th-Century Music* 21 (1997): 208–222.

Kivy, Peter, *The Possessor and the Possessed: Handel, Mozart, Beethoven, and the Idea of Musical Genius* (New Haven and London: Yale University Press, 2001).

Kopp, David, *Chromatic Transformations in Nineteenth-Century Music* (Cambridge University Press, 2002).

Kramer, Lawrence, *Franz Schubert: Sexuality, Subjectivity, Song* (Cambridge University Press, 1998).

Music as Cultural Practice, 1800–1900 (Berkeley and Los Angeles: University of California Press, 1990).

"Odradek Analysis: Reflections on Musical Ontology," *Music Analysis* 23 (2004): 287–309.

"The Schubert Lied: Romantic Form and Romantic Consciousness," in Walter Frisch (ed.), *Schubert: Critical and Analytical Studies* (Lincoln and London: University of Nebraska Press, 1986), 200–237.

Kramer, Richard, *Distant Cycles: Schubert and the Conceiving of Song* (Chicago University Press, 1994).

"The Hedgehog: Of Fragments Finished and Unfinished," *19th-Century Music* 21 (1997): 134–148.

Krebs, Harald, "Alternatives to Monotonality in Early Nineteenth-Century Music," *Journal of Music Theory* 25 (1981): 1–16.

review of Charles Fisk, *Returning Cycles*, in *Music Theory Spectrum* 25 (2003): 388–400.

"Some Early Examples of Tonal Pairing: Schubert's 'Meeres Stille' and 'Der Wanderer'," in William Kinderman and Harald Krebs (eds.), *The Second Practice of Nineteenth-Century Tonality* (Lincoln and London: University of Nebraska Press, 1996), 17–33.

"The Background Level in Some Tonally Deviating Works of Franz Schubert," *In Theory Only* 8/8 (1985): 5–18.

"Third Relation and Dominant in Late 18th- and Early 19th-Century Music," 2 vols. (PhD thesis, Yale University, 1980).

"Tonart und Text in Schuberts Liedern mit abweichenden Schlüssen," *Archiv für Musikwissenschaft* 47 (1990): 264–271.

"Wandern und Heimkehr: Zentrifugale und Zentripetale Tendenzen in Schuberts Frühen Liedern," *Musiktheorie* 13 (1998): 111–122.

Kreissle von Hellborn, Heinrich, *Franz Schubert* (Vienna: Carl Gerold's Sohn, 1865).

Franz Schubert: Eine biographische Skizze (Vienna: L. C. Zamarski and C. Dittmarsch, 1861).

Krones, Hartmut, "'Ein Accumulat aller musikalischen Modulationen und Ausweichungen ohne Sinn, Ordnung und Zweck': Zu Schuberts 'schauerlichen' Werken der Jahre 1817–28," *Österreichische Musikzeitschrift* 52 (1997): 32–40.

Laitz, Steven, "The Submediant Complex: Its Musical and Poetic Roles in Schubert's Songs," *Theory and Practice* 21 (1996): 123–166.

Laufer, Edward, "Revised Sketch of Mozart, K. 545/I and Commentary," appendix to Gordon Sly, "Schubert's Innovations in Sonata Form: Compositional Logic and Structural Interpretation," *Journal of Music Theory* 45 (2001): 144–150.

Lek, Robbert van der, "Zum Verhältnis von Text und Harmonik in Schuberts 'Daß sie hier gewesen,'" *Archiv für Musikwissenschaft* 53 (1996): 124–134.

Lendvai, Ernö, *Béla Bartók: An Analysis of His Music* (London: Kahn & Averill, 1971).

Lerdahl, Fred, *Tonal Pitch Space* (Oxford University Press, 2001).

Lewin, David, "A Formal Theory of Generalized Tonal Functions," *Journal of Music Theory* 26 (1982): 41–48.

    "*Auf dem Flusse*: Image and Background in a Schubert Song," *19th-Century Music* 6 (1982): 47–59. Reprinted in Walter Frisch (ed.), *Schubert: Critical and Analytical Studies* (Lincoln and London: University of Nebraska Press, 1986), 126–152.

    Generalized Musical Intervals and Transformations (New Haven: Yale University Press, 1987).

Macdonald, Hugh, "Schubert's Volcanic Temper," *Musical Times* 119 (1978): 949–952.

Mak, Su Yin, "Schubert's Sonata Forms and the Poetics of the Lyric," *Journal of Musicology* 23 (2006): 263–306.

Malin, Yonatan, "Metric Displacement Dissonance and Romantic Longing in the German Lied," *Music Analysis* 25 (2006): 251–288.

Marston, Nicholas, "Analysing Variations: The Finale of Beethoven's String Quartet op. 74," *Music Analysis* 8 (1989): 303–324.

    "Schubert's Homecoming," *Journal of the Royal Musical Association* 125 (2000): 248–270.

Marx, A. B., *Musical Form in the Age of Beethoven: Selected Writings on Theory and Method*, ed. and trans. Scott G. Burnham (Cambridge University Press, 1997), 86.

Mason, Daniel Gregory, *Masters in Music: Volume IV* (Boston: Bates and Guild Co., 1904).

    The Romantic Composers (New York and London: Macmillan, 1906).

Mathews, William S. B., *How to Understand Music*, vol. II (Philadelphia: Theodore Presser, 1888).

Mattheson, Johann, *Kleine General-Bass-Schule* (Hamburg: Johann Christoph Kissner, 1735).

Mayer, Andreas, "Der psychoanalytische Schubert," *Schubert durch die Brille* 9 (1992): 7–31.

McClary, Susan, "Constructions of Subjectivity in Schubert's Music," in Philip Brett, Elizabeth Wood, and Gary C. Thomas (eds.), *Queering the Pitch: The New Gay and Lesbian Musicology* (New York: Routledge, 1994), 205–233.

    Conventional Wisdom: The Content of Musical Form (Berkeley and Los Angeles: University of California Press, 2000).

    Feminine Endings: Music, Gender, and Sexuality (University of Minnesota Press, 1991).

Gay/Lesbian Study Group Newsletter 2, no. 1 (April 1991): 8–14.

"Music and Sexuality: On the Steblin/Solomon Debate," *19th-Century Music* 17 (1993): 83–88.

McKay, Elizabeth Norman, *Franz Schubert: A Biography* (Oxford: Clarendon Press, 1996).

McKinney, Howard D. and W. R. Anderson, *Music in History: The Evolution of an Art* (New York: American Book Company, 1940).

Messing, Scott, *Schubert in the European Imagination: The Romantic and Victorian Eras*, vol. I (New York: University of Rochester Press, 2006).

Montgomery, David, "Franz Schubert's Music in Performance: A Brief History of People, Events, and Issues," in Christopher H. Gibbs (ed.), *The Cambridge Companion to Schubert* (Cambridge University Press, 1997), 270–283.

Muxfeldt, Kristina, "Schubert's Songs: The Transformation of a Genre," in Christopher H. Gibbs (ed.), *The Cambridge Companion to Schubert* (Cambridge University Press, 1997), 121–137.

Nature: International Journal of Science 26, no. 656 (1882): xxix and 26, no. 657 (1882): xxxvii.

Newbould, Brian, *Schubert: The Music and the Man* (Berkeley and Los Angeles: University of California Press, 1997).

Newcomb, Anthony, "Structure and Expression in a Schubert Song: *Noch einmal* Auf dem Flusse *zu hören*," in Walter Frisch (ed.), *Schubert: Critical and Analytical Studies* (Lincoln and London: University of Nebraska Press, 1986).

Noeske, Nina, "Schubert, das Erhabene und die letzte Sonate D. 960 – oder: Die Frage nach dem Subjekt," *Schubert: Perspektiven* 7 (2007): 22–36.

Parry, Hubert, *Summary of the History and Development of Mediæval and Modern European Music* (London: Novello and Company, 1904).

The Evolution of the Art of Music (London: Kegan Paul, Trench, Trubner, & Co. Ltd., 1897).

Perry, Jeffrey, "The Wanderer's Many Returns: Schubert's Variations Reconsidered," *Journal of Musicology* 19 (2002): 374–416.

Pesic, Peter, "Schubert's Dream," *19th-Century Music* 23 (1999): 136–144.

Porter, Ernest G., *Schubert's Song Technique* (London: Dennis Dobson, 1961).

Reed, John, *Schubert* (London: The Master Musicians, 1987).

The Schubert Song Companion (Manchester: Mandolin, 1997).

Roden, Timothy, Craig Wright, and Bryan Simms, *Anthology for Music in Western Civilization*, vol. II (Boston: Schirmer Cengage Learning, 2010).

Rosen, Charles, *Frontiers of Meaning: Three Informal Lectures on Music* (New York: Hill and Wang, 1994).

"Schubert's Inflections of Classical Form," in Christopher H. Gibbs (ed.), *The Cambridge Companion to Schubert* (Cambridge University Press, 1997), 72–98.

Sonata Forms, rev. edn. (New York: W. W. Norton, 1988).

Salzer, Felix, "Die Sonatenform bei Franz Schubert," *Studien zur Musikwissenschaft* 15 (1928): 86–125.

Schachter, Carl, "Motive and Text in Four Schubert Songs," in David Beach (ed.), *Aspects of Schenkerian Theory* (New Haven: Yale University Press, 1983), 61–76.

Schenker, Heinrich, *Der freie Satz* (Vienna: Universal Edition, 1935; rev. edn. 1956).

  Der Tonwille: Pamphlets in Witness of the Immutable Laws of Music, Offered to a New Generation of Youth, vol. I, ed. William Drabkin (Oxford University Press, 2004).

  Der Tonwille: Pamphlets in Witness of the Immutable Laws of Music, Offered to a New Generation of Youth, vol. II, ed. William Drabkin (Oxford University Press, 2005).

  Five Graphic Music Analyses (New York: Dover, 1969).

  Free Composition, 2 vols., trans. and ed. Ernst Oster (New York: Longman, 1979).

  Harmony, trans. Elisabeth Mann Borgese, ed. Oswald Jonas (Cambridge, MA: MIT Press, 1973).

Schoenberg, Arnold, *Fundamentals of Musical Composition*, ed. Gerald Strang and Leonard Stein (London: Faber and Faber, 1967).

  Theory of Harmony, trans. Roy E. Carter (Berkeley and Los Angeles: University of California Press, 1983).

Schwarz, Boris and Nicholas E. Taw, "Mason, Daniel Gregory (ii)," *New Grove Dictionary of Music and Musicians*, vol. XVI, ed. Stanley Sadie and John Tyrell (New York: Macmillan, 2001), 34–35.

Shamgar, Beth, "Schubert's Classic Legacy: Some Thoughts on Exposition-Recap. Form," *Journal of Musicology* 18 (2001): 150–169.

Siciliano, Michael, "Neo-Riemannian Transformations and the Harmony of Franz Schubert" (PhD thesis, University of Chicago, 2002).

  "Two Neo-Riemannian Analyses," *College Music Symposium* 45 (2005): 81–107.

Sly, Gordon, "Schubert's Innovations in Sonata Form: Compositional Logic and Structural Interpretation," *Journal of Music Theory* 45 (2001): 119–150.

Smith, Charles J., "Musical Form and Fundamental Structure: An Investigation of Schenker's *Formenlehre*," *Music Analysis* 15 (1996): 191–297.

Snyder, John, "Schenker and the First Movement of Mozart's Sonata K. 545: An Uninterrupted Sonata-Form Movement?" *Theory and Practice* 16 (1991): 51–78.

Solie, Ruth A., review of *Queering the Pitch: The New Gay and Lesbian Musicology*, in *Journal of the American Musicological Society* 48 (1995): 311–323.

Solomon, Maynard, "Franz Schubert and the Peacocks of Benvenuto Cellini," *19th-Century Music* 12 (1989): 193–206.

  "Franz Schubert's 'My Dream,'" *American Imago* 38 (1981): 137–154.

Spalding, Walter Raymond, *Music: An Art and a Language* (Boston and New York: Arthur P. Schmidt Co., 1920).

Statham, Henry Heathcote, "Grove's Dictionary of Music," *Edinburgh Review* 153 (1881): 212–240.

  My Thoughts on Music and Musicians (London: Chapman and Hall, 1892).

  "Schubert – Chopin – Liszt," *Edinburgh Review* 158 (1883): 475–509.

Steblin, Rita, "Schubert durch das Kaleidoskop: Die Unsinnsgesellschaft und ihre illustren Mitglieder," *Österreichische Musikzeitschrift* 52 (1997): 52–61.

Stein, Deborah, *Hugo Wolf's Lieder and Extensions of Tonality* (Ann Arbor: UMI, 1985).

"Schubert's *Erlkönig*: Motivic Parallelism and Motivic Transformation," *19th-Century Music* 13 (1989): 145–158.

Straus, Joseph N., "Normalizing the Abnormal: Disability in Music and Music Theory," *Journal of the American Musicological Society* 59 (2006): 113–184.

Taruskin, Richard, "Chernomor to Kashchei: Harmonic Sorcery, or, Stravinsky's 'Angle'," *Journal of the American Musicological Society* 38 (1985): 72–142.

Stravinsky and the Russian Traditions: A Biography of the Works through Mavra, 2 vols. (Berkeley and Los Angeles: University of California Press, 1996).

The Oxford History of Western Music: The Nineteenth Century, vol. III (New York: Oxford University Press, 2005).

Taylor, John, *The Student's Text-book of the Science of Music* (London: George Philip and Son, 1876).

Temperley, Nicholas, "Schubert and Beethoven's Eight-Six Chord," *Nineteenth-Century Music* 5 (1981): 142–154.

Thym, Jürgen and Ann C. Fehn, "Schubert's Strategies in Setting Free Verse," in Jürgen Thym (ed.), *Of Poetry and Song: Approaches to the Nineteenth-Century Lied* (Rochester, NY: University of Rochester Press, 2010), 261–280.

Tobin, Robert, *Warm Brothers: Queer Theory and the Age of Goethe* (Philadelphia: University of Pennsylvania Press, 2000).

Tovey, Donald Francis, *Essays in Musical Analysis*, vol. I, *Symphonies* (London: Oxford University Press, 1946).

"Franz Schubert (1797–1828)," in Hubert J. Foss (ed.), *The Mainstream of Music and Other Essays* (Oxford University Press, 1949), 103–133.

"Tonality," *Music and Letters* 9 (1928): 341–363.

"Tonality in Schubert," in Hubert J. Foss (ed.), *The Mainstream of Music and Other Essays* (Oxford University Press, 1949), 134–159.

Tymoczko, Dmitri, "The Geometry of Musical Chords," *Science* 313, no. 5783 (2006): 72–74.

Tschense, Astrid, *Goethe-Gedichte in Schuberts Vertonungen: Komposition als Textinterpretation* (Hamburg: von Bockel, 2004).

Van Tassel, Eric, "'Something Utterly New:' Listening to Schubert Lieder," *Early Music* 25 (1997): 702–714.

Vogler, Abbé Georg Joseph, *Handbuch zur Harmonielehre und für den Generalbaß* (Prague: K. Brath, 1802).

Wagner, Richard, *Beethoven*, trans. Edward Dannreuther (London: William Reeves, 1880).

Walsh, William Shepard, *Handy-book of Literary Curiosities* (Philadelphia: J. B. Lippincott Co., 1892).

Weber, Gottfried, *Versuch einer geordneten Theorie der Tonsetzkunst zum Selbstunterricht mit Anmerkungen für Gelehrtere*, 3 vols. (Mainz: B. Schott, 1817, 1818, 1821).

Webster, James, "Music, Pathology, Sexuality, Beethoven, Schubert," *19th-Century Music* 17 (1993): 89–93.

"Schubert's Sonata Form and Brahms's First Maturity (I)," *19th-Century Music* 2 (1978): 18–35.

"Sonata Form," in *New Grove Dictionary of Music and Musicians*, vol. XXIII, ed. Stanley Sadie and John Tyrrell (London: Macmillan Publishers Ltd, 2001), 687–710.

Wen, Eric, "A Response to Gordon Sly and Edward Laufer: An Alternative Interpretation of the First Movement of Mozart's K. 545," *Journal of Music Theory* 46 (2002): 364–368.

Wilberforce, Edward (trans.), *Schubert: A Musical Biography* (London: Wm. H. Allen & Co., 1866).

Winter, Robert, "The Bifocal Close and the Evolution of the Viennese Classical Style," *Journal of the American Musicological Society* 42 (1989): 275–337.

Wolff, Christoph (ed.), *The String Quartets of Haydn, Mozart and Beethoven: Studies of the Autograph Manuscripts* (Cambridge, MA: Harvard University Department of Music, 1980).

Wollenberg, Susan, "Schubert's Poetic Transitions," in Xavier Hascher (ed.), *Le style instrumental de Schubert: sources, analyse, évolution* (Paris: Sorbonne, 2007), 261–277.

"Schubert's Transitions," in Brian Newbould (ed.), *Schubert Studies* (Ashgate: Aldershot, 1998), 16–61.

Woodford, Peggy, *Schubert* (London: Omnibus Press, 1984).

Youens, Susan, "Franz Schubert: The Prince of Song," in Rufus Hallmark (ed.), *German Lieder in the Nineteenth Century* (New York: G. Schirmer, 1996), 31–74.

"Of Dwarves, Perversion, and Patriotism: Schubert's *Der Zwerg*, D. 771," *19th-Century Music* 21 (1997): 177–207.

Retracing a Winter's Journey: Schubert's Winterreise (Ithaca, NY: Cornell University Press, 1991).

Index